Hand Book of

Computer Science & Engineering

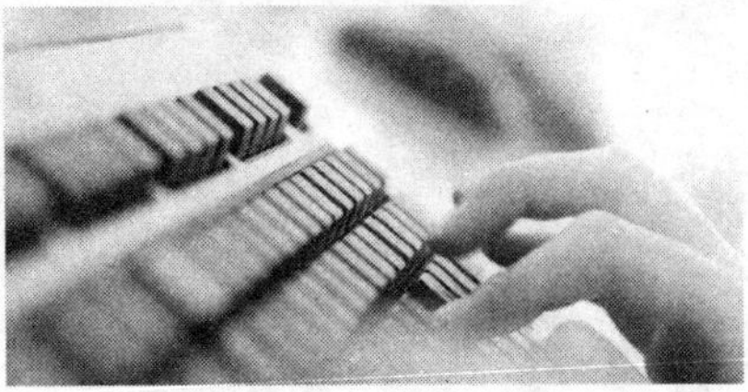

G K Publications (P) Ltd

CL MEDIA (P) LTD.

Edition : 2017

Typeset by : *CL Media DTP Unit*

Administrative and Production Offices

Published by : **CL Media (P) Ltd.**
KH No. 1027, Ramnagar, Salempur,
Rajputana, Roorkee (U.K.)-247667

Marketed by : **G.K. Publications (P) Ltd.**
A-41, Lower Ground Floor,
Espire Building,
Mohan Cooperative Industrial Area,
Main Mathura Road,
New Delhi - 110 044

For product information :
Visit ***www.gkpublications.com*** or email to ***gkp@gkpublications.com***

Preface

If you've got technical examinations such as GATE, ESE & PSUs around the corner and having to quickly go through a wide range of topics in a limited time, this is the book would be a complete solution for you. Technical exams being difficult in nature, has to be given enough priority and time during exam preparation. But it is also quite easy to score in these exams as you just need to be thorough with formulas, key points and techniques to quickly solve the questions.

GKP's Handbook Series is a collection of handbooks for Mechanical Engineering, Civil Engineering, Electrical Engineering, Computer Science Engineering and Electronics & Communication Engineering. This series serves as a quick reference guide for students preparing for exams such as GATE, ESE, PSUs recruitment and any other technical exam. The handbooks include last minute preparation points, formulae with conceptual clarity and definitions and equations with explanatory figures.

We, at GK Publications have specially designed this book in line with the varying needs of each aspirant. This book is not only to prepare you for the technical exams but is also a good asset for your semester exam preparations.

Hard work in the right direction will surely fulfill your desires. Have a lot of self-belief; load it with a lot of practice, top it off with a little smart work and you are good to go.

We hope this little effort of ours will be helpful in achieving your dreams. If you have any suggestions on improvement of this book, you can write to us at gkp@gkpublications.com.

All the Best!

Team GKP

Contents

Unit-1 Engineering Mathematics

Unit-2 Digital Logic

Unit-3 Machine Instructions

Unit-4 Programming and Data Structure

Unit-9 Database

Unit-10 Software Engineering Gate

Unit-11 Computer Network

Unit-12 Web Technologies

Computer Science

1

Engineering Mathematics

CONTENTS

1 Mathematical Logic

INTRODUCTION

Proposition: A declarative statement that is either True (T) or False (F) but not both.

Compound proposition: When propositions are combined using logical operators.

Connectors: Operators that combine proposition to form compound proposition.

(*a*) **Conjunction:**
- ANDing of two statements
- symbol → ∧
- $p \wedge q$. (p, q are statements)

(*b*) **Disjunction:**
- ORing of two statements
- symbol → V
- $p \vee q$

(*c*) **Negation:**
- statement is opposite of original statement
- symbol → ~, – ⌉
- eg. $\tilde{p}$, $\bar{p}$, $\neg p$

(*d*) **Conditional:**
- Implication statement "*i.e.*, if p then q" where p and q are two statements
- symbol '→'
- eg. $p \rightarrow q$.

(*e*) **Bi-conditional:**
- statement of form "if and only if"
- symbol '↔'
- eg. $p \leftrightarrow q$.

PRIORITIZATION OF OPERATORS

- $\urcorner$(negate)
- $\wedge$ (conjunction)
- $\vee$ (disjunction)
- $\rightarrow$ (conditional)
- $\leftrightarrow$ (Bi conditional)

Note

Few Variations:

(*i*) Contrapositive: $p \rightarrow q \equiv \sim p \rightarrow \sim p$.

(*ii*) Converse: $p \rightarrow q \equiv q \rightarrow p$

(*iii*) Inverse: $p \rightarrow q \equiv \sim p \rightarrow \sim q$

Tautology: When compound proposition is always True (T).
e.g. $p \vee \sim p$.

Contradiction: When compound proposition is always false (F).
e.g. $p \wedge \sim p$.

Contingency: When proposition is neither tautology nor contradiction.
e.g. p.

Logical Equivalence: P $\Leftrightarrow$ Q is tautology if P and Q are logically equivalent.

Functionally Complete: When only equivalent formula for a give formula can be written by only connectives in set of operators then it is called functionally complete set of operator
e.g. $\{\sim, \vee\}$, $\{\sim, \wedge\}$, $\{\sim, \vee, \wedge\}$.

Consistent: if $H_1 \wedge H_2 \wedge H_3 \wedge \ldots H_n$ is satisfiable then;
$H_1, H_2 \ldots$ and H_n are consistent

Inconsistent: If $H_1 \wedge H_2 \wedge H_3 \ldots H_n$ is **unsatisfiable** then;
$H_1, H_2 \ldots$ and H_n are inconsistent

EQUIVALENCES

$$P \vee (P \wedge Q) \equiv P$$

$$P \rightarrow Q \equiv \neg P \vee Q \equiv \neg Q \rightarrow \neg P$$

$$P \wedge (P \vee Q) \equiv P$$

$$P \leftrightarrow Q \equiv (P \rightarrow Q) \wedge (Q \rightarrow P)$$

$$P \leftrightarrow Q \equiv (P \wedge Q) \vee (\neg P \wedge \neg Q)$$

$$P \leftrightarrow Q \equiv \neg P \leftrightarrow \neg Q$$

$$P \rightarrow (Q \rightarrow R) \equiv (P \wedge Q) \rightarrow R$$

$$\neg(P \leftrightarrow Q) \equiv P \leftrightarrow (\sim Q) \equiv (\sim P) \leftrightarrow Q \equiv P \oplus Q)$$

$$(P \rightarrow Q) \wedge (P \rightarrow R) \equiv P \rightarrow (Q \wedge R)$$

$$(P \rightarrow R) \wedge (Q \rightarrow R) \equiv (P \vee Q) \rightarrow R$$

$$(P \to Q) \vee (P \to R) \equiv P \to (Q \vee R)$$
$$(P \to R) \vee (Q \to R) \equiv (P \wedge Q) \to R$$
$$P \vee Q \equiv \neg P \to Q$$
$$P \wedge Q \equiv \neg(P \to \neg Q)$$
$$\neg(P \to Q) \equiv (P \wedge \neg Q)$$

Identity Laws: (i) $P \wedge T = P$ (ii) $P \vee F = P$

Domination Laws: (i) $P \vee T = T$ (ii) $P \wedge F = F$

Idempotent Laws: (i) $P \wedge P = P$ (ii) $P \vee P = P$

Commutative Laws: (i) $P \vee Q = Q \vee P$ (ii) $P \wedge Q = Q \wedge P$

Associative Laws: (i) $(P \vee Q) \vee R = P \vee (Q \vee R)$
(ii) $(P \wedge Q) \wedge R = P \wedge (Q \wedge R)$

Distributive Laws: (i) $P \vee (Q \wedge R) = (P \vee Q) \wedge (P \vee R)$
(ii) $P \wedge (Q \vee R) = (P \wedge Q) \vee (P \wedge R)$

Demorgan's Laws: (i) $\neg(P \wedge Q) = \neg P \vee \neg Q$
(ii) $\neg(P \vee Q) = \neg P \wedge \neg Q$

Absorption Laws: (i) $P \vee (P \wedge Q) = P$ (ii) $P \wedge (P \vee Q) = P$

Negation Laws: (i) $P \vee \neg P = T$ (ii) $P \wedge \neg P = F$

Double Negation Laws: $\neg(\neg P) = P$

Rules of Inference (Tautological Implications).

Simplification: $(P \wedge Q) \Rightarrow P$
$(P \wedge Q) \Rightarrow Q$

Addition: $P \Rightarrow (P \vee Q)$
$Q \Rightarrow (P \vee Q)$

Disjunctive Syllogism: $(\sim P, P \vee Q) \Rightarrow Q$

Modus Ponens: $(P, P \to Q) \Rightarrow Q$

Modus Tollens: $(\sim Q, P \to Q) \Rightarrow \sim P$

Hypothetical Syllogism: $(P \to Q, Q \to R) \Rightarrow (P \to R)$

Conjunctive Syllogism: $(\sim(P \wedge Q), P) \Rightarrow \sim Q$

Dilemma: $(P \vee Q, P \to R, Q \to R) \Rightarrow R$

Constructive Dilemma: $(P \vee Q, P \to R, Q \to S) \Rightarrow R \vee S$

Destructive Dilemma: $(\sim R \vee \sim S, P \to R, Q \to S) \Rightarrow \sim P \vee \sim Q$

Other Rules: $\sim P \Rightarrow (P \to Q)$
$Q \Rightarrow (P \to Q)$
$\sim(P \to Q) \Rightarrow P$
$\sim(P \to Q) \Rightarrow \sim Q$

Normal Form

- PCNF
  - Principle conjunctive normal form
  - Products of sum or conjunction of max term only
  - $[P(x_1) \vee P(x_2)] \wedge [P(x_3) \vee P(x_4)]$
- PDNF
  - Principle disjunctive normal form
  - Sums of product or disjunction of min terms only
  - $[P(x_1) \wedge P(x_2)] \vee [P(x_3) \wedge P(x_4)]$

PREDICATE LOGIC

Quantifier

- Existential ($\exists$)
  - ↳ 'there exist'
  - ↳ if $p(x)$ is proposition over universe U then; $\exists\, xp(x)$
- Universal ($\forall$)
  - ↳ 'for all' | 'for every'
  - ↳ if $p(x)$ is proposition over universe U; $\forall x, p(x)$

Predicates

- P(x): propositional statement with one variable.
- Q(x, y): propositional statement with two variable

Logical Equivalences:

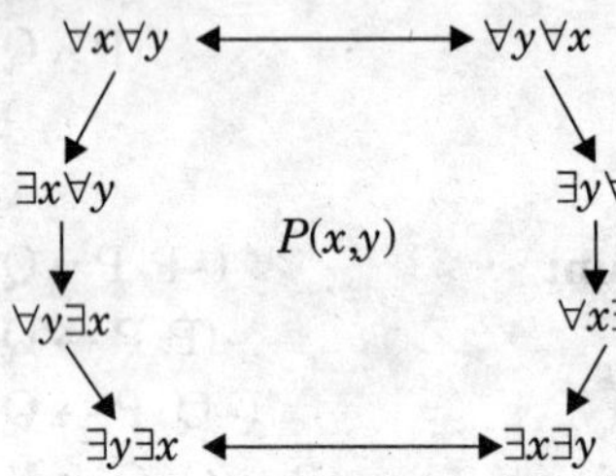

1. $\forall x\, [P(x) \wedge Q(x)] \equiv \forall x\, P(x) \wedge \forall x\, Q(x)$
2. $\exists x\, [P(x) \vee Q(x)] \equiv \exists x\, P(x) \vee \exists x\, Q(x)$
3. $\forall x\, (P(x) \vee Q) \equiv \forall x\, P(x) \vee Q$
4. $\forall x\, (P(x) \wedge Q) \equiv \forall x\, P(x) \wedge Q$
5. $\exists x\, (P(x) \vee Q) \equiv \exists x\, P(x) \vee Q$
6. $\exists x\, (P(x) \wedge Q) \equiv \exists x\, P(x) \wedge Q$
7. $\forall x\, P(x) \wedge \exists y Q(y) \equiv \forall x \exists y\, [P(x) \wedge Q(y)]$
8. $\forall x\, P(x) \vee \exists y Q(y) \equiv \forall x \exists y [P(x) \vee Q(y)]$

Combinatorics

2

PERMUTATIONS (ORDERED SELECTION OR ARRANGEMENT)

- P = permutation
- n = number of objects
- r = objects under consideration at a time.

Number of permutations of n objects

1. 'r' at a time = ${}^nP_r = P(n, r) = (n)_r$.
2. 'r' at a time = n^r ($\therefore$ with repetition)
3. 'all' at time = $n!$
4. '$\leq r$' at a time = $\dfrac{(n^{r+1} - 1)}{n - 1}$ ($\therefore$ with repetition)
5. 'r' at a time = $n^r - {}^nP_r$ ($\therefore$ atleast one repetition)
6. 'all' at a time = $\dfrac{n!}{r!}$ (when, 'r' are identical)
7. 'all' at a time = $\dfrac{n!}{n_1!n_2!...n_r!}$ (n_1 are alike; n_2 are alike; ... n_r are a like)
8. 'r' at a time;
   (*a*) m-particular objects never included = ${}^{(n-m)}P_r$
   (*b*) m-particular objects always included = ${}^{(n-m)}P_{(r-m)} \cdot {}^rP_m$ ($n \geq m$ and $r \geq m$)
9. ${}^nP_r = P(n-1, r) + r \cdot P(n-1, r-1)$
10. ${}^nP_r = r! \cdot {}^nC_r = n \times {}^{(n-1)}P_{(r-1)}$

CIRCULAR PERMUTATIONS

1. Taking all at a time

$= (n-1)!$ [when; direction not specified]

$= \dfrac{(n-1)!}{2}$ [when; direction *i.e.*, clockwise or anticlockwise is specified]

2. Taking 'r' at a time = $\frac{^nP_r}{r}$ (direction not specified)

$$= \frac{1}{2} \cdot \frac{^nP_r}{r} \text{ (direction is specified)}$$

DERANGEMENTS

- Number of derangements for n-objects = D_n

$$= n! \sum_{i=0}^{n} \frac{(-1)^i}{i!} \qquad \left(D_n \simeq \frac{n!}{e} \text{ for large value of } n \right)$$

(The prob. of a given permutation being a derangement

$$= \frac{D_n}{n!} = \sum_{i=0}^{n} \frac{(-1)^i}{i!} \simeq \frac{1}{e} \text{ for large } n \Bigg)$$

- **Binomial theorem:**

$$(a + b)^n = {}^nC_0 a^n b^0 + {}^nC_1 a^{n-1} b + \ldots + {}^nC_n a^0 b^n = \sum_{r=0}^{n} {}^nC_r \, a^{n-r} \, b^r$$

- **Multi-nomial coefficients:**

$$\binom{n}{n_1, n_2, \ldots\ldots, n_r} = \frac{n!}{n_1!\, n_2! \ldots\ldots n_r!}$$

Note

- Number of ways to distribute 'r' apples to n-persons = $^{(n+r-1)}C_r$.
- Number of permutation of $(n_1 + n_2)$ objects; taking all at a time $= \frac{(n_1 + n_2)!}{n_1!\, n_2!}$ (where; n_1 are alike and n_2 are alike)

COMBINATIONS (UNORDERED SELECTION)

- The number of combinations of n objects;
  1. Considering 'r' at a time = ^nC_r
  2. Considering zero or more at a time = 2^n
  3. Considering one or more at a time = $2^n - 1$

4. **Non empty selection:**

Number of ways = $[(p + 1)(q + 1)....]-1$

(where; objects are of p-type and q-types)

5. Considering 'r' at a time with m-particular objects;

(*a*) Included = $C(n - m, r - m)$

(*b*) Not included = $C(n - m, r)$

COUNTING

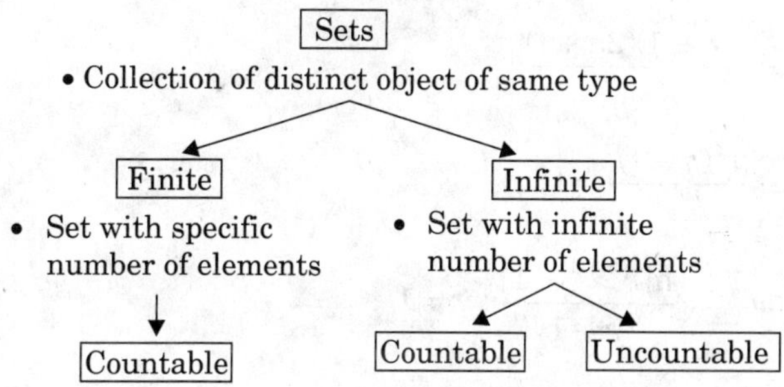

Countable: Set of real numbers that are solution to quadratic equation ($ax^2 + bx + c = 0$; where a, b and c are integer)

Uncountable: Set of lines through the origin.

COUNTING PRINCIPLE (INCLUSION-EXCLUSION)

- $n(A \cup B) = n(A) + n(B) - n(A \cap B)$
- $n(A \cup B \cup C) = n(A) + n(B) + n(C) - n(A \cap B) - n(A \cap C) - n(B \cap C) + n(A \cap B \cap C)$
- Let $A_1, A_2, ..., A_n$ are finite sets. $n(A_1 \cup A_2 \cup ... \cup A_n)$

$$= \sum_{1 \le i \le n} n(A_i) - \sum_{1 \le i < j \le n} n(A_i \cap A_j) + \sum_{1 \le i < j < k \le n} n(A_i \cap A_j \cap A_k) - ... + (-1)^{n-1} n(A_1 \cap A_2 ... \cap A_n)$$

- If A and B are disjoint $n(A \cup B) = n(A) + n(B)$.
- The set of functions "from" the positive integers to (0, 1, 2, 3, 4, 5, 6, 7, 8, 9,) is '**uncountable**' since the power set of positive integers is uncountable.

PIGEONHOLE PRINCIPLE

If n pigeons are assigned to m pigeonholes then atleast $\left[\frac{(n-1)}{m}\right] + 1$ pigeons share the same pigeonhole.

FUNDAMENTAL COUNTING PRINCIPLE

If an event can occur in r different steps where step 1 can occur in n_1 ways followed by step 2 that occur in n_2 ways ... till step r to occur in n_r ways then; number of possible ways for an event to occur is; $\boldsymbol{n_1 \cdot n_2 \cdot n_3 \ldots n_r}$.

SUMMATION

- $\Sigma n = \dfrac{n(n+1)}{2}$
- $\Sigma n^2 = \dfrac{n(n+1)(2n+1)}{6}$
- $\Sigma n^3 = \dfrac{n^2(n+1)^2}{4} = [\Sigma n]^2$
- $\sum_{k=0}^{n} a \cdot r^k = \dfrac{a[r^{n+1} - 1]}{r-1}$; $r \neq 1$
- $S_n = \sum_{k=1}^{n} f(k) = S_{n-1} + f(n)$
- $\sum_{k=n_1}^{n_2} f(k) = f(n_1) + f(n_1 + 1) + f(n_1 + 2) + \ldots + f(n_2)$; for $n_1 \leq n_2$
- $\sum_{k=1}^{n} \left[f(k) + g(k)\right] = \sum_{k=1}^{n} f(k) + \sum_{k=1}^{n} g(k)$

GENERATING FUNCTIONS

- $G(x) = \sum_{r=0}^{\infty} a_r x^r = a_0 + a_1 x + a_2 x^2 + \ldots + a_r x^r + \ldots$
- $(1 + ax)^n = \sum_{r=0}^{n} {}^nC_r \cdot a^r \cdot x^r = \sum_{r=0}^{n} {}^nC_r (ax)^r$
- $(1 + x^k)^n = \sum_{r=0}^{n} {}^nC_r \cdot x^{kr}$
- $\dfrac{1 - x^{n+1}}{1 - x} = \sum_{r=0}^{n} x^r$

- $e^x = \sum_{r=0}^{\infty} \frac{x^r}{r!} = 1 + \frac{x}{1!} + \frac{x^2}{2!} + ...$

- $\log(1 + x) = \sum_{r=0}^{\infty} \frac{(-1)^{r+1} \cdot x^r}{r!} = -1 + \frac{x}{1!} - \frac{x^2}{2!} + \frac{x^3}{3!} ...$

- $\frac{1}{1-ax} = \sum_{r=0}^{\infty} (ax)^r = \sum_{r=0}^{\infty} a^r \cdot x^r$

- $\frac{1}{1-x^n} = \sum_{r=0}^{\infty} (x^n)^r = \sum_{r=0}^{\infty} x^{nr}$

- $\frac{1}{(1-ax)^n} = \sum_{r=0}^{\infty} {}^{n+r-1}C_r \cdot (ax)^r$

- $\frac{1}{(1+ax)^n} = \sum_{r=0}^{\infty} {}^{n+r-1}C_r \cdot (-1)^r \cdot (ax)^r$

- $\sin x = \sum_{r=0}^{\infty} (-1)^r \frac{x^{2r+1}}{(2r+1)!} = x - \frac{x^3}{3!} + \frac{x^5}{5!} - ...\infty$

- $\sinh x = \sum_{r=0}^{\infty} \frac{x^{2r+1}}{(2r+1)!} = x + \frac{x^3}{3!} + \frac{x^5}{4!} + ...\infty$

- $\cos x = \sum_{r=0}^{\infty} (-1)^r \cdot \frac{x^{2r}}{(2r)!} = 1 - \frac{x^2}{2!} + \frac{x^4}{4!} - ...\infty$

- $\cosh x = \sum_{r=0}^{\infty} \frac{x^{2r}}{(2r)!} = 1 + \frac{x^2}{2!} + \frac{x^4}{4!} + ...\infty$

RECURRENCE RELATION

$a_n = a_n^H + a_n^P$

where

$a_n^H \rightarrow$ complementary solution

$a_n^P \rightarrow$ particular solution

- Complementary function $[a_n^H]$ (Solution to homogenous part)

Root	a_n^H
1. $t_1, t_2, t_3, \ldots t_k$ are distinct real numbers	$C_1 \cdot t_1^n + C_2 t_2^n + \ldots + C_k t_k^n$
2. $t_1 = t_2 = t_3$	$(C_1 + C_2 n + C_3 n^2)$
3. Pair of roots are complex $(\alpha \pm i\beta)$	$r^n[C_1 \cos n\theta + C_2 \sin n\theta]$ where $r = \sqrt{\alpha^2 + \beta^2}$ $\theta = \tan^{-1} \frac{\beta}{\alpha}$

- Particular function $[a_n^P]$

R.H.S	a_n^P
1. Constant	d_1
2. $C_1 + C_2 n$	$d_1 + d_2 n$
3. $C_1 + C_2 n + C_3 n^2$	$d_1 + d_2 n + d_3 n^2$
4. a^n	$d_1 a^n$
5. $n \cdot a^n$	$(d_1 + d_2 n)a^n$

d_1, d_2 and d_3 values are obtained by substituting a_n^P in given recurrence relation.

Example 1. *Given* $a_n - 3a_{n-1} = n + 2$

Sol. $a_n^H : a_n - 3a_{n-1} = 0$

$\Rightarrow \quad a_{n+1} - 3a_n = 0$

$\Rightarrow \quad t - 3 = 0$

$\Rightarrow \quad t = 3$

$\therefore \quad a_n^H = C_1 3^n \quad \ldots(i)$

$a_n^P : d_1 + d_2 n$ is substituted in recurrence relation

$(d_1 + d_2 n) - 3(d_1 + d_2(n - 1)) = n + 2$

By comparing co-efficients of 'n' and constants, we get $d_1 = -7/4$ and $d_2 = -1/2$.

$\therefore a_n = a_n^H + a_n^P$

$$= C_1 \cdot 3^n + \left(-\frac{7}{4} - \frac{n}{2}\right)$$

Now C_1 can be evaluated if initial conditions are given.

3 Set Theory and Algebra

Set: It is a collection of distinct objects of same type. The objects are elements or members of the set.

where;

$N \rightarrow$ set of natural numbers {1, 2, 3 ...}
$Z \rightarrow$ set of integers {... –2, –1, 0, 1, 2, ...}
$Q \rightarrow$ set of rational numbers.
$\phi \rightarrow$ empty set
$U \rightarrow$ universal set
$R \rightarrow$ set of real numbers
$C \rightarrow$ set of complex numbers
$\subseteq \rightarrow$ subset

Note $N \subseteq Z \subseteq Q \subseteq R \subseteq C$

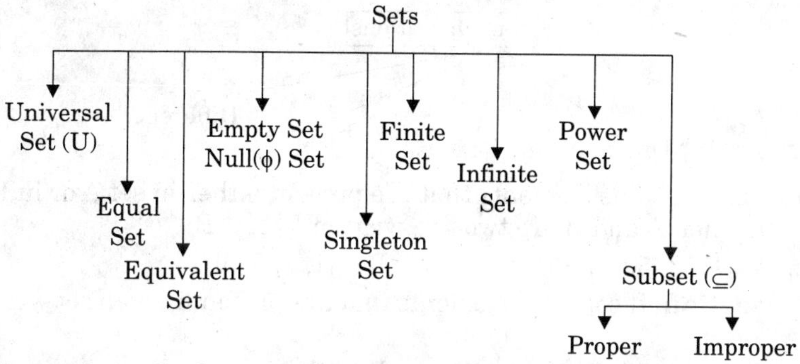

Universal set: Set having all objects under consideration denoted by 'U'.

Equal set: Set having same elements. denoted by A = B.

$[A = B \Leftrightarrow (x \in A \leftrightarrow x \in B]$

Equivalent set: Set having same number of elements.

i.e. $|A| = |B|$

Empty/Null set: Set having zero elements. denoted by 'ϕ' or '{ }'.

Singleton Set: Set having a single element.

Finite set: Set with finite or countable number of elements *i.e.*, Cardinality of a set can be obtained as a number.

Infinite set: Set that is not finite.

e.g. Set of positive integer.

Power set: Power set of a set A is set of all subsets of A and is denoted as P(A).

e.g. $P(\{0, 1, 2\}) = \{\phi, \{0\}, \{1\}, \{2\}, \{0, 1\}, \{0, 2\}, \{1, 2\}, \{0, 1, 2\}\}$

Subset: When every element of set R is also an element of set Q then, R is subset of Q.

- Written as $R \subseteq Q$.
- Here; Q is **SUPERSET** of R.

$R \subseteq Q = \{x : x \in R \Rightarrow x \in Q\}$.

Proper subset: If R is subset of Q and $R \neq Q$ then it is proper subset denoted by $R \subset Q$.

e.g., R = {2, 3, 4}, Q = {2, 3, 4, 5}

$R \subset Q \Leftrightarrow \forall x(x \in R \rightarrow x \in Q) \wedge \exists x\,(x \in Q \wedge x \notin R)$

Improper: If R is subset of Q and R = Q

Note
- For every set A: $\phi \subseteq A$ and $A \subseteq A$
- Comparable: If $A \subseteq B$ or $B \subseteq A$; then A and B are comparable.
- If set has n-elements then, power set has 2^n elements.

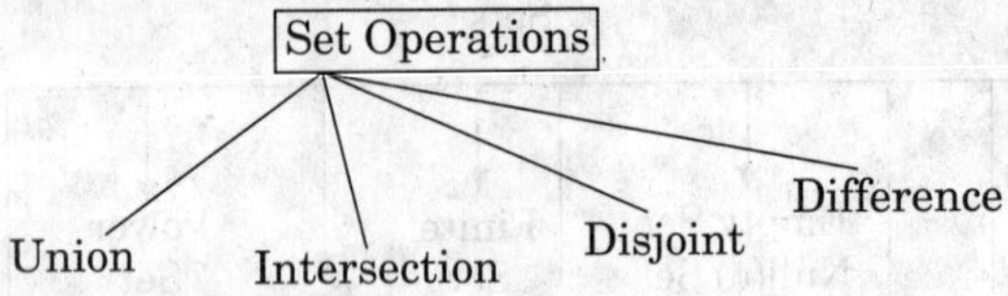

Union: It contains elements that are present either in set A or in B or in both when A and B are two set, written as $A \cup B$.

e.g., A = {1, 3, 5}; B = {1, 2, 3}; $A \cup B = \{1, 2, 3, 5\}$

Intersection: It contains elements that are present in both set written as $A \cap B$.

e.g., A = {1, 3, 5}; B = {1, 2, 3}; $A \cap B = \{1, 3\}$.

Disjoint: A and B are disjoint sets if their intersection is empty set.

$$A \cap B = \phi$$

Difference: Set containing that are present in A but not in B.

e.g., A = {1, 3, 5}, B = {1, 2, 3} $A - B = \{5\}$

Note
- $\text{Max}\,(|A|\ |B|) \leq |A \cup B| \leq (|A| + |B|)$
- $|A \cup B| = |A| + |B| - 1\ |A \cap B|$
- The difference of A and B is also called the complement of B with respect to A or relative complement of B in A.

Inclusion exclusion principle:

$$n(A_1 \cup A_2 \cup \ldots \cup A_n)$$
$$= \sum_{1 \le i \le n} n(A_i) - \sum_{1 \le i < j \le n} n(A_i \cap A_j) + \sum_{1 \le i < j < k \le n} n(A_i \cap A_j \cap A_k) - \ldots$$
$$+ (-1)^{n-1} n(A_1 \cap A_2 \cap \ldots \cap A_n)$$

Properties of sets:

Let: A, B and C $\rightarrow$ sets

U $\rightarrow$ Universal sets

ϕ $\rightarrow$ Empty sets

Identity	Name
$A \cup B = B \cup A$ $A \cap B = B \cap A$	Commutative Laws
$A \cup (B \cup C) = (A \cup B) \cup C$ $A \cap (B \cap C) = (A \cap B) \cap C$	Associative Laws
$A \cap (B \cup C) = (A \cap B) \cup (A \cap C)$ $A \cup (B \cap C) = (A \cup B) \cap (A \cup C)$	Distributive Laws
$A \cup \phi = A$ $A \cap U = A$	Identity Laws
$A \cup \overline{A} = U$ $A \cap \overline{A} = \phi$	Complement Laws
$A \cup A = A$ $A \cap A = A$	Idempotent Laws
$A \cup (A \cap B) = A$ $A \cap (A \cup B) = A$	Absorption Laws
$(\overline{\overline{A}}) = A$	Double Complement Laws
$A \cup U = U$ $A \cap \phi = \phi$	Domination Laws
$\overline{A \cup B} = \overline{A} \cap \overline{B}$ $\overline{A \cap B} = \overline{A} \cup \overline{B}$	De Morgans Laws

Cartesian Product of Sets: Let A and B be sets. The cartesian product of A and B, denoted by $A \times B$, is the set of all ordered pairs (a, b) $a \in A$ and $b \in B$.

Note

- If $|A| = m$ and $|B| = n$ then $|A \times B| = mn$
- In general $A \times B \neq B \times A$ but $A \times B = B \times A$ iff $A = B$ or $A = \phi$, $B = \phi$. However, $|A \times B| = |B \times A|$ always.

Multi set: Set with element that can appear more than once.

Example: $\{a, a, b, b, b, c, c, c, c, c, d\} = \{2\cdot a, 3\cdot b, 5\cdot c, 1\cdot d\}$

Let $A = \{m_1\cdot a_1, m_2\cdot a_2, \ldots, m_k\cdot a_k\}$ where m_i = multiplicity of a_i

$B = \{n_1\cdot a_1, n_2\cdot a_2, \ldots, n_k\cdot a_k\}$ where n_i = multiplicity of a_i

Then $A \cup B$ = a multiset, in which multiplicity of a_i is max $\{m_i, n_i\}$

$A \cap B$ = a multiset, in which multiplicity of a_i is min $\{m_i, n_i\}$

$A + B$ = a multiset, in which multiplicity of a_i is $(m_i + n_i)$

$A - B$ = a multiset, in which multiplicity of

$$a_i = \begin{cases} m_i - n_i & \text{if} \quad m_i > n_i \\ 0 & , \quad \text{otherwise} \end{cases}$$

FUNCTIONS

Definition:

- If P and Q are non empty sets, a function 'f' from P to Q is an assignment of exactly one elements of Q to each element of P.
  Here; $f(P) = q$; q is unique element of Q assigned to P element of A by function 'f'
  $f = P \to Q$ (f is function from P to Q).
- Functions can sometimes be called as mappings or transformation.
  Domain: Let $f = P \to Q$; set P is domain of function f.
  Codomain: Let $f = P \to Q$; set co-domain of function f.
  Image of an element: If $f(P) = q$; q is image of p and p is pre-image of q.

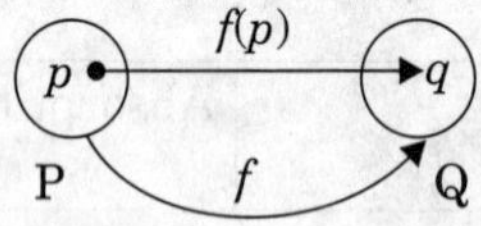

Note

- if number of elements $|P| = m$ and $|Q| = n$; then number of functions possible from P to Q = n^m.
- $f : P \to P$ is a function on set P, if; $|P| = n$ then number of functions possible on P = n^n.

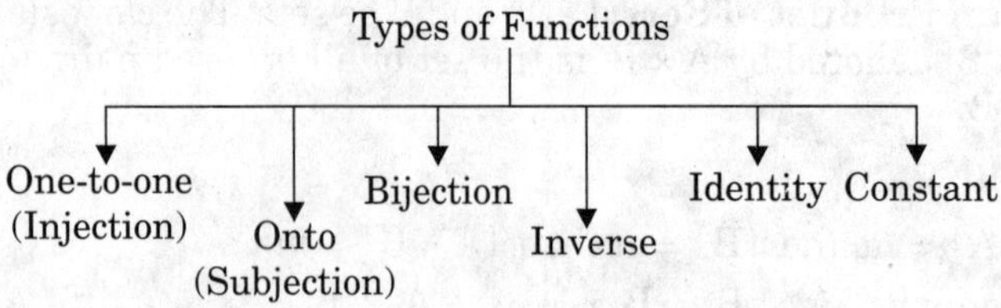

1. **One-to-one:** $f(P) = f(q)$ implies that $P = q$ for all P & q in domain of f.
   - if P and Q are finite sets then one-to-one from P & Q is possible if $|P| \leq |Q|$
   - if $|P| = m$ and $|Q| = n$; $(m > n)$; number of functions from P to Q in $X(n, n) = n(n-1)(n-2) \ldots 1 = n!$
2. **Onto function:** $f: P \rightarrow Q$ is onto if for every element $q \in Q$ there is an element $p \in P$ if $f(p) = q$

   $$\text{Range}(f) = \text{Co-domain } (f) = Q.$$

   - if P & Q are finite sets then;

     $f: P \rightarrow Q$ is onto when $|Q| \leq |P|$
   - if $|P| = |Q|$ then every one-to-one $f: P \rightarrow Q$ is onto and vice versa
   - if $|P| = |Q| = n$ then number of $f: P \rightarrow Q = n!$
   - if $|P| = m$ and $|Q| = n$ $(n < m)$ then number of onto $f: P \rightarrow Q = n^m - {}^nC_1 (n-1)^m + {}^nC_2 (n-2)^m \ldots + (-1)^{n-1}\, {}^nC_{n-1} (1^m)$
3. **Bijection:** One-to-one function + onto function
   - if P & Q are finite sets then; bijection is possible when $|P| = |Q|$.
   - if $|P| = |Q|$ then number of bijection

     = number of one-to-one

     = number of onto possible from P to Q = $n!$
4. **Inverse function:** Let $f: P \rightarrow Q$ be one-to-one. The inverse of f denoted by f^{-1} is function that assigns to an element q of Q the unique element p in P such that $f(P) = q$.

   $f^{-1}(q) = p$ when $f(p) = q$

   Inverse is possible only when function is bijective.
5. **Identity function:** Let $f: P \rightarrow P$; here f is identity function if each element of set p has image on itself.

   Identity function is written as I.

   Identity function on $P = I_P$

   It is bijection if $f(p) = P$; $\forall\, p \in P$.
6. **Constant function:** $f: P \rightarrow Q$ is constant function if $f(x) = r$; $\forall x \in P$ i.e all the elements of domain are mapped to only one element of co-domain. Therefore, range of constant function contains only single element.

   Function composition:

   Let f and $g \rightarrow$ two functions defined on set P;

   (fog): $P \rightarrow P$ defined by $(fog)x = f(g)(x))$

   (gof): $P \rightarrow P$ defined by $(gof)x = g(f)(x))$

Note

- In general $(fog)x \neq (gof)x$
- Let $f : A \rightarrow B$ and $g : B \rightarrow C$ then $(gof) : A \rightarrow C$
  but (fog) may not be defined
  (fog) is defined if range of $g(x)$ is a subset of A
- If $f : A \rightarrow A$ is a bijection then
  $fo\,f^{-1} = f^{-1}\,of = I$ where I is identity function on A.
- If $f : A \rightarrow B$ is a bijection then $fof^{-1} = I_B$, $f^{-1}\,of = I_A$, $f^{-1} : B \rightarrow A$
- If $f : A \rightarrow B$ and $g : B \rightarrow C$ are injective (one-one) then $gof : A \rightarrow$ C is also injective.
- If $f : A \rightarrow B$ and $g : B \rightarrow C$ are surjective (onto) then $gof : A \rightarrow C$ is also surjective.
- If $f : A \rightarrow B$ and $g : B \rightarrow C$ are functions and $gof : A \rightarrow C$ is injective then f is also injective.
- If $f : A \rightarrow B$ and $g : B \rightarrow C$ are functions, and $gof : A \rightarrow C$ is surjective then g is also surjective (onto)

RELATION

Let P and Q be two non empty sets. Then binary relation R from P to Q is a subset of P × Q.

$R \subseteq P \times Q$

Relations on a set: Relation of set P is relation from P × P i.e. a relation on a set P is a subset of P × P.

- if $|P| = m$ and $|Q| = n$ then; number of relation on P = 2^{mn}
- if $|P| = n$ and $|Q| = n$ then; number of relation on P = $2^{(n2)}$

Types of Relation

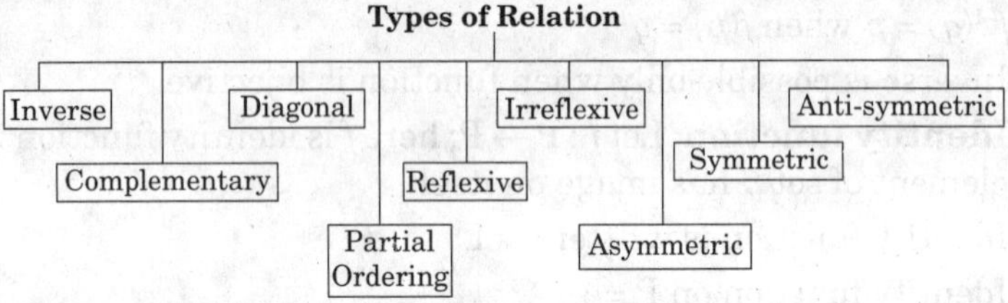

1. **Inverse relation (R^{-1}):**
   - R is relation from a set P to Q.
   - Inverse of R = R^{-1} relation from Q to P consisting of ordered pair which when reversed belongs to R.
     i.e., $R^{-1} = \{(q, p) \mid (p, q) \in R\}$
2. **Complementary relation (R^C):**
   $$R^C = \overline{R} = \{(p, q) \mid (p, q) \notin R\} = (P \times Q) - R$$
3. **Diagonal relation (Δ_n):**
   - or identity relation
   - Relation R on set P is diagonal if; $R = \{(p, p) \mid p \in P\} = \Delta_P$

4. Reflexive relation:

- $P^R P \ \forall\ P \in P$ (i.e. $(p, p) \in R \ \forall\ p \in P$)
- if $|P| = n$; number of reflexive relations possible an $P = 2^{n(n-1)}$
- Smallest reflexive relation an $P = \Delta_P$ (diagonal relation)
- Largest reflexive relation on $P = P \times P$
- A diagonal relation on set A is reflexive and any superset of it is also reflexive.

5. Irreflexive relation:

- A relation R on a set P is irreflexive;
  if; $P \not R\ P$ (i.e. $(P, P) \notin R, \forall_p \in P$)
  if $|P| = n$; number of irreflexive relation on $P = 2^{n(n-1)}$
- smallest irreflexive relation on $P = \phi$
- largest irreflexive relation on $P = (P \times P) - \Delta_P$.

6. Symmetric relation:

- R is symmetric if; $p^R q$ then $q^R p$, $\forall p, q \in P$
- number of symmetric relation possible when;
- if $|P| = n$; $2^n \times 2^{\frac{n^2 - n}{2}} = 2^{n(n+1)/2}$
- diagonal pairs $= 2^n$
- Non-diagoual pairs $= 2^{(n2-2)/2}$
- smallest $= \phi$
- largest $= P \times P$.

7. Antisymmetric relation:

- Relation on set P is antisymmetric if; $P^R q$ and $q^R P$ then $P = q$, $\forall p, q \in P$.
- Smallest antisymmetric relation is ϕ
- Largest $\rightarrow$ not unique number of elements in largest antisymmetric relation includes $\rightarrow$ all diagonal pairs and half non diagonal pairs.

  $$i.e.\ n + \frac{(n^2 - n)}{2} = \left(\frac{n^2 + n}{2}\right) \text{ elements.}$$

- Subset of antisymmetric relation = antisymmetric relation.
- If $P = \{1, 2, \ldots n\}$ then; number of antisymmetric relation of $P = 2n \times 3^{n(n-1)/2}$ with: n diagonal pairs and 2^n choices. $\frac{n(n-1)}{2}$ non diagonal pairs and $3^{n(n-1)/2}$ choices
- Relation is antisymmetric if; $R \cap R^{-1} \subseteq \Delta P$.

8. Asymmetric relation:

- R on set P is asymmetric if; $(q, p) \notin R$ wherever $(p, q) \in R$, $\forall\ p, q \in P$.
- Relation is asymmetric if is this both antisymmetric and reflexive.
- If $P = \{1, 2, \ldots n)$ then no. of asymmetric relation $= 3^{n(n-1)/2}$.

9. Partial ordering relation:

- Relation R on a set P is partial order if R is reflexive, antisymmatric and transitive
- **Poset:** Partially ordered set P with partial ordered relation R defined on P is called poset
- Totally ordered set: A POSET [P; Q] is totally ordered set, if every pair of elements in P are comparable i.e. either $P^R q$ or $q^R P$ $\forall$ P, $q \in$ A.

Note

- Number of reflexive and symmetric relations with n-elements = $2^{n(n-1)/2}$.
- Number of neither reflexive nor irreflexive relation = $2n^2 - 2.2^{n(n-1)}$
- ϕ is not reflexive [empty relation]
- **A relation R on a set A is:**
  (*i*) Symmetric $\Leftrightarrow R = R^{-1}$
  (*ii*) Antisymmetric $\Leftrightarrow (R \cap R^{-1}) \subseteq \Delta_A$
  (*iii*) Reflexive $\Leftrightarrow R^{-1}$ is also reflexive
  (*iv*) Reflexive $\Leftrightarrow R^C$ or $\overline{R}$ is reflexive

If R and S are antisymmetric then $(R \cap S)$ is also antisymmetric for any relation S on A.

If R is antisymmetric then every subset of R is also antisymmetric.

If R is relation on a set A then $R \cup R^{-1}$ is always symmetric and $R \cup \Delta$ is always reflexive.

- **If R and S on set A are any two:**
  (*i*) Reflexive relations then $(R \cup S)$ and $(R \cap S)$ are also reflexive.
  (*ii*) Symmetric relations then$(R \cup S)$ and $(R \cap S)$ are also symmetric.
  (*iii*) Antisymmetric relations the $(R \cap S)$ is always antisymmetric.
  (*iv*) Transitive relations then $(R \cap S)$ is always transitive.
  (*v*) Equivalence relations then $(R \cap S)$ is always equivalence relation.

Closures of Relations

Transitive (R^*)	Reflexive (R^+)	Symmetric ($R^\#$)
• smallest transitive relation on set P which contains R. e.g. P = {1, 2, 3} and R = {(1, 2), (2, 3)} R^* = {(1, 2), (2, 3), (1, 3)}	• smallest reflexive relation on set P which contains $R = (R \cup \Delta_P)$ e.g. P = {1, 2, 3}; R = {(1, 2), (2, 3)} R^+ = {(1 ,2), (2, 3), (1, 1), (2, 2), (3, 3)}	• smallest symmetric relation on set P which contains $R = (R \cup R^{-1})$ e.g. P = {1, 2, 3} R = {(1, 2), (2, 3)} $R^\#$ = {(1, 2), (2, 3), (2, 1), (3, 2)}

PARTITION OF A SET

Let A be a set with 'n' elements dividing the set A into subsets $\{A_1, A_2, \ldots, A_n)$ is called partition of A, if

(*i*) every subset is a non-empty set and

(*ii*) $\forall_{i,j}\ A_i \cap A_j = \phi$; $(i \neq j)$ and

(*iii*) $(A_1 \cup A_2 \cup A_3 \cup \ldots \cup A_n) = A$

Example. *Let A = [1, 2, 3]. Then there are 5 partitions possible on A.*

$P_1 = \{\{1, 2, 3\}\}$, $P_2 = \{\{1\}, \{2, 3\}\}$, $P_3 = \{\{2\}, \{1, 3\}\}$, $P_4 = \{\{3\}, \{1, 2\}\}$, and $P_5 = \{\{1\}, \{2\}, \{3\}\}$

GROUPS

Closure: Binary operator * is said to be closed on an non-empty set A, if $a * b \in A$ for all $a, b \in A$

Number of binary operations on set 'G' = $|G|^{|G| \times |G|}$

Associativity: $(a * b) * c = a * (b * c)$; $\forall a, b, c \in G$

Identity:

- $\exists e \in G\ \forall \partial \in G\ (a * e = e * a = a)$ where 'e' is identity
- If there exist an identity element in G then it must be unique.

Inverse: $\forall a \in G\ \exists\ b \in G\ (a * b = b * a = e)$

This also means and $a^{-1} = b$ and $b^{-1} = a$

Commutative: $\forall a, b \in G\ (a * b = b * a)$

Groupoid:

- An algebric system (G, *) is groupoid if it is closed operation G.

Semigroup:

- An algebric system which is groupoid and associative

Monoid:

- An algebric system (G, *) which is semigroup and there is an identity in G.

Group:

- An algebric system (G, *) which is monoid and every element in G has inverse

Abelian group:

- An algebric system (G, *) which is a group and it is also commutative *i.e.* $a * b = b * a$; $\forall a, b \in G$.

Order of an element of a group:

1. Let G be a group & $g \in G$ then, order of g = smallest positive number k so that $ak = e$.
2. Let G $\rightarrow$ finite group & $g \in G$; The order of g divides the order of G
3. Any group of even order contains an element or order 2.

Cyclic group:

- Let G be a group, it is cyclic if it is generated by one element. *i.e.* $G = \{a^i \mid i \in Z\}$
- Let G be cyclic group generated by a then
  - G is abelian and group of prime order.
  - Every subgroup of G is cyclic
  - If G is infinite; elements are precisely ... $a^{-3}, a^{-2}, a^{-1}, e, a, a^2, a^3$ ...
  - if G is finite; elements are precisely $e, a, a^2 \ldots an^{-2}, an^{-1}$ & $an = e$.
  - For finite cyclic group;
- There should be $g \in G$ with same order as of G and g will be generator or of that group.
- When $G = \langle g \rangle$ of order n then for every positive integer d/n; there is exactly one subgroup of G of order d.

SUBGROUP

- H is subgroup of G if;

  (*i*) Subset: $H \subseteq G$

  (*ii*) Closure: $ab \in H$ for $a, b \in H$

  (*iii*) Identity: identity elements of G is contained in H

  (*iv*) Inverse: for $a \in H_i$ there exist $a^{-1} \in H$.
- For G as group and H_i where $i \in I$ is collection of subgroup f_G

  then; $H = \bigcap_{i=I} H_i \rightarrow$ subgroup of G.
- **Lagrange's Theorem:** In finite group G; H is subgroup then $|H|$ divides $|G|$.

COSET

Left coset

- For $G \subseteq H$; left H-coset in G is a set of the form aH: = $\{ah \mid h \in H\}$
- left coset of a subgroup $H < G$ is a subset of G of the form $gH = (gh : h \in H)$
- 2 left cosets are either equal or disjoint:

$$gH = g'H \Leftrightarrow g^{-1} g' \in H$$

Right coset:

- For $G \subseteq H$; right H-coset in G is a set of the form Ha: = $\{ha \mid h \in H\}$.
- Number of distinct right cosets (equivalently left closets) of G is called the index of H in G and is denoted by [G : H].
- A right coset of H in H is a subset of the form $Hg = (hg : h \in H)$. Two right cosets are either disjoint or equal; we have $Hg = Hg' \leftrightarrow g^{-1} g' \in H$.

  * Any elements of coset is representative of that coset.

  * For finite H, cosets have cardinality $|H|$

  * There are equal number of left and right coset in group.

GROUP THEORY CLASSIFICATION

Groupoid	Semigroup	Monoid	Group	Abelian
Closure	closure + Associative	closure + Associative + identity	closure + Associative + identity + Inverse	Group + Commutative
Example: (N, +, *) (Z, +, –, *) (R, +, –) (R – {0}, *, /)	*Example:* (N, +, *) (Z, +, *) (R, +) (R – {0}, *) [– and / are always not associative]	*Example:* (N, *) (Z, +, ×) ({0, 1}, ×) ($\{a, b\}^b$, +)	*Example:* Non-singular matrices closed under '*' (multiplication)	*Example:* ({0, 1, 2, 3}, $+_4$) (Z, +) (R, +) (R – {0}, *) (Q, +) (Q – {0}, *) ({1, –1, i, –i}) ({1, ω, ω²}, *) ({1, –1}, *)

- Order of a group → number of elements in the group
- O(G) ≤ 5; Abelian group.
- Every group of prime order is a cyclic group and every cyclic group is an Abelian group.
- ({0, 1, 2, ..., m – 1}, $+_m$) Addition modulo and ({1, 2, 3, ..., q – 1}, X_q) multiplication modulo is Abelian group
- G be finite group and g ∈ G, then $g^{|G|} = e$ where $|g|$ is order of element g and it divides $|G|$.
- All non-singular matrices are grouped under matrix multiplication but not Abelian.
- If O(G) = $2n$, there exist one 'self invertible' element other than identity element.
- The set {0, 1, 2, ... m–1} with $\oplus_m$ is always a group with identity, $e = 0$ where $\oplus_m$ is addition modulo m defined as $a \oplus_m b = r\left(\frac{a+b}{m}\right)$
- The set {1, 2, ... P – 1} with $\otimes_P$ is always a group with identity $e = 1$, where $\otimes_P$ is multiplication modulo P defined as:

$$a \otimes_P b = r\left(\frac{a \times b}{P}\right)$$

- Order of an element O(a) = n and O(a) = O(a^{-1}) where, a ∈ G and $a^n = e$.

LATTICE THEORY

- **First Element (Least):** Let A be unordered set, the element 'a' in 'A' is first element of A if for every element 'x' in A, $a \leq x$.
  Last Element (Greatest): Let a be unordered set, the element 'b' in 'A' is last element of A if for every element 'x' in A, $x \leq b$.
  e.g. • For N = set of natural elements; then first element = 1; last element = nil.
  • For any set 'A' with P(A) as its power set.
  First elements of P(A) = ϕ; last elements of P(A) = A.
- **Minimal Element:** elements without predecessors.
  - if only one minimal exist then it is always 'least'
- **Maximal Element:** elements with no successors if only one maximal exist then it is always greatest.
  - Any number of minimal and maximal may exist.
- **Least Element:** a is least element of Poset P; if $a \leq x$; $\forall x \in P$
- **Greatest Element:** b is greatest element of P if; $x \leq b$; $\forall x \in P$
- **Lower Bound:** Let $A \subseteq P$; and if $a \in p$ & $a \leq x \; \forall x \in A$ then element a is lower bound
  - Immediate successor of lower bound are known as ATOMS.
- **Upper Bound:** Let $A \subseteq P$; then if $b \in P$ and $x \leq b \; \forall x \in A$ then, element b is upper bound
- **Greatest Lower Bound (Infimum):** 'y' is infimum of A, if y is lower bound of 'A' and 'z' is any other lower bound of then $z \leq y$, $\forall z \in P$
- **Least upper bound (Supremum):** 'x' is supremum of A, if x is an upper bound of 'A' and if 'z' is any other upper bound, then $x \leq z$, $\forall z \in P$.

Note

- If only one minimal exist then it is always "least"
- If only one maximal exist then it is always 'greatest"
- Immediate successors of lower bound are called 'atoms"

Example: *Consider the following hasse diagram for a poset P.*
Given P = {a, b, c, d, e, f}. Let S = {b, c, d} and $S \subseteq P$.
Then
Lower bound of S = b, a
Upper bound S = e, f
Infimum = b
No supremum element exist.
Minimal = a
Maximal = e, f
Least = a
No greatest elements exist.

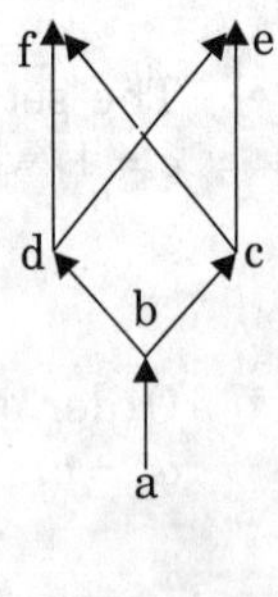

LATTICE

- A lattice L is a poset with every pair of element having a supremum and infimum.
- Let L be a non empty set closed under two binary operations called meet ($\wedge$) and join ($\vee$), then 'L' is a lattice if for any elements a, b and c of 'L' the following axioms hold.

1. **Commutative Laws:**

   (*i*) $a \wedge b = b \wedge a$

   (*ii*) $a \vee b = b \vee a$

2. **Associative Laws:**

   (*i*) $(a \wedge b) \wedge c = a \wedge (b \wedge c)$

   (*ii*) $(a \vee b) \vee c = a \vee (b \vee c)$

3. **Absorption Laws:**

   (*i*) $a \wedge (a \vee b) = a$

   (*ii*) $a \vee (a \wedge b) = a$

4. **Following hasse diagrams are "lattices".**

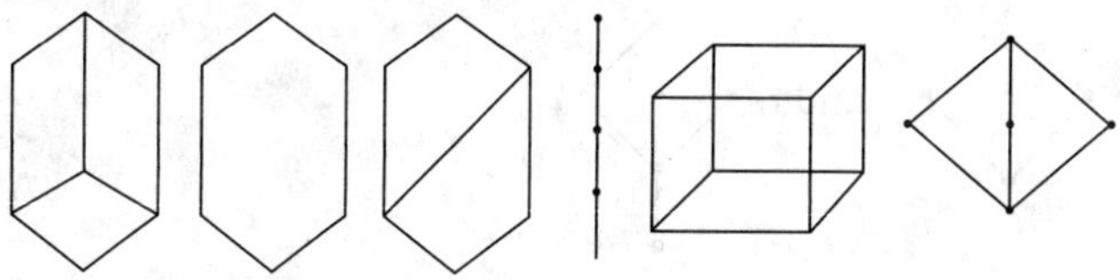

(*a*) (*b*) (*c*) (*d*) (*e*) (*f*)

- Every chain is a lattice.
- in lattice L; $a \wedge b = a$ if $a \vee b = b$.
- $x \wedge y$ = infimum (x, y) and $x \vee y$ = supremum (x, y).
- In lattice; every 2-element subset has infimum and supremum.

Types of Lattices

- **Bounded lattices:** Lattice with 1 as greatest element and 0 as least element i.e., if $0 \in$ L and $1 \in$ L then $0 \leq x \leq 1$, $\forall\, x \in$ L.
  - (L $\leq$, $\wedge$, $\vee$) and (P(s), $\subseteq$, $\cap$, $\cup$): bounded lattices.
  - (N, $\leq$, min, max) and (N, l, gcd, 1 cm) are not bounded.
  - Every finite lattice is bounded lattice.
- **Complemented lattice:**
  - It is bounded lattice where every element has atleast one complement.
  - x and y are complement if $x \vee y = 1$ and $x \wedge y = 0$.

- **Distributive lattice:**
  - For a lattice to be distributive, following conditions should be satisfied:

    (i) $a \wedge (b \vee c) = (a \wedge b) \vee (a \wedge c)\ \forall\ a, b, c \in L$

    (ii) $a \vee (b \wedge c) = (a \vee b) \wedge (a \vee c)\ \forall\ a, b, c \in L$
- Every element has a unique complement if distributive lattice is complemented.
- Lattice with elements less than 5 is always distributive.

e.g. 

- **Non distributive lattice:** Lattice with sublattice that is isomorphic to following lattices:

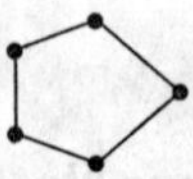 and 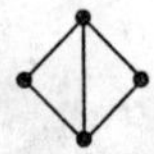

e.g., 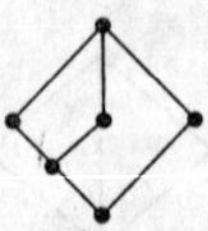 and 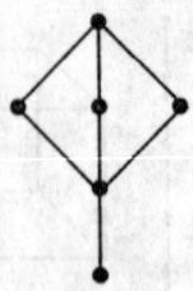

- **Modular lattice**
  - if a lattice satisfies; $a \vee (b \wedge c) = (a \vee b) \wedge c\ \forall\ a, b, c \in L$ and $a \leq c$.
  - every distributive lattice is modular.
- **Sub lattice:** Lattice with same meet ($\wedge$) and join ($\vee$) as the parent lattice.

  e.g. (D_{12}, /, *gcd*, *l* cm) is sublattice of (N, /, *gcd*, 1 cm) where '/' defines divide relation.
- **Dual Poset:** If (P, $\leq$) is poset then (P, $\geq$) is also a poset, such poset are dual poset.
- **Dual Lattice:** Lattice is dual if (L, $\leq$, $\wedge$, $\vee$) is a lattice and (L, $\geq$, $\vee$, $\wedge$) is also a lattice.
- **Complete lattice:** When every subset of lattice L has infimum and supremum in L then it is complete lattice.
- **Lexicographical Order (Dictionary order):** Let A_1 and A_2 $\rightarrow$ partial ordered sets, then lexicographical ordering ($\leq$) on $A_1 \times A_2$ is defined as:

  $(a_1, a_2) < (b_1, b_2)$; either "if $a_1 < b_1$" or both "$a_1 = b_1$ and $a_2 \leq b_2$"

- **Well ordered set**
  - For an ordered set A to be well-ordered;
    - it should be ordered linearly
    - must be a discrete set
    - every subset of A contains first element
  - Every 'Finite linearly ordered set' is well ordered.
- **Boolean Algebra (B, $\leq$, $\wedge$, $\vee$)**
  - When lattice is complemented and distributive
    e.g. (P(s), $\subseteq$, $\cap$, $\cup$)

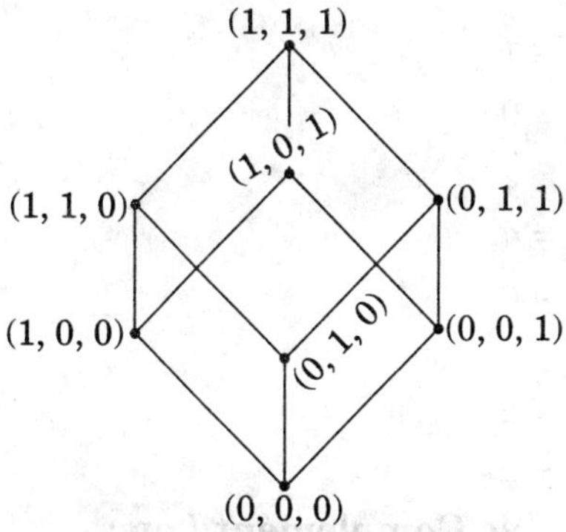

Boolean algebra
(complemented & distributive)

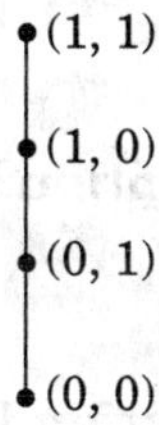

Not boolean algebra
(not complemented)

- It satisfies:
  - Lattice [poset, meet, join]
  - Bounded [lower, upper]
  - distributed and complemented lattice
- Let B be finite boolean algebra with n-atoms then B has 2^n elements and every non-zero element of B is sum of unique set of atoms.

  e.g. B is Boolean algebra with less than 100 elements then B can have 2^1, 2^2, 2^3, 2^4, 2^5, and 2^6 elements.
- Let a, b, c be any elements in a Boolean algebra B(B, +,', 0, 1) then;

1. Commutative Laws:

$$a + b = b + a$$
$$a * b = b * a$$

2. Associative Laws:

$$(a + b) + c = a + (b + c)$$
$$(a * b) * c = a\ 6* (b * c)$$

3. Distributive Laws:

$$a + (b * c) = (a + b) * (a + c)$$
$$a * (b + c) = (a * b) + (a * c)$$

4. Identity Laws:

$$a + 0 = a$$
$$a * 1 = a$$

5. Complement Laws:

$$a + a' = 1$$
$$a * a' = 0$$

6. Idempotent Laws:

$$a + a = a$$
$$a * a = a$$

7. Absorption Laws:

$$a + (a * b) = a$$
$$a * (a + b) = a$$

8. Involution Law or Double Complement Law:

$$[(a')' = a]$$
$$0' = 1$$
$$1' = 0 \quad \Rightarrow \quad (0')' = 0$$

9. DeMorgan's Law:

$$(a + b)' = a' * b'$$
$$(a * b)' = a' + b'$$

10. Domination Law:

$$a + 1 = 1$$
$$a * 0 = 0$$

Graph Theory

4

TERMINOLOGY

- **Isolated vertex:** Vertex with degree zero or **cone vertex.**
- **Pendent vertex:** Vertex with degree 1.
- **Degree of vertex:** Number of incident edges on a vertex. Self loop is counted twice denoted by $d(v)$.
- **Pendent edge:** Edge incident to pendent vertex.
- **Path:** Sequence of edge without vertex repetition.
- **Network:** Graph with one source and one sink.
- **Trial/Tour/walk:** Sequence of edge without repetition of edges, vertex may repeat.
- **Independence number:** Number of vertices in largest maximal independent set.
- **Diameter of graph:** Maximum distance between any 2 vertices.
- **Loop:** Edge drawn from a vertex to itself
- **Cut vertex (Articulation point):** Vertex when removed makes graph disconnected.
- **Cut Edge (Bridge):** Edge when removed, makes the graph disconnected.
- **Cut set:** Set of edges which when removed makes graph disconnected provided no proper subset of these edges disconnects the graph.
- **Edge connectivity:** Number of edges in smallest cutset of G, minimum number of edges whose removal disconnects the graph.
- **Weakly connected:** A digraph is weakly connected if the underlying undirected graph (remove all arrows in directed graph) is connected.
- **Vertex connectivity:** Minimum number of vertices which when removed results in disconnected graph or reduced to trivial graph.
- **Strongly connected:** In digraph, if path exist between any vertex to any other vertex. *i.e.*, for given vertices u and v; there exist a path from u to v as well as from v to u.
- **Unilaterally connected:** In digraph, if for every two vertices u and v there exist a path from either u to v or v to u and not necessarily both.

Points to Remember

- One or more cut set may exist in connected graph.
- For every cut edge; there exist a cut vertex as atleast one vertex of the cut edge is a cut vertex but not true for vice-versa.
- For an edge of connected graph G to be cut edge; the edge should not be part of any cycle in G.

GRAPHS

- Vertices when connected by directed or undirected lines called edge then it is known as graph.
- Graph G is defined by G = (V, E) where;
  V → vertices; E → edges.

  Types of graph:

  1. Directed graph:
  - also known as digraph.
  - the edges have defined direction.
  - edge (u, v) then edge is from u to v and not v to u.

  2. Undirected graph:
  - edges do to have direction defined, *i.e.*, they can be in any direction.
  - e.g. edge $\{u, v\}$ is either joining (u to v) or (v to u).

  3. Null graph/Discrete graph:
  - graph with 0 edge, only isolated vertices.

  4. Trivial graph:
  - graph with one vertex and no edges.

  5. Pseudo graph:
  - graph with self loops, parallel edges or multiple edges.

  6. Simple graph:
  - graph without self loop and no parallel edges.

  7. Regular graph:
  - graph with same degree vertices.
  - for 'k' as degree of vertices, it is called as 'k-regular graph'.

  8. Complete graph:
  - simple graph with 'n-mutually adjacent vertices'.
  - represented by k_n.
  - every complete graph is regular.
  - degree of each vertex in $k_n = n - 1$.
  - number of edges in

$$k_n = |E(k_n)| = \frac{n(n-1)}{2}$$

9. Cycle graph:

- simple graph with edges forming a cycle of length n where n vertices and n edges are present and $n \geq 3$.

10. Wheel graph:

- W_n or wheel graph is simple graph with n-vertices ($n \geq 4$) obtained from C_{n-1}, by adding a new vertex which is adjacent to all vertices of C_{n-1}.

  Number of edges = $|E(w_n)| = 2(n-1)$

11. Bi-connected graph:

- not cut vertices and no bridges

12. k-connected graph:

- removal of k-vertices results in disconnected graph

13. k-line connected graph:

- removal of k-edges results in disconnected graph

14. Non-separable graph:

- graph without any cut vertices hence, no cut edges (bridges)

Points to remember

In simple graph:

- maximum number of edges possible with n vertices

$$= n(n-1)/2 = nC_2$$

- number of graphs with n labelled vertices = $2^{n(n-1)/2}$
- is connected if;

$$|E| > \frac{(n-1)(n-2)}{2}$$

- with n-vertices and 'k' component has:
  - atleast $(n-k)$ *i.e.*, $|E| \geq (n-k)$ edges.
  - atmost $[(n-k)(n-k+1)]/2$ edges.

- In Any Graph;
  - ➢ number of vertices with odd degree is always even
  - ➢ if degree of each vertex = k then; graph is k-regular graph where;

$$|E| = \frac{k|v|}{2} = \frac{nk}{2} \quad (|v| = n)$$

  - ➢ if degree of each vertex is atleast k;

    i.e., minimum degree = k

    then $\quad |E| \geq \dfrac{k|v|}{2}$

Hand Shaking Theorem: Let G = (V, E) be non-directed graph with $V = \{v_1, v_2, \ldots v_n\}$

Then; $$\sum_{i=1}^{n} \deg(v_i) = 2|E|$$

TREE

- An acyclic graph or graph with no cycle.

Spanning Tree

- Considering a connected graph G = (V, E); spanning tree T is a sub-graph of G if T is a tree and T includes all the vertices of G.
- Number of spanning trees for $k_n = n^{n-2}$.
- Number bridges for spanning tree with n-edges = $n - 1$.
- Number of binary trees with n-vertices

$$= \frac{^{2n}C_n}{n+1} = \frac{2n!}{n!(n+1)!}$$

- k-tree (forest) with total n-vertices have $(n - k)$ edges.
- **Circuit Rank of graph:** Number of edges that must be removed from connected graph with n-vertices and e-edge to produce spanning tree.
- Circuit Rank/Nullity/Cyclomatic Complexity

$$= e - (n - 1) \text{ edges.}$$

- Number of edges that need to be removed to produce forest with n-vertices, e-edges and k-components

$$= e - (n - k) \text{ edges.}$$

- A finite tree has atleast two degree of vertices of degree 1.
- The number of different trees with vertex set $\{V_1, V_2, \ldots V_n\}$ in which the vertices have degree $d_1, d_2, \ldots d_n$ respectively

$$= \frac{(n-2)!}{(d_1 - 1)!\,(d_2 - 1)!\ldots(d_n - 1)!}$$

Bipartite graph

- Graph G = (V, E) is bipartite if its vertices V can be partitioned into two subsets V_1 and V_2 so that each edge of G connects a vertex of V_1 to a vertex of V_2. *i.e.*, $V = V_1 \cup V_2$ and $V_1 \cap V_2 = \phi$.
- Maximum number of edges with 'n' vertices = $\left[\frac{n^2}{4}\right]$.
- It is either even length cycle or acyclic.

Complete Bipartite graph

- Bipartite graph is complete when every vertex in V_1 is adjacent to every vertex in V_2.
- Denoted by $(k_{m,n})$. It is regular graph of degree m.
- Vertices → $(m + n)$ and edges → (mn)

Planar graph

- Graph or a multigraph that can be drawn on a plane so that no edges cross.

$$\sum_{i=1}^{n} \deg(V_i) = 2|E| \quad \text{and} \quad \sum_{i=1}^{n} \deg(r_i) = 2|E|$$

where r_i are regions

- if degree of each region is:

  k then $k \cdot |R| = 2|E|$; atleast 3 then $3|R| \le 2|E|$
- For simple planar graph:

Euler's formula

Connected graph: $|R| = |E| - |V| + 2$

k components: $|R| = |E| - |V| + (k + 1)$

Connected planar simple

$$|E| \le \{3|V| - 6\}$$

Connected planar simple graph with no triangles:

$$|R| \le \{2|V| - 4\}$$

- There exist atleast one vertex; $V \in G$ such that degree $(V) \le 5$.
- $k_{m,n}$ is planar $\leftrightarrow$ $(m \le 2$ or $n \le 2)$
- k_n is planar $\leftrightarrow n \le 4$
- A non planar graph with minimum number of

  vertices → k_5; edges → $k_{3,3}$

Polyhedral graph

- Simple connected planar graph. $G = (V, E)$
- Every interior region is a polygon of same degree and degree of every vertex deg $(v) \ge 3$

  $3|V| \le 2|E|$; $3|R| \le 2|E|$

Complementary graph

- Complement of $G = \overline{G}$.
- It is simple graph with same vertices as of G and two vertices are adjacent in $\overline{G}$ if the two vertices are not adjacent in G.
- $G \cup \overline{G} = k_n$
- $|E(G)| + |E(\overline{G})| = |E(k_n)| = \dfrac{n(n-1)}{2}$

Isomorphic graph

- Two graphs G and G* are isomorphic if there is a function $f : V(G) \to V(G^*)$ such that, f is bijection and "for each pair of vertices u and v of G : $\{u, v\} \in E(G)$ if $\{f(u), f(v)\} \in E(G^*)$".
- It G and $\overline{G}$ are isomorphic then; number of edges, number of vertices, degree sequence and number of cycles of every length are same.
- If G is a simple graph such that $G \cong \overline{G}$ then G is said to be "self complementary". Where;

$$|E(G)| = \frac{n(n-1)}{4};$$

where n is number of vertices in G.

Homomorphism

G_1 is homomorphic to G if it can be obtained by dividing some edge of G.

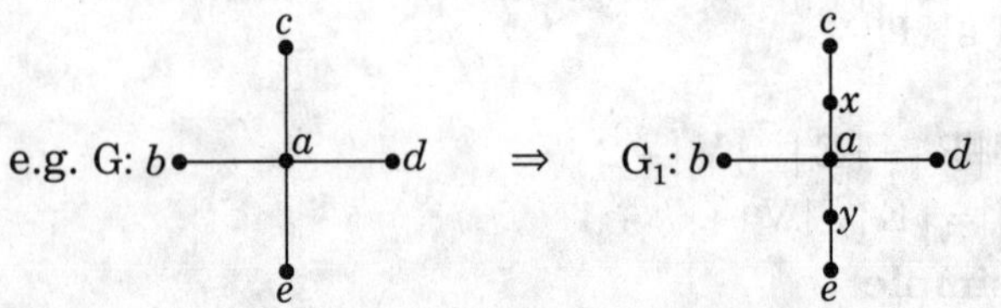

Here: $\{a, c\}$ of G is divided into $\{c, x\}$ and $\{x, a\}$ edges.
$\{e, a\}$ of G is divided into $\{e, y\}$ and $\{y, a\}$ edges.

Colouring or Proper Colouring

- The vertices of graph G = (V, E) are coloured such that adjacent vertices have different colours.
- Proper colouring is when two adjacent vertices u and v have different colours otherwise it is improper colouring.

Chromatic Number x(G)

- Minimum number of colours needed to colour the vertex.
- $x(G)$ of $k_n = x(k_n) = n$
- Tree and Bipartite graph are 2-colourable.
- It can also be said that for non-empty to be bichromatic, it must be Bipartite.
- Any planar graph is 4-colorable *i.e.*, x(planar graph) ≤ 4.
- k cycle graph:
  2-colorable; k is even length cycle
  3-colorable; k is odd length cycle
- Chromatic partition is given by equivalence relation between vertices of the same colour in a connected graph.

MATCHING

When atmost 1 edge is incident on every vertex in a set of edges in graph G = (V, E).

$$\text{Degree (V)} \leq 1$$

Maximal Matching: No edge of the graph can be added to matching.

Maximum Matching: Matching with maximum number of edges.

Perfect Matching

- Matching that is also a covering *i.e.*, every vertex contain exactly one edge incident to it in graph (G = V, E).

$$\text{Degree (V)} = 1$$

Number of perfect matching for $k_{2n} = \dfrac{(2n)!}{2^n \times n!}$ $(n \rightarrow \text{even})$

Complete Matching: In a bipartite graph with vertex partition, V_1 and V_2; complete matching between two partition is when every vertex in V_1 is matched against certain vertex in V_2, such that no two vertices of V_1 is matched against single vertex in V_2.

Covering

- In graph G = (V, E); it is set of edges where every vertex is incident with atleast one edge

$$[\deg (V_i) \geq 1] \ (V_i \in G)$$

- **line covering** of graph has atleast $n/2$ edges for n vertices
- Cycle cannot be present in **minimal line covering.** The components are always stargraphs and no edge can be deleted.

Minimal Covering : Edges are not deleted while still covering the vertices.

Minimum Covering: Smallest minimal covering (less number of edges)

Covering Number: Number of edges in minimum covering.

Traversable Multigraph

- When a path that include all the vertices and uses each edge exactly once exist in a graph *i.e.*, either Euler cycle or Euler trail) Then such graph is traversable.
- **Eularian graph:** When graph have closed traversable path with no edge repetition (vertices may repeat).
- Condition for graph G to be traversable: number of vertices with odd degree = 0 or 2.
- If number of vertices with odd degree is;

  exactly 2: Euler path exists but Euler circuit does not exist

  0: Euler circuit exist not Euler path
- **Hamiltonian path:** path where vertex of the graph are present exactly once without any repetition.
- **Hamiltonian cycle:** hamiltonian path with some first and last vertex.

Probability

5

MEAN, MEDIAN AND MODE

- Mean $(\bar{X}) = \dfrac{\sum_{i=1}^{n} x_i}{n} = \dfrac{\sum_{i=1}^{n} f_i x_i}{\sum f_i}$

- Median $= \dfrac{x_{n/2} + (x_{n/2} + 1)}{2}$; n is even

  $= x_{n+1/2}$; n is odd

  $= L_{med} + \left(\dfrac{N/2 - F}{f}\right) \times W$

  where L_{med} = lower limit of median class
  $N = \Sigma f_i$
  F = Cumulative frequency upto the median class (cumulative frequency of the preceding class)
  f = frequency of the median class

- **Mode:** Value of 'x' corresponding to maximum frequency.

  $L_{mode} + \dfrac{f_m - f_1}{(2f_m - f_1 - f_2)} \times h$

  Where L_{mode} = lower limit of modal class
  f_m = frequency of modal class
  f_1 = preceding frequency of modal class
  f_2 = Following frequency of modal class

  Mode = 3 Median – 2 Mean [for Asymmetric distribution]
  Mean = Mode = Median [for Symmetric distribution]

Points to remember

- For Asymmetric distribution ; Mode = 3 median – 2 mean
- For Symmetric distribution, Mean = Mode = Median.

AXIOMS OF PROBABILITY

Let A and B be two events. Then

1. $P(\bar{A}) = 1 - P(A)$
2. $P(\phi) = 0$; ϕ is the empty set
3. $P(A - B) = P(A) - P(A \cap B)$
4. $P(A - B) = P(A \cap \bar{B})$
5. $P(A \cup B) = P(A) + P(B) - P(A \cap B)$
6. $P(A \cup B) = P(A) + P(B)$; mutually exclusive events.
7. $P(A \cap B) = P(A) . P(B/A) = P(B). P(A/B)$
8. $P(A \cap B) = P(A) . P(B)$; independent events.
9. $P(A \cap B) = \phi$; mutually exclusive events.
10. $P(S) = 1$; S is sample space.
11. $\max(0, P(A) + P(B) - 1) \leq P(A \cap B) \leq \min(P(A), P(B))$
12. $\max(P(A), P(B)) \leq P(A \cup B) \leq \min(1, P(A) + P(B))$
13. $\max(0, P(A_1) + P(A_2) .... + P(A_n) - (n - 1)) \leq P(A_1 \cap A_2 ... \cap A_n) \leq \min(P(A_1), P(A_2) ...., P(A_n))$
14. $\max(P(A_1), P(A_2)...., P(A_n)) \leq P(A_1 \cup A_2.... \cup A_n) \leq \min(1, P(A_1) + P(A_2) .... + P(A_n))$
15. $P(A \mid B) = \dfrac{P(A \cap B)}{P(B)}$
16. $P(A \mid B) = P(A)$; independent events.
17. $P(E_1 \cap E_2 \cap .... \cap E_n) = P(E_1) .P(E_2).... P(E_n)$; independent events.
18. Rule of total probability : $P(X) = \sum_{i=1}^{n} P(E_i)P(X \mid E_i)$
19. Baye's Theorem:

$$P(E_1 \mid X) = \frac{P(E_1) \cdot P(X \mid E_1)}{P(E_1) \cdot P(X \mid E_1) + P(E_2) \cdot P(X \mid E_2) + P(E_3)P(X \mid E_3)}$$

In general, $$P(E_i \mid X) = \frac{P(E_i) \cdot P(X \mid E_i)}{\sum_{j=1}^{n} P(E_j) \cdot P(X \mid E_j)}$$

RANDOM VARIABLE (STOCHASTIC VARIABLE)

Random variable assigns a real number to each possible outcome. Let X be a discrete random variable, then

1. $P(x) = P(X \leq x)$ is called distribution function $\sum_{i=0}^{n} P(i)$ *of* X.

2. Mean or Expectation of X = μ = E(X) = $\sum_{i=1}^{n} x_i \, P(x_i)$

3. Variance of X = σ^2 = E(X^2) – [E(X)]^2 = $\sum_{i=1}^{n} (x_i - \mu)^2 \, P(x_i)$

4. Standard deviation of X = σ = $\sqrt{\text{Variance}}$

5. $\sum_{i=1}^{n} P(x_i) = 1$

Types of Random Variables

Discrete
- Finite set of values or countably infinite

Continuous/non-discrete
- Infinite number of uncountable values.

DISCRETE DISTRIBUTION

1. **Binomial distribution:** Probability of an event to occur with r successes and $n–r$ failures *i.e.* event will occur exactly $\underline{r}$ times in n trials.

$$P(x = r) = P(r) = \sum {}^nC_r p^r q^{n-r}$$

$$\text{Mean} = E(x) = np$$

$$\text{Variance} = \sigma^2 = V(x) = npq = np(1-p)$$

$$\text{Standard deviation} = \sigma = \sqrt{npq} = \sqrt{np(1-p)}$$

where; $r = 0, 1 \ldots n$

$q = 1 - p$

n = fixed number of trial

p = probability of success.

2. **Poisson Distribution:** Frequency distribution that gives probability of number of independent events occuring in a fixed time.

$$P(X = x) = \sum \frac{e^{-\lambda} \cdot \lambda^x}{x!} \; ; x = 0, 1, 2 \ldots, \infty$$

Where; X = discrete random variables

λ = Parameter of distribution (positive constant)

- Mean (μ) = Variance (σ^2) = λ
- Standard deviation (σ) = $\sqrt{\lambda}$
- Poisson is limiting case of Binomial as $n \to \infty$ and P$\to$ 0.

CONTINUOUS DISTRIBUTION

Let X be continuous random variable. Then

(*i*) Density functions:

- $P(X \le a) = \int_{-\infty}^{a} f(x) \cdot dx$
- $P(a \le X \le b) = \int_{a}^{b} f(x) \cdot dx$

(*ii*) Mean = $E(x) = \int_{-\infty}^{\infty} x \cdot f(x) \cdot dx$

(*iii*) Variance of X = V(X)

$$= \int_{-\infty}^{\infty} [x - E(x)]^2 \cdot f(x)dx = E(x^2) - (E(x))^2$$

$$= \int_{-\infty}^{\infty} x^2 f(X)dx - \left[\int_{-\infty}^{\infty} xf(x)dX\right]^2$$

(*iv*) $\int^{\infty} f(x)dx = 1$

1. **Uniform distribution** also called Rectangular distribution

   (*i*) Density function

   $$f(x) = \frac{1}{b-a}\ ;\ a \le x \le b = 0\ ;\ \text{otherwise}$$

   (*ii*) Cumulative function

   $$P(X \le x) = \int_{-\infty}^{x} f(x) \cdot dx$$

   $$= \begin{cases} 0 & ;\ \textit{if } x \le a \\ \dfrac{x-a}{b-a} & ;\ \textit{if } a \le x \le b \\ 1 & ;\ \textit{if } x > b \end{cases}$$

   (*iii*) Mean (μ) = $(a + b)/2$ = E(X)

   (*iv*) Variance (σ^2) = $(b - a)^2/12$

2. **Normal distribution**

   (*i*) Density function

   $$f(x) = \frac{1}{\sigma\sqrt{2\pi}} \cdot e^{-\frac{1}{2}\left(\frac{x-\mu}{\sigma}\right)^2}\ ;\ -\infty \le x \le \infty,\ \sigma > 0,\ -\infty < \mu < \infty$$

   (*ii*) Normal distribution is symmertrical

(*iii*) Mean = μ; Variance = σ^2

(*iv*) $f(x) \geq 0$ for all x

(*v*) $\int^{m} f(x) \cdot dx = 1$

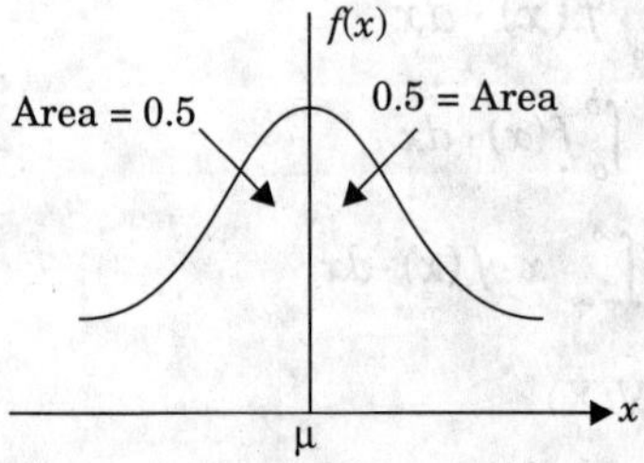

(*vi*) $P(Z) = \frac{1}{\sqrt{2\pi}} e^{-\frac{Z^2}{2}}$; $-\infty \leq Z \leq \infty$ and $Z = \frac{x-\mu}{\sigma}$

$Z = \frac{x - np}{\sqrt{npq}}$ (when approximating binomial by normal)

Z = Standard normal variate

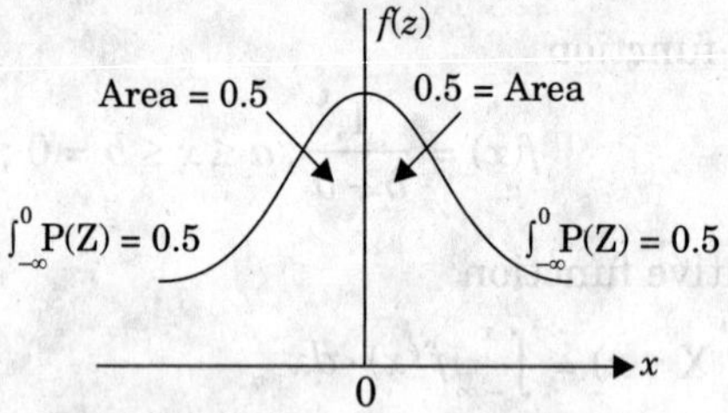

3. Exponential distribution.

(*i*) Density function:

$$f(x)\ \lambda.e^{-\lambda x} ; x > 0 = 0 \text{ ; Otherwise}$$

(*ii*) Mean $(\mu) = \frac{1}{\lambda}$ = S.D(σ)

(*iii*) Variance $(\sigma^2) = \frac{1}{\lambda^2}$

6 Linear Algebra

Definition: Study of linear transformations.

Matrix

- A rectangular array of numbers, symbols or repression arranged in rows and columns.
- Plural is called matrices.
- **Principal Diagonal:** In a square matrix all elements a_{ij} for which $i = j$ are elements of principal diagonal.
  (i = rows; j = column of matrix)
- **Upper triangular matrix:** A square matrix will all elements as zero below principal diagonal.
- **Lower triangular matrix:** Square matrix with all elements as zero above the principal diagonal.
- **Diagonal matrix:** Square matrix will all elements as zero except elements of principal diagonal.
- **Scalar matrix:** Diagonal matrix with all elements of principle diagonal being same.
- **Idempotent matrix:** $A^2 = A$ (A is square matrix).
- **Involuntary matrix:** $A^2 = I$ (A is square matrix).
- **Nilpotent matrix:** A is square matrix where $A^m = 0$ (m is least positive integer and also known as Index of class of Nilpotent matrix A)
- **Transpose matrix:** Matrix obtained by switching rows to columns and columns to rows.
  A^T is transpose matrix of A
- **Symmetric matrix:** When $A^T = A$ for A being square matrix.
- **Skew-Symmetric matrix:** When $A^T = -A$.
- **Conjugate matrix:** Matrix obtained by replacing the elements by conjugate complex number.
  $(\overline{A})$ or $(\sim A)$ is conjugate of (A).
- **Orthogonal matrix:** If $A^T = A^{-1}$ or $AA^T = I = A^TA$ then A is orthogonal matrix.

- **Transpose conjugate matrix:** → (A^θ) or $A^* = (\overline{A})^T$
- **Hermitian matrix:** A is a square matrix where $A^\theta = A$ matrix with all diagonal elements as real numbers and all off-diagonal elements above and below principal diagonal are conjugate of each other *i.e.*, $a_{ij} = \overline{a}_{ji}$

  e.g. $\begin{bmatrix} 2 & 3-4i \\ 3+4i & 5 \end{bmatrix}$

- **Skew Hermitian matrix:** A is square matrix and $A^\theta = -A$ matrix with zero or purely imaginary diagonal elements and all off diagonal elements above and below the principle diagonal are conjugate of each other with opposite sign *i.e.*, $a_{ij} = -\overline{a}_{ji}$

  e.g. $\begin{bmatrix} 2i & 3-4i \\ -3-4i & 5i \end{bmatrix}$

- **Unitary matrix:** A is square matrix; $A^\theta = A^{-1}$ or $AA^\theta = I = A^\theta A$
- **Boolean matrix:** Matrix with only '0' and '1' element.
- **Sparse matrix:** Matrix with more zero elements.
- **Dense matrix:** Non-sparse matrix.
- **Singular matrix:** $|A| = 0$; it also have inverse.
- **Non singular matrix:** $|A| \neq 0$.
- **Adjoint matrix:** Transpose of cofactors matrix.

  i.e., $\text{Adj}(A) = (\text{cof}(A))^t$.

Properties of Matrix

- **Commutative:**

  $$A + B = B + A$$

- **Associative:**

  $$-(A + B) + C = A + (B + C)$$

  $$-(AB)C = A(BC)$$

- **Non-Commutative:**

  $$AB \neq BA$$

- **Distributive:**

  $$A(B + C) = AB + AC$$

- $A = \frac{1}{2}(A + A^T) + \frac{1}{2}(A - A^T)$

- $A(\text{Adj } A) = (\text{Adj } A)\, A = A\, I_n$
- $\text{Adj } (AB) = (\text{Adj } B) \,.\, (\text{Adj } A)$
- $A^{-1} = \dfrac{\text{Adj } A}{|A|}$; $|A| \neq 0$
- $(A^{-1})^{-1} = A$ and $(A^{-1})^T = (A^T)^{-1}$
- $(AB)^{-1} = B^{-1} A^{-1}$
- If A is a square matrix of n order then,
  - ➢ $|\text{Adj } A| = (\det A)^{n-1^2} = |A|^{n-1}$
  - ➢ $|\text{Adj } (\text{Adj } A)| = |A|^{(n-1)^2}$
  - ➢ $A + A^T$: Symmetric
  - ➢ $A - A^T$: Skew symmetric
- If $|A| \neq 0$ then $|A^{-1}| = \dfrac{1}{|A|}$
- If $A_{n \times n}$ matrix then, $|kA| = k^n |A|$
- If A and B are symmetric;
  - ➢ $(A + B)$, $(A - B)$, $(AB + BA)$ and (A^n and B^n) all are symmetric
  - ➢ $(AB - BA)$ is skew-symmetric
- If A and B are skew symmetric then;
  - ➢ $(A + B)$ and $(A - B)$ are skew symmetric.
  - ➢ (A^n and B^n) are skew symmetric if n = odd.
  - ➢ (A^n and B^n) are symmetric for n = even.
- The determinant of orthogonal matrix and unitary matrix A has absolute value '1'.

  If $A_{m \times n}$ and $B_{n \times p}$ then product of AB requires

  (*i*) mnp multiplications

  (*ii*) $m(n - 1)p$ additions

  (*iii*) for each entry, n multiplications and $(n - 1)$ additions.

$$(A^T)^T = A,\ (kA)^T = k(A^T)$$

$$(A + B)^T = A^T + B^T,\ (AB)^T = B^T A^T$$

Rank of matrix or (r(A))

- it is number of linearly independent rows or columns in the matrix.
- it is the order of its largest non-vanishing *i.e.*, non-zero minor of the matrix.
- A and B are 2 matrices;
  - ➢ $r(A + B) \leq r(A) + r(B)$
  - ➢ $r(A - B) \geq r(A) - r(B)$
  - ➢ $r(AB) \leq \min \{r(A), r(B)\}$

- Rank of diagonal matrix = number of non-zero elements in diagonal.
- If rank (A) = r and number of variables = n then number of linearly independent infinite solutions of AX = 0 is $(n - r)$.
- The system of linear equation AX = B has.
  - Consistent; if $r(A) = r(A \mid B)$
  - Unique solution; $r(A) = r(A \mid B)$ = number of variables
  - Infinitely many solution; $r(A) = r(A \mid B)$ < number of variables
  - No solution; $r(A) \neq r(A \mid B)$ *i.e.*, $r(A) < r(A \mid B)$
- The system of linear equation AX = 0;
  - Unique | zero | trivial solution; $r(A)$ = number of variables.
  - Infinitely many solution or non-trivial; $r(A)$ < number of variables.
- In system with homogenous linear equation AX = 0;
  - A is singular; nontrivial solution/infinite solution.
  - A is non singular; Trivial/zero/unique solution.

EIGEN VALUE

- Roots of characteristic equation of a matrix is eigen value or latent roots or characteristic roots.
- If A is square matrix of n order and λ be scalar then $|A - \lambda I| = 0$ is its characteristic equation.
- **Spectrum of matrix:** set of eigen values of a matrix.
- Matrix with n order will have n latent roots that might not be distinct.

EIGEN VECTOR

There exist a non-zero solution X, corresponding to each eigen value λ such that $(A - \lambda I)X = 0$. X is eigen vector or latent vector or characteristic vector of A.

Properties : Eigenvalues of

- symmetric matrix $\rightarrow$ real
- skew symmetric matrix $\rightarrow$ purely imaginary or zero.

Properties of Eigen Values

Sum of eigen values of a matrix = sum of elements of principal diagonal (trace).

$$\Sigma\lambda_i = \lambda_1 + \lambda_2 + \lambda_3 + ... + \lambda_n = \text{Trace of A}$$

Product of eigen values = Determinant of matrix.

$$\Pi\lambda_i = \lambda_1 \cdot \lambda_2 \cdot .... \lambda_n = |A|$$

If λ is eigen value of A then $\frac{1}{\lambda}$ is eigen value of A^{-1}. (provided $\lambda \neq 0$ *i.e.*, A is non-singular).

Eigen values of A and A^T are same

If λ is eigen value of orthogonal matrix then $\frac{1}{\lambda}$ is also its eigen value $[\because A^T = A^{-1}]$

If $\lambda_1, \lambda_2, ..., \lambda_n$ are eigen values of matrix 'A', then

(*i*) $\lambda_1^m, \lambda_2^m, ..., \lambda_n^m$ are eigen values of matrix A^m.

(*ii*) $\lambda_1 + K, \lambda_2 + K, ..., + K$ are eigen values of $A + KI$

(*iii*) $(\lambda_1 - K)^2, (\lambda_2 - K)^2, ..., \lambda_n (\lambda_n - K)^2$ are eigen values of $(A - KI)^2$

(*iv*) $K\lambda_1, K\lambda_2, ..., K\lambda_n$ are eigen values of KA.

The eigen values of symmetric matrix are real.

The eigen values of skew-symmetric matrix are either purely imaginary or zero.

The modulus of the eigen values of orthogonal and unitary matrices = 1.

If a matrix is either lower or upper triangular or diagonal then the principal diagonal elements themselves are the eigen values.

Zero is eigen value of a matrix iff the matrix is singular.

7 Numerical Methods

Linear Algebraic Equations

$$a_{11}x_1 + a_{12}x_2 + a_{13}x_3 = b_1$$
$$a_{21}x_1 + a_{22}x_2 + a_{23}x_3 = b_2$$
$$a_{31}x_1 + a_{32}x_2 + a_{33}x_3 = b_3$$

$$A = \begin{bmatrix} a_{11} & a_{12} & a_{13} \\ a_{21} & a_{22} & a_{23} \\ a_{31} & a_{32} & a_{33} \end{bmatrix}_{3\times 3}, X = \begin{bmatrix} x_1 \\ x_2 \\ x_3 \end{bmatrix}_{3\times 1}, B = \begin{bmatrix} b_1 \\ b_2 \\ b_3 \end{bmatrix}_{3\times 1}$$

LU Decomposition or LU Factorization or Triangularization (Doolittle's Crout's triangularisation Method)

- Principle minors of A are non-singular.

$AX = B \Rightarrow LUX = B$ [since $A = LU$]

- $A = \begin{bmatrix} a_{11} & a_{12} & a_{13} \\ a_{21} & a_{22} & a_{23} \\ a_{31} & a_{32} & a_{33} \end{bmatrix} = \begin{bmatrix} 1 & 0 & 0 \\ l_{21} & 1 & 0 \\ l_{31} & l_{32} & 1 \end{bmatrix} \begin{bmatrix} u_{11} & u_{12} & u_{13} \\ 0 & u_{22} & u_{23} \\ 0 & 0 & u_{33} \end{bmatrix}$ (Doolittle's method)

- $A = \begin{bmatrix} a_{11} & a_{12} & a_{13} \\ a_{21} & a_{22} & a_{23} \\ a_{31} & a_{32} & a_{33} \end{bmatrix} = \begin{bmatrix} l_{11} & 0 & 0 \\ l_{21} & l_{22} & 0 \\ l_{31} & l_{32} & l_{33} \end{bmatrix} \begin{bmatrix} 1 & u_{12} & u_{13} \\ 0 & 1 & u_{23} \\ 0 & 0 & 1 \end{bmatrix}$ (Crout's method)

Order of Computation in Doolittle's Method:

In Doolittle's method the equations are set-up row-wise for A's elements.

(*a*) First row of $A \Rightarrow u_{11} = a_{11}; = u_{12} = a_{12}; u_{13} = a_{13}$

(*b*) Second row of $A \Rightarrow l_{21} = \dfrac{a_{21}}{a_{11}}; u_{22} = a_{22} - \dfrac{a_{21}}{a_{11}} \cdot a_{12}; u_{23} = a_{23} - l_{21}u_{13}$

(*c*) Third row of $A \Rightarrow$

$$l_{31} = \frac{a_{31}}{a_{11}}; l_{33} = \frac{1}{u_{22}}\left[a_{32} - \frac{a_{31}}{a_{11}} \cdot a_{12}\right]; u_{33} = a_{33} - l_{31} \cdot u_{13} - l_{33}u_{23}$$

Similarly, in Crout's method the equations are set-up column-wise for A elements.

ROOT FINDING METHODS

1. Bisection/Binary Chopping/Half-Interval/Bolzano Method

$x_2 = \frac{x_0 + x_1}{2}$ (x_2 is the new value and x_0, x_1 are the old values)

For next step if $f(x_0) \cdot f(x_2) < 0$ then replace $x_1 \leftarrow x_2$ else replace $x_0 \leftarrow x_2$

(*i*) Convergence is slow but sure (guaranteed).

(*ii*) Rate of convergence is 1 (Linear/First order)

(*iii*) It cannot find complex roots of equation. After n bisections, the length of subinterval, which contains $x_n = \frac{b-a}{2^n}$.

i.e., after n bisections $\qquad$ $\text{error}_{max} = \frac{b-a}{2^n}$

(*iv*) If the error is to be made less than the error tolerance ε,

$$\text{number of iterations 'n'} = \left\lceil \frac{\log\left(\frac{b-a}{\varepsilon}\right)}{\log 2} \right\rceil = \left\lceil \log_2\left(\frac{b-a}{\varepsilon}\right) \right\rceil$$

2. Regular-Falsi Method (Method of False Position)

$$x_2 = \frac{f_1 x_0 - f_0 x_1}{f_1 - f_0}$$

For next step if $f(x_0) \cdot f(x_2) < 0$ then replace $x_1 \leftarrow x_2$ else replace $x_0 \leftarrow x_2$

(*i*) Convergence is guaranteed.

(*ii*) Order of convergence = 1 (linear/First order)

(*iii*) It cannot find complex roots.

3. Secant Method (Interpolation Method)

$$x_2 = \frac{f_1 x_0 - f_0 x_1}{f_1 - f_0}$$

Successive iteration takes last two iterations *i.e.*, both may be (+ve) or both may be (–ve), or one is (+ve) another is (–ve).

(*i*) It can find complex roots.

(*ii*) Faster convergence, no guarantee of convergence.

(*iii*) Order of convergence = 1.62.

4. **Newton Raphson Method (Method of Tangents)**

(*i*) Two functions are evaluated per iteration.

(*ii*) Best method to find complex roots of equation.

(*iii*) Choice of initial approximation x_0 is very important for converges.

(*iv*) If $f(a)$ and $f(b)$ are of opposite signs, a root of $f(x) = 0$ lies between 'a' and 'b', this idea can be used to fix the approximate root.

(*v*) If $f'(x_n) \neq 0$,

$$x_{n+1} = x_n - \frac{f(x_n)}{f'(x_n)}$$

(*vi*) Order of convergence = 2 (*i.e.*, quadratic convergence)

(*vii*) When $f'(x)$ is very large, then correct value of root can be find with "minimum" number of iterations.

(*viii*) The error at any stage is proportional to the square of error previous stage $\varepsilon_{i+1} \propto \varepsilon_i^2$.

(*ix*) Condition for convergence $f'(x) \neq 0$ and $|f(x) \cdot f''(x)| < |f'(x)|^2$.

(*x*) The number of accurate significant digits doubles after a iteration.

Numerical Integration

It is the process of finding or evaluating a definite integral $I = \int_a^b f(x)dx$ from a set of numerical values of the integrand $f(x)$.

1. **Trapezoidal Rule:**

(*i*) $I = \int_{x_0}^{x_n} y \cdot dx = \frac{h}{2}[(y_0 + y_n) + 2(y_1 + y_2 + ... + y_{n-1})]$

(*ii*) $h = (x_n - x_0)/n_i$ (where n_i = Number of intervals)

(*iii*) It gives exact result when the integrand is polynomial of degrand or '1'.

(*iv*) If we are evaluating $I = \int_a^b f(x)dx$ by trapezoidal rule then

$$\text{Error} = -\frac{h^3}{12} \cdot f''(\xi) \times n_i \quad (a \leq \xi \leq b)$$

(*v*) Error is order of h^2 and error term is h^3

(*vi*) If for the same integration limits, tabulation (step size) is halved then error is reduced by factor '4'.

2. Simpson's Rule:

(*i*) It gives exact result when polynomial of degree ≤ 3.

(*ii*) If we are evaluating $I = \int_a^b f(x)dx$ by Simpson's rule then

$$\text{Error} = -\frac{h^5}{90} \cdot f^{iv}(\xi) \times n_i \quad (a \le \xi \le b)$$

(*iii*) Simpson's rule is more accurate as compare to trapezoidal rule, since it is a fourth order method as compared to trapezoidal rule which is second order.

(*iv*) Simpson's 1/3rd Rule:

$$\int_{x_0}^{x_n} ydx = \frac{h}{3} [(y_0 + y_n) + 2(y_2 + y_4 + \ldots + y_{n-2}) + 4(y_1 + y_3 + \ldots + y_{n-1})]$$

(*v*) Simpson's 3/8 Rule:

$$\int_{x_0}^{x_n} ydx = \frac{3h}{8} [(y_0 + y_n) + 2(y_3 + y_6 + \ldots + y_{n-3}) + 3(y_1 + y_2 + \ldots + y_{n-1})]$$

(*vi*) If tabulation (step size) is halved, the error in Simpson's rule evaluation of the integral is reduced by a factor of '16'.

Calculus

8

LIMIT, CONTINUITY AND DIFFERENTIABILITY

Limit Existence at a Point

- Left Limit (LHL): $\lim_{x \to a^-} f(x) = \lim_{h \to 0} f(a-h)$

  Right Limit (RHL): $\lim_{x \to a^+} f(x) = \lim_{h \to 0} f(a+h)$

  $\lim_{x \to a} f(x)$ exists, iff LHL and RHL exits.

- Indeterminate forms 0/0, ∞/∞, $0 \times \infty$, $\infty - \infty$, $0^0, 1^\infty, 0^\infty$

  L Hospital's Rule: If $\lim_{x \to a} [f(x)/g(x)]$ is of the form either 0/0 or ∞/∞ then $\lim_{x \to a} [f(x)/g(x)] = \lim_{x \to a} [f'(x)/g'(x)]$

Continuity

A function $f(x)$ is said to be continuous at $x = a$ if:

$$\lim_{x \to a^+} f(x) = \lim_{x \to a^-} f(x) = f(a)$$

- If $f(x)$ and $g(x)$ is continuous function then following are also continuous

  (i) $f(x) + g(x)$ (ii) $f(x) \cdot g(x)$

  (iii) $f(x) - g(x)$ (iv) $f(x)/g(x)$ $[g(x) \neq 0]$

- Polynomial, Exponential, Sin and Cos functions are continuous everywhere.

Differentiability

A function $f(x)$ is said to be differentiable at $x = a$ if it is continuous at $x = a$ and if left derivative = $f'(a)$ = right derivative

- *i.e.* $\lim_{h \to 0^-} \dfrac{f(a) - f(a-h)}{h} = f'(a) = \lim_{h \to 0^+} \dfrac{f(a+h) - f(a)}{h}$

- If $f(x)$ is differentiable in (a, b), then it is always continuous at (a, b), but converse need not be true.

MEAN VALUE THEOREMS

Rolle's Mean Value Theorem

If

(i) '$f(x)$' is continuous is $[a, b]$

(ii) '$f(x)$' is differentiable in (a, b)

(iii) $f(a) = f(b)$ then $\exists\ c \in (a, b)$ such that $f'(c) = 0$

Larange's Mean Value Theorem

If

(i) '$f(x)$' is continuous in $[a, b]$

(ii) '$f(x)$' is differentiable in (a, b) then $\exists\ c \in (a, b)$ such that

$$f'(c) = \frac{f(b) - f(a)}{b - a}$$

Cauchy's Mean Value Theorem

Let $f(x)$ and $g(x)$ are two functions if

(i) $f(x)$ and $g(x)$ are continuous in $[a, b]$

(ii) $f(x)$ and $g(x)$ are differentiable in (a, b)

(iii) $g'(x) \neq 0\ \forall x \in (a, b)$

then $\exists\ c \in (a, b)$ such that $\dfrac{f'(c)}{g'(c)} = \dfrac{f(b) - f(a)}{g(b) - g(a)}$

Derivatives

- $\dfrac{d}{dx}(\sin x) = \cos x$
- $\dfrac{d}{dx}(\cos x) = -\sin x$
- $\dfrac{d}{dx}(\tan x) = \sec^2 x$
- $\dfrac{d}{dx}(\cot x) = -\operatorname{cosec}^2 x$
- $\dfrac{d}{dx}(\sec x) = \sec x \cdot \tan x$
- $\dfrac{d}{dx}(\operatorname{cosec} x) = \operatorname{cosec} x \cot x$
- $\dfrac{d}{dx}(\sin^{-1} x) = \dfrac{1}{\sqrt{1 - x^2}}$
- $\dfrac{d}{dx}(\cos^{-1} x) = \dfrac{-1}{\sqrt{1 - x^2}}$
- $\dfrac{d}{dx}(\tan^{-1} x) = \dfrac{1}{1 + x^2}$
- $\dfrac{d}{dx}(\cot^{-1} x) = \dfrac{-1}{1 + x^2}$
- $\dfrac{d}{dx}(\sec^{-1} x) = \dfrac{1}{x\sqrt{x^2 - 1}}$
- $\dfrac{d}{dx}(\operatorname{cosec}^{-1} x) = \dfrac{-1}{x\sqrt{x^2 - 1}}$

- $\frac{d}{dx}(\sinh x) = \cosh x$
- $\frac{d}{dx}(\cosh x) = \sinh x$
- $\frac{d}{dx}(e^x) = e^x$
- $\frac{d}{dx}(a^x) = a^x \cdot \log a$
- $\frac{d}{dx}[f(x)]^n = n\cdot [f(x)]^{n-1}$
- $\frac{d}{dx}(ax+b)^n = n\cdot (ax+b)^{n-1}\cdot a$
- $\frac{du}{dx} = \frac{du}{dy}\frac{dy}{dx}$ (chain rule)
- $\frac{d}{dx}(uv) = u.\frac{dv}{dx} + v.\frac{du}{dx}$
- $\frac{d}{dx}\left(\frac{u}{v}\right) = \frac{v.\frac{du}{dx} - u.\frac{dv}{dx}}{v^2}$
- $\sinh x = \frac{e^x - e^{-x}}{2}$
- $\cosh x = \frac{e^x + e^{-x}}{2}$
- $\frac{d}{dx}(\log_e x) = \frac{1}{x}$

INTEGRALS

- $\int x^n \cdot dx = \frac{x^{n+1}}{n+1}; (n \neq -1)$
- $\int \frac{1}{x} \cdot dx = \log_e x$
- $\int e^x \cdot dx = e^x$
- $\int a^x dx = \frac{a^x}{\log a}$
- $\int \frac{f'(x)}{f(x)} . dx = \log [f(x)]$
- $\int [f(x)]^n \cdot f'(x) \cdot dx = \frac{[f(x)^{n+1}]}{n+1}$
- $\int \frac{1}{a^2+x^2} dx = \frac{1}{a} . \tan^{-1}\frac{x}{a}$
- $\int \frac{1}{a^2-x^2} dx = \frac{1}{2a} \cdot \log\left[\frac{a+x}{a-x}\right]$
- $\int \frac{1}{x^2-a^2} dx = \frac{1}{2a} \cdot \log\left[\frac{x-a}{x+a}\right]$
- $\int \frac{dx}{\sqrt{a^2-x^2}} = \sin^{-1}\frac{x}{a}$
- $\int \frac{dx}{\sqrt{a^2+x^2}} = \sinh^{-1}\frac{x}{a}$
- $\int \frac{dx}{x^2-a^2} = \cosh^{-1}\frac{x}{a}$
- $\int \sinh x\, dx = \cosh x$
- $\int \cosh x\, dx = \sinh x$
- $\int \sin x \cdot dx = -\cos x$
- $\int \cos x \cdot dx = \sin x$

- $\int \tan x \cdot dx = \log \cos x = \log \sec x$
- $\int \cot x \, dx = \log \sin x$
- $\int \sec x \cdot dx = \log (\sec x + \tan x)$
- $\int \text{cosec } x \cdot dx = \log (\text{cosec } x - \cot x)$
- $\int \sec^2 x \cdot dx = \tan x$
- $\int \text{cosec}^2 x \cdot dx = -\cot x$
- $\int e^{ax} \sin bx \, dx = \dfrac{e^{ax}}{a^2 + b^2} (a \sin bx - b \cos bx)$
- $\int e^{ax} \cos bx \, dx = \dfrac{e^{ax}}{a^2 + b^2} (a \cos bx + b \sin bx)$
- $\int \sqrt{a^2 - x^2} \cdot dx = \dfrac{x}{2} \sqrt{a^2 - x^2} + \dfrac{a^2}{2} \sin^{-1} \dfrac{x}{a}$
- $\int \sqrt{a^2 - x^2} \cdot dx = \dfrac{x}{2} \sqrt{a^2 + x^2} + \dfrac{a^2}{2} \sinh^{-1} \dfrac{x}{a}$
- $\int \sqrt{x^2 - a^2} \cdot dx = \dfrac{x}{2} \sqrt{x^2 - a^2} - \dfrac{a^2}{2} \cosh^{-1} \dfrac{x}{a}$

DEFINITE INTEGRALS

Theorem 1: If $f(x)$ is continuous in $[a, b]$ and $F(x)$ is any antiderivative of $f(x)$ in $[a, b]$ then $\int_a^b f(x)\, dx = F(b) - F(a)$

Theorem 2: If $f(x)$ is continuous on $[a, b]$ then $F(x) = \int_a^b f(t) \cdot dt$ is differentiable at every point of x in $[a, b]$ and $\dfrac{dF}{dx} = \dfrac{d}{dx} \int_a^b f(t) \cdot dt = f(x)$.

i.e., If $f(x)$ is continuous on $[a, b]$ then $\exists$ a function $F(x)$ whose derivative on $[a, b]$ is $f(x)$

Theorem 3: If $f(x)$ is continuous on $[a, b]$ and $u(x)$ and $v(x)$ are differentiable functions of x whose values lie in $[a, b]$ then $\dfrac{d}{dx} \int_{u(x)}^{v(x)} f(t) \cdot dt$

$$= f(v(x)) \frac{dv}{dx} - f(u(x)) \cdot \frac{du}{dx}$$

PROPERTIES OF DEFINITE INTEGRALS

1. $\int_a^a f(x) \cdot dx = 0$

2. $\int_a^b f(x) \cdot dx = \int_b^a f(z) \cdot dz$

3. $\int_a^b f(x) \cdot dx = -\int_b^a f(x) \cdot dx$

4. $\int_a^b k \cdot dx = k(b-a)$

5. $\int_a^b f(x) \cdot dx = \int_a^c f(x) \cdot dx + \int_c^b f(x) \cdot dx$

6. $\int_0^a f(x) \cdot dx = \int_0^a f(a-x) \cdot dx$

7. $\int_{-a}^a f(x) \cdot (dx) = 2\int_0^a f(x) \cdot dx$; if (x) is even function $f(-x) = f(x) = 0$; if $f(x)$ is odd function $f(-x) = -f(x)$

8. $\int_a^b f(x) \cdot dx = \int_a^b f(a+b-x) \cdot dx$

9. $\int_0^{2a} f(x) \cdot dx = \int_0^a f(x) \cdot dx + \int_0^a f(2a-x) \cdot dx$

10. $\int_0^{2a} f(x) \cdot dx = 2\int_0^a f(x) \cdot dx$; if $f(2a-x) = f(x) = 0$; If $f(2a-x) = -f(x)$

11. $\int_0^{na} f(x) \cdot dx = n \cdot \int_0^a f(x) \cdot dx$; if $f(x+a) = f(x)$

    [$f(x)$ is periodic function with period 'a']

12. $\int_0^a x \cdot f(x) \cdot dx = \frac{a}{2}\int_0^a f(x) \cdot dx$; if $f(a-x) = f(x)$

13. **Mean value theorem for definite integrals:** Let f be continuous in (a, b) then $\exists c \in (a, b)$ such that $f(c) = \frac{\int_a^b f(x)dx}{(b-a)}$

    $f(c)$ is the average value of the function in the interval (a, b).

14. $\int_a^b f(x)dx \le \int_a^b g(x)dx$ If $f(x) \le g(x)$ on (a, b)

15. $\int_0^{\pi/2} \sin^n x \cdot dx = \int_0^{\pi/2} \cos^n x \cdot dx = \frac{(n-1)\cdot(n-3)\cdot(n-5)\ldots}{n\cdot(n-2)\,(n-4)\ldots} \times k$

    Where, K = 1; if n is odd and K = $\pi/2$; if n is even

IMPROPER INTEGRALS

1. $\int_a^b f(x) \cdot dx$ is "improper integral";

   (*i*) If $a = -\infty$ or $b = \infty$ or both

   (*ii*) If $f(x) = \infty$ for one or more values of x in $[a, b]$.

2. $\int_a^b f(x) \cdot dx$ is "convergent", if the value of integral is "finite".

3. $\int_a^b f(x) \cdot dx$ is "divergent" if the value of integral is "infinite".

4. If $0 \le f(x) \le g(x)$; $\forall x$ and $\int_a^\infty g(x) \cdot dx \cdot$ converges then $\int_a^\infty f(x)$ also converges.

5. If $0 \le g(x) \le f(x)$; $\forall x$ and $\int_a^\infty g(x) \cdot dx$ diverges then $\int_a^\infty f(x)$ also diverges.

6. If $f(x)$ and $g(x)$ are two functions, such that $\lim\limits_{n \to \infty} \dfrac{f(x)}{g(x)} = k$

   where k = finite and $k \ne 0$ then

   $\int_a^\infty f(x) \cdot dx$ and $\int_a^\infty g(x) \cdot dx$ "converge" or "diverge" together.

7. $\int_a^\infty e^{-Px} \cdot dx$ and $\int_{-\infty}^b e^{Px} \cdot dx$ converges for any constant $P > 0$ and diverges for $P \le 0$.

8. $\int_a^b \dfrac{dx}{(b-x)^P}$ is convergent iff $P < 1$.

9. $\int_a^b \dfrac{dx}{(x-a)^P}$ is convergent iff $P < 1$.

10. $\int_1^\infty \dfrac{dx}{x^P}$ converges if $P > 1$ and diverges if $P < 1$.

TOTAL DERIVATIVES

If $u = f(x, y)$ where x and y are functions of t, then the "total derivative" of u with respect to t is

$$\frac{du}{dt} = \frac{\partial u}{\partial x}\left(\frac{dx}{dt}\right) + \frac{\partial u}{\partial y}\left(\frac{dy}{dt}\right)$$

By putting $t = x$ in above equation, we get

$$\frac{du}{dx} = \frac{\partial u}{\partial x} + \frac{\partial u}{\partial y} \cdot \frac{dy}{dx}$$; where x and y are connected by some relation.

PARTIAL DERIVATIVES

1. If $u = f(x, y)$ then $\frac{\partial u}{\partial x} = \lim_{h \to 0} \frac{[f(x+h, y) - f(x, y)]}{h}$

   and $\frac{\partial u}{\partial y} = \lim_{k \to 0} \frac{[f(x, y+k) - f(x, y)]}{k}$.

2. If $u = f(x, y)$, where $x = g(r, s)$ and $y = h(r, s)$ then

$$\frac{\partial u}{\partial r} = \frac{\partial u}{\partial x} \cdot \frac{\partial x}{\partial r} + \frac{\partial u}{\partial y} \cdot \frac{\partial y}{\partial r}$$

$$\frac{\partial u}{\partial s} = \frac{\partial u}{\partial x} \cdot \frac{\partial x}{\partial s} + \frac{\partial u}{\partial y} \cdot \frac{\partial y}{\partial s}$$

3. If $u = f(x, y)$ is a homogenous function of degree 'n' then

$$x \cdot u_x + y \cdot u_y = n.u$$

$$x^2 u_{xx} + 2xy \cdot u_{xy} + y^2 u_{yy} = n(n-1)\, u$$

   If $u = f(x, y, z)$ is a homogenous function of degree 'n', then

$$x \cdot u_x + y \cdot u_y + z \cdot u_z = n.u$$

   If $u = f(x, y)$ is not homogenous function, but $F(u)$ is a homogenous function of degree 'n', then

$$x \cdot u_x + y \cdot u_y = n \left[\frac{F(u)}{F'(u)}\right] = G(u)$$

$$x^2 \cdot u_{xx} + 2xy \cdot u_{xy} + y^2 \cdot u_{yy} = G(u)\,[G'(u) - 1]$$

MAXIMUM AND MINIMA [EXTREMUM]

1. A necessary condition for $f(a)$ to be an extreme value of $f(x)$ is $f'(a) = 0$.
2. The vanishing of $f'(a) = 0$ is only a necessary but not a sufficient condition for $f(a)$ to be an extreme value of $f(x)$.
3. **Stationary Values:** A function $f(x)$ is said to be stationary for $x = C$ and $f(C)$ is a stationary value of $f(x)$ if $f'(C) = 0$.
4. To find points of maximum, points of minimum and saddle points the following steps are required:

   (*i*) Put $f'(x) = 0$ and find stationary points (x_i)

Computer Science

2

Digital Logic

CONTENTS

1 Logic Functions

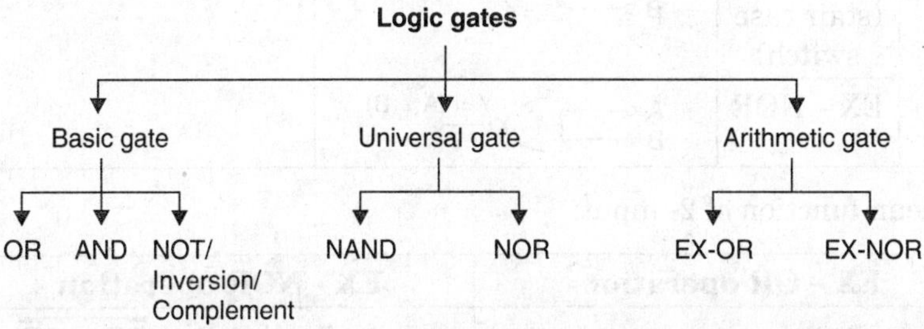

<table>
<tr><th colspan="2">Name</th><th>Symbol</th><th>Truth Table</th></tr>
<tr><td>(i)</td><td>NOT</td><td>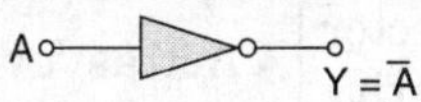
</td><td>
<table>
<tr><th>A (Input)</th><th>Output $Y = \overline{A}$</th></tr>
<tr><td>0</td><td>1</td></tr>
<tr><td>1</td><td>0</td></tr>
</table></td></tr>
<tr><td>(ii)</td><td>AND</td><td>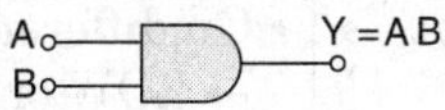
</td><td>
<table>
<tr><th colspan="2">Input</th><th>Output</th></tr>
<tr><td>A</td><td>B</td><td>Y = AB</td></tr>
<tr><td>0</td><td>0</td><td>0</td></tr>
<tr><td>0</td><td>1</td><td>0</td></tr>
<tr><td>1</td><td>0</td><td>0</td></tr>
<tr><td>1</td><td>1</td><td>1</td></tr>
</table></td></tr>
<tr><td>(iii)</td><td>OR</td><td>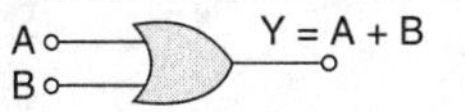
</td><td>
<table>
<tr><th colspan="2">Input</th><th>Output</th></tr>
<tr><td>A</td><td>B</td><td>Y = A+ B</td></tr>
<tr><td>0</td><td>0</td><td>0</td></tr>
<tr><td>0</td><td>1</td><td>1</td></tr>
<tr><td>1</td><td>0</td><td>1</td></tr>
<tr><td>1</td><td>1</td><td>1</td></tr>
</table></td></tr>
</table>

(iv)	NAND (NOT + AND)	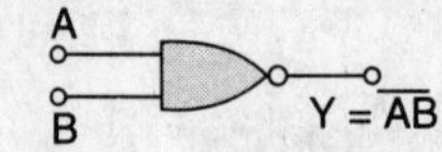	
(v)	NOR (NOT + OR)	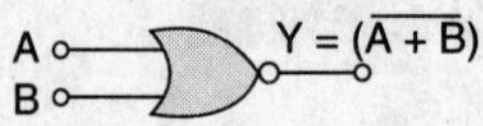	
(vi)	EX – OR (stair case switch)	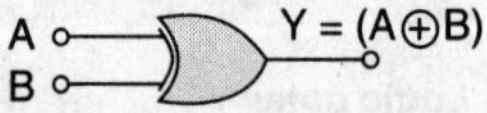	
(vii)	EX – NOR	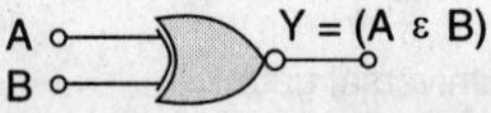	

Boolean function of 2- input:

EX – OR operation	**EX – NOR operation**
• $Y = A \oplus B = \bar{A}B + A\bar{B}$	• $y = A \odot B = \overline{A \oplus B} = (\overline{\bar{A}B + A\bar{B}})$ $= AB + \bar{A}\,\bar{B}$
• Act as "odd number of 1's detector in the input" and used in parity generation & detection.	• Act as 'even number of 1's detector.
• On same input, output → LOW or logic '0'.	• On same input; output → HIGH or logic '0'.
• On different input, output → HIGH or logic '1'.	• On different input; output → LOW or logic '0'.
• $A \oplus A = 0, A \oplus 0 = A$ $A \oplus \bar{A} = 1, A \oplus 1 = \bar{A}$	• $A \odot A = 1, A \odot 1 = A$ • $A \odot \bar{A} = 0, A \odot 0 1 = \bar{A}$
• $A \oplus A \oplus A \oplus$ ... upto n terms $= 0$, when n = even	• $A \odot A \odot A \odot$ ... upto n terms $= 1$, when n is even
• $A \oplus A \oplus A \oplus$ ... upto n terms $= A$, when n = odd	• $A \odot A \odot A \odot$ ... upto n terms $= A$, when n is odd

Points to Remember:

- $\bar{A} \oplus B = A \oplus \bar{B} = A \odot B$
- $\bar{A} \odot B = A \odot \bar{B} = A \oplus B$
- For odd no. of inputs EXOR and EXNOR are same and for even number of variables they are complements to each other.

i.e., $A \oplus B \oplus C = A \odot B \odot C$

as $A \oplus B \oplus C = \overline{A \oplus B}\, C + (A \oplus B)\, \overline{C}$

$$= (A \odot B)\, C + (A \oplus B)\, \overline{C}$$
$$= (A \odot B)\, C + \overline{A \odot B}\, \overline{C}$$
$$= A \odot B \odot C$$

- $\overline{A \oplus B \oplus C} = A \odot B \oplus C = A \oplus B \odot C$
- $\overline{A \odot B \odot C} = A \oplus B \odot C = A \odot B \oplus C$
- $A \oplus B \oplus AB = A + B$

- EXOR and EXNOR are also called arithmetic gates as they are used in addition, subtraction, comparator circuits.

IMPLEMENTATION OF GATES USING NAND

- AND gate :

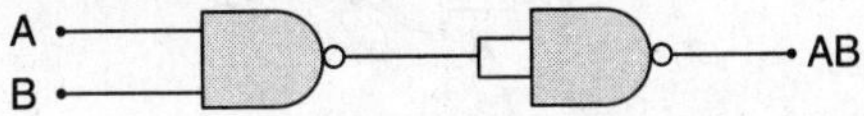

- OR gate :

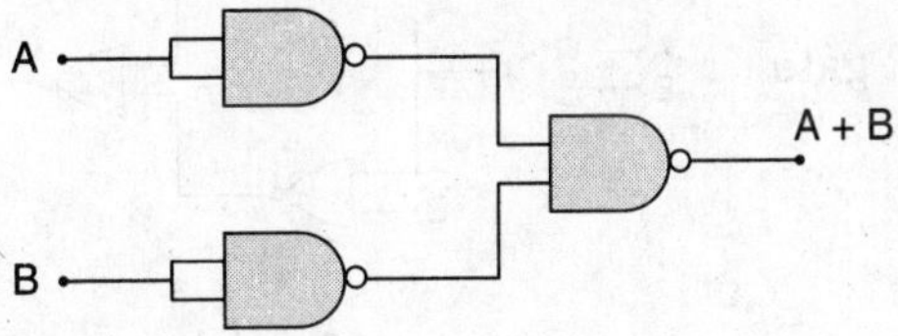

- NOT gate :

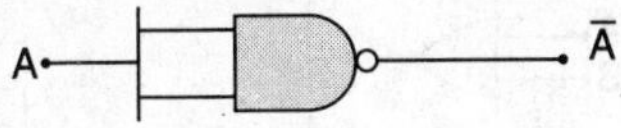

- EXOR gate :

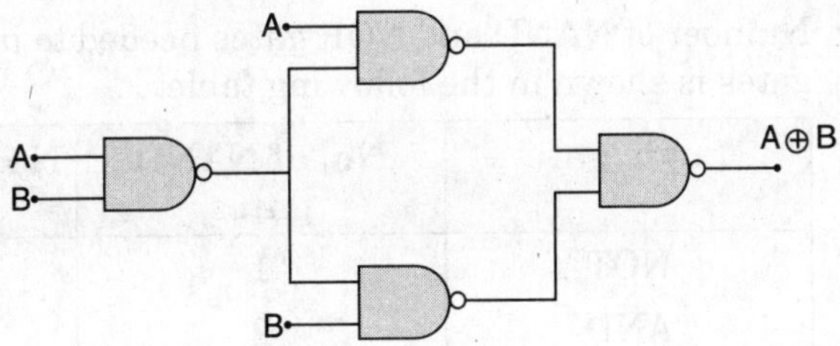

- EXNOR gate :

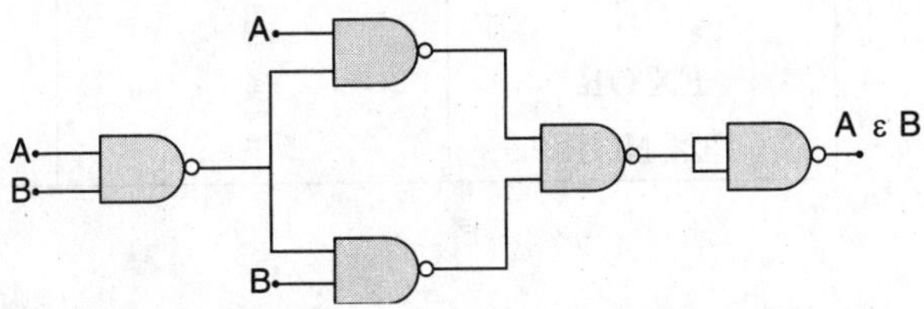

IMPLEMENTATION OF GATES USING NOR

- AND gate :

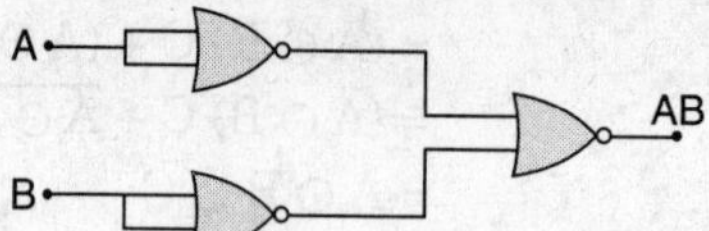

- OR gate :

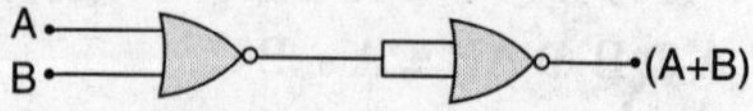

- NOT gate :

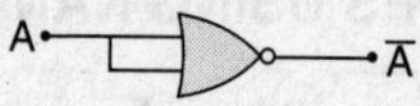

- EXOR gate :

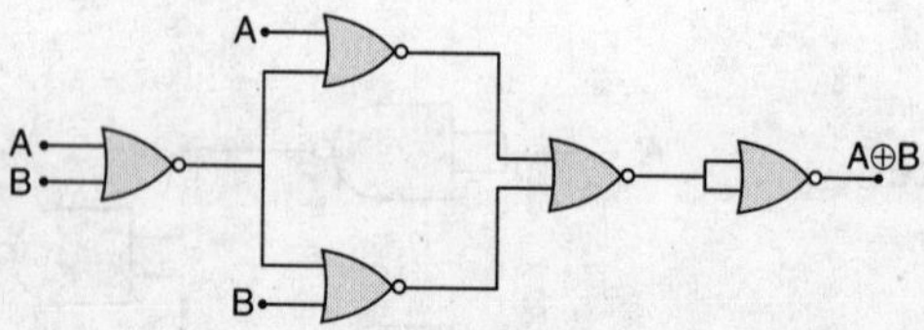

- EX-NOR gate :

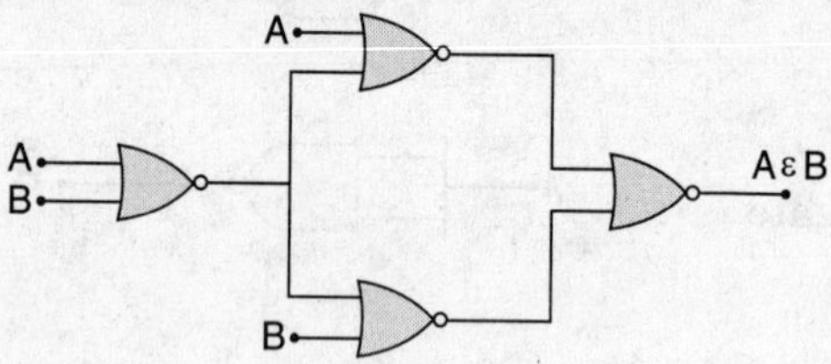

Note:

- Number of NAND and NOR gates needed to implement other logic gates is shown in the following table.

Logic gate	No. of NAND gates	No. of NOR gates
NOT	1	1
AND	2	3
OR	3	2
EX OR	4	5
EX NOR	5	4

- **Alternative Symbols of Gates :**
  1. Bubbled – OR gate ≡ NAND gate
  2. Bubbled – NAND gate ≡ OR gate
  3. Bubble – NOR gate ≡ AND gate
  4. Bubbled – AND gate ≡ NOR gate

Minimization

2

Boolean Algebra Laws

	Name	
1.	Identity law	$\rightarrow A + A = A$ $\rightarrow A.\ A = A$
2.	Commutative law	$\rightarrow A + B = B + A$ $\rightarrow A.\ B = B.\ A$
3.	Associative law	$\rightarrow A + (B + C) = (A + B) + C = A + B + C$ $\rightarrow A.\ (B.\ C) = (A.\ B)\ C = ABC$
4.	Distributive	$\rightarrow A\ (B + C) = AB + AC$ $\rightarrow A + (BC) = (A + B)\ (A + C)$
5.	De Morgan's law	$\rightarrow (A + B)' = A'\ B'$ $\rightarrow (AB)' = A' + B'$

Points to Remember :

- $A + AB = A$
- $A\ (A + B) = A$
- $A + A'\ B = A + B$
- $A\ (A' + B) = AB$
- NAND and NOR gates → do not follow associative law but follow commutative law
- OR, AND, EX-OR, EX-NOR → follow associative & commutative both.

Boolean Algebraic Theorems:

- AND operation theorems

  (*i*) $A\ .\ A = A$ (*ii*) $A\ .\ 0 = 0$

  (*iii*) $A\ .\ 1 = A$ (*iv*) $A\ .\ \overline{A} = 0$

- Involution theorem : $(A')' = \overline{\overline{A}} = A$

- OR operation theorem :
  (*i*) A + A = A　　(*ii*) A + 0 = A
  (*iii*) A + 1 = 1　　(*iv*) $A + \bar{A} = 1$
- De Morgan's theorem :
  (*i*) $\overline{(A_1 \cdot A_2 \cdot A_3 \cdot ... A_n)} = \bar{A}_1 + \bar{A}_2 + \bar{A}_3 + ... + \bar{A}_n$
  (*ii*) $\overline{(A_1 + A_2 + A_3 + ... + A_n)} = \bar{A}_1 \cdot \bar{A}_2 \cdot \bar{A}_3 ... \bar{A}_n$
- Transposition theorem : (A + B) (A + C) = A + BC
- Distribution theorem : A + BC = (A + B) (A + C)
  Boolean Algebraic Theorem :
- $(A + B). (A + \bar{B}) = A$
- $AB + \bar{A}C = (A + C) + (\bar{A} + B)$
- $(A + B) (\bar{A} + C) = AC + \bar{A}B$
- $AB + \bar{A}C + BC = AB + \bar{A}C$
- $(A + B) (\bar{A} + C) (B + C) = (A + B) (\bar{A} + C)$
- $\overline{A \cdot B \cdot C \cdot ...} = \bar{A} + \bar{B} + \bar{C} + ...$
- $\overline{A + B + C + ...} = \bar{A}. \bar{B}. \bar{C}...$

Duality theorem:

- Theorem that helps to convert the sum of products to product of sums and vice versa.

i.e., each OR gate is changed to AND gate and vice versa and all O's and 1's are complemented keeping in mind;

$$A + 1 = 1 ; A + 0 = A ; A.1 = A ; A. 0 = 0;$$
$$A + B = B + A ; A.B = B.A.$$

- Expression is known as 'dual expression' and for 1- time dual; it is 'self dual expression'.

Note:

- For n-variables, maximum possible self-dual function = $(2)^{2^{n-1}} = 2^{(2^n/2)}$
- Number of Boolean functions formed over
  (*i*) *n*-boolean variables = 2^{2^n}
  (*ii*) *n*-*n* valued variables = 2^{n^n}
- Number of *n*-valued functions formed over
  (*i*) *n*-boolean variables = n^{2^n}
  (*ii*) *n*-*n* valued variables = n^{n^n}

Boolean Function Representation

Canonical form | **Standard form**

- All terms contain each literal
  Ex. $F(A, B, C) = \overline{A}BC + ABC + \overline{A}\overline{BC}$
- All terms do not have each and every literal
  Ex. $F(A, B, C) = \overline{A} + BC + A\overline{BC}$

Literals: Single logic variable or its complement.

Minterm: Product of all the literals with or without compliment involved *e.g.* if X = 1, Y = 0, Z = 1 then minterm = XYZ′

e.g., if X = 0; Y = 0 minterm = X′ Y′

Maxterm: Sum of all the literals with or without complement involved.

e.g., if X = 0, Y = 0 ; maxterm = X + Y

if X = 1, Y = 0, Z = 1; maxterm = X′ + Y + Z′

Karnaugh Map (Complete Simplification Rules)

- *k*-map is truth table graph, which aids in visually simplifying the logic.
- Valuable tool for logic minimization.
- Considers most boolean theorem and postules automatically.
- Maximum number of product terms for irreducible expression with *n*-variables are 2^{n-1} and maximum number of literals = $n \times 2^{n-1}$

Now;

- Generate *k*-map.
  → Put a 1 in all specified minterms
  → Put a O in all other boxes.
- Group all adjacent 1's without including any Os.
  → All groups must be rectangular & contains a 'power of 2' *i.e.*, 1, 2, 4, 8...

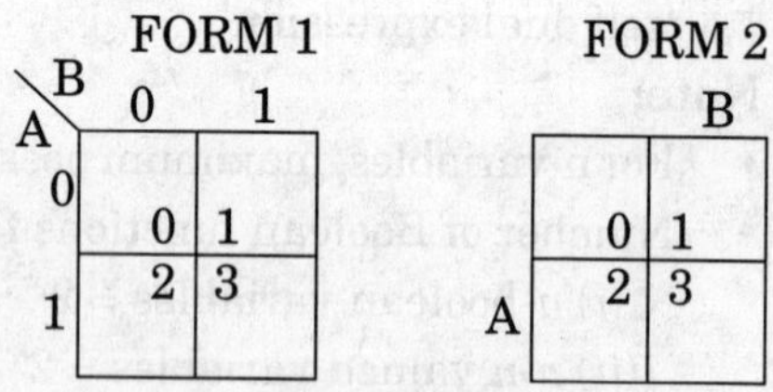

2-variable k-map

→ An essential group contains at least one minterm not included in any other groups.

- Using minimum number of loops, pair the 1's. Any 1 already been looped can also be looped again.
- Define product terms using variables common to all minterms in group.
- Sum all essential groups plus a minimal set of remaining groups to obtain a minimum sum of product.

3 Combinational Circuits

Combinational Circuits

→ Circuit combining different gates in a single circuit eg. encoder, decoder multiplexer and demultiplexer

→ Output of the circuit depends on present input

→ No feedback required

→ No memory required.

ADDER

<table>
<tr><th></th><th>Half</th><th>Full</th></tr>
<tr><td>Intro</td><td>• Addition of two single bit numbers.</td><td>• addition of two single bit numbers with carry</td></tr>
<tr><td>No. of input and output</td><td>• Two input (A and B) and 2 output (sum and carry)</td><td>• 3 input (A,B and carry) and 2 output (sum and carry)</td></tr>
<tr><td>Logical expression</td><td>• Sum = S = $\overline{A}B + A\overline{B}$ = $A \oplus B$ carry = C = AB.</td><td>• $S = A \oplus B \oplus C$ C = AB + BC + CA = AB + C $(A \oplus B)$</td></tr>
<tr><td>NAND/NOR gates</td><td>• 5</td><td>• 9.</td></tr>
<tr><td>Circuit diagram</td><td>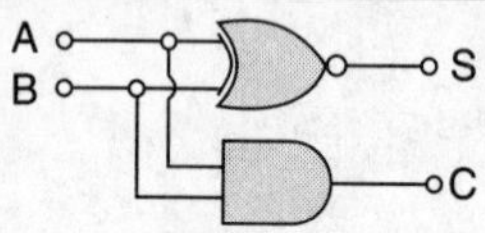
</td><td>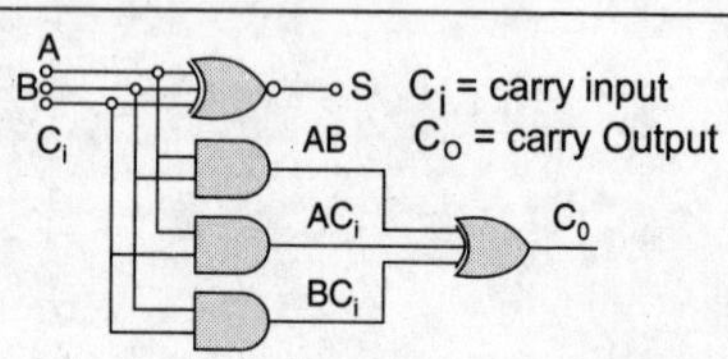
</td></tr>
</table>

Truth Table

Input		Output	
A	B	S	C
0	0	0	0
0	1	1	0
1	0	1	0
1	1	0	1

Input			Output	
A	B	C_i	S	C_o
0	0	0	0	0
0	0	1	1	0
0	1	0	1	0
0	1	1	0	1
1	0	0	1	0
1	0	1	0	1
1	1	0	0	1
1	1	1	1	1

Subtractor

	Half	Full
Intro	• Produces difference between two binary bits at the input and produces an output (Borrow)	• Also produces difference between binary bits but overcome disadvantage of a half subtractor
Inputs	• Two inputs A and B. in A – B; A is minuend and B is subtrahend bit and 2 output D and Borrow. D is difference	• Three inputs A, B, C and two output D and C′. A - minuend B-Subtrahend C-Borrow by previous stage D-Difference output C-Borrow output
NAND/NOR gates	• 5	• 9.
Logical expression	Difference = D $= \overline{A}B + A\overline{B} = A \oplus B$ Borrow = B = $\overline{A}B$	• $D = A \oplus B \oplus C$ $B = \overline{A}B + \overline{A}C + BC$ $= \overline{A}B + \overline{(A \oplus B)} \cdot C$

Circuit diagram

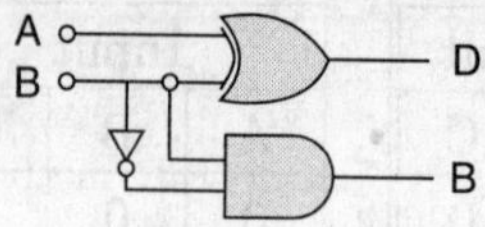

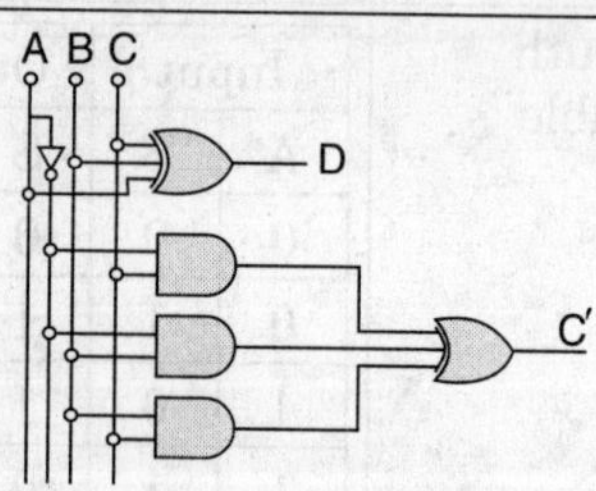

Truth Table

Input		Output	
A	B	A-B	Borrow
0	0	0	0
0	1	1	1
1	0	1	0
1	1	0	0

Input			Output	
A	B	C	(A-B-C)	C′
0	0	0	0	0
0	0	1	1	1
0	1	0	1	1
0	1	1	0	1
1	0	0	1	0
1	0	1	0	0
1	1	0	0	0
1	1	1	1	1

Note:

- Full adder can be implemented by 2 half adder and one OR gate or 1 full subtractor and 1 NOT gate.
- Full subtractor can be implemented with 2 half subtractor and 1 OR gate or 1 full adder and 1 NOT gate.

Multiplexer

- Also known as MUX or data selector or many to one circuit or universal logic circuit or parallel to serial convertor.
- It selects one of the *n* data inputs and routes it to the output. Selection is done by selection lines.
- E is strobe or enable input responsible for cascading, it is an active low terminal.
- There are 2^n input lines where *n* – select line
- If there are M number of data inputs and *n* is number of select lines then $n = \log_2 M$.

Block Diagram

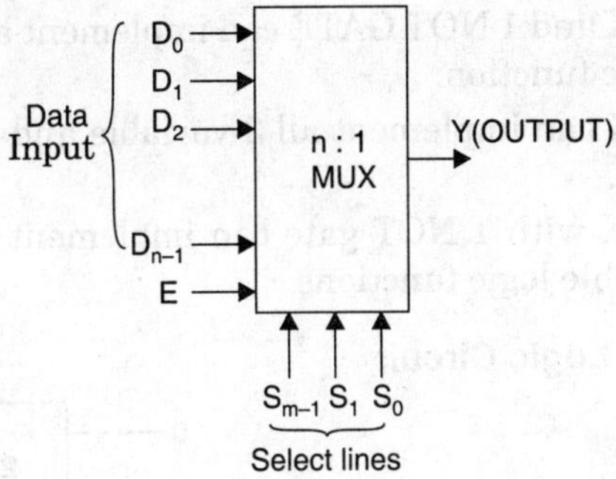

Multiple variations;

- 2 : 1 Multiplexer
- 4 : 1 Multiplexer
- 8 : 1 Multiplexer
- 16 :1 Multiplexer and so on.

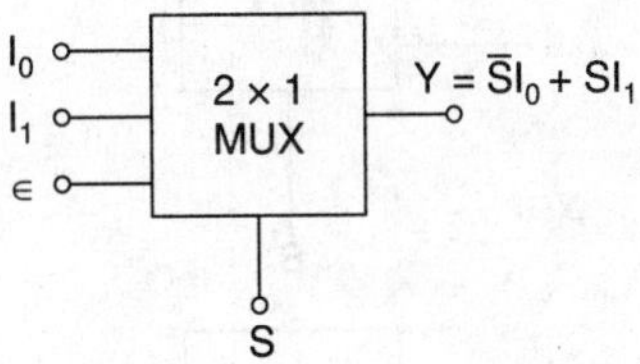

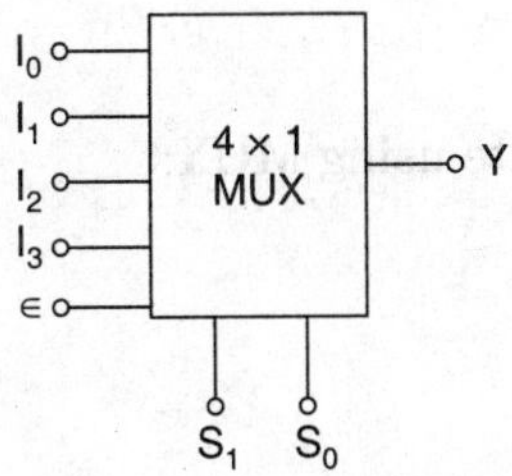

$$Y = \bar{S}_1 + \bar{S}_0\ I_0 + \bar{S}_1\ S_0\ I_1 + S_1\ \bar{S}_0\ I_2 + S_1\ S_0\ I_3$$

Implementation of High order MUX using low order MUX

Given MUX	To Be Implemented	Required number of MUX
2 : 1	$2^n : 1$	$2^n - 1$
(nx1) MUX	m x 1	$\left[\dfrac{m-1}{n-1}\right]$
2 : 1	4 : 1	3
4 : 1	16 : 1	4 + 1 = 5
4 : 1	64 : 1	16 + 4 + 1 = 21
8 : 1	64 : 1	8 + 1 = 9
8 : 1	256 : 1	32 + 4 + 1 = 37

Points to Remember

- One 4 : 1 MUX and 1 NOT GATE can implement all 2-variable and 3-variable logic function.
- One 8 : 1 MUX can implement all 3-variable and few of 4-variable logic functions.
- One 8 : 1 MUX with 1 NOT gate can implement all 3-variable as well as 4-variable logic functions.

MUX as Universal Logic Circuit

- AND gate using MUX:

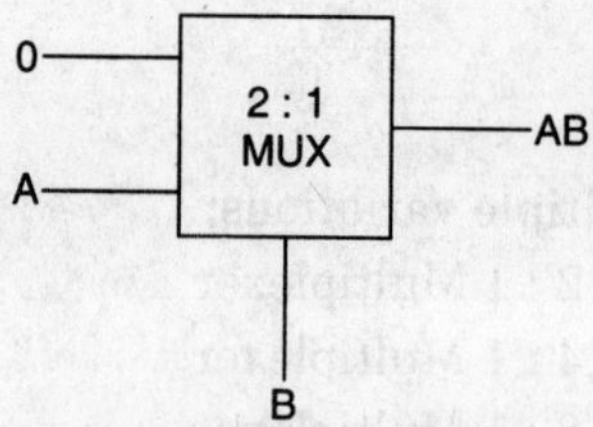

- OR gate using MUX:

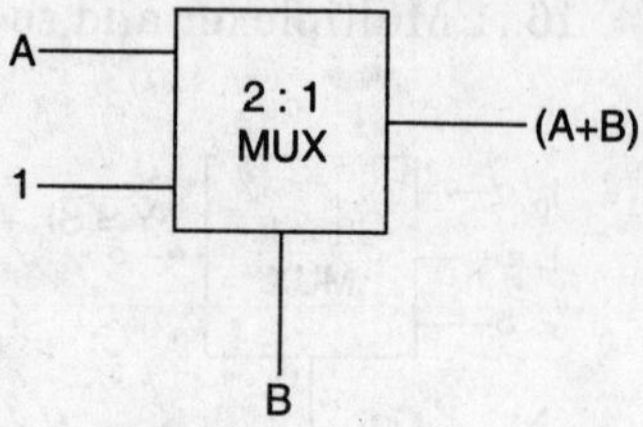

- NOT gate using MUX:

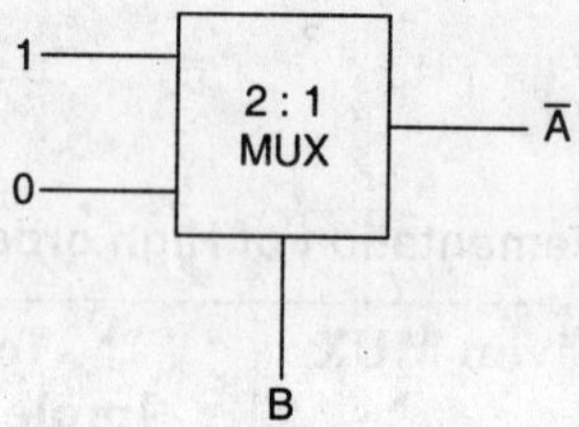

- NAND gate using two 2 : 1 MUXs:

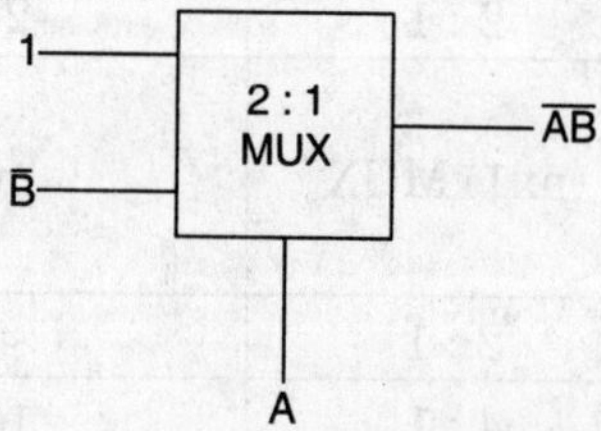

- NOR gate using 2 : 1 MUXs:

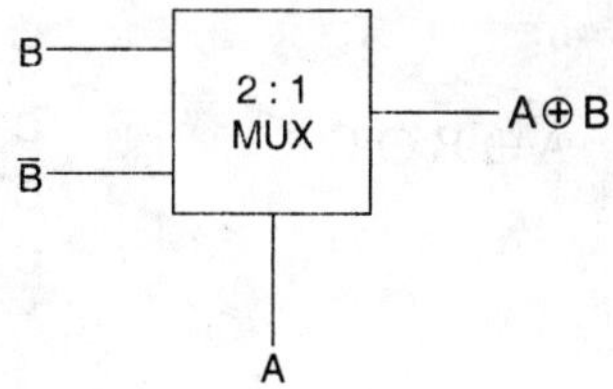

- EXOR gate using two 2 : 1 MUXs:

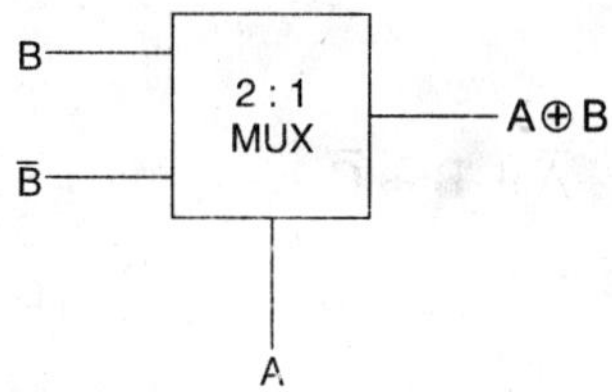

- EXNOR gate using two 2 : 1 MUXs:

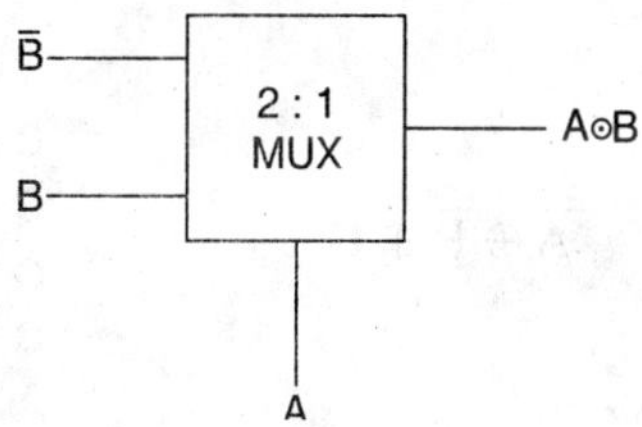

Three Input EXOR and EXNOR Gate Using MUX

- $A \oplus B \oplus C$

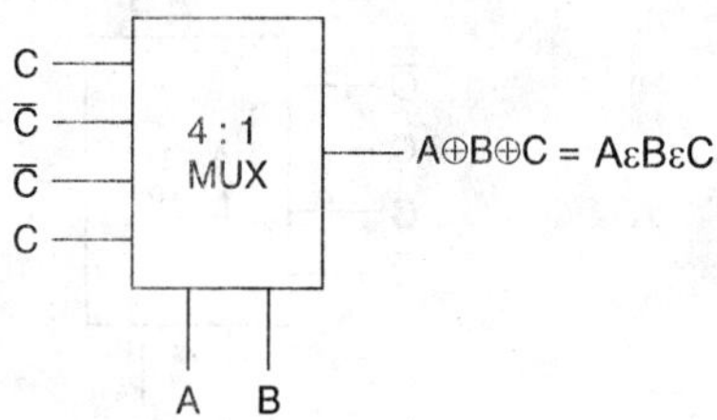

- $A \oplus B \oplus \overline{C}$

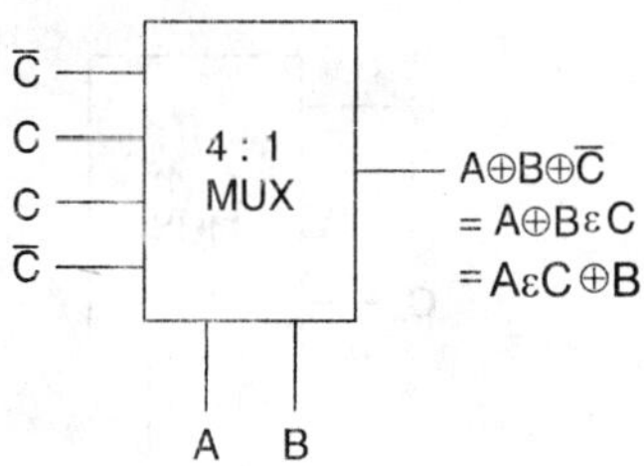

- $\overline{A} \oplus B \oplus C$

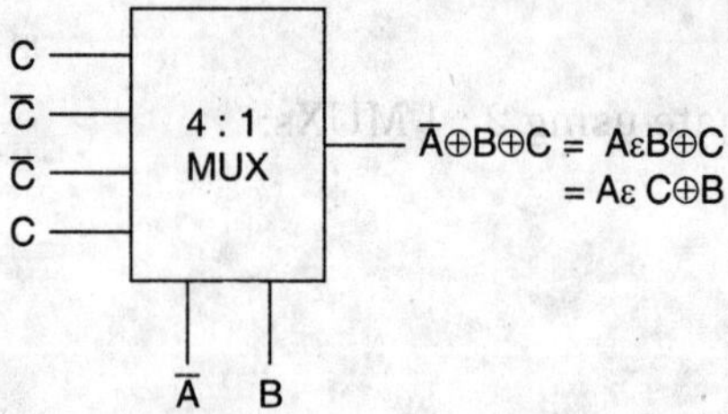

- $\overline{A} \oplus B \oplus \overline{C}$

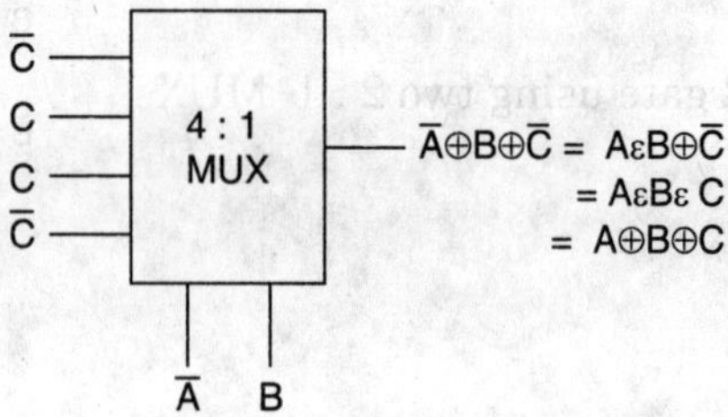

$\overline{A} \oplus \overline{B} \oplus C$

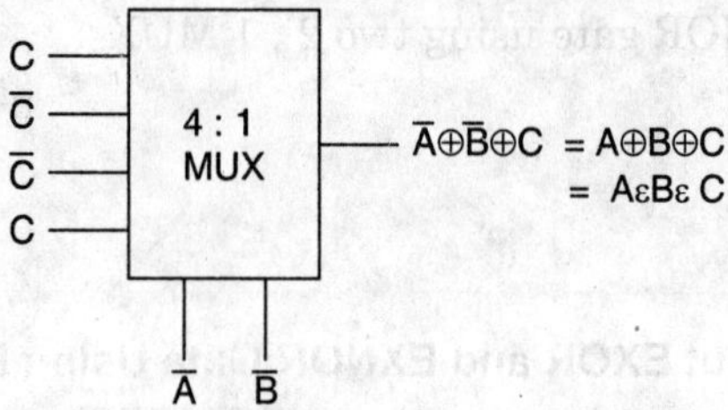

- $\overline{A} \oplus \overline{B} \oplus \overline{C}$

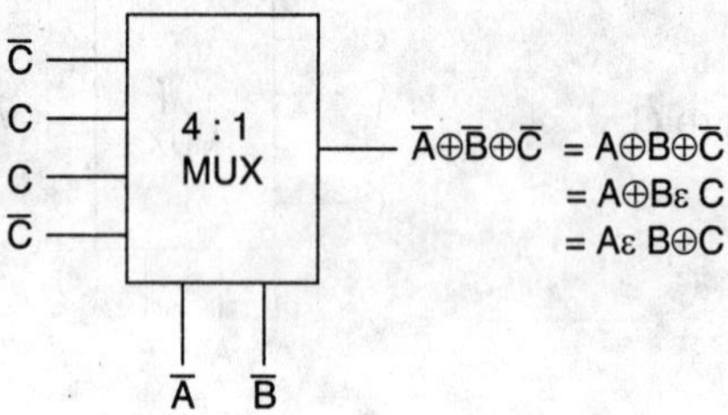

- $A \oplus \overline{B} \oplus C$

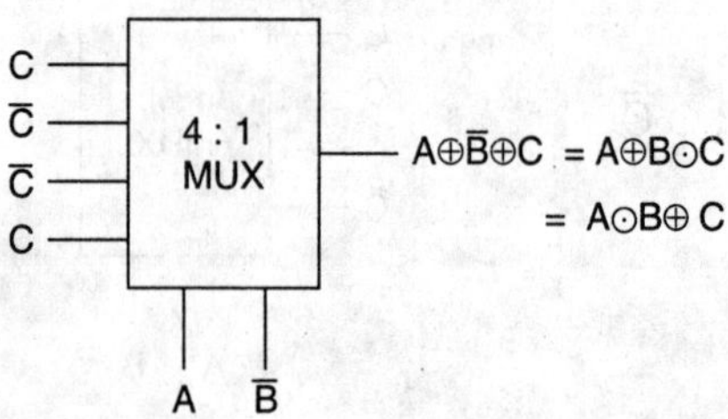

- $A \oplus \overline{B} \oplus \overline{C}$

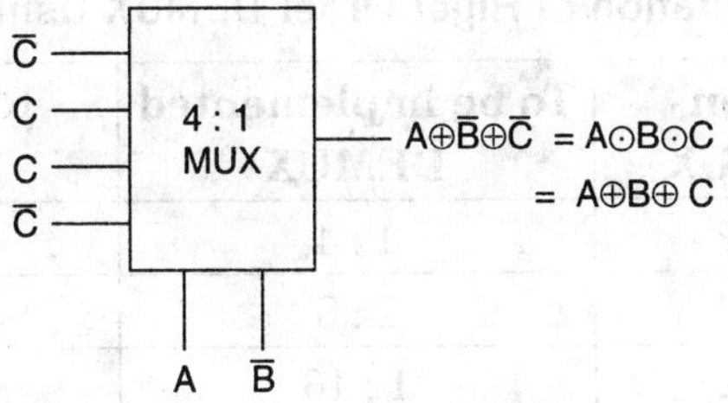

DEMULTIPLEXER (DEMUX)

- Also known as DEMUX or data distribution or one to many circuit
- Performs reverse operation of a multiplexer.
- It receives one input and distribute it over several outputs. It has 1 input, n-outputs and m select input.
- The number of select lines required in a single input and 'n' output DEMUX is $\log_2 n$.

Block Diag: (1 : 2 DEMUX)

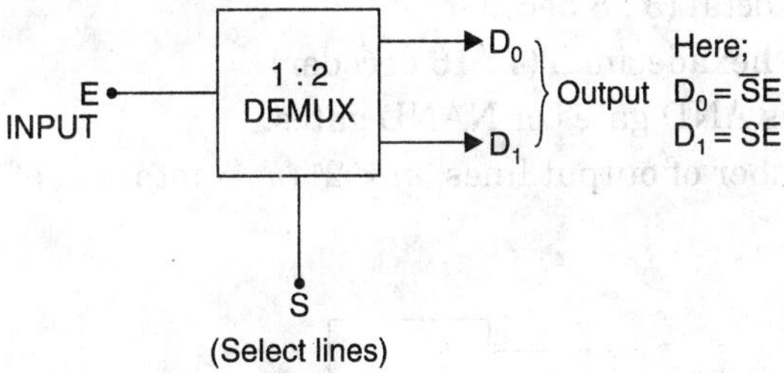

1 : 4 DEMUX

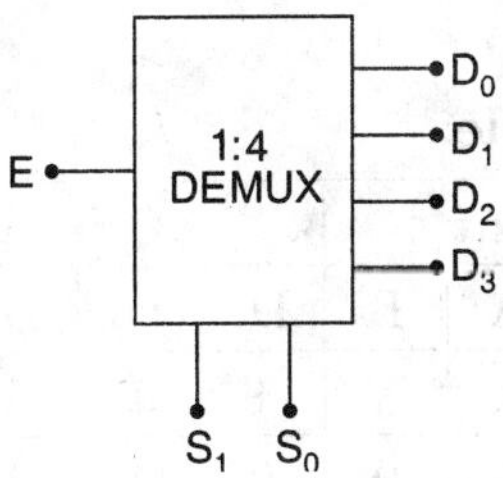

Select lines		Outputs			
S_1	S_0	D_3	D_2	D_1	D_0
0	0	0	0	0	E
0	1	0	0	E	0
1	0	0	E	0	0
1	1	E	0	0	0

$$D_0 = \overline{S}_1 \overline{S}_0 E,\ D_1 = \overline{S}_1 S_0 E,\ D_2 = S_1 \overline{S}_0 E,\ D_3 = S_1 S_0 E$$

Implementation of Higer Order DEMUX Using Lower Order DEMUX

Given DEMUX	To be implemented DEMUX	Required Number of DEMUX
1 : 2	1 : 4	1 + 2 = 3
1 : 2	1 : 8	1 + 2 ⊕ 4 = 7
1 : 2	1 : 16	1 + 2 + 4 + 8 = 15
1 : 2	1 : 64	1 + 2 + 4 + 8 + 16 + 32 = 63
1 : 4	1 : 16	1 + 4 = 5

Decoder

- It is identical to demultiplexer without any data input.
- It has many input and output lines
- It converts binary information from n input lines to a maximum 2 unique output lines.
- It converts binary data into other codes like
- Binary to octal (3 : 8 decoder)
- Binary to hexadecimal (4 : 16 decoder)
- It contains AND gates or NAND gates.
- Total number of output lines: $m < 2^n$ ($n \rightarrow$ total no. of input lines)

Block Diagram

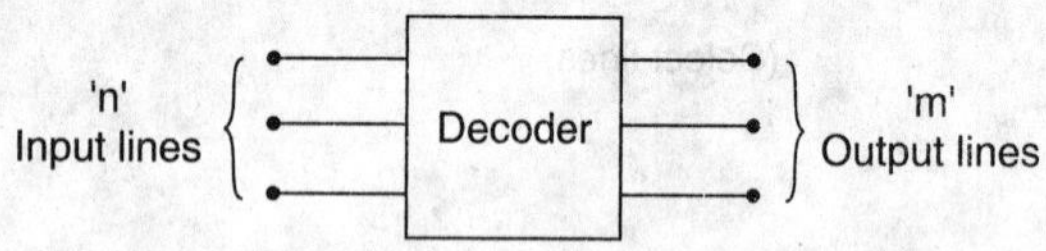

2 × 4 Decoder

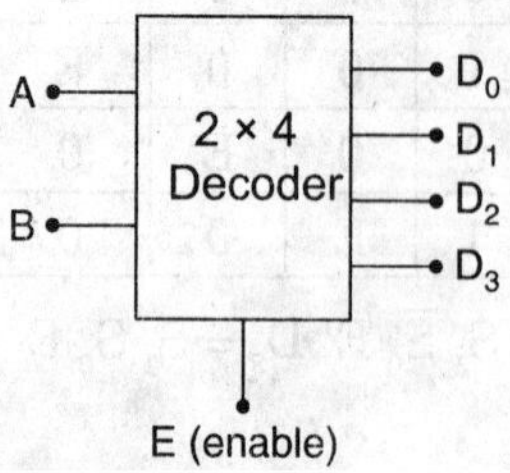

Truth Table:

Input			Output			
E	A	B	D_0	D_1	D_2	D_3
1	X	X	1	1	1	1
0	0	0	0	1	1	1
0	0	1	1	0	1	1
0	1	0	1	1	0	1
0	1	1	1	1	1	0

Note:

- 2×4 Decoder may act like a 1 : 4 DEMUX and vice-versa.
- to implement n-functions, we unique; require
  - (a) n-muxs or
  - (b) One $n \times 2n$ decoder and n OR gates.

  Implementation of decoders using decoder.

Given Decoder	To be implemented Decoder	Required Number of Decoder
2 : 4	4 : 16	1 + 4 = 5
2 : 4	3 : 8	2 + 1 NOT Gate
4 : 16	8 : 256	1 + 16 = 17

Encoder

- performs inverse operation of the decoder.
- it has n-input line and m-output lines.
- it converts n-digital word and into another m digital word like octal to Binary, Hexadecimal to Binary.
- Normally, only one input line is high at a time.
- But in priority encoder; more than one input line can be high but only for highest priority input line, binary output is available at output.

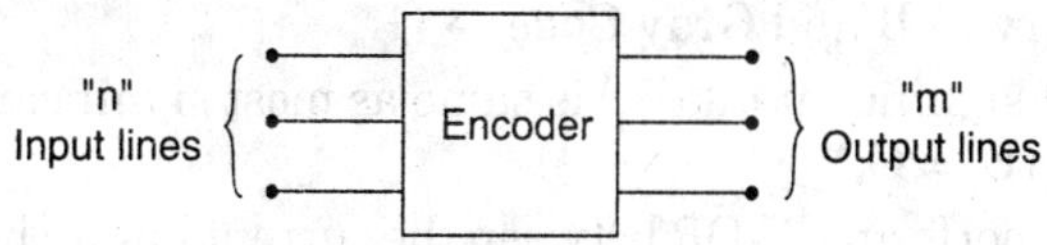

Example : Priority encoder
Decimal to BCD convertor.

CODE CONVERTERS

1. **BCD to Excess – 3 Code**
   - ⇨ Convert BCD to decimal
   - ⇨ Add 3_{10} to the decimal number
   - ⇨ Convert into Binary to get excess – 3 code.

let. Input BCD be A,B,C,D and excess – 3 output be W, X, Y, Z

Truth table: (BCD + 0011) = excess – 3

Inputs				Output			
A	**B**	**C**	**D**	**W**	**X**	**Y**	**Z**
0	0	0	0	0	0	1	1
0	0	0	1	0	1	0	0
0	0	1	0	0	1	0	1
0	0	1	1	0	1	1	0
0	1	0	0	0	1	1	1
0	1	0	1	1	0	0	0
0	1	1	0	1	0	0	1
0	1	1	1	1	0	1	0
1	0	0	0	1	0	1	1
1	0	0	1	1	1	0	0

Minimized Boolean Function:

$$Z = \overline{D}$$
$$Y = CD + \overline{C}\,\overline{D}$$
$$X = \overline{B}C + \overline{B}D + B\overline{C}\,\overline{D}$$
$$W = A + BC + BD$$

2. Binary to gray code converter

⇨ Binary → B and Gray Code → G

⇨ Most significant bit (B_1) is same as most significant bit in gray code ($B_1 = G_1$)

⇨ Now, perform EX-OR between the current binary bit & previous bit *i.e.*, $Gn = Bn$ (EX – OR) B_{n-1}

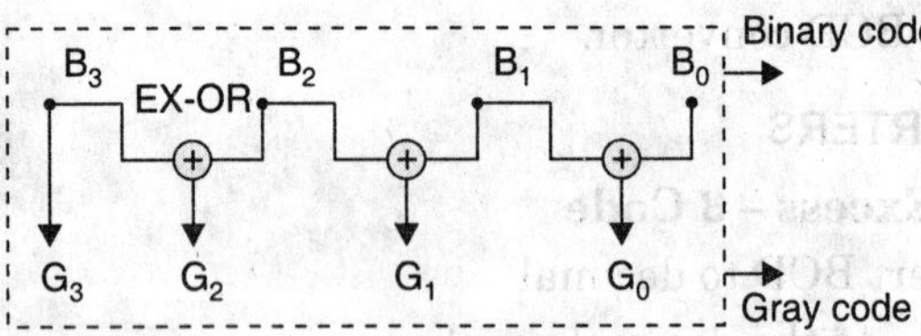

Equivalent logic gate diagram:

$$G_3 = B_3$$
$$G_2 = B_3 \oplus B_2$$
$$G_1 = B_2 \oplus B_1$$
$$G_0 = B_1 \oplus B_0$$

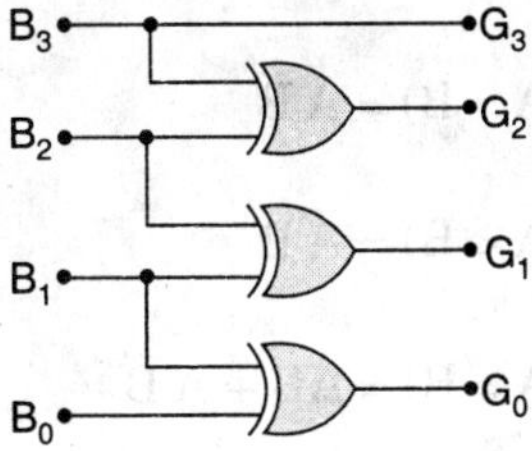

Gray to Binary Converter

- $G_1 = B_1$
- Take EX–OR between the previous binary bit and current gray code bit.

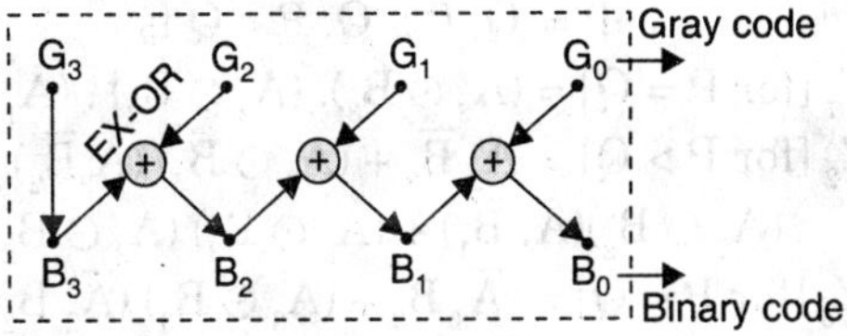

- **Equivalent logical gate diagram:**

$$B_3 = G_3$$
$$B_2 = B_3 \oplus G_2$$
$$B_1 = B_2 \oplus G_1$$
$$B_0 = B_1 \oplus G_0$$

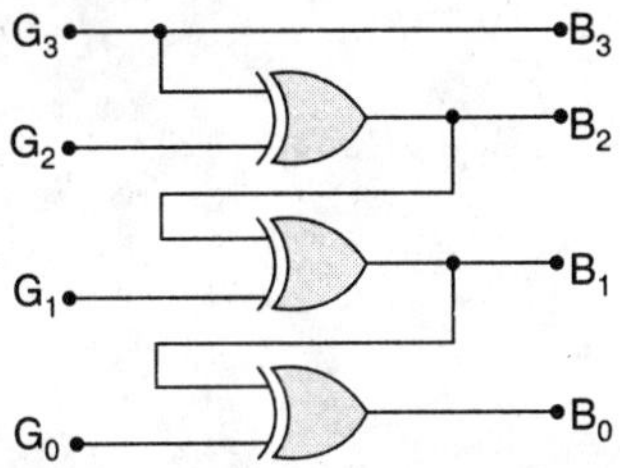

Carry look ahead adder

- Commonly known as CLA solves the problem of carry delay by calculating the carry signals in advance, based on the input signal.
- Makes addition faster →.
- Requires 4 logic gate array to provide sum.
- Carry circuit is implemented using two levels AND-OR gate circuit
- Number of AND gates required in carry circuit for n bit CLA is

$$N_{AND} = \frac{n(n+1)}{2}$$

- Number of OR gates required in CLA is 'n' →.

Comparator

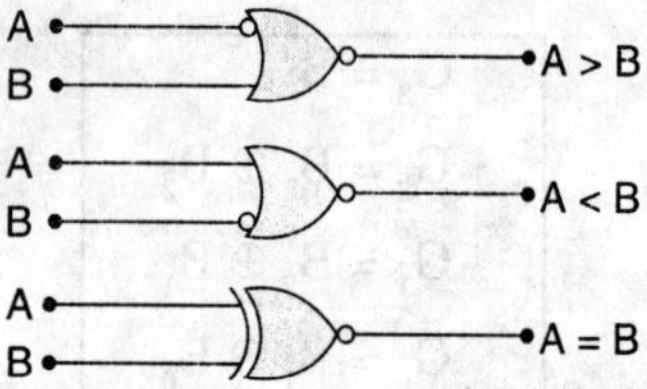

- $(A > B) = A\overline{B}$
- $(A < B) = \overline{A}B$
- $(A = B) = AB + \overline{A}\,\overline{B}$
- **Example:**

  Suppose we have

  $P = A_3 A_2 A_1 A_0$

  $Q = B_3 B_2 B_1 B_0$

  Logic expression for

  $P = Q,\ P > Q,\ P < Q$ is

  Y_1 [for $P = Q$] $= (A_2 \odot B_3).(A_2 \odot B_2).(A_1 \odot B_1).(A_0 \odot B_0)$

  Y_2 [for $P > Q$] $= A_3\overline{B}_3 + (A_3 \odot B_3)(A_2\overline{B}_2) + (A_3 \odot B_3)(A_2 \odot B_2)(A_1\overline{B}_1) + (A_3 \odot B_3)(A_2 \odot B_2)(A_1 \odot B_1)(A_0\overline{B}_0)$

  Y_3 [for $P < Q$] $= \overline{A}_3 B_3 + (A_3 \odot B_3)(\overline{A}_2 B_2) + (A_3 \odot B_3)(A_2 \odot B_2)(A_1 B_1) + (A_3 \odot B_3)(A_2 \odot B_2)(A_1 \odot B_1)(\overline{A}_0 B_0)$

4 Sequential Circuits

Sequential Circuit

- Circuit where output values depends on present input values as well as input values in the past.
- Memory is required
- It has previous input, output, clock and a memory element.

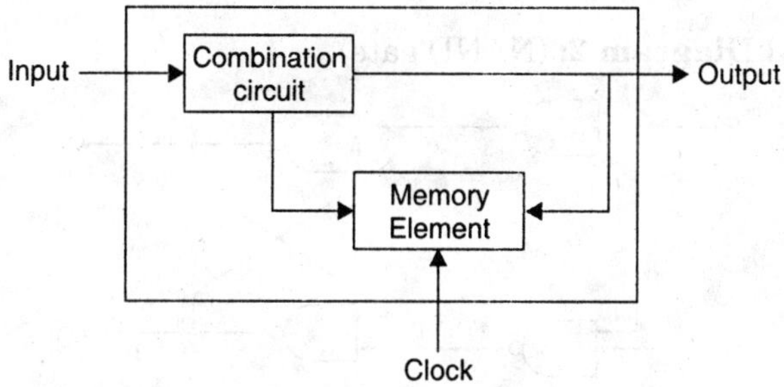

Flip-Flops

- samples the inputs and changes its output only at particular instants of time and not continuously.
- can store 'one-bit of information'.
- also called as 'Bistable Multivibrator' or 'Latch'.
- 2 NAND gates or 2 NOR gates are required to construct Flip Flop circuit.

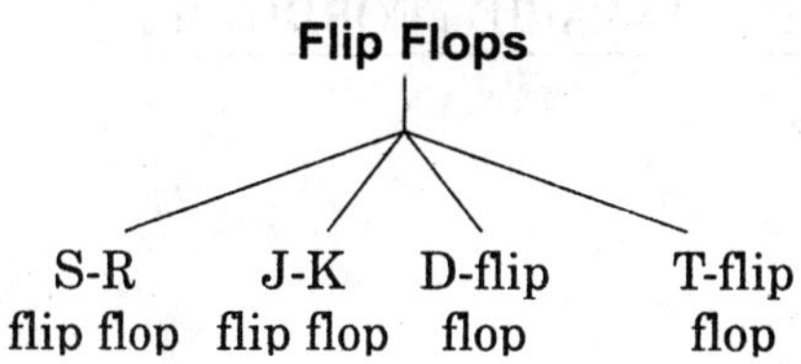

S-R Flip Flop

- Also called SR Latch
- Here, output will take place if and only if the enable input is made active.
- Input S stands for SET and R for RESET.

Logical Diagram 1: (NOR gate)

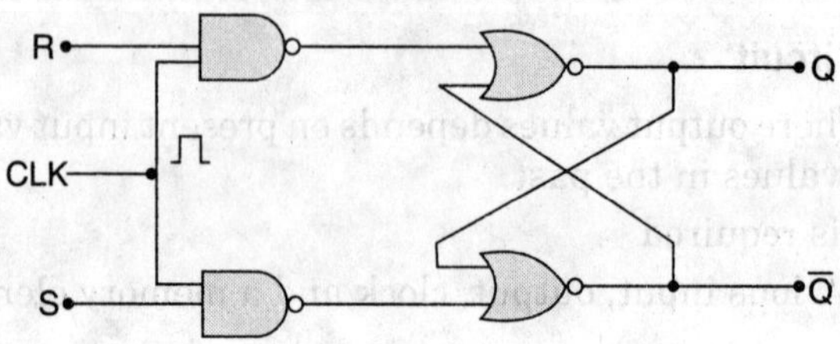

Logical Diagram 2: (NAND gate)

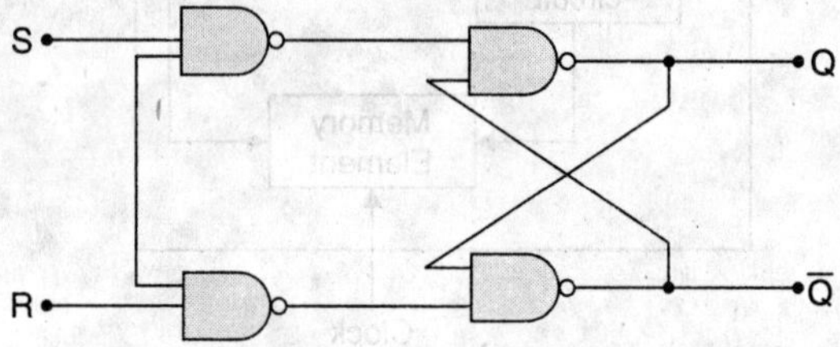

Truth Table:

Clock	S_n	R_n	Q_{n+1}	STATE
0	X	X	Q_n	
1	0	0	Q_n	HOLD
1	0	1	0	RESET
1	1	0	1	SET
1	1	1	INVALID	FORBIDDEN

Inputs (S_n, R_n)

$Q_n \rightarrow$ Output during bit time '*n*'.

$Q_{n+1} \rightarrow$ Output after CLK passes *i.e.*, bit time '*n + 1*'.

Characteristic table of SR-FF

S	R	Q_n	Q_{n+1}	
0	0	0	0	→ Q_n
0	0	1	1	
0	1	0	0	→ n
0	1	1	0	
1	0	0	1	→ 1
1	0	1	1	
1	1	0	X	→ Invalid
1	1	1	X	

Excitation table of S-R-F

Q_n	Q_{n+1}	S	R
0	0	0	X
0	1	1	0
1	0	0	1
1	1	X	0

Characteristic equation:

$$Q_{n+1} = S + \overline{R}Q_n$$

(valid only for S.R = 0)

Note:

- When both input S and R are HIGH → Invalid state

D-Flip Flop

- Delay Flip Flop is simple gated S-R Latch with a NAND inverter connected between S and R inputs.
- only one input.
- it is FF with delay to exactly one cycle of CLK.

Logical diagram

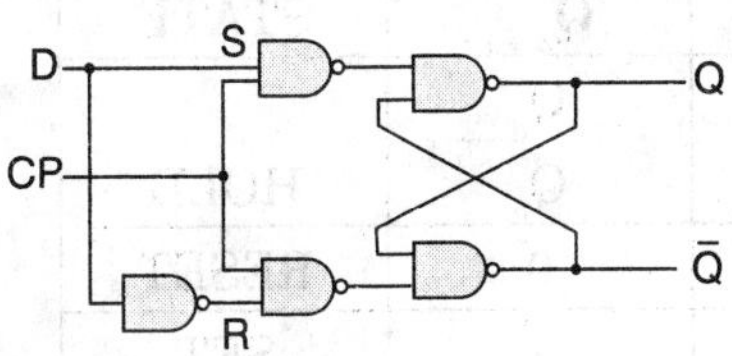

Graphical diagram

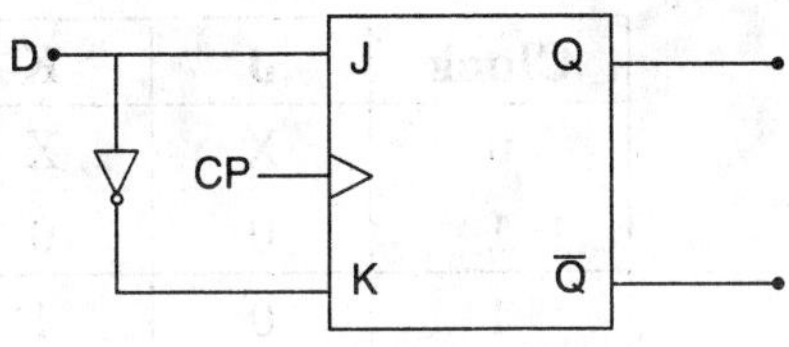

J = D and K = $\overline{D}$

Truth Table

CLK	D	Q_{n+1}
0	X	Q_n
1	0	0
1	1	1

Characteristic Table

D	Q_n	Q_{n+1}
0	0	0
0	1	0
1	0	1
1	1	1

Excitation Table

Q_n	Q_{n+1}	D
0	0	0
0	1	1
1	0	0
1	1	1

Characteristic Equation

$$Q_{n+1} = D$$

J-K Flip Flop

- Universal flip flop because other flip flops can be derived from it.
- Input J stand for SET and K for CLEAR.
- $S = J\overline{Q}$ and $R = KQ$

Logic Diagram 1

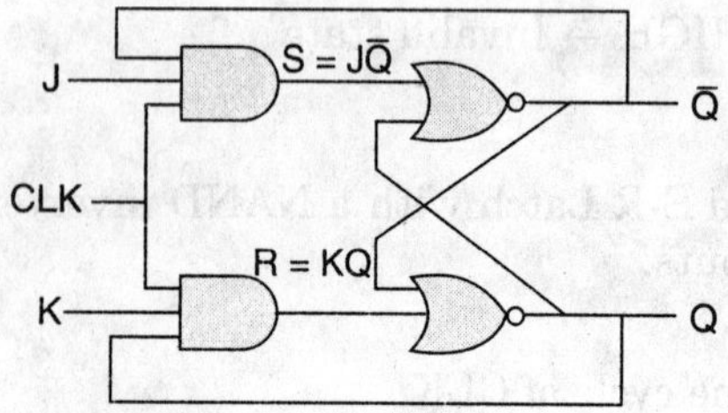

Logic Diagram 2

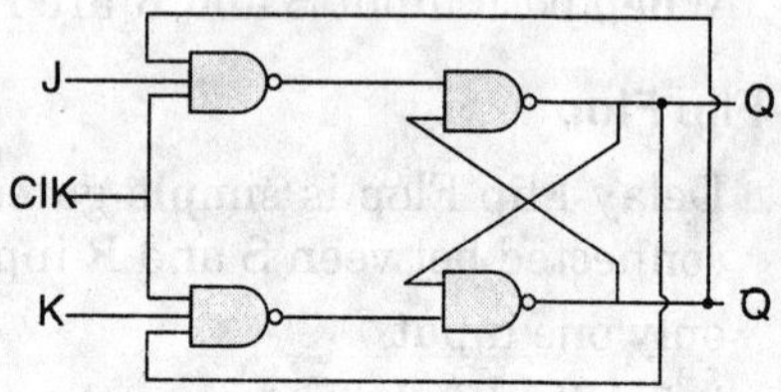

Truth Table

Clock	J	K	Q_{n+1}	STATE
0	X	X	Q_n	
1	0	0	Q_n	HOLD
1	0	1	0	RESET
1	1	0	1	SET
1	1	1	$\overline{Q}_n$	TOGGLE

Characteristic Table

J	K	Q_n	Q_{n+1}	
0	0	0	0	→ Q_n
0	0	1	1	
0	1	0	0	→ 0
0	1	1	0	
1	0	0	1	→ 1
1	0	1	1	
1	1	0 →	1	→ $\overline{Q}_n$
1	1	1 →	0	

Excitation Table

Q_n	Q_{n+1}	J	K
0	0	0	X
0	1	1	X
1	0	X	1
1	1	X	0

Characteristic equation; $\boxed{Q_{n+1} = J\overline{Q}_n + \overline{K}Q_n}$

Race Around Condition:

Also called toggling output.

Occurs when; $J = K = 1$ and $t_{Pd(FF)} < t_{PW}$

To Avoid; $t_{PW} < t_{pd(FF)} < T$.

T-Flip Flop

- Toggle Flip Flop is JK flip flop with J and K permanently connected together. It has only single input T.

Graphical symbol

J = K = T

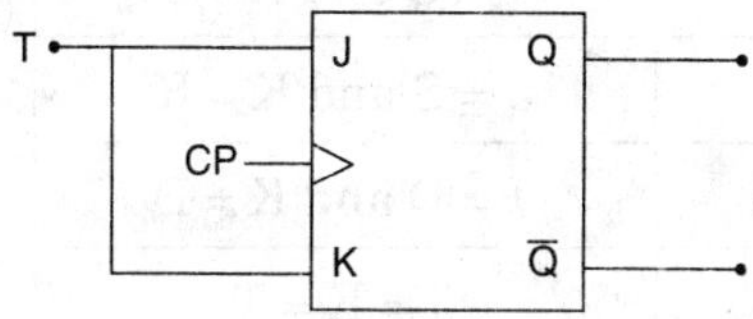

Logic Diagram

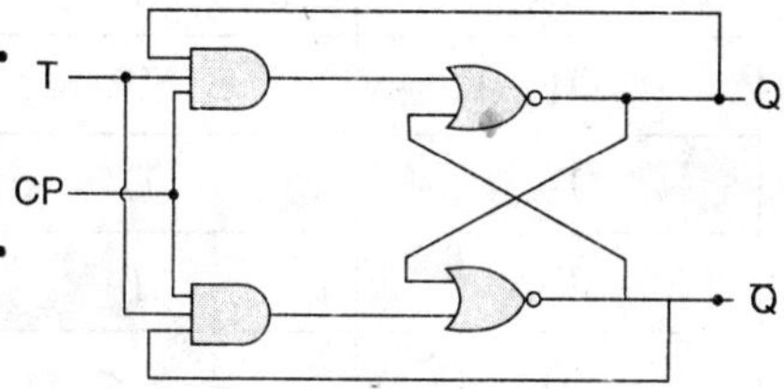

Truth Table

CLK	T	Q_{n+1}	STATE
0	X	Q_n	--
1	0	Q_n	HOLD
1	1	$\overline{Q}_n$	RESET

Characteristic Table

T	Q_n	Q_{n+1}
0	0	0
0	1	1
1	0	1
1	1	0

Characteristic equation; $Q_{n+1} = \overline{T}Q_n + T\overline{Q}_n + T \oplus Q_n$

Excitation Table

Q_n	Q_{n+1}	T
0	0	0
0	1	1
1	0	0
1	1	0

Note:

- Race around condition occurs in JK-FF and T-FF to store 2-bit of information. It arises in Asynchronous circuits.

- A master slave FF consist of a SR-FF and a T-FF.
- Frequency is halved at the output of any FF whose behaviour is same as TOGGLED-FF.

Conversion of Flip Flops

Source Flip-Flop	Destination Flip-Flop	Condition
SR	JK	$S = J\overline{Q}_n$ and $R = KQ_n$
SR	D	$S = D$ and $R = \overline{D}$
SR	T	$S = T\overline{Q}$ and $R = TQ$
JK	SR	$J = S$ and $K = R$
JK	D	$J = D$ and $K = \overline{D}$
JK	T	$J = K = T$
D	SR	$D = S + \overline{R}Q_n$
D	JK	$D = J\overline{Q} + \overline{K}Q$
D	T	$D = T \oplus Q$
T	SR	$T = J\overline{Q} + KQ$
T	JK	$T = S\overline{Q} + RQ$
T	D	$T = D \oplus Q$

Toggle Mode of operation

1.

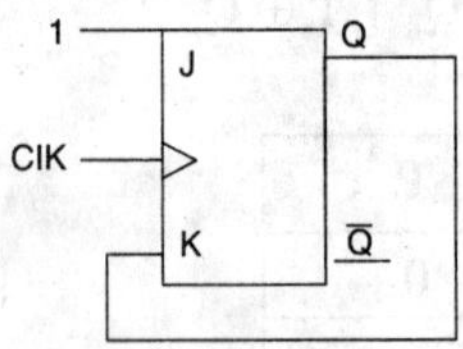

$Q(n+1) = \overline{Q}(n)$

2.

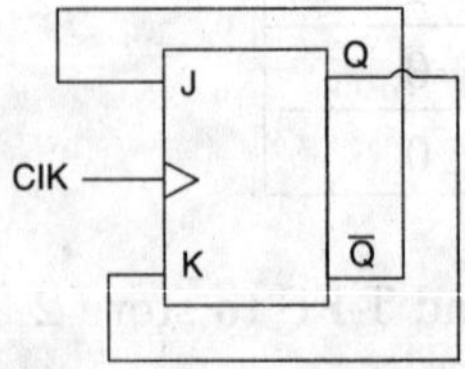

$Q(n+1) = \overline{Q}(n)$

3. 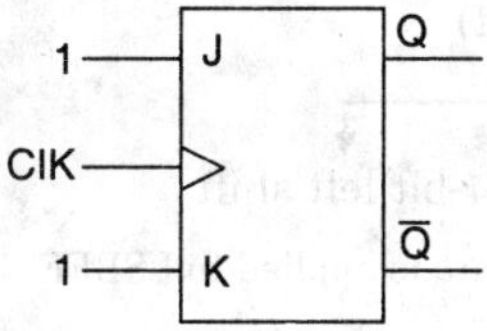

$Q(n+1) = \overline{Q}(n)$

4. 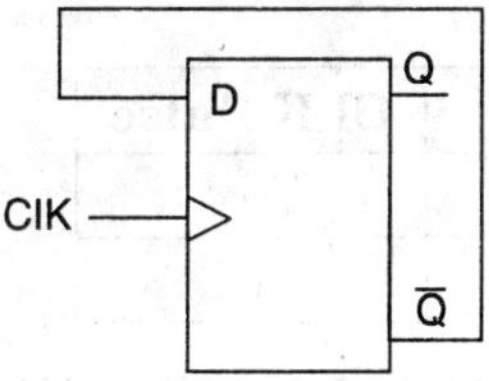

$Q(n+1) = \overline{Q}(n)$

5. 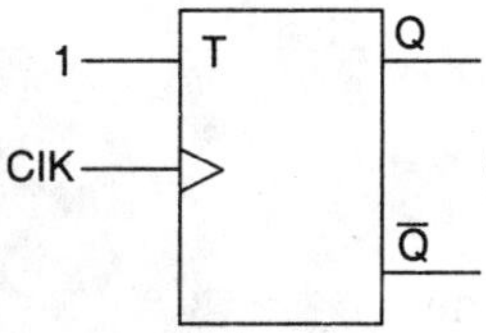

$Q(n+1) = \overline{Q}(n)$

Shift Registers

- To increase storage capacity of number of bits, we have to use group of flip flop called registers.
- The binary data in a register can be moved within the register from one flip flop to another. Such registers are called Shift Registers.

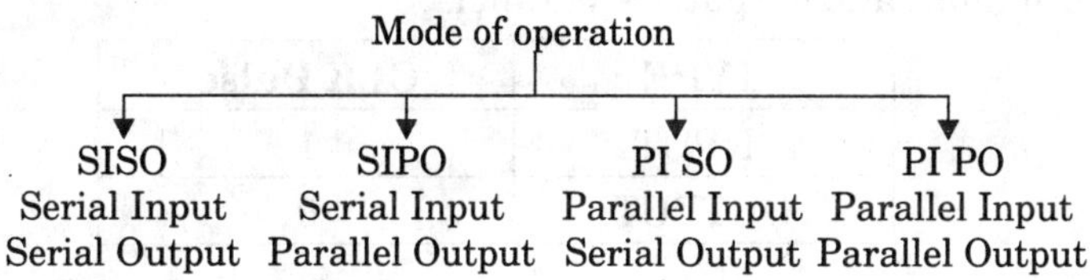

SISO

- For entering '*n*' bit data in '*n*' bit register; '*n*' clock pulse is required.
- $(n - 1)$ clock pulse is required if n bit data is stored in SISO register for output to take serially.
- SISO is used to provide '*n*' clock pulse delay to input data.
- If T = time period of clock pulse then delay = nT.

SISO (4-bit)

4-bit right shift	4-bit left shift
LSB is applid to MSB FF (D-FF)	MSB data is applied to LSBFF (D-FF).

SIPO

DATA	TYPE	BIT	CLK Pulse
Serial	INPUT	n	n
Parallel	OUTPUT	n	0

- Here; data is entered serially and taken out in parallel manner.
- Speed of SIPO is same as that of SISO.

PISO

- data is entered in parallel manner.
- circuit works in shift mode and load mode.

DATA	TYPE	CLK PULSE
Parallel	Input	1
Serial	Output	$n - 1$

PIPO

- Both input and output are parallel.

TYPE	CLK Pulse
INPUT	1
OUTPUT	0

TIME DELAY (D*t*)

- SISO shift registers introduce time delay in digital signals.

$$\Delta t = N \times T = N \times \frac{1}{fc}$$

where N = number of FF

T = time period of CLK pulse

fc = CLK frequency

POINTS TO REMEMBER:

- All shift registers are JK-FF.
- PIPO register is storage register made Up of D-FF
- Each shift left operation: multiply data by 2.
- Shift right operation: divide data by 2.
- Temporal → spatial: SIPO register
  code code
  Spatial → Temporal: PISO register
  code code

COUNTERS:

On the basis of clock pulse applied;

Counters

Asynchronous

- FF with different clocks
- Slow
- Count sequence is fixed
- Decoding error

Synchronous

- FF with same clock
- Fast
- Any count sequence
- No decoding error

MOD Counter:

- Modulus counter.
- 'MOD number' indicates number of states in counting sequence and frequency division obtained from last FF.
- For n-FF; 2^n different states; counter is "MOD-2^n counter" *i.e.*, it it is capable of counting upto $(2^n - 1)$.

Up-Down Counter:

- Combination of Up and Down Counter.
- It can count in any direction depending upon the control input.
- A mode control (M) input is provided to select the mode.

Ripple Counter:

- It is also known as Asynchronous counter.
- With n-FF; 2^n possible states
- & 2^{n-1} maximum counts that can be counted

Disadvantage

- Propagation delay of FFs leads to decoding error.

  i.e., $t_{Pd(FF)}$
- For proper operation of Ripple Counter;

$$T_{CLK} \geq nt_{Pd(FF)}\ ; \qquad f_{CLK} \leq \frac{1}{nt_{Pd(FF)}}$$

- Maximum CLK frequency ; $f_{CLK,\,m} = \dfrac{1}{nt_{pd(FF)}}$

Note:

- For determination of UP/DOWN Counter:

TRIGGERING EDGE	CLK CONNECTION	ACCESS AS
–ve	Q	UP Counter
–ve	$\overline{Q}$	Down Counter
+ve	Q	Down Counter
+ve	$\overline{Q}$	UP Counter

- Ripple counter; flip flop applied with external clock will act as LSB bit.
- Asynchronous input to FF are Clear and Preset
- $N \leq 2^n$ and $n \geq 3.32 \log_{10} N$

  if N = total number of states

  and n = number of FFs
  - BINARY Counter; $N = 2^n$
  - Non-Binary Counter; $N < 2^n$
  - In 'MOD-n' Counter;

    Input frequency = f then

    Output frequency = f/N
  - "MOD-MN" Counter
- When 2-counters are cascaded with MOD-M followed by MOD-N then overall cascaded counter is (MXN) or 'MOD-MN'

Non-Binary Ripple Counter

Decade Counter or MOD-10 Counter

- 10 used states and 6 unused states
- Decade counters require resetting to zero when output count reaches the decimal value of 10.

- For down counter, MOD Number = $2^n - N$
- Output frequency of MOD-10 counter = $f/10$

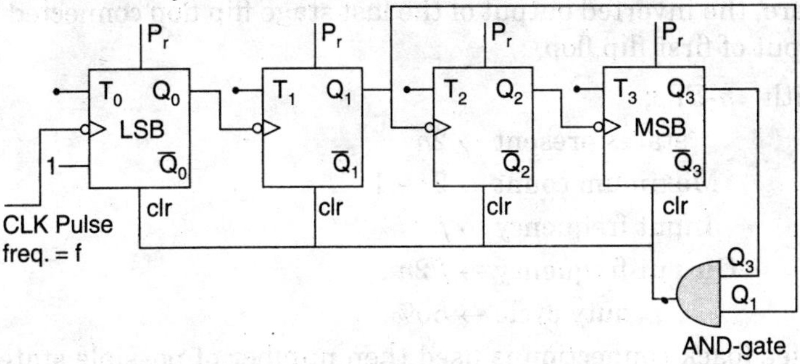

Synchronous (Parallel) Counters

NOT-Self Starting Ring Counter

- It is SISO Shift Register

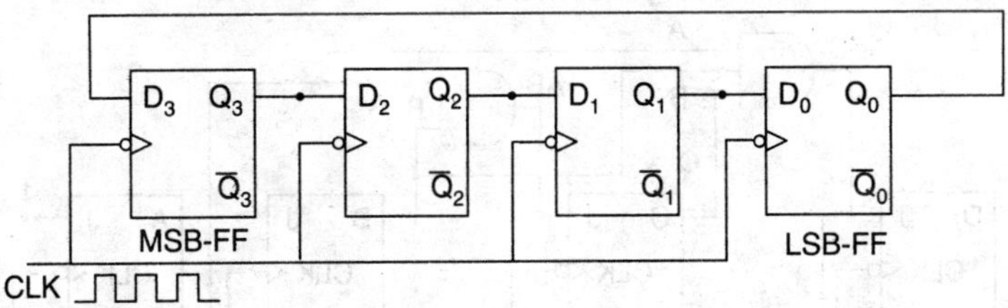

In 4-bit ring counter:

- used states = 4; unused states = $2^4 - 4 = 12$

Self Starting Ring Counter

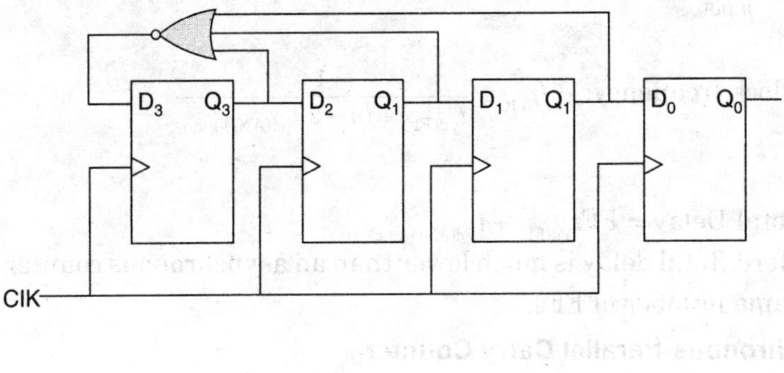

Twisted-Ring Counter

- Commonly known as Johnson Counter or Switch Tail Ring Counter.
- Here, the inverted output of the last stage flip flop connected to the Input of first flip flop.
- With n-FFs;

$$\begin{aligned} \text{states present} &\rightarrow 2n \\ \text{Maximum count} &\rightarrow 2^n - 1 \\ \text{Input frequency} &\rightarrow f \\ \text{Output frequency} &\rightarrow f/2n \\ \text{duty cycle} &\rightarrow 50\% \end{aligned}$$

- If feedback connection is used then number of possible states will decrease.
- For decoding; 2 input AND or NOR-gate is used
- Lockout may occur when counter enters into unused stage.

Synchronous-Series Carry Counter

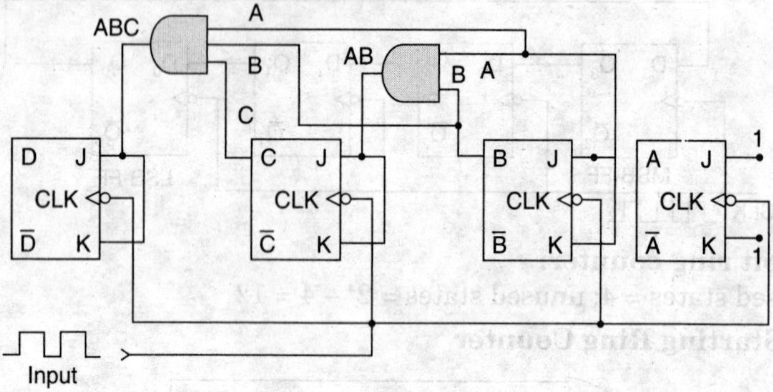

- Clock frequency: $f_{\text{CLK}} \leq \dfrac{1}{t_{\text{pd(FF)}} + (n-2)t_{\text{pd(AND-gate)}}}$

- Total Delay = $\text{FF}t_{\text{Pd(FF)}} + t_{\text{Pd(AND-gate)}}$
  Here; Total delay is much lower than an asynchronous counter with same number of FFs.

Synchronous-Parallel Carry Counter

- Fastest Counter
- Clock frequency: $f_{\text{CLK}} = \dfrac{1}{t_{\text{pd(FF)}} + t_{\text{pd(AND-gate)}}}$

POINTS TO REMEMBER:

For Ring Counter →

- CLK frequency = f then output frequency = f/N
  (N = number of states)
- n-FFs; number of states → n.
  maximum count → 2^{n-1}
- Decoding is easy as no aid of extra circuit.

Number Representation and Computer Arithmetic

5

Digital Number System

- Number system with symbols called digits and these symbols representing different values depending on the position they occupy in the number.
- Number system with base '*b*' will have '*b*' different digits from 0 to $(b - 1)$.

Representation:

$$\{(N)_b = d_{n-1}\, d_{n-2} \ldots d_i \ldots d_1 d_0 \,.\, d_{-1} d_{-2} \ldots d_{-f} \ldots d_{-m}\}$$

Where;

N = number

b = base or radix

$d_{n-1}\, d_{n-2} \ldots$ = integer portion of number N_b

$d_{-1}\, d_{-2} \ldots$ = fraction portion of number and between these two there is a radical sign.

Number System

- Weighted Number System
  - Binary, Octal, Hexa decimal, BCD.
- Unweighted Number System
  - Gray code, Excess-3 code.

- In Binary number system; a group of four bits is known as 'Nibble' and group of eight bits is known as 'Byte'.

  4 bit = 1 Nibble;

  8 bits = 1 byte.

NUMBER SYSTEM	BASE	DIGITS
Binary	2	0, 1
Octal	8	0, 1, 2, 3, 4, 5, 6, 7
Decimal	10	0, 1, 2, 3, 4, 5, 6, 7, 8, 9
Hexadecimal	16	0, 1, 2, 3, 4, 5, 6, 7, 8, 9 A, B, C, D, E, F

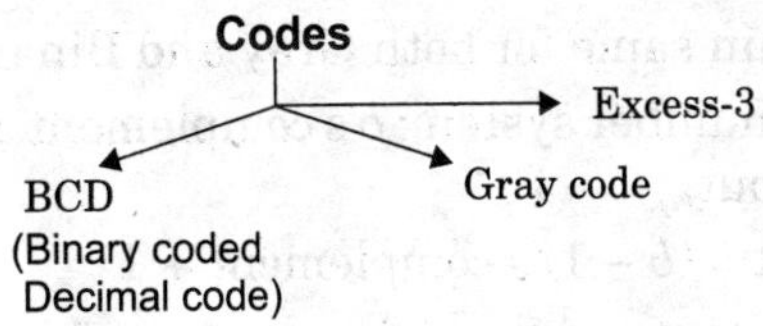

BCD

- Decimal number is represented by binary equivalent. Also known as 8421-code.
- **4 Bit Binary Formula:**

  Total number of representation = 2^4 = 16

  Valid BCD codes = 10

  Invalid BCD codes = 6

In 8-bit Binary format

Valid BCD codes = 100

Invalid = 256 – 100 = 156

Note:

- During arithmetic operation; if invalid BCD is present then add (0110) to get correct result.
- BCD is not self complementing code.

Excess-3 code

- A 4-bit code derived by adding 3 to each coded number
- It is self complementing code and unweighted

Gray Code

- Known as minimum change code/cyclic code/Reflective code
- While proceeding to neat step; only one bit in the code group get changed.
- It has minimum error so also known as minimum error code.

CONVERSION

Binary to Gray Conversion:

- Binary and Gray have same number of bits.
- MSB of both Binary and Gray will always be same.
- To get next digit (start from left to right), each adjacent pair of binary digit is EXOR to get next gray code digit.

Gray to Binary Conversion

- MSB will remain same for both Gray and Binary.
- With base b in number system; b's complement and $(b-1)'$s complement is found out.
- b's complement = $(b-1)'$s complement + 1
- $(b-1)'$s complement: subtract given number from maximum number possible to the given base *i.e.*, $r^n - 1$
- if $(X_3 X_2 X_1 X_0)_b = (A)_{10}$ Then;
  $$A = X_0 + X_1 b^1 + X_2 b^2 + X_3 b^3).$$

Digital Number Representation

- Possible integer value is $[0 \text{ to } (2^n - 1)]$ in unsigned magnitude representation with n bits.
- Extra bit is **'Sign bit'** (MSB)
  - if MSB = 0; Positive number
    MSB = 1; negative number
  - range of number: $-(2^{n-1}-1)$ to $+(2^{n-1}-1)$
- **1's complement**
  - Positive number are represented similar to positive number in sign magnitude but negative number first considers the positive number then take 1's complement
  - Range: $-(2^{n-1}-1)$ to $+(2^{n-1}-1)$
- **In 2's complement**
  - Positive number are similar to positive number in sign magnitude and for negative number, 2's complement of positive number is taken.
  - Range: $-(2^{n-1}-1)$ to $+(2^{n-1}-1)$

Binary Arithmetic

- Only magnitude is added for numbers with same sign using the sign as MSB.

1's Complement Addition

- With different sign numbers; one of them is kept as it is and 1's complement of other one is taken and then only magnitude is added.
- In case of carry:
  - Add it to LSB
  - Sign of the result is sign of number that was not complemented
- In case of no carry:
  - 1's complement is considered as result
  - Sign of result is sign of complemented number

2's Complement Addition :

- If numbers are of same sign; they are added.
- Carry if generated is discarded
- In case of no carry; 2's complement of result is taken.

Overflow

- Addition of two same signed number in signed representation leads to Overflow.
- For detecting an Overflow; XOR gate is used, where; C_{in} (input carry to MSB) and C_{out} (output carry from MSB) are inputs.

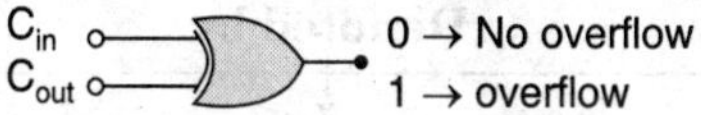

- Representing zero;
  In 2's complement: only one representation *i.e.*, 0.
  In 1's complement: + 0 and – 0.

Fixed Point and Floating Point Representation

Fixed point: used for small range of values like Integer
Floating point: used for large range of values like Float/Real.

Fixed Point Representation

- **Fixed point unsigned integers:** Let the following n-bit number represent fixed point unsigned integer.

  $(a_{n-1}\, a_{n-2}\, a_{n-3} \dots a_1\, a_0)_2$

  $$V = \sum_{i=0}^{n-1} a_i * 2^i = a_0 * 2^0 + a_1 * 2^1 + \dots + a_{n-1} * 2^{n-1};\ a_i \in (0, 1)$$

  (*i*) $V \to V_{min}$, Iff $\forall i, a_i = 0 \Rightarrow V_{min} = 0$
  (*ii*) $V \to V_{max}$, Iff $\forall i, a_i = 1 \Rightarrow V_{max} = 2^0 + 2^1 + \dots\dots\dots 2^{n-1}$

  (*iii*) Range: $(0 \text{ to } 2^n - 1)$

- **Fixed point unsigned fraction:** Let the following n-bit number represent fixed point fraction

$(a_1 a_2 a_3 \dots a_n)_2$

$$V = \sum_{i=1}^{n} a_i * 2^{-i} \quad ; \; a_i \in (0, 1)$$

(*i*) $V \to V_{min}$, Iff $\forall\, i, a_i = 0 \Rightarrow V_{min} = 0$

(*ii*) $V \to V_{max}$, Iff $\forall\, i, a_i = 1$

(*iii*) $\text{Error} = \dfrac{1}{2^{n+1}} + \dfrac{1}{2^{n+2}} + \dots\infty = \dfrac{1}{2^n}\left[\dfrac{1}{2} + \dfrac{1}{2^2} + \dots\infty\right]$

(*iv*) Error = 2^{-n} ≡ Weight of least significant bit of a fraction.

(*v*) Range: $(0 \text{ to } 1 - 2^{-n})$

(*vi*) The more the bits in the fraction, less the error, and more the accuracy (precision).

Fixed Point Signed Number

Denoted by

Singed Magnitude Form	1's Complement Form	2's Complement Form
• Sign bit is explicitly considered	• Sign bit not explicitly considered	• Sign bit not explicitly considered
• Additional hardware is required for resultant sign of arithmatic	• No additional hardware required	• No additional hardware
• Addition subtraction is done on additional software.	• Addition and Subtraction is done using adder only	• Addition Subtraction done using adder only.
• O has 2 representation + 0: 0000 0000 – 0: 1000 0000	• O has 2 representation + 0: 0000 0000 – 0: 1111 1111	• O has 1 representation

Floating Point Representation

- The numbers are stored in mantissa exponent form.

  i.e., $\pm m \times r^{\pm e}$

where; m = mantissa/significant
e = exponent
r = radix/base

- Representation is in normalised form where MSB of mantissa must be non-zero as zero cannot be normalized.
- The value of expression is given by:
  (*i*) Explicit Normalization: $V = (-1)^{sign} [0.M]_2 \times 2^{E\text{-}Bias}$
  (*ii*) Implicit Normalization: $V = (-1)^{sign} [1.M]_2 \times 2^{E\text{-}Bias}$
- Biased exponent: an unsigned number that can represent signed exponent of original number.
- True Exponent = Biased Exponent – Bias

Sign	E(K) Biased Exponent	Mantissa

Bias = 2^{k-1}

$0 < E < 2^K - 1$, Bias = 2^{K-1}

- The IEEE 754 is concerned with floating point standard. Some of its features are:
  (*i*) The base of the system is 2.
  (*ii*) There is a provision for the values ± 0 and ± ∞.
  (*iii*) The floating point number is stored either with single precision or with double precision.
  (*iv*) Certain mantissa exponent combinations does not represent any number representing NAN.
  (*v*) The value represented in single precision.
  (*vi*)

S(1)	E(8)	M(23)	Value
0/1	000....0 E = 0	000....0 M = 0	± 0
0/1	11....1 E = 255	00....0 M = 0	± ∞
0/1	111....1 E = 255	Not all zeros	NAN (Not A Number)
0/1	000....0 E = 0	M ≠ 0	$(-1)^s (0.M)_2 \times 2^{-126}$
0/1	1 ≤ E ≤ 254	XXX....X	$(-1)^s (0.M)_2 \times 2^{E-127}$

Single Precision

← 32 bites →

S	E	M
1	8	23

$0 \le E \le 255$

Double Precision

← 64 bites →

S	E	M
1	11	52

$0 \le E \le 2047$

MEMORY

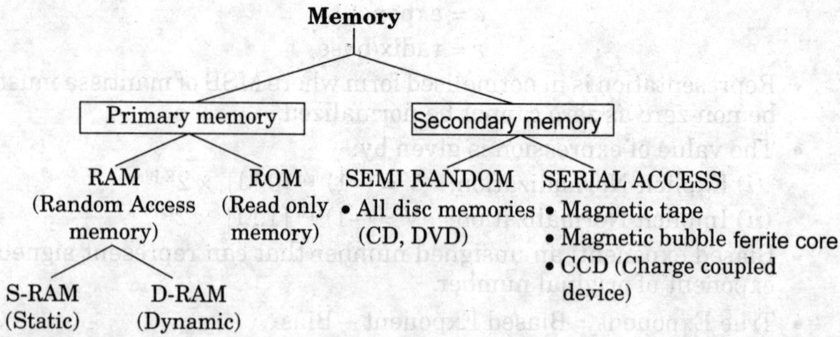

DIFFERENCES

1. RAM & ROM

RAM	ROM
• it is read/write memory (Random Access Memory)	• read only memory.
• volatile memory or temporary storage	• non-volatile or permanent storage

2. Static Ram AND Dynamic RAM

Static RAM	Dynamic RAM
• Uses latches to store data	• Used capacitors to store data
• BJT, MOSFET is used	• MOSFET is used
• Faster	• Slower
• Bigger in size	• Smaller in size
• Less capacity	• 5 to 10 times more capacity
• Used as cache momory	• Used as main memory
• More expensive per bit	• Less expensive difficult
• Acess is easy	• Acess is difficult
• Power consumption is less	• Power consumption is more
• Low density	• High density
• No refreshing required	• Refreshing required

Computer Science

3

Machine Instructions

Contents

1 Machine Instructions & Addressing Modes

MACHINE INSTRUCTIONS

Types

Zero address instructions	One address instructions	Two address instructions
• NOP	• PUSH • POP	• ADD • MULT • SUB

Opcode	Address 1 (m)	Address 2 (m)

← n →

$$P \times 2^{2m} + Q \times 2^{2m} + R = 2^n \text{ (Total Instructions)}$$

P → 2-address instruction

Q → 1-address instruction

R → 0-address instruction

ADDRESSING MODES

Types of Addressing Mode

Sequential control flow
- Program is stored in sequential memory locations.
- Program counter itself points the next instruction address.
- Addressing mode is focused on data.

Transfer of control flow
- Program is stored in random memory locations.
- Special instructions and addressing modes are needed to calculate the next instruction address.

Sequential Control Flow Addressing Mode

- Register Based
- Memory Based

1. Register Based Addressing Mode:

(*i*) Access the data when available in the registers.

(*ii*) Register / Register Direct Addressing Mode:

➢ Used to access the local variables.

➢ Here, data is present in the register whose address is available in address field of instruction.

Effective address = Address field value

Data = [EA] = [Register Name]

Ex. MOV R_1, R_2.

2. Memory Based Addressing Modes

➢ Data available in memory is accessed where EA is always the memory address.

➢ Different addressing modes are:

(*i*) Implied/ Implicit Addressing Mode:

➢ No use of effective address as data is available in op-code itself.

e.g. CMA

(*ii*) Immediate Addressing Mode:

➢ Registers are initialized to a constant value or constants are accessed in this mode.

Range of values is limited by size of the address field.

➢ Data is present in instructions address field. If its size is n-bit then possible range of immediate constants or data is 0 to $2^n - 1$.

➢ e.g. MOVA, 10.

(*iii*) Direct/ Absolute Addressing Mode:

➢ Static variables are accessed. Data is present in the memory and memory cell address is present in address field of the instruction.

Data = [EA]= [Memory Address]

➢ Using direct addressing mode, read or write the data requires one memory reference.

e.g. MOVR_1, [1000]

(*iv*) Auto Indexed Addressing Mode:

➢ Here data is accessed using "base address". Data is linear array elements.

➢ Base register maintains the base address.

Data 0 = EA = Base Register ± step size.

➢ Step size: Dependency on amount of data to be accessed from the memory.

Auto Indexed Addressing Mode

- Auto Increment
  - Pre-Auto increment: Move R_0, + (R_1)
  - Post-Auto increment: Move R_0, (R_1) +
- Auto Decrement
  - Pre-Auto Decrement: Move R_0, – (R_1)
  - Post-Auto Decrement: Move R_0, (R_1) –

(*v*) Indirect Addressing Mode:

➢ It implements pointers and EA is available in either register or memory.

Types

- Register Indirect Addressing Mode
  - EA = [Address field value] ⇒ [Register name]
  - EA is present in address register whose name is available in address field of instruction.
- Memory Indirect Addressing Mode
  - EA = [Address field value] ⇒ [Memory address].
  - Data = EA = Memory address.
  - EA is present in memory whose address is in address field of instruction.

(*vi*) Indexed Addressing Mode:

➢ Array indexing is done where
EA = Base address + Index Value

➢ Register Indexed Addressing Mode:
It holds the Index values and access random array element

➢ Indirect Index Addressing Mode:
Base address is present in memory whose address is in address field of instruction.

TRANSFER OF CONTROL FLOW ADDRESSING MODE

- The control is transferred from one location to other during execution of:
  - ➢ selection statement – if, then, else, goto, switch
  - ➢ iterative statement – For loop, while loop, do – while loop
  - ➢ subprogram concept
- It can be implemented by three mnemonics jump, branch and skip
- Instruction is of two types:

(*i*) Unconditional Transfer of Control:

- Program control is transferred to target address while executing an instruction, without checking any condition.

  eg. HALT.

(ii) Conditional Transfer of Control:

- While executing the instruction, evaluation is done for associated condition. If it results true then target address is loaded into Program Counter (PC) else no change in PC.
- Status of previous instruction are used to evaluate the conditions. Ex. They are used to implement 'if', 'switch', 'for', 'do while' and 'while' statements.

COMPUTATION OF EA FOR THE NEXT INSTRUCTION

Relative/PC Relative Addressing Mode

- Only the offset address is required to access the instruction 'within' the segment.

  Offset address is present in instruction's address field.
- EA = Base Address + offset Address

  ↓ PC   ↓ Address field value
- PC ← PC + IR [Address Field]

Base register Addressing Mode

- Base address along with offset address is required to access the instruction 'between' the segment.
- Base address is in base register and offset address is in address field of instruction.
- EA = [Base register] + IR [Address field]
- PC ← [Base register] + IR [Address field].

ALU & Data-Path, CPU Control Design

2

INTRODUCTION

CPU

- Data section/Data path
  - Registers and ALU performs operations.
- Control section/Control unit
  - Control signal is issued to data path

ALU AND DATA PATH

Type of Data Path

- One bus data path
  - CPU and ALU uses same bus for all incoming and outgoing data.
- Two bus data path
  - General purpose registers are connected to 2 buses.
  - At same time; input to ALU can be secured from 2 different registers.
- Three bus data path
  - 2 buses are source bus that moves data out called in-bus and third bus or out-bus is destination that moves data into register.

- The ALU, registers and interconnecting path is 'ALU data path'.
- To increment PC; constant is used.

  If select = 0; MUX output is constant

  1; MUX output is Y.

One-bus Datapath

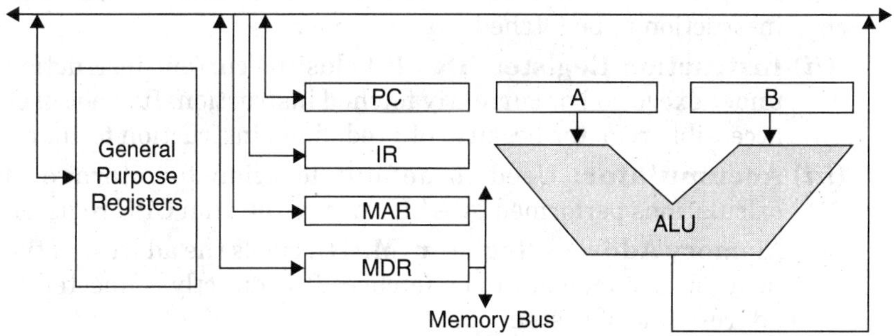

One-bus Datapath

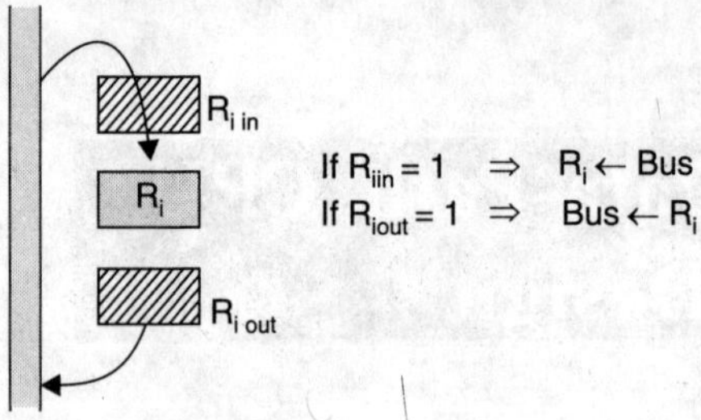

Data flow Into register and Out from register

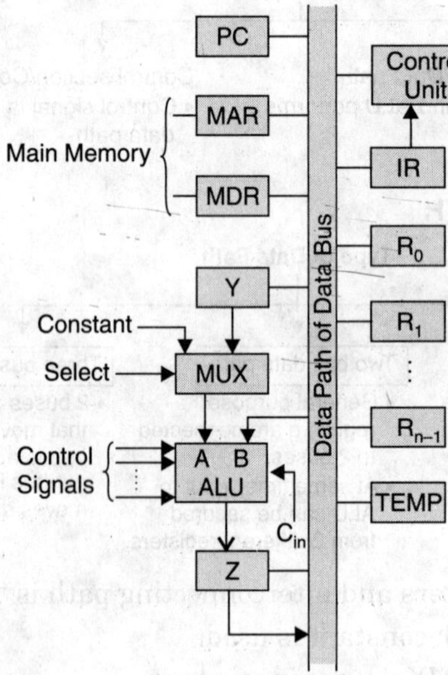

- **CPU Registers**

  Different Registers are:

  (*i*) **Program Counter (PC):** It holds the location of the next instruction to be fetched from memory.

  (*ii*) **Instruction Register (IR):** It holds the current instruction under execution or currently fetched instruction. It is not user accessible register because of predefined instruction format.

  (*iii*) **Accumulator:** Used to default location for storage of calculations performed by ALU. It is an internal CPU register.

  (*iv*) **Memory Address Register (MAR):** Holds the address of the next piece of memory to be fetched. It is directly connected to address line of system bus.

(v) **Memory Data Register (MDR)/Memory Buffer Register (MBR) Data Buffer:** Holds the data pieces fetched from memory. It is directly connected to address line of the system bus.

- **Micro-operations**
  - ➢ Operations that can be performed by system on data stored in registers. It includes data transfer between registers or register and external bus of CPU and performing Arithmetic and logic operations on registers.
  - ➢ The operations must be complete in single cycle.
  - ➢ Control operations executes them.

Ex. I_1: $R_1 \longrightarrow R_2$

$\boxed{R_1} \longrightarrow \boxed{R_2}$

R_{1out} R_{2in}

- **Microprogram**
  - ➢ Sequence of micro operations
  - ➢ To fetch cycle:

    T_1 : PC → MAR ; PC_{out}, MAR_{in}

    T_2 : M [MAR] → MBR; MAR_{out}, MBR_{in}

    T_3 : MBR → IR; MBR_{out}, IR_{in}

    PC ← PC + Step size; PC_{out}, PC_{in}
  - ➢ The basic operations performed are:

(i) Register transfer ($R_2 \leftarrow R_1$):

$R_{1\ out}$, $R_{2\ in}$, (only one clock cycle required)

(ii) ALU operation ($R_3 \leftarrow R_1 + R_2$):

$R_{1\ out}$, Y_{in}

$R_{2\ out}$, Selecet = 1, Add

Z_{out}, $R_{3\ in}$

Minimum number of clocks = 3

(iii) If two data paths are used:

$R_{1\ out}$, Y_{in}, $R_{2\ out}$, Select = 1, Add

Z_{out}, $R_{3\ in}$

Minimum number of clocks = 2

(iv) Memory Read

$R_2 \leftarrow M[(R_1)]$

$R_{1\ out}$, MAR_{in}, read

Wait for memory function to complete (WMFC).

MDR_{out}, $R_{2\ in}$

Hence number of clocks can be 2 or 3 depending on WMFC

(*v*) Memory Write:

$M[(R_1)] \leftarrow R_2$

$R_{1\,out}$, MAR_{in},

$R_{2\,out}$, MDR_{in}, write

WMFC

Minimum number of clocks = 3

CONTROL UNIT

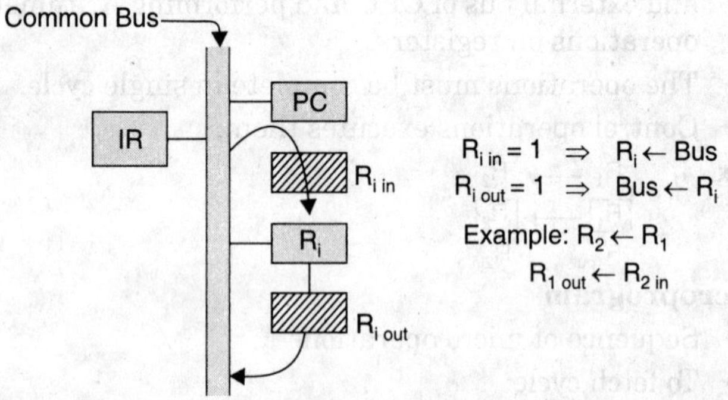

- It provides appropriate timing and control signal required for execution of micro-operations and are directly executed on base machine.
- Instruction is executed using instruction cycle whose sub cycle invokes micro-program.
- Program is a sequence of instruction along with data.

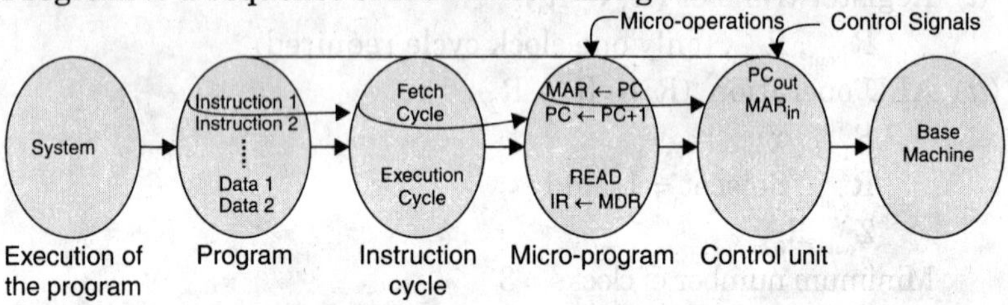

Program Execution using Control Unit

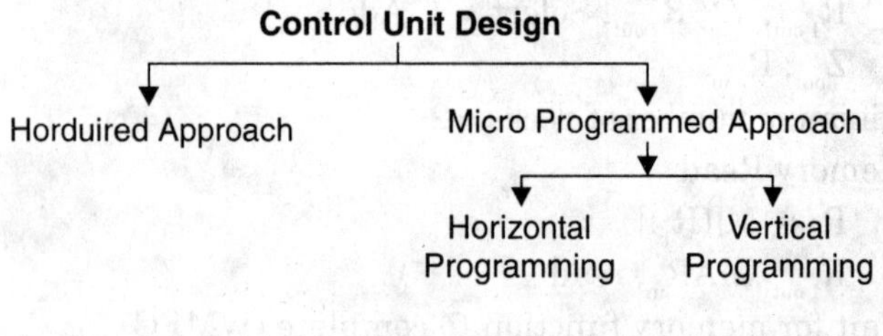

Hardwired Control Unit

- Fastest CU due to independent circuits where control signals are expressed as Sum-of-product (SOP).

  eg. $Y_{in} = T_1 + T_3 \cdot ADD + T_5 \cdot BR + ...$.

  (Y_{in} is enabled during T_1 for all instructions, during T_3 for ADD and so on ....)

  It can be realised as:

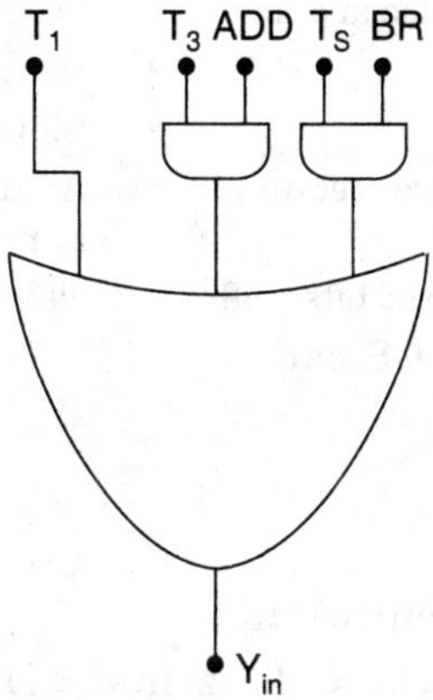

- It is implemented in RISC processor and used in Real time application like air craft simulation and weather forecasting.
- Hardware complexity is more for large number of instructions and control signal.

Micro-programmed Control Unit

- Control Memory (CM) is permanent memory i.e., ROM used to store microprogram that contains sequence of micro-operations or control word.
- Generations of control signal is slower than in hardwired.
- System is flexible for large number of instructions and control signal.
- On basis of type of control word (cw) in CM;

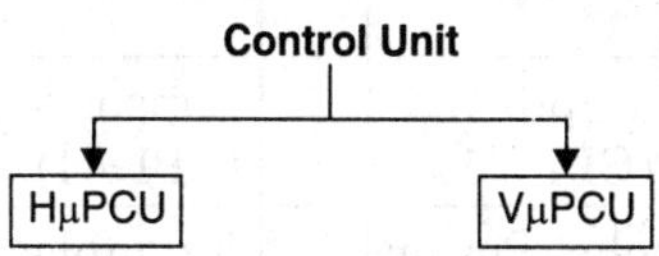

- Horizontal microprogrammed control unit
- Control signals are in decoded binary Format (1 bit/cs)
- Longer control word
- High degree of parallelism i.e., if degree is n; nCS are enabled at a time.
- Flexibility is less
- Faster
- No additional hardware required (decoders)

  eg. If CS = 68 then required bits = 68.

  ⇒ More than one CS can be enabled at a time

- Vertical microprogrammed control unit.
- Control signals are in encoded binary format.
- Shorter control word.
- Low degree of parallelism i.e. degree is 1 of 0.
- More flexible
- Slower
- Additional hardware (decoder) is required to generate control signal.

  eg. if N = 68 than $\log_2 68$ = 7 bits required.

POINTS TO REMEMBER

- Ascending order of Control Unit:

  w.r.t. speed: Vertical < Horizontal < Hardwired

  w.r.t. flexibility: Hardwired < Horizontal < Vertical

RISC AND CISC

	RISC		CISC
1.	Reduced instruction set computer	1.	Complex instruction set computer
2.	Supports rich register set	2.	Supports less number of registers
3.	Supports less number of addressing modes	3.	Supports more number of addressing modes
4.	Supports fixed length instructions	4.	Supports variable length instructions
5.	One instruction/cycle (CPI = 1)	5.	(CPI ≠ 1)
6.	Allows successful pipeline implementation (CPI = 1)	6.	Supports unsuccessful pipeline (CPI ≠ 1)
7.	Example: Motorola, Power PC, Advance Risk Machine.	7.	Example: Pentium

Memory and I/O Interfaces

3

INTRODUCTION

- The I/O interface provides a method for transferring information between internal storage and external I/O devices.
- Isolated I/O → CPU has distinct I/O instructions which are associated with the address of interface register.
- Memory mapped I/O → Memory and I/O share same address space. Interface register is treated as part of memory system.

INPUT OUTPUT ORGANIZATION

- The input and output devices are very slow.
- CPU is an electronic devices and input/output devices are electromagnetic which does not let them to be directly connected with system bus.
- There is difference in operating mode, data transfer and word format.
- For synchronization high speed interface or I/O Module is needed.

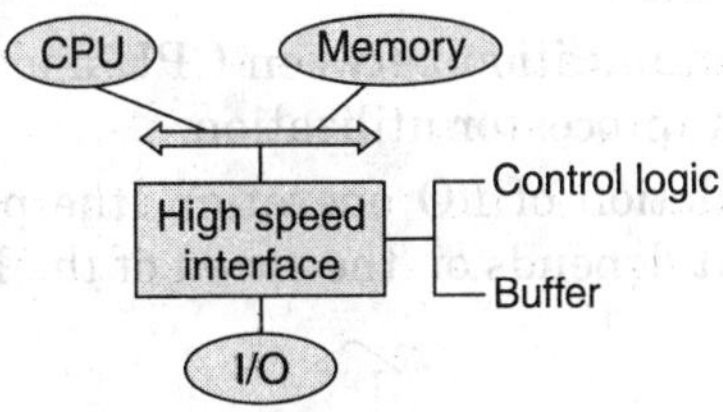

I/O Interface

- This I/O module enables the device for the operation. It prepares the data and then transfer it to the Buffer.
- When data is in Buffer then signal is sent to CPU by high speed interface and acknowledgement is awaited.
- On receiving the acknowledgement, data is transferred to the CPU with high rate thus minimizing the speed gap.

Types of Interfaces

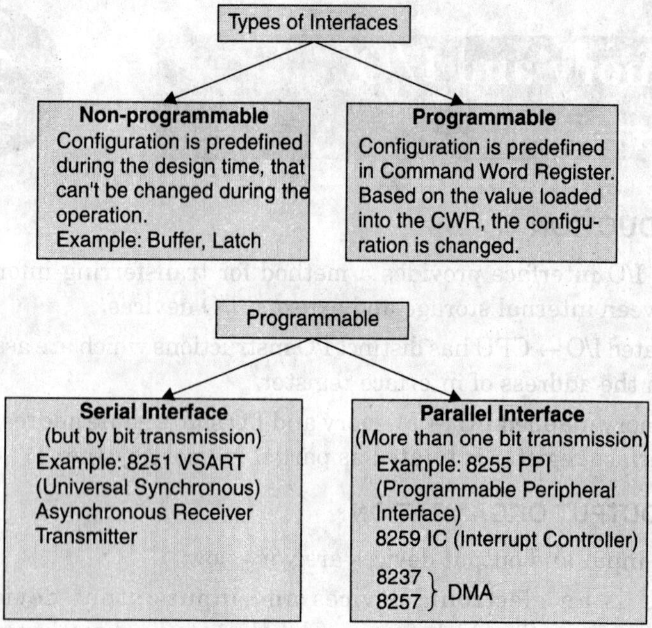

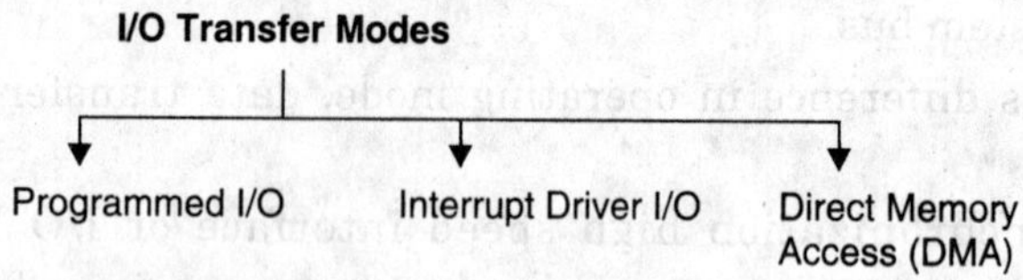

(*i*) Programmed I/O

- ➢ Direct communication between CPU and I/O devices leading to inefficient processor utilization.
- ➢ Until completion of I/O operation, the processor undergoes waiting that depends on the speed of the I/O device.

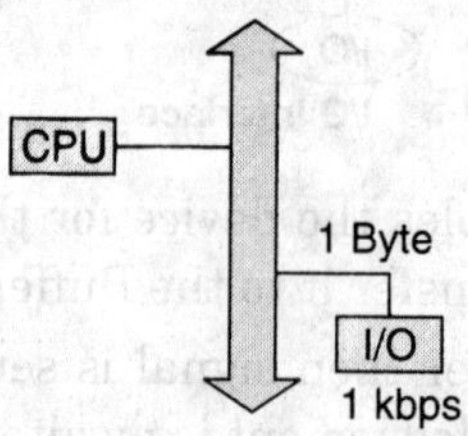

(*ii*) Interrupt Driven I/O

- For high speed interface between I/O devices and CPU, IC or Interrupt controller is used thus resulting in efficient processor utilization.
- The time of execution/transfer depends on latency of IC and not speed of I/O devices because CPU is communicating with IC.

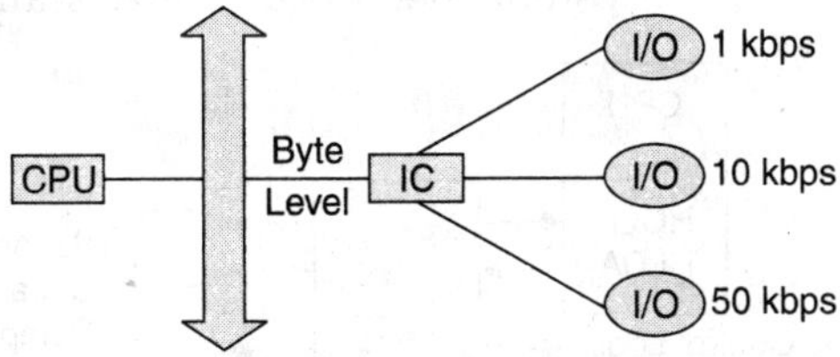

(*iii*) Direct Memory Access (DMA)

- CPU has no involvement in transfer of data as it is directly transferred to main memory from I/O devices.
- The secondary storage devices are connected through DMA with system bus.
- The program is transferred page by page through DMA during user program execution from auxiliary memory to main memory.

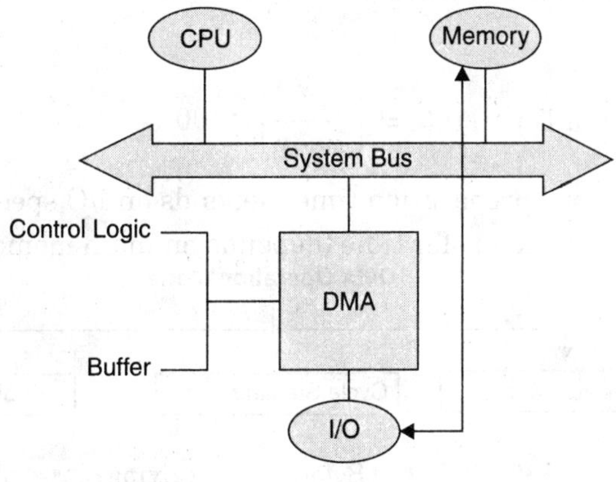

- DMA is initialized with source and destinations address, control signals and count value by CPU.
- The device is enabled by request interpretation by DMA control logic and then prepared data is transferred to the buffer.
- When data is available in buffer then;

- ✦ DMA enables the HOLD signal: It gains control of the bus and wait for the acknowledgement.
- ✦ HLDA signal is received.
- ✦ Data is transferred from I/O to main memory by DMA until count bcomes zero.
- ✦ Connection is established to CPU after transfer operation.

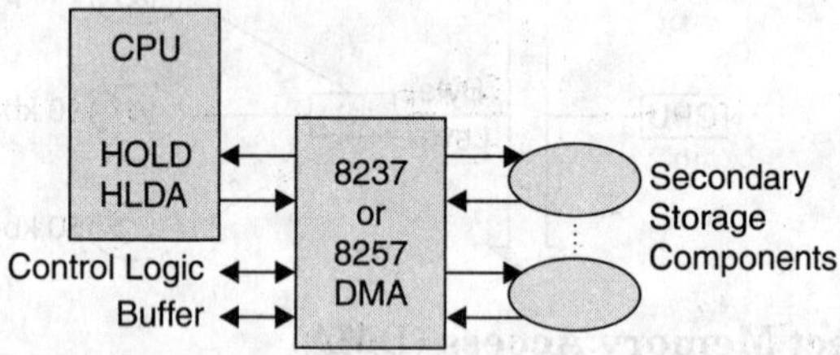

➢ During DMA operation; CPU is in either 'Busy state' or 'Block/ Hold state'.

➢ CPU is in **busy state** while data is being prepared and after transfer of data it changes to blocked state.

➢ % time for :

$$\text{CPU in Block state} = \left(\frac{y}{x+y}\right) \times 100$$

$$\text{CPU in Busy state} = \left(\frac{x}{x+y}\right) \times 100$$

where; x = preparation time (depends on I/O speed)

y = Transfer time (depends on main memory speed)

DMA Operation Mode

Burst Mode	Cycle Stealing Mode	Block Mode
• When Bulk amount of data is transferred to main memory after HLDA signal is received.	• Before receiving HLDA signal; CPU operation is suspended forcefully and important data is transferred to main memory.	• After receiving HLDA signal; Data is transferred to the main memory in block wise.

Instruction Pipelining

4

INTRODUCTION

- Instruction pipelining is a technique used in the design of modern microprocessors, microcontrollers and CPU to increase their instruction throughut.
- There are certain set of phrases for an instruction execution cycle:

  ***(i)* Instruction Fetch (IF)**
  - MAR ← PC [MAR ← 2000]
  - PC ← PC + 1 [Next Instruction : 2004]
  - READ CONTROl signal is enabled
  - IR ← MDR

  ***(ii)* Instruction Decode (ID)**

  Purpose of the instruction is highlighted

  ***(iii)* Operand Fetch (OF)**
  - Memory Read : MAR ← LOCX
  - Write into any general purpose register:

  ***(iv)* Execute (EX) and store**

  ➢ MAR ← LOCZ

  ➢ MDR ← R_i

  ➢ Write into memory.

  ***(v)* Indirect phase:**

Here, EA = 300
(Disect Address)

Here, EA = 450
(Indirect Address)
(2 memory cycled required

  ***(vi)* Interrupt phase:**

  ➢ Every instruction involves sequence of micro-operations which are register transfer operation that complete in 1 clock cycle.

  ➢ For T = total time for instruction cycle then;

  ➢ T = T_1, T_2, T_3 .... (division of T)

Interrupt type

External/Hardware Interrupt
- Due to timing and I/O devices

Software Interrupt
- Due to switching from user to system mode and receivers

Internal Interrupt
- Due to incorrect use of instruction and data.

Modes of CPU Operation

User mode/
Non-privileged mode
- Executer user program

System mode/Supervisor/
Kernel/Privileged mode
- executes operating system to obtain system service.

PIPELINING

- Acceptance of an input at one end even before appearance of output of previously accepted input at other end is pipelining.
- Here, excution is overlapping.
- In pipelining; A new instruction must be inserted for every new cycle. ∴ CPI = 1.

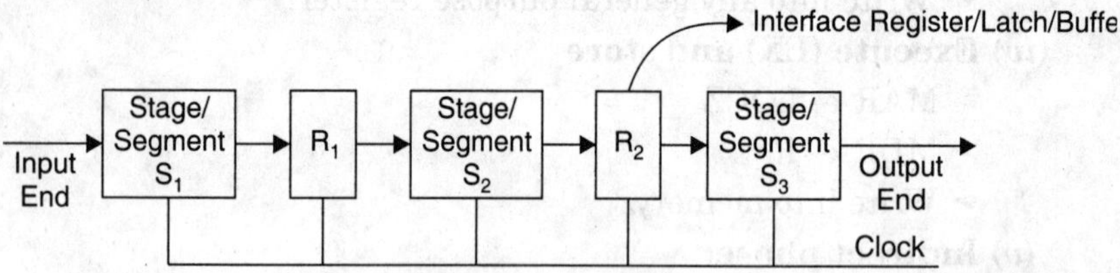

Types of Pipelines

Linear pipeline
- Performs only one specific function

Non linear pipeline
- Perform multiple functionalists.
- Uses feed forward and feed backward connections.

Synchronous Pipeline
- On common clock, all registers transfer data to the next page simultaneously

Synchronous Pipeline
- Handshake protocol is used to control data flow.

Performance Evaluation of Pipeline Processor

- Considering 'k' segment pipeline with clock cycle time t_p to execute n-tasks. k cycles are required to complete the operation because first task is executed in the non-overlapping time span.

- The remaining $(n - 1)$ tasks emerge from the pipe at the rate of one cycle per task, so $(n - 1)$ tasks requires $(n - 1)$ cycles to complete the operation execution time (ET) of k segment pipeline is

$$ET_{pipe} = k + (n - 1) \text{ cycles}$$
$$ET_{pipe} = (k + (n + 1) \cdot t_p$$

- The performance gain of the pipeline processor over the non-pipeline is:

$$\text{Speed up (S)} = \frac{\text{Performance}_{pipe}}{\text{Performance}_{nonpipe}} = \frac{\frac{1}{ET_{pipe}}}{\frac{1}{ET_{nonpipe}}} = \frac{ET_{nonpine}}{ET_{pipe}}$$

$$S = \frac{nt_n}{(K + (n - 1))t_p}$$

- For large number of tasks or instructions $K + (n - 1)$ approaches to n

$$S = \frac{nt_n}{nt_p} \Rightarrow S = \frac{t_n}{t_p}$$

- When all the instructions are taking the same number of cycles then one instruction execution time is equal to the number of stages in the pipeline (K) *i.e.,*

$$t_n = K_{tp} \Rightarrow S = \frac{K \cdot t_p}{t_p} \Rightarrow S = K$$

Instruction Pipeline

The instruction pipeline operates on a stream of instructions by overlapping the phases of instruction cycle.

Stall cycle

- No meaningful operation performed for an instruction.
- It arises due to:
  - ➢ uneven clock cycles needed by each stage for instructions.
  - ➢ Increased buffer overhead
  - ➢ Memory operands
  - ➢ Pipelined dependencies

$$S_{eff} = \frac{S_{ideal}}{(1 + \text{Stall frequency} \times \text{Stall cycles})}$$

$$= \frac{K}{(1 + \text{Stall frequency} \times \text{Stall cycles})}$$

- The maximum speedup that can be achieved by using a pipelined processor= number of stages.

$$S_{max} = S_{ideal} = K$$

- Efficiency $E_K = \frac{S}{K} = \frac{n}{K + (n - 1)}$

- $$\text{Throughput} = \frac{\text{Number of tasks processed}}{\text{Total time required to process the tasks}}$$

$$\text{Throughput} = \frac{n}{(K + (n - 1)) \cdot t_p}$$

Advance Pipeline (RISC Pipeline)

- In RISC processor, instruction pipeline is implemented for instruction execution.

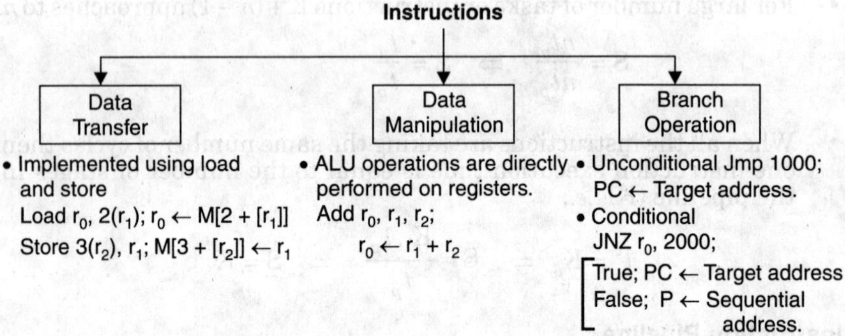

- Branch instruction execution is completed at the end of the second stage.

Dependencies in the pipeline

→ Stall is an extra cycle created in pipeline with NOP that are caused by dependency.

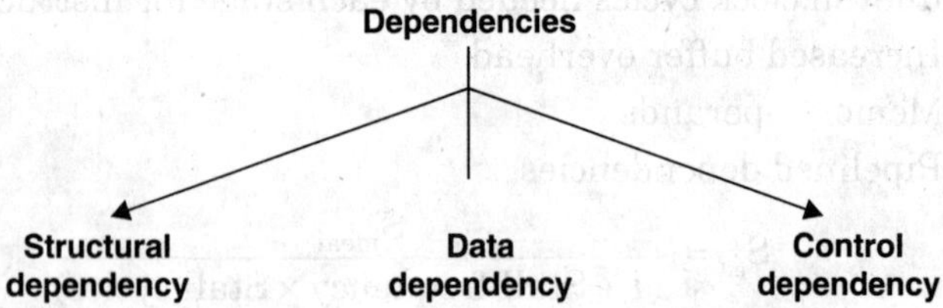

(*i*) Structural Dependency

➢ It arises due to the resource conflict which is a situation when more than one instruction tries to access the same resources in same cycle.

It creates stalls in the pipeline.

➢ 'Renaming' minimize the number of stalls.

It is concept where we divide the memory into two independent modules used to store the instruction and data separately called code memory (CM) and data memory (DM) respectively.

(*ii*) Data dependency

➢ When *i* and *j* are first and second instruction respectively, then data dependency exist between *i* and *j* when the instruction *j* tries to read the data before instruction *i* writes it.

(*iii*) Control dependency

➢ It occurs during transfer of control instructions such as BRANCH, CALL, JMP etc.

➢ The sequential instruction is a wanted instruction if current instruction is decoded as data transfer or data manipulation.

➢ Flush or Freeze → process of removal of unwanted instruction from pipeline. It creates stalls.

➢ Branch penalty are number of stall cycle created in the pipeline due to branch operation.

Branch penalty = At what stage the target address is available – 1.

➢ To reduce branch penalty; Branch prediction buffer or loop buffer or branch target buffer is used.

Branch Target Buffer → High speed buffer maintained at the instruction fetch stage to store the predicted target address.

➢ The out-of-order execution creates two more dependencies in the pipeline.

- **Anti dependency**
  Exits when instruction *j* tries to write before instructions *i* reads the register.
- **Output dependency**
  Exits when instruction *j* tries to write the destination before instruction *i* reads it.

- Above dependencies are handled by register renaining.
- **Register renaming**: Temporary storage is used for holding out-of-order execution output. The register file is later updated with temporary storage once exception is received from dependent instruction.

Hazards

- Hazards or danger on delay that creates extra cycles which creates stalls due to being non-operational.
- Consider a program segment in order;

  i: instruction

  j: instruction

Hazards

RAW Read-After-Write	WAR Write-After-Read	WAW Write-After-Write
• True data dependency	• Anti-dependency	• Output dependency
• *j* reads the data before *i* writes it.	• *j* writes the data before *i* reads it	• *j* writer the data before *i* writes it.

Performance Evaluation of the Pipeline with stalls.

$$S = \frac{CPI_{Nonpipe} \times \text{Cycle Time}_{Nonpipe}}{CPI_{pipe} \times \text{Cycle Time}_{Pipe}} \quad \text{for ideal } CPI_{pipe} = 1$$

$$S = \frac{CPI_{Nonpipe} \times \text{Cycle Time}_{Nonpine}}{\left(\text{Ideal CPI} + \frac{\text{No. of stall cycles}}{\text{Instruction}}\right) \times \text{Cycle Time}_{pipe}}$$

- When there is no setup time overhead then both the cycle times are equal.

$$S = \frac{CPI_{Nonpipe}}{1 + \left(\frac{\text{No. of the stall cycles}}{\text{Instruction}}\right)}$$

- When all instruction are taking the same number of cycles then one instruction requires cycle equal to number of stages in pipeline to complete the execution.

$$S = \frac{\text{Pipeline Depth}}{1 + \frac{\text{No. of stall cycles}}{\text{Instruction}}}$$

- When efficiency is 100% no stalls.

$$S = \text{Pipeline depth}$$

5 Cache & Main Memory, Secondary Storage

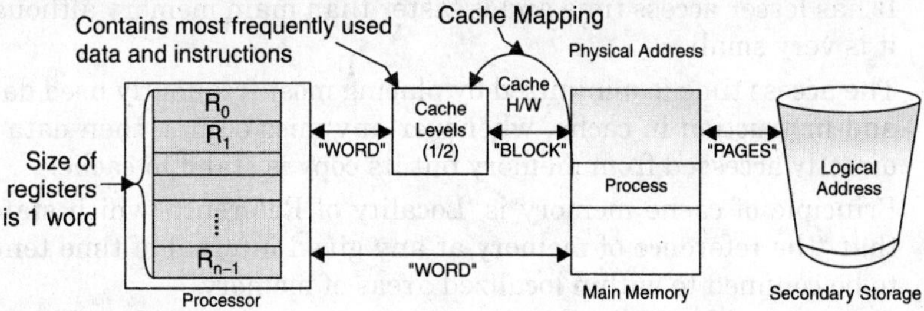

Memory Hierarchy

- Highlights the accessing order of existing memory system .
- It is used to bridge the speed mismatch between fastest processor to the slowest memories at reasonable cost.
- When the processor refers to I[th] level memory if it is found then 'hit' else 'miss'.

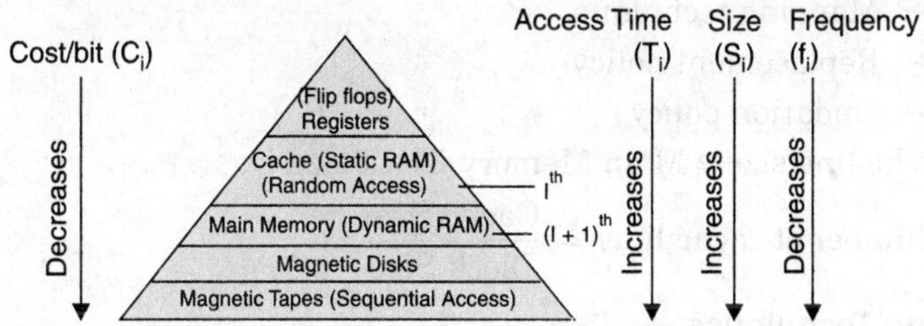

- On basis of order of accessing the memory system;

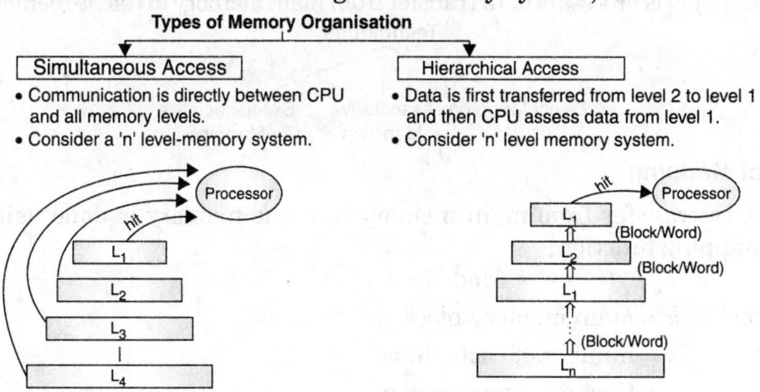

CACHE MEMORY

- An intermediate memory between CPU and main memory,

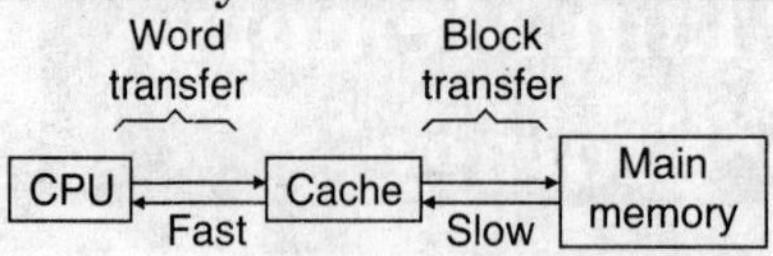

- It has lesser access time and is faster than main memory although it is very small.
- The access time is minimized by placing most frequently used data and instruction in cache, whenever any miss occurs, then data is directly accessed from memory but its copy is stand in cache.
- Principle of cache memory is 'Locality of Reference' which states that "the reference of memory at any given internal of time tends to be confined to within localized areas of memory."
- Cache is divided into equal pants called cache blocks on cache lines.
- Following factors effects performance of cache:
  - ➢ Size
  - ➢ Block size
  - ➢ Number of level
  - ➢ Mapping technique
  - ➢ Replacement policy
  - ➢ Updation policy
- Cache line size = Main Memory Block size

$$\text{Number of cache lines} = \frac{\text{Cache Size}}{\text{Block Size}}$$

Mapping Techniques

- Mapping is process of data transfer from main memory to Cache memory.

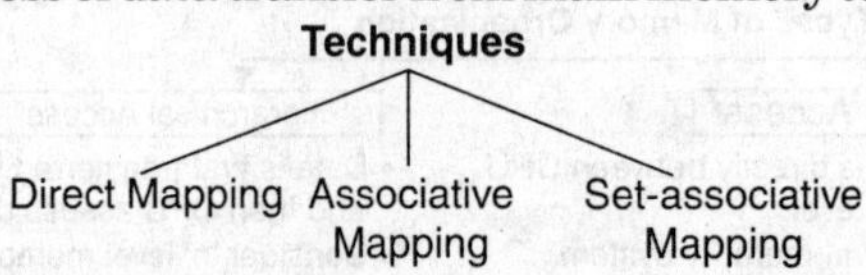

Direct Mapping

- Data transfer from main memory to cache memory is done using mapping function;

$$k \text{ Mod N} = i.$$

where; k = main memory block no.

N = number of cache lines

i = Cache memory line no.

- Address representation:

← Physical Address (in bits) →

Tag	Block	Word

- The Hit ratio is less. When same block is accessed from different pages it is always a miss and replacement is done when 'conflict miss' occurs.
- The high order address bits are compared with each cache tag.
  - ➢ if match is not found: a Miss and Reference is forwarded to main memory.
- The request is interpreted by main memory in its know format.

Tag	Word

(Here tag field is directly connected with address logic so is corresponding block is enabled)

- Now; the block of main memory along with complete tag is transferred to cache line using mapping function.
- CPU then access the data from the cache.
- Tag size/tag length: number of bits in the tag.

Associative Mapping

- Cache address is not used as any memory block can be mapped to anywhere in cache.
- Data is transferred along with complete tag.
- Physical representation

← Physical Address (in bits) →

Tag	Word

- Replacement is done when either cache is full or capacity miss occurs.
- Block number is updated in cache field. Miss occurs when high order address bits are sequentially compared with each tag.
- Complexity of tag comparator is more.
- Maximum number of tag comparisons =N.

  N → number of cache block
- Cache size = Tag memory size + Data Memory size
- Data memory suze = Number of Cache line × Number of bits in the line

Set Associative Mapping

- Cache memory is organised into sets that are capable to hold multiple main memory blocks.

- Address representation:

← Physical Address (in bits) →

Tag	Set offset	Word offset

- Number of sets = $\frac{N}{P-\text{way}}$;

    N = number of cache lines

    P = number of MM blocks possible on each cache lines.
- Mapping Function; K mods = i where;

    K = main memory block number

    S = number of cache sets

    i = cache memory set number.
- Replacement is when set is full.
- The existing tag and CPU generated tags are compared by multiplexers.
- Hit ratio of tag comparator and complexity is optimal.
- Maximum number of tag comparisons = P but when P = 1 then direct mapping.
- Tag memory size = Number of sets in cache × Number of blocks in the set × Number of Tag bits in each block.

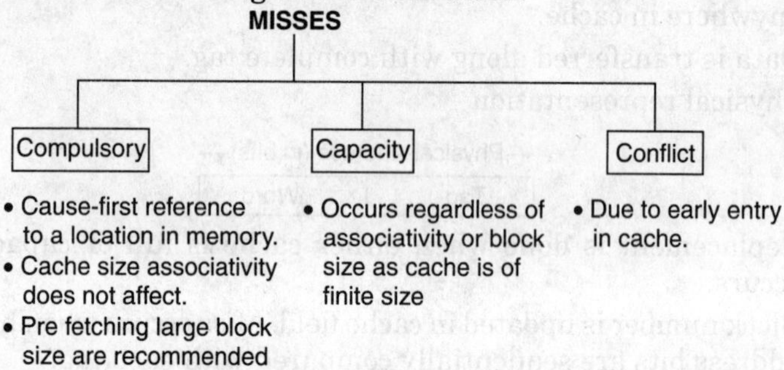

- **Double the associativity**
    - ➢ Capacity and line size → Constant
    - ➢ Number of sets → Half
    - ➢ Conflict Misses → Decreased
    - ➢ Capacity and compulsory misses → no effect.

    Higher associativity reduces conflict misses due to more place to put same element.

- **Halving the line size:**
  - ➢ Associativity and number of sets → constant
  - ➢ Capacity → Half
  - ➢ Conflict Miss → no effect
  - ➢ Capacity and Compulsory misses → Increased
  - ➢ Line size → Short
    (Shorts line means pre-fetching that reduces caches ability to exploit spatial locality.
- **Doubling the number of Sets:**
  - ➢ Capacity line size → Constant
  - ➢ Associativity → Half and less
  - ➢ Conflict Misses → Increased
  - ➢ Compulsory and capacity misses → no effect.

REPLACEMENT ALGORITHM

When old block is replaced with new block then replacement algo is used.

FIFO
- First-In-First-out
- Cache block with longest time span is replaced with new block

LRU
- Least recently used
- Cache block having less number of reference with longest time span is replaced.

UPDATING TECHNIQUES

The less of data is created when cache is updated while main memory is not updated i.e. same address contains different values at different places this is known as **Coherence.**

To avoid coherence, updating is done using techniques

- Write through
- Write Back

Write through

- Coherence is avoided by simultaneously updating cache memory and main memory.
- Word updation (T_W) Time

$$= \max\left(\text{Word updation time in cache} \;\middle|\; \text{Word updation time in main memory}\right)$$

- $T_{avg_{read}} = H_r \; T_c + (1 - H_r) + (T_m + T_c)$

  H_r → read hit, T_c → read data, $(1 - H_r)$ → read miss, T_m → read allocate, T_c → read data

- $T_{avg_{write}} = H_w \; T_w + (1 - H_w) + (T_m + T_w)$

  (H_w → write hit; T_w → word updation time; $(1 - H_w)$ → write miss; T_m → write allocate; T_w → word updation time)

- Total access time of memory, when both read and write cycle is considered is:

$$T_{avg} = f_{read} \times T_{avg_{read}} + f_{write} \times T_{avg_{write}}$$

- Throughput $\eta_{WT_{cache}} = \dfrac{1}{T_{avg\,WT}}$ word/sec

- The hit ratio for the wire operation is always 1,
- $T_{avg_{write}} = H_w \; T_m$; where T_m = Main memory access time

Write Back

- The write operation is done only on cache memory by CPU thus creating coherence but before replacement of cache block with new memory block, updation is done in main memory.
- Modified bit or update bit is present in each cache line which is 'set' when block is updated.

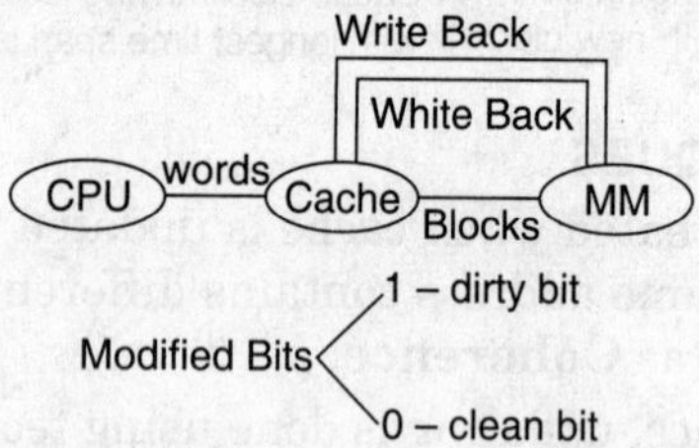

$$T_{avg_{read}} = H_r \; T_c + (1 - H_r) + [\% \text{ dirty bits } (T_m + T_m + T_c) + \% \text{ clean bits } (T_m + T_c)]$$

(H_r → read hit; T_c → read data; $(1 - H_r)$ → read miss; dirty bits: T_m → write back, T_m → read allocate, T_c → read data; clean bits: T_m → read alocate, T_c → read data)

$$T_{avg_{write}} = H_w \; T_c + (1 - H_w) + [\% \text{ dirty bits } (T_m + T_m + T_c) + \% \text{ clean bits } (T_m + T_c)]$$

(dirty bits: T_m → write back, T_m → write allocate, T_c → write data; clean bits: T_m → write alocate, T_c → write data)

- $T_{avg_{write\,back}} = f_{read} \times T_{avg_{read}} + f_{write} \times T_{avg_{write}}$

- Through put η_{write} back $= \dfrac{1}{T_{avg_{write\,back}}}$ word/sec

MULTILEVEL CACHES

- These are used to reduce miss penalty

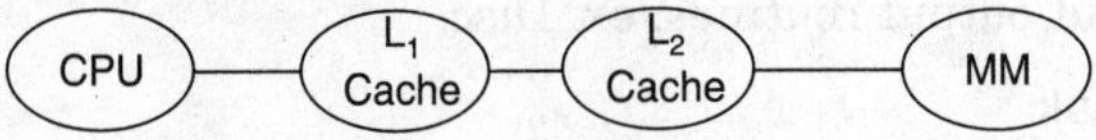

- two kinds of miss rates are calculated:

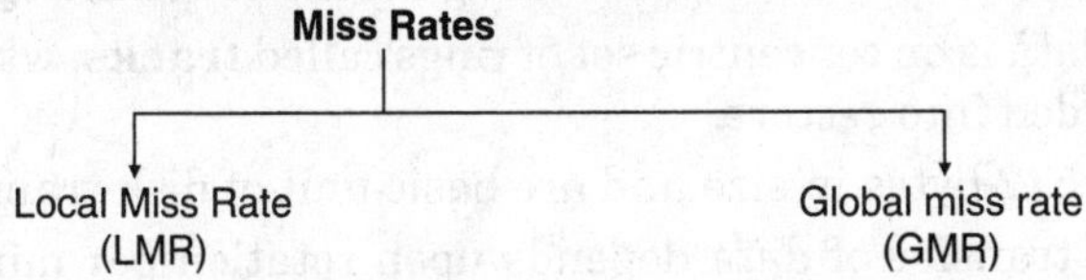

$$LMR = \frac{\text{No. of misses in the cache}}{\text{total No. of references to that cache}} \qquad GMR = \frac{\text{No. Of misses in the cache}}{\text{total no. of CPU generated references}}$$

- Average access time can be calculate as

$$T_{avg} = \text{Hit time}_{L_1} + \text{Miss rate}_{L_1}\text{ (Local miss rate)} \times \text{Miss penalty}_{L_1}$$

$$\text{Miss penalty}_{L_1} = \text{Hit time}_{L_2} + \text{Miss rate}_{L_2} \times \text{Miss penalty}_{L_2}$$

$$\text{Miss Penalty}_{L_2} = \text{MM Access time}$$

- Average memory stall cycles

$$= (\text{No. of miss}_{L_1} / \text{Instruction} \times \text{Hit time}_{L_2})$$

$$+ (\text{No. of misses}_{L_2} / \text{Instruction} \times \text{Miss penalty}_{L_2})$$

POINT TO REMEMBER

- On basis of index and tag correspondence to physical or virtual addresses;

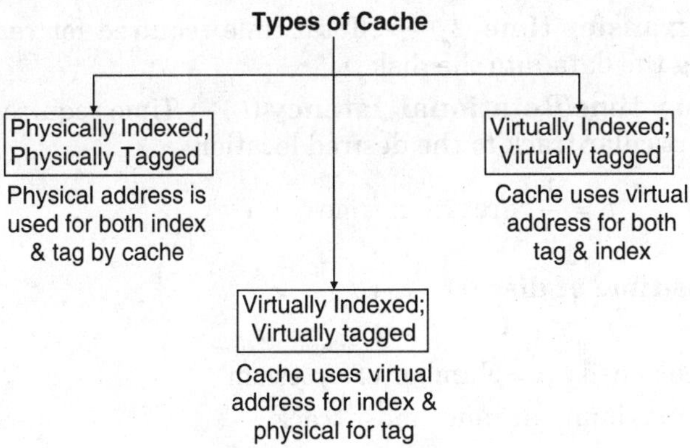

SECONDARY MEMORY

Permanents storage external and non volatile memory, that is accessed through input/output routines. ex. Disc.

Magnetic Disk

- Circulator disk used to store data using magnetic technology.
- Storage of data is on concentric set of rings called **tracks**, which are further divided into sectors.
- Sectors are 512 bytes in size and are basic unit of disk transfer.
- The rate of transfer of data depends upon rotation per minute or rpm. Each rotation covers 1 track.

Disk Construction

- Constant track Capacity Disc
  - Second density –variable
  - Disk moves with angular velocity
- Variable track capacity disk
  - Second density – constant

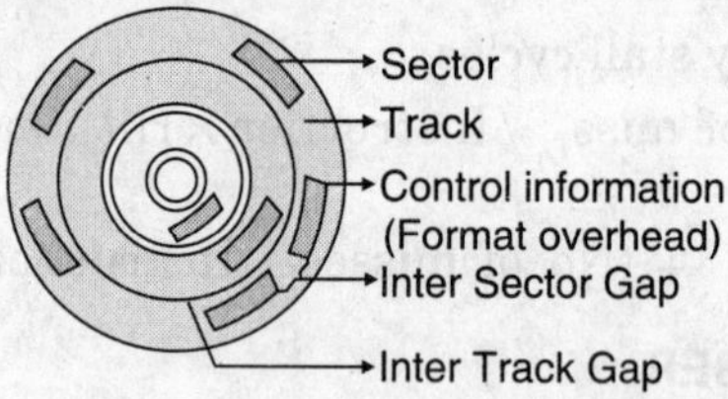

- **Seek time** (t_s) → Total time taken to move on desired track measured in milliseconds
- **Data transfer time** (t_d) → Total time required for reading and writing the data into the disk.
- **Latency time/Rotational latency** (t_r) → Time required to bring the particular track to the desired location.

$$t_r = \frac{1}{2} \times \text{rotation time}$$

- **Access-time of disc** $(t) = t_s + t_r$
- $t_{avg.} = t_s + t_r + t_a + t_{overhead}$.
- Storage density ρ = Number of bytes/cm

  (It is maximum at inner most track.)

- Data transfer rate (D) = Number of bytes/sec.
- Organisation of multiple disk:

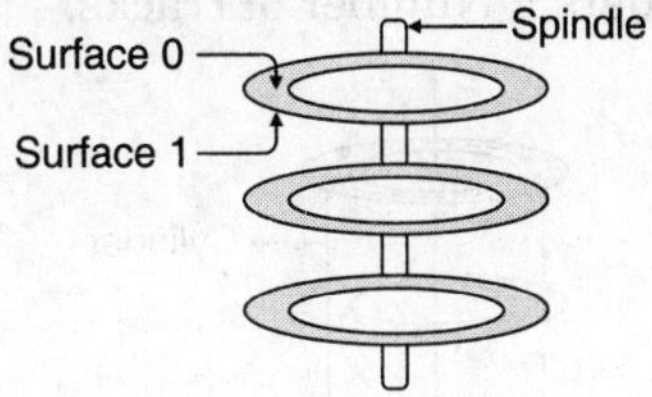

- **Disk Characteristic**

  (a) Single sided or double sided disk →

  By default ; double sided disk are used as recording is done on both the surface.

  (b) Fixed read/write (R/W) head or Movable (R/W) head

Fixed R/W Head 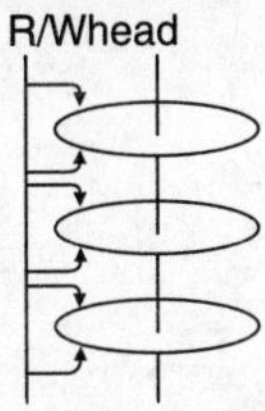	**Moveable R/W Head** 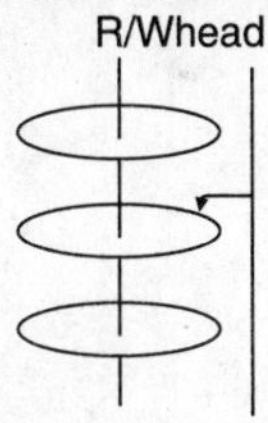
(*a*) One R/W head per surface (*b*) Each rotation covers '*n*' tracks *n* = no. of surfaces. (*c*) Hardware increases and hence cost is more	(*a*) One R/W head for all surface (*b*) Each rotation covers 1 track (*c*) Less hardware required but access time increases

  (c) Single Platter on Multiple platter disk

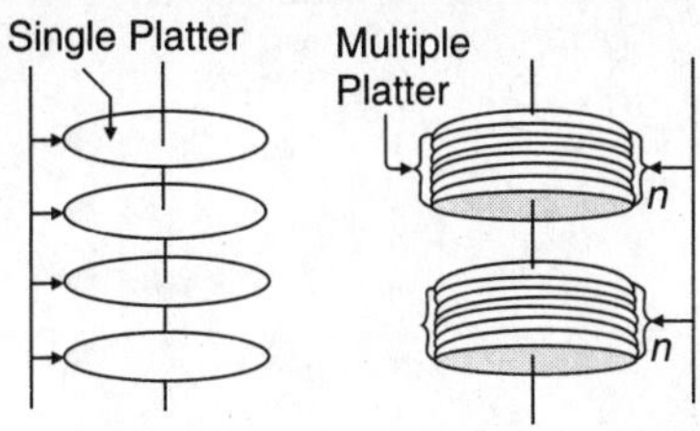

- A vertical set of all the tracks from the same position in a disk pack forms a cylinder.

  Number of cylinders = Number of tracks.

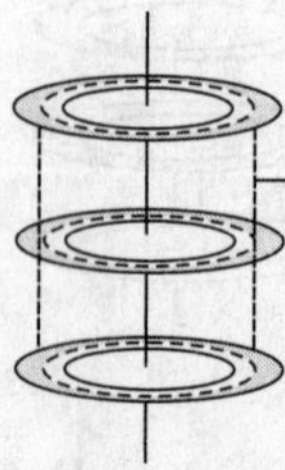

Note:

- Capacity = Track × Sectors/Track × Bytes/Sector.
- $\text{Capacity}_{\text{formatted}}$ = Tracks × Sectors/Track × Bytes/Sector – Format overhead).

Computer Science

4

Programming and Data Structure

CONTENTS

1 Programming in C

C was adopted as a system development language as it produces code that runs nearly as fast as the assembly language code.

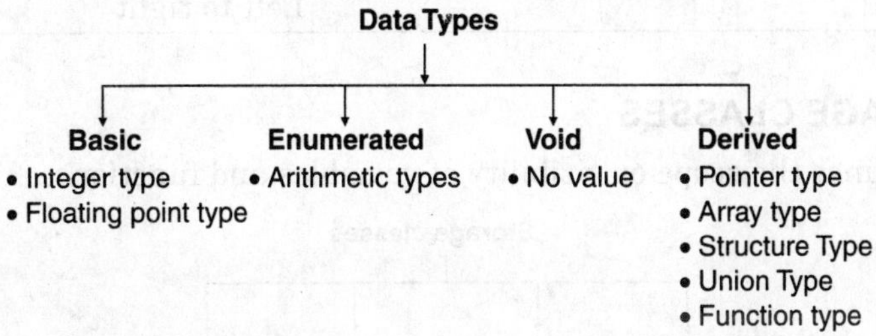

Note:
char → 8 bits → 1 byte
int → 16 bits | 32 bits → 2 or 4 bytes
float → 32 bits → 4 bytes
double → 64 bits → 8 bytes
void → generic pointer

Operator precedence table

S. No.	Operator	Associativity
1.	(,), [,], →,	Left to right
2.	!, ~, ++, – –, + (unary), – (unary), *, &, size of	Right to left
3.	*, /, %	Left to right
4.	+, –	Right to left
5.	<< , >>	Left to right
6.	<, <=, >, >=	Right to left
7.	==, !=	Left to right
8.	&	Right to left
9.	^	Left to right

(Highest) ↔ (Lowest)

<table>
<tr><th>S. No.</th><th>Operator</th><th>Associativity</th></tr>
<tr><td>10.</td><td>|</td><td>Right to left</td></tr>
<tr><td>11.</td><td>&&</td><td>Left to right</td></tr>
<tr><td>12.</td><td>| |</td><td>Right to left</td></tr>
<tr><td>13.</td><td>? :</td><td>Left to right</td></tr>
<tr><td>14.</td><td>=, +=, −=, *=, /=, %=, &=, ^=, | =,
<<=, >>=</td><td>Right to left</td></tr>
<tr><td>15.</td><td>,</td><td>Left to right</td></tr>
</table>

STORAGE CLASSES

- Defines the scope or visibility of variables and functions.

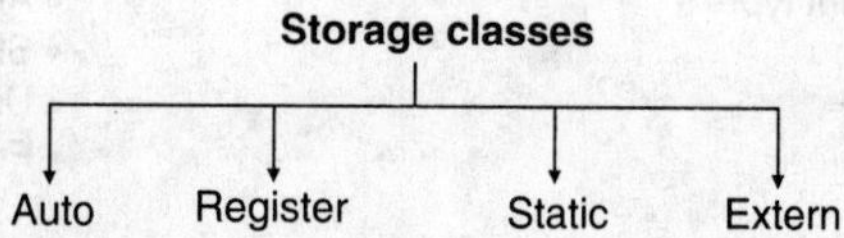

Auto

- Default storage class for all local variables.

Register

- Defines local variables that should be stored in register instead of RAM.
- Requests the compiler to store variable making is quickly accessible from CPU register.

Static

- Keeps local variables in existence during lifetime of program instead of creating and destroying each time, hence maintaining their values between function calls.

Extern

- Gives reference of a global variable that is visible to all the program files.

FORMAT SPECIFIERS

- % c : Character
- % d : Signed integer
- % i : Signed integer

- % u : Unsigned integer
- % ld : Signed long
- % lu : Unsigned long
- % f : Floating point
- % lf : Double floating point
- % e : Exponential notation
- % s : String
- % x : Unsigned hexadecimal
- % o : Unsigned octal
- % % : Prints a % sign

OPERATORS

- Assignment Operators: =
- Arithmetic Operators: +, –, *, /, %
- Relational Operators: >, >=, <, <=, ==, !=
- Logical Operators: &&, | |
- Bitwise Operators: &, ^, >>, l, ~, <<

CONTROL STATEMENTS

- if statement
- nested if statement
- conditional operator? :
- switch statement
- for statement
- while statement
- do-while statement
- break statement
- continue statement

POINTER

It is a variable whose value is the address of another variable i.e, direct address of memory location. It needs to be declared like any other variable.

ARRAY

It is a kind of data structure that can store a fixed-size sequential collection of elements of the same type. It is collection of variables of same type.

Functions and Recursions

2

RECURSION

- It is a function that calls itself directly or indirectly.

```
void recursion () {
        recursion ();    /* Function calls itself */
    }
    int main () {
    recursion ();
    }
```

- **Factorial function:**

```
int fact (int n)
if (n == 0) return 1;
else return n*fact (n – 1);
```

- **Fibonacci sequence:**

```
int fib (int n)
{
if (n < 2) return n;
else return fib (n – 1) + fib (n – 2);
}
```

(*i*) The number of function calls on fib(n) = 2 × fib (n + 1) – 1

(*ii*) The number of addition in fib(n) = fib (n + 1) – 1

(*iii*) In fib(n) after (n + 1) function calls first addition will be performed.

- **Tower of Hanoi:** (A : source, B : temporary, C : destination)

```
    TOH (A, B, C, n)
    {
if (n – 1) C.PUSH (POP)(A)).
    {
        TOH (A, B, C, n – 1);
        C.PUSH (POP (A));
      TOH (B, C, A, n – 1);
      }
    }
```

(*i*) Number of function calls in TOH(n) = $2^{n+1} - 1$
(*ii*) Number of moves in TOH(n) = $2^n - 1$

- **GCD of two number (iteration)**

```
f(a, b)
{
while (b ≠ 0)
{
        t = b;
        b = a mod b;
        a = t;
}
return a;
}
```

- **GCD of two number (recursive function)**

```
f (a, b)
{
        if (a = b) reture a;
        else if (a > b) returen f (a –b, b);
        else f(a, b –a); // if (a < b)
}
```

- **Finding the second maximum of three (distinct) numbers**:

```
int trial (int a , int b, int c)
{
        if (a > = b) && (c < b)) return b;
        else if (a > = b) return trial (a, c, b);
        else return trial (b, a, c);
}
```

Declarations and Notations

- int*p; — *p* can be a pointer to an integer.
- int*p[10]; — *p* is a 10 element array of pointers to integer.
- int(*p)[10]; — *p* is a pointer to a 10-element integer array.
- int*p(); — *p* is a function that returns a pointer to integer.
- intp(char *a); — *p* is a function that takes an argument as pointer to a character and returns an integer.
- int *p(char *a); — *p* is a function that takes an argument as pointer to a character and returns a pointer to an integer.
- int (*p)(char *a); — *p* is a pointer to a function that takes an argument as pointer to a character and returns an integer.

- int (*p(char *a))[10]; — p is a function that takes an argument as pointer to a character and returns a pointer to a 10 element integer array.
- int p(char (*a)[]); — p is a function that takes an argument as pointer to a character array and returns an integer.
- int p(char *a[]); — p is a function that takes an argument as array of pointers to characters and returns a pointer to an integer.
- int *p(char a []); — p is function that takes an argument as character array and returns a pointer to an integer.
- int *p(char (*a)[]); — p is a function that takes an argument as character array returns a pointer to an integer.
- int *p(char *a []); — p is a function that takes an argument as array of pointers to characters and returns a pointer to an integer.
- int (*p)(char (*a)[]); — p is pointer to a function that takes an argument as pointer to a character array and returns an integer.
- int *(*p)(char (*a)[]); — p is a pointer to a function that takes an argument as pointer to a character array and returns a pointer to an integer.
- int *(*p)(char *a[]); — p is a pointer to a function that takes an argument as array of pointers to characters and returns a pointer to an integer.
- int (*p[10])(); — p is a 10 element array of pointers to functions, each function returns an integer.
- int (*p[10]) (char a); — p is a 10 element array of pointers to functions, each functions takes an argument as character and returns an integer.
- int *(*p[10]) (char a); — p is a 10 element array of pointers to functions, each function takes an argument as character and returns a pointer to an integer.
- int *(*p[10])(char *a); — p is a 10 element array of pointers to functions, each function takes an argument as pointer to a character, and returns a pointer to an integer.

3 Parameter Passing

Parameter passing is mechanism used to pass parameters to a procedure or function.

Methods

- **Formal parameter:** Parameters associated with the function.
- **Actual parameter:** Parameters used to call the function.
- **Call by copy:** Values are copied into and out of the procedure parameter.
- Call by value, call by result and call by value–result are its special cases.

1. **Call by value:** Copy going into the procedure or Actuals copied to formals.
    - Used for passing objects whose reference is passed by value.
2. **Call by result:** Copy going out of procedure, formals are copied back into actuals.
3. **Call by value result:** (Restore) $\rightarrow$ copy going in, and again going out. i.e., Actuals copied to formals and vice versa.
4. **Call by reference:** Actuals and formals are identified and uses same address space.
5. **Call by name:** Re-evaluate actuals on every use.
6. **Call by Constant:** Formal values are never changed.
7. **Call by Text:** Same as call by name but if variables are named as local variables then it refers local.
8. **Call by Need:** Memory allocates only if formals are used in function.

	Actuals used	Actuals changed	Formals changed	Similar technique
Call by value	Yes	No	Yes	–
Call by reference	Yes	Yes	Yes	–
Call by result	No	Yes	Yes	Call by reference
Call by restore (value-result)	Yes	Yes	Yes	Call by reference
Call by need	Yes	No	Yes	Call by value
Call by text	Yes	Yes	–	Call by reference
Call by name	Yes	Yes	–	Call by reference
Call by constant	Yes	No	No	–

Pass-by-Name or Call by Name:

If actual parameter is:

1. Scalar variable→ Call by name is equivalent to pass by reference.
2. Constant expression→ Call by name is equivalent to pass by value.
3. Array element → pass by name is different as value of subscript expression can change during execution between time of various reference.
4. Expression containing variable → pass by name is different as expression is evaluated for each access to the formals at the time the variable is reached.

Points to Remember :

1. While passing address of an array element as parameter → "call by reference" and "call by name" gives different result.
2. In presence of loop → "call by reference" and "call by value-result" gives different result.

4 Scope and Binding

SCOPE

- Visibity of variables is its scope. It is the range of statement in which variable is visible.

<table>
<tr><th>Static Scoping</th><th>Dynamic Scoping</th></tr>
<tr><td>• Bind name to non local variables</td><td>• Based on calling sequence of subprograms</td></tr>
<tr><td>• Scope can be statically determined prior to execution</td><td>• Scope can be determined at runtime</td></tr>
<tr><td>• Easy to read, reliable and executes faster</td><td>• Difficult to read, reliability less and less efficient</td></tr>
<tr><td>• Less flexible</td><td>• More flexible</td></tr>
<tr><td>eg. const int b = 5;
int foo ()
{
int a = b + 5;
return a;
}
int bar ()
{
int b = 2;
return foo ();
}
int main ()
{
foo (); || returns 10
bar (); || returns 10
return 0;
}</td><td>eg. const int b = 5;
int foo ()
{
int a = b + 5;
return a;
}
int bar ()
{
int b = 2;
rturn foo ();
}
int main ()
{
foo (); || returns 10
bar (); || returns 7
return 0;
}</td></tr>
</table>

Consider the following program with function call

```
main ()
{
    x(x)
    ⋮
    y()
}
```

```
x
{
    z()
    }
```

```
z
   {
         }
```

```
y
    {
p ()
}
```

```
p
{
     }
```

Static Scope:

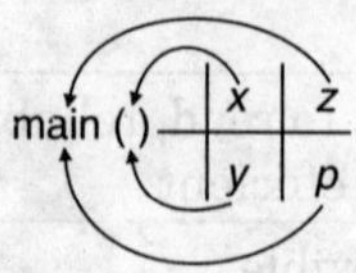

Dynamic Scope:

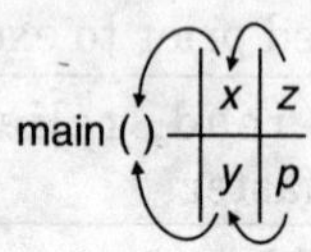

BINDING

Association of attributes with program entities that can take place at language design time, language implementation time, compile time, linktime, load time or runtime.

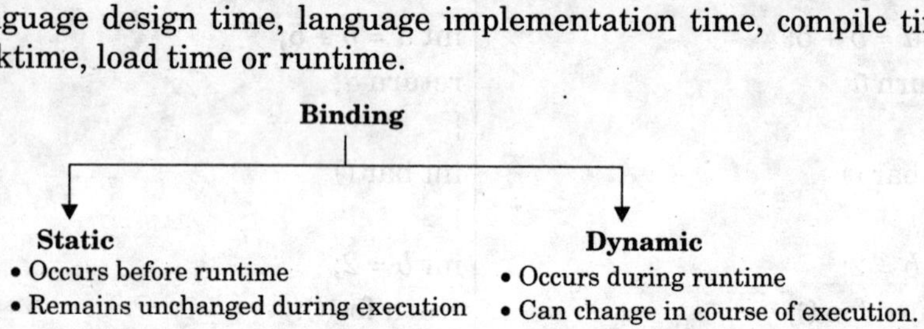

5 Abstract Data Types, Arrays & Linked Lists

INTRODUCTION

- Data structure is a way of data organization to make it used efficiently in a computer.
- Based on manipulation criteria it is divided into.

Primitive
Integers, Real numbers, Character, Boolean Values

Non-primitive
Arrays, stacks, Queue, records, file, linked list tree, graph etc.

Linear
- Arrays, record, stacks, queues etc.

Non-linear
- Trees and graphs

- Based on storage criteria;

LINKED LIST

- Sequence of data structures which are connected together via links. Each link contains connection to another link.
- It is dynamically allocated and is non-contiguous in nature.

Operations on single linked set

- When item navigation is forward only.

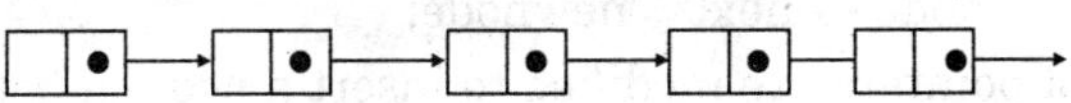

Insertion

- Number of pointers modified to insert a new node at end = 2

node → next = newnode;

newnode → next = null;

- Number of pointers modified to insert a new node at beginning = 2

  newnode → next = root;

  root = newnode;

- Number of pointers modified to insert a new node in mid = 2

  newnode → next = node → next;

  node → next = newnode;

Deletion

- Number of pointers modified to insert a new node at beginning = 1

  head → next = head → next → next;

Operations on double linked set

- When items can be navigated forward and backward way.

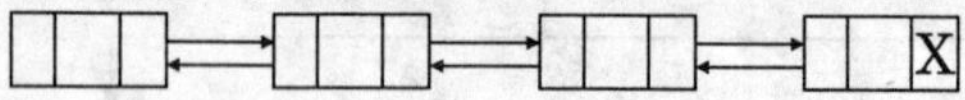

Struct node

```
{
int data;
struct node * prev;
struct node * next;
}
```

Insertion

- Number of pointers are modified to insert a node at beginning = 4

  newnode → next = root;

  newnode → prev = null;

  root → prev = newnode;

  root = newnode;

- Number of pointers are modified to insert a node at the end = 3

  newnode → next = null;

  newnode → prev = node;

  node → next = newnode;

- Number of pointers are modified to insert a node in between = 4

  newnode → next = node → next;

  newnode → prve = node;

  (node → next) → prev = newnode;

  node → next = newnode;

Deletion

- Number of pointers are modified to delete a node in middle = 2
  (node → prev) → next = node → next;
  (node → next) → prev = node → prev; free (node)

Array

- It is collection of homogenous elements stored in contiguous memory location.
- They are static in nature, compile time carry binding and user friendly.

1-D Array

- Single sub-scripted or one dimensional array.
- When only one variable name can be given using one subscript.
- Let A be array of n-elements
  Address of element A[i] : Base (A) + (i – start index × size of element)

2-D Array

- Two dimensional array or matrix array.
- 2-D array is similar to 1-D but it is organized as a matrix.
- Let A[m][n] be a 2-D array with m rows and n columns. Then;
  - Address of an element A[i][j] in "row major order":
    Base (A) + (j-start index) × size of element + (i-start index) × size of element × n.
  - Address of an element A[i][j] in "column major order"
    Base (A) + (i-start index) × size of element + (j-start index) × m × size of element.

Array Operations

(i) **Insertion**

- Best case → At end, takes constant time *i.e.*, Ω(1).
- Worst case → At beginning, takes O(n) time.
- Average case → In middle, takes O(n) time.

(ii) **Deletion:**

- Best case → At end, takes constant time *i.e.*, Ω(1).
- Worst case → At beginning, takes O(n) time.
- Average case → In middle, takes θ(n) time.

***(iii)* Traversal:**

Direct access: O(1).

TRIANGULAR MATRICES

- **Lower Triangular** [◺]$_{n \times n}$:

  (i) Size $= n + \dfrac{n^2 - n}{2} = \dfrac{n(n+1)}{2}$

  (ii) **Row Major Order (RMO):** $(j-1) + \dfrac{i(i-1)}{2}$

  (iii) **Column Major Order (CMO):**

  $$a[i][j] = (i-j) + \left[(j-1)n - \frac{(j-1)(j-2)}{2}\right]$$

- **Upper Triangular** [◹]$_{n \times n}$:

  (i) Size $= \dfrac{n(n+1)}{2}$

  (ii) **RMO:** $a[i][j] = (i-j) + \left[(i-1)n - \dfrac{(i-1)(i-2)}{2}\right]$

  (iii) **CMO:** $a[i][j] = \left[(i-1) + \dfrac{j(j-1)}{2}\right]$

- **Strictly lower triangular** [◺]$_{n \times n}$:

  (i) Size $= \dfrac{n^2 - n}{2}$

  (ii) **RMO:** $a[i][j] = (j-1) + \dfrac{(i-1)(i-2)}{2}$

  (iii) **CMO:** $a[i][j] = (i-1) + \dfrac{(j-1)(j-2)}{2}$

- **Tridiagonal** [⋱]$_{n \times n}$:

  (i) Size $= 3n - 2$

  (ii) Row: $2i + j - 3$

  (iii) Column: $i + 2j - 3$

Stacks and Queues 6

STACK

- Linear data structure where insertion and deletion of items takes place at one end called top of the stack.

APPLICATIONS

- Recursion
- Evaluation of expression-Postfix
- Conversion of arithmetic expression from infix to post/prefix
- Tower of hanoi
- Permutation
- Fibonacci series
- Balancing of symbols
- Subroutines

OPERATIONS

- push () → pushing/storing an element on the stack.
- pop () → removing/accessing an element.
- peek () → getting top data element without removing.
- is Full () → check if stack is full
- is Empty () → check if stack is empty.
- stack follows last in-first out algorithm.

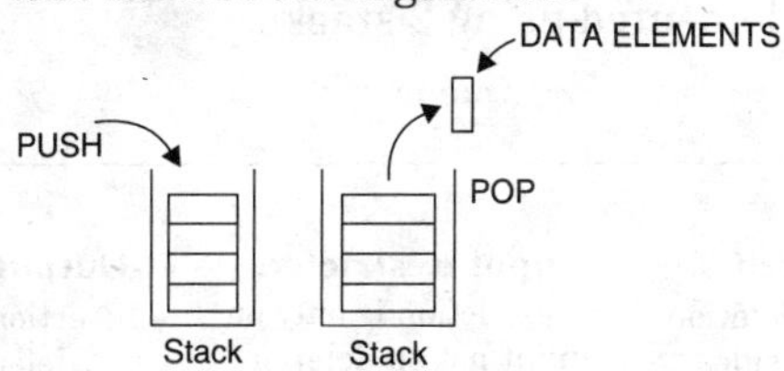

- **Push operation**
  - ➢ **Push operation on stack:** Let N is the maximum stack size and x is the element to be inserted on to stack S.

```
push(S, Top, N, x)
{
   if (Top == N – 1)
{
printf ("stack is overflow");
exit(1);
```

```
}
Top ++;
S [Top] = x
}
```

➢ **Pop operation on stack:**

```
pop (S, Top, N)
{
   int y;
   if (Top == –1)
{
print f("under flow");
exit(1);
}
y = S [Top];
Top – –;
return (y);
}
```

QUEUE

- Queue is an abtract data structure with both end open. One end is used for insertion called 'enque' and other to remove data 'dequeue'.
- It follows First-in-First out method.

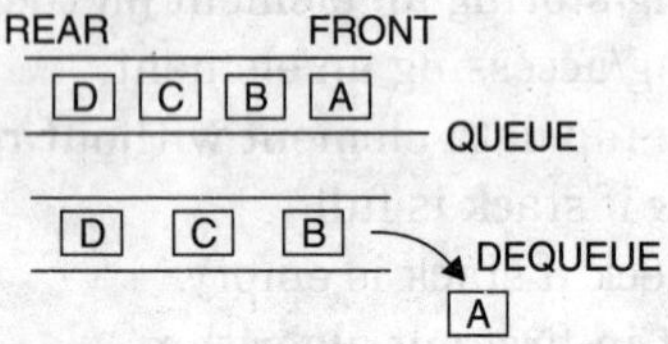

- It can be implemented using 2 stacks.

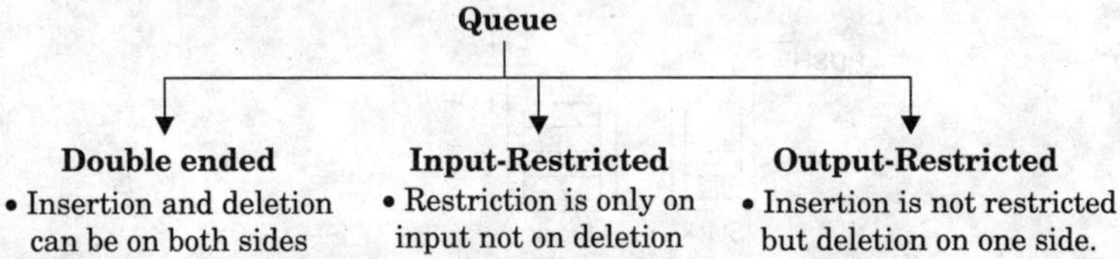

- **Priority Queue:** Special queue with each element having priority assigned.

  It can be ascending priority queue or descending priority queue.

Application

- Multiprogramming
- BFS
- Radix sort
- Resource Sharing
- CPU Scheduling
- Real time system
- Storing operands in evaluation of prefix expressions.

Operations

enqueue (): add/store an item .
dequeue (): remove/access an item.
peek (): get the front element without removing it.
is full (): check if queue is full.
is empty (): check if queue is empty.
Queue [o : n – 1] is an array;

- 'front': stores subscript value of the first element of the queue.
- 'rear': stores subscript value of last element of the queue.
- when queue is empty: front and rear = –1 and new element is to be inserted in the queue.

```
Enqueue (QUEUE, n, front, rear, element)
{
If (((front == 0) and (rear == n –1)) or (rear == front –1))
{
  Print "Overflow"
  exit();
}
if (front == –1)
  front = rear = 0;
else if (rear == n –1)
  rear = 0;
else
  rear = rear + 1;
QUEUE [rear] = element;
exit();
```

Dequeue Operation for QUEUE

```
Dequeue (QUEUE, n, front, rear)
{
if (front == –1)
{
  Print "Underflow"
  exit();
}
element = QUEUE [front];
if (front == rear)
  front = rear = –1;
else if (front == n –1)
  front = 0;
else
  front = front + 1;
exit();
}
```

7 Trees, BSTs and Binary Heaps

TREE

- It is represented as nodes connected by edges. Its a type of graph defined as T(V, E) where V = set of vertices and E = set of edges.
- It has exactly one edge between pair of vertices with no cycles or self loops.
- Degree of tree = maximum number of children a node can hold.
- Nodes in tree:
  - (*i*) Root node – initial node
  - (*ii*) Internal node – node with minimum or parent node – 1 child
  - (*iii*) External node or leaf nodes – nodes having no child.

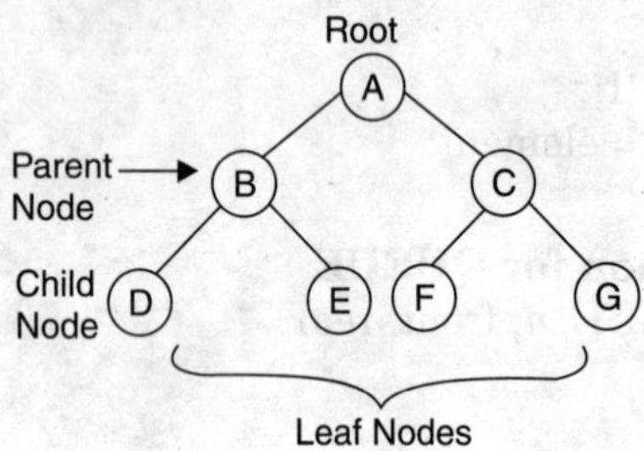

Properties

(*i*) For nodes = n; edges = $(n - 1)$

(*ii*) Let n_0 = number of nodes with degree O
n_2 = number of nodes with degree Q
$n_0 = n_2 + 1$

(*iii*) In a linked representation of Binary tree; for n nodes; NULL links = $n + 1$.

(*iv*) In heap array;
location of child → location of parent.
i (index starts from 0) → $[(i - 1)/2]$
i (indexing at 1) → $[i/2]$

Now:

location of parent → location of child

	Right	Left
i (index starts from 0)	$2i + 1$	$2i + 1$
i (indexing at 1)	$2i + 1$	$2i$

BINARY TREE

- Tree data structure with each node having at most two children referred as left child and the right child.
- Let T(n) be number of different binary trees on n distinct elements, then

$$T(n) = \sum_{k=1}^{n} T(k-1)\,T(n-k+1)$$

- Rank/Index of any node:

  Rank (i) = (number of nodes in left sub tree of i) + 1.
- In a m-ary tree (degree = m); if n_i = number of nodes of i degree.

  (i = 0, 1, ... m)

  then; $n_0 = 1 + \sum_{i=2}^{m} (i-1)n_i$

  (leaf nodes)
- For Binary tree with n nodes:
- Maximum array size = $2^n - 1$
- Minimum array size = $2^{[\log (n-1)]} - 1$
- Maximum height = n
- Minimum height = $\log_2 n$
- Maximum number of nodes = $2^{h+1} - 1$ (h = height)
- Total possible trees = ${}^{2n}C_n/(n + 1)$
- Non-empty tree; with n node and e edges; $n = e + 1$.

Types

1. **Complete Binary tree:**
   - tree with nodes being inserted or filled from left to right.
   - leaves may not be at same level.
   - complete n-ary tree is one with every node having 'o' or 'n' sons.
   - if x = number of internal nodes,

     then number of leaves = $x (n - 1) + 1$.

2. **Full Binary tree:**
   - Tree with every node having exactly 2 children and all leaves are at same level.
   - All full binary trees are complete but not vice versa.
3. **Strict Binary tree:**
   - Tree with each node having 0 or 2 children.

Binary tree Traversal

- Process of visiting/checking or updating each node of the tree exactly once.

Techniques

- Preorder: (Root → Left → Right)
- In order: (Left → Root → Right)
- Post order: (Left → Right → Root)

Example.

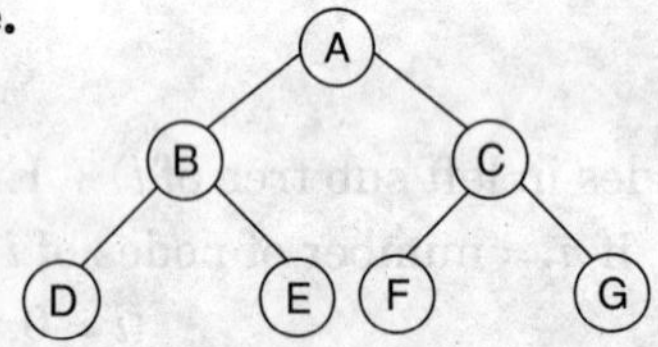

Preorder traversal → ABDECFG.

In order traversal → DBEAFCG.

Post order traversal → DEBFGCA.

BINARY SEARCH TREE (BST)

- It divides the sub tree in two segment → left and right subtree. Where;

  left subtree ≤ node/Root ≤ Right subtree.
- Recursion of left child from the root gives minimum element and recursion of right child from the root gives maximum element
- In order traversal of BST is called "Binary sort".

	Average Case	Worst Case
Space	$O(n)$	$O(n)$
Search	$O(\log n)$	$O(n)$
Insert	$O(\log n)$	$O(n)$
Delete	$O(\log n)$	$O(n)$
Build		$O(n^2)$

- **"Deletion of a node" in BST**
  - (*i*) If node has no child, simply delete that node.
  - (*ii*) If node has 1 child, delete that node and replace it with child.
  - (*iii*) If node has 2 children, that node and replace it with inorder successor or predecessor of that node.

HEAP TREE

- Special tree-based structure. It is balanced binary tree where root node value is compared with its children and arranged accordingly. It α has child β then;

$$\text{value}(\alpha) \geq \text{value}(\beta).$$

- **Two types of heap trees:**
  - **(*i*) Min heap:** When value of root node is less than either of its children
  - **(*ii*) Max heap:** When value of root node is greater than either of its children.

Heap Sort

- It deletes the root from heap tree placing it as output until all nodes are deleted.
- It gives either ascending order (or min heap) or descending order (or max heap).

AVL SEARCH TREE

- Invented by Adelson, Velski and Landis; AVL is height balancing binary search tree.
- It checks the height of left and right sub tree assuring the difference no more than 1.

  This difference is called Balance Factor (b_f)

$$|b_f| = |h_L - h_R| \leq 1$$

$$b_f = -1 \mid 0 \mid 1$$

- Height is balanced using rotation technique.

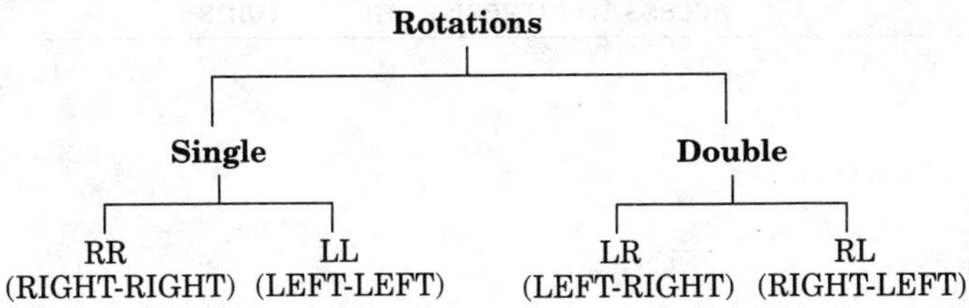

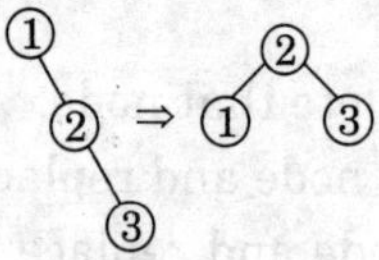

RR Rotation

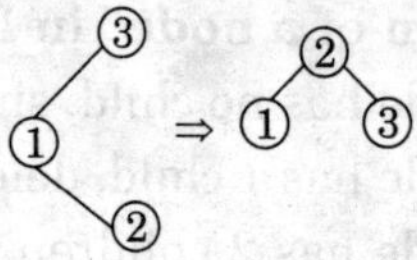

LR Rotation

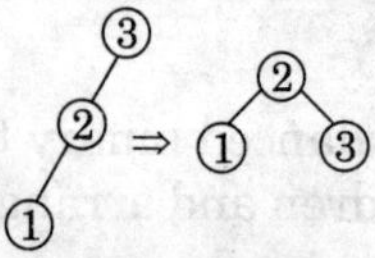

LL Rotation

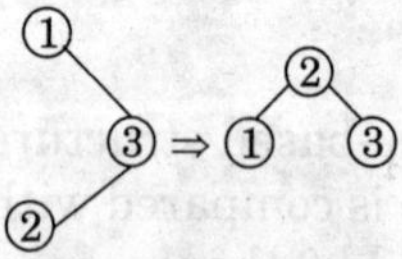

RL Rotation

Advantages and disadvantages of Data Structures

Data Structure	Advantages	Disadvantages
Array	Quick insertion, fast access if index known	Slow search, slow deletion, fixed size
Sorted array	Quicker search than unsorted array	Slow insertion and deletion, fixed size
Stack	Last-in first-out access (LIFO)	Slow access to other items
Queue	First-in first-out access (FIFO)	Slow access to other items
Linked list	Quick insertion, quick deletion	Slow search
Binary tree	Quick search, insertion, deletion (if tree remains balanced)	Deletion algorithm is complex
Hash table	Fast access if key known, Fast insertion	Slow deletion, access slow key not known, inefficiency
Heap	Fast insertion, deletion, access to largest item	Slow access to other items

Computer Science

5

Algorithms

CONTENTS

Analysis and Asymptotic Notations

1

ALGORITHM

- It is sequence of computational steps performed to solve a problem.

ASYMPTOTIC NOTATIONS

It is shorthand way to tell about running time of an algorithm.

1. **Big – oh [0]:** It is measure for longest amount of time that algorithm can possibly take to complete.

   Let $f(n)$ and $g(n) \rightarrow$ non negative functions then if there exist an integer n_0 and constant c such that $n > n_0$; $f(n) \leq c\, g(n) \Rightarrow f(n)$ is big oh of $g(n)$ "$f(n) \in O(g(n))$".

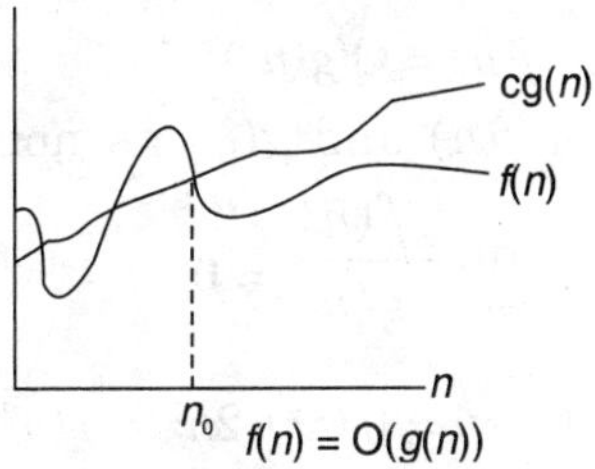

$f(n) = O(g(n))$

Example:

$$3n + 8 = O(n)$$

$$n^4 + 100n^2 + 50 = O(n^4)$$

$$1000n \log_2 n = O\left(\frac{n \log_2 n}{1000}\right)$$

$$n^x \text{ is } O(n^y);\ 0 < x < y,$$

$$(n + k)^m = O(n^m);\ k \text{ is constant}$$

2. **Big omega (Ω):**

- It describes best that can happen for a given data size.
- For non-negative functions $f(n)$ and $g(n)$ if there exits integer n_0 and a constant c such that $n > n_0$, $f(n) \geq cg(n)$ then $f(n)$ is big omega of $g(n)$

$$\text{"}f(n) \in \Omega(g(n))\text{"}$$

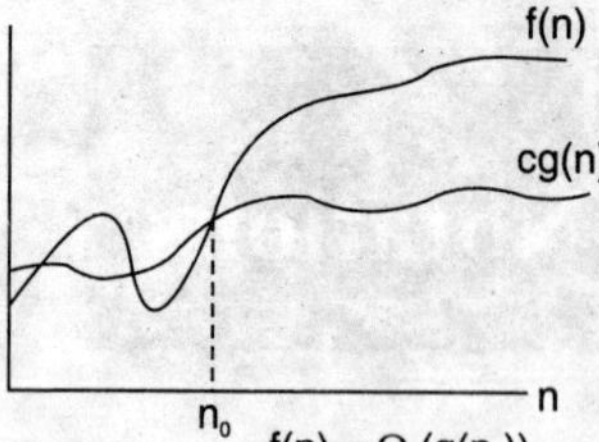

$f(n) = \Omega(g(n))$

3. **Theta notation** (θ): For non-negative functions $f(n)$ and $g(n)$, if there exit positive constant c_1 and c_2 and integer n_0 such that $n > n_0$; $c_1 g(n) \le f(n) \le c_2 g(n)$ then $f(n)$ is theta of $g(n)$;

"$f(n) = O(g(n))$"

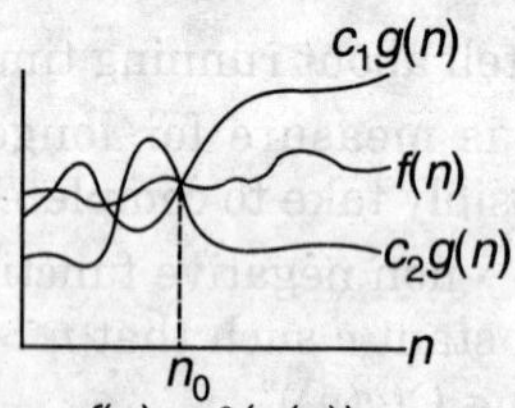

$f(n) = \theta(g(n))$

"$f(n) = O(g(n))$"

4. **Little oh (o):** For $f(n)$ and $g(n)$ as non-negative functions;

for "$f(n) = 0\ (g(n))$"; $\lim_{n\to\infty} \frac{f(n)}{g(n)} = 0.$

if $2n = 0\ (n^2); 2n^2 \ne 0\ (n^2).$

5. **Little omega** (ω)**:** For non-negative functions $f(n)$ and $g(n)$;

for "$f(n) = \omega\ (g(n))$"; $\lim_{n\to\infty} \frac{g(n)}{f(n)} = 0$

Complexity Types (Lowest to Greatest)

1. Constant: $O(1)$
2. Logarithmic: $O(\log_2 n)$
3. Linear: $O(n)$
4. Quadratic: $O(n^2)$
5. Cubic: $O(n^3)$
6. Polynomial: $O(n^k)\ \forall k > 3$
7. Exponential: $O(a^n)\ \forall a > 1$
8. Factorial: $O(n!)$

Properties of Asymptotic Notation

1. **Reflexive property:** If $f(n) = O(f(n))$ and $f(n) = \Omega\,(f(n))$ then; $f(n)\ \Theta\ (f(n))$
2. **Transitive property:** If $f(n) = O(g(n))$ and $g(n) = O(h(n))$ then; $f(n) = O(h(n))$
3. **Symmetric property:** If $f(n) = \Theta\ (g(n))$ then; $g(n) = \Theta\ (f(n))$
4. If $f(n) = O\ (g(n))$ and $e(n) = O\ (h(n))$ then.
   (a) $f(n) + e(n) = O(g(n) + h\ (n))\ /\ O \max\ (g(n), h(n))$
   (b) $f(n) \cdot e(n) = O\ (g(n) \cdot h(n))$
   (c) $h(n) \cdot f(n) = 0\ (h(n) \cdot g(n)$
5. $f(n) = O\ (g(n))$ if $g(n) = \Omega\ (f(n))$

Formulae

1. $\log x^y = y \log x$
2. $\log^k n = (\log n)^k$
3. $\log_b^x = \log_a^x / \log_a^b$
4. $\log_b^x = \log x^a / \log b^a$
5. $\log (xy) = \log x + \log y$
6. $\log (x/y) = \log x - \log y$
7. $n! = O(n^n)$
8. $2^n = O(n^n)$
9. $\sum_{i=1}^{n} 2^i = 2^n = O(2^n)$
10. $\sum_{k=1}^{n} \log k = n \log n$
11. $\sum_{k=1}^{n} \frac{1}{k} \log k = n \log n$
12. $\sum_{i=1}^{n} i^2 = \frac{n(n+1)(2n+1)}{6} = O(n^3)$
13. $\sum_{k=1}^{n} k^p = 1^p + 2^p + \ldots + n^p = \frac{1}{p+1} n^{p+1}$
14. $\sum_{i=1}^{n} i = 1 + 2 + 3 \ldots + n = \left(\frac{n+1}{2}\right) = O(n^2)$

15. $\sum_{k=0}^{n} x^k = 1 + x + x^2 + x^3 + \ldots x^n = \frac{x^{n+1}}{x-1}; \ (x \neq 1)$

16. If $\lim_{n \to \infty} \frac{f(n)}{g(n)} = 0$ then $f(n) = O(g(n))$ [*i.e.*, $f(n) < g(n)$]

17. If $\lim_{n \to \infty} \frac{g(n)}{f(n)} = 0$ then $f(n) = \omega(g(n))$ [*i.e.*, $f(n) > g(n)$]

Asymptotic Analysis

1. **Loops:** Running time of a loop is atmost product of statement inside the loop running time and total iterations.

Example:

```
main ()                        →    1
{
  x = y + z;                   →    1
  for (i = 1; i < = n; i + +)  →  2n + 1
  {
        x = y + z;             →    n
  }
}
Total time                     →  = cn = O(n)
```

2. **Nested loop:** Analysis is from inner to outer loop. Total running time is product of the size of all loops.

Example:

```
for (i = 1, i < = n, i + +)    →    2n + 1
{
   for (j = 1, j < = n, j ++)  →    O(n²)
       k = k + 1;              →    O(n²)
}
Total Time                     →  = cn² = O(n²)
```

3. **Consecutive 'for' statement:** Time complexity of 'for' statement are added up.

```
x = x + 1;                     →    O(1)
for (i = 1; i < n; i ++)       →    O(n)
m = m + 2;                     →    O(n)
for (i = 1; i ≤ n; i ++)       →    O(n)
{
for (j = 1 ;j < n ; k + + )    →    O(n²)
        k = k + 1;             →    O(n²)
}
Total Time                     →  = O(n²)
```

4. **'if – then – else' statement:** Either 'then' or 'else' whichever takes larger time is worst case running time.

   Example:

```
if (length() = = 0)                        →    O(1)
{
    return false;                          →    O(1)
}
else
{
    for (n = 0; n < length(); n ++)        →    O(n)
    {
    if (! list [n] = (otherlist [n]))      →    O(n)
    return false;                          →    O(n)
    }
}
Total Time =                               →    O(n)
```

Logarithmic Complexity

An algorithm is O (log n) if it takes constant time to cut the problem size by a fraction (usually by 1/2)

Example:

```
for (i = 1; i < n;)     →    O(log n)
{
    i = i * 2.          →    O(log n)
}
Total Time              →    = O(log n)
```

RECURRENCE RELATIONS

- **Substitution Method:** Substituting the function again and again until it is removed.

1. $T(n) = \begin{cases} T(n-1) + n & \text{if } n > 1 \\ 1 & \text{if } n = 1 \end{cases} \rightarrow O(n^2)$

2. $T(n) = \begin{cases} T(n-1) * n & \text{if } n > 1 \\ 1 & \text{if } n = 1 \end{cases} \rightarrow O(n^n)$

3. $T(n) = \begin{cases} T(n/2) + c & \text{if } n > 1 \\ 1 & \text{if } n = 1 \end{cases} \rightarrow O(\log_2 n)$

4. $T(n) = \begin{cases} T(n/2) + n & \text{if } n > 1 \\ 1 & \text{if } n = 1 \end{cases} \rightarrow O(n)$

5. $T(n) = \begin{cases} T(n-1) + \log n & \text{if } n > 1 \\ 1 & \text{if } n = 1 \end{cases} \rightarrow O(n \log n)$

RECURSIVE TREE METHOD:

If T(n) can be divided into parts then recursive tree method is used.

1. $T(n) = \begin{cases} C & \text{if } n = 1 \\ 2T(n/2) + \Theta(n) & \text{otherwise} \end{cases} \rightarrow O(n \log_2 n)$

2. $T(n) = T(n/3) + T(2n/3) + cn \rightarrow O(n \log n)$
3. $T(n) = 3T(n/4) + cn^2 \rightarrow O(n^2)$

MASTER METHOD

Let $f(n)$ be a function and T(n) → defined on non-negative integer by recurrence relation

$T(n) = aT(n/b) + f(n)$ where; $a \geq 1$ and $b > 1$

Then, T(n) is bounded asymptotically as;

(a) If $f(n) = O(n^{\log_b a - \in})$ for some constant $\in > O$;

$$T(n) = \Theta(n^{\log_b a})$$

(b) If $f(n) = \Theta(n^{\log_b a} \log^k n)$ k = constant $\forall\ k \geq O$

$$T(n) = \Theta(n^{\log_b a} \cdot \log^{k+1} n)$$

(c) If $f(n) = \Omega(n^{\log_b a + \in})$ for constant $\in > O$; and $a \cdot f(n/b) \leq c \cdot f(n)$ for $c < 1$

$$T(n) = \Theta(f(n))$$

Example:

1. $T(n) = 9T(n/3) + n \rightarrow \Theta(n^2)$
2. $T(n) = T(2n/3) + 1 \rightarrow \Theta(\log n)$
3. $T(n) = 3T(n/4) + n \log n \rightarrow \Theta(n \log n)$
4. $T(n) = 2T((\sqrt{n})) + \log_2 n \rightarrow O(\log_2 n \cdot \log_2(\log_2 n))$

Divide and Conquer

2

DIVIDE AND CONQUER (DAC)

- The problem is divided into smaller sub problems and then each one is solved independently.

```
DAC (P)
{
if (P is small) return solution (P);
    else
    {
k = Divide (P);
return (combine (DAC(P1), DAC (P2), ... DAC (Pk)));
    }
}
```

DIVIDE AND CONQUER ALGORITHMS

- **Maximum Minimum:**

  ➢ **Recurrence Relation:** $T(n) = \begin{cases} 0; & \text{if } n = 1 \\ 1; & \text{if } n = 2 \\ T\left(\frac{n}{2}\right) + T\left(\frac{n}{2}\right) + 1; & \text{if } n > 2 \end{cases}$

  ➢ Time complexity with DAC = $O(n)$

  ➢ Best case = $(n - 1) = O(n)$

  ➢ Worst case = $2(n - 1) = O(n)$

  ➢ Average case = $\left(\frac{3}{2}(n-1)\right) = O(n)$

Binary Search

- **Recurrence Relation:** $T_n = \begin{cases} 1; & \text{if } n = 1 \\ c + T(n/2) & \text{if } n > 2 \end{cases}$

- Best Case = $O(1)$
- Average Case = Worst Case = $O(\log_2 n)$

Merge Sort

- **Recurrence Relation:** $T(n) = \begin{cases} c & \text{if } n = 1 \\ T(n/2) + T(n/2) + cn & \text{if } n > 1 \end{cases}$
- Time complexity: $O(n \log n)$
- Worst case complexity = $O(n \log n)$
- Best case complexity = $O(n \log n)$
- Average case complexity = $O(n \log n)$
- $S(n) = 2n + \log n + c$; space complexity
- Worst case space complexity = $O(n)$

Quick Sort

- Best case: each partition splits array into two halves then
  $$T(n) = T(n/2) + T(n/2) + n = O(n \log n).$$
- Worst case: each partition gives unbalanced splits we get
  $$T(n) = T(n - k) + T(k - 1) + cn = O(n^2)$$
- **Average case:** In the average case, we do not know where the split happens for this reason we take all the possible value of split locations.
  $$T(n) = \frac{1}{n}\sum_{i=1}^{n} T(i-1) + T(n-i) + n + 1 = O(n \log n)$$
- **Space complexity:** $S(n) = 2n = n + \log n$

Matrix Multiplication

- **Using DAC:**
  $$T(n) = \begin{cases} O(1), & \text{for } n = 1 \\ 8T(n/2) + O(n^2), & \text{for } n > 1 \end{cases}$$
  Time complexity = $O(n^3)$
- Strassen's Matrix Multiplication:
  $$T(n) = \begin{cases} O(1) & \text{for } n = 1 \\ 7T(n/2) + an^2, & \text{for } n > 1 \end{cases}$$
  Time complexity = $O(n^{2.81})$

Power of an Element

- $T(n) = \begin{cases} 1, & \text{if } n = 0 \\ a, & \text{if } n = 1 \\ T(n/2) + c & \text{otherwise} \end{cases}$

  Time complexity = $O(\log_2 n)$

Greedy Approach

3

GREEDY ALGORITHM

It follows the problem solving heuristic of making the locally optimal choice of each stage with the hope of finding global optimum.

OPTIMAL MERGE PATTERN (HUFFMAN CODING)

- At every step file of least length is merged.

```
Optimal Merge pattern (int A [], int n)
{
    Initialize a priority queue, PQ, to contain n elements in A;
    Struct binary tree node* temp;
    for (i = 1; i < n; i++)
    {
        temp = (struct*) malloc (size of (binary tree node));
        temp → left = Delete_min (PQ);
        temp → right = Delete_min (PQ);
        temp → data = (temp → left → data) + (temp → right → data);
        insert temp to PQ;
    }
    return PQ:
}
```

- Time complexity: $O(n \log n)$
- The number of bits per message = Σ(frequency of external node 'i') × (Number of bits required for q_i)
- Weighted external path length = $\Sigma q_i\, d_i$

  (d_i = distance from 'i' root to external nodes 'i')

FRACTIONAL KNAPSACK PROBLEM

- Given weights and values of n items, the items are to be kept in knapsack of capacity W to get maximum total value in it.

Here we can break the items for maximising the value.

for ($i = 1$; $i \leq n$; i ++)

$$a[i] = p_i / w_i$$

- Time complexity = O (n log n) + O(n) = O (n logn).

JOB SEQUENCING WITH DEADLINE

- Sort all jobs in decreasing order of profit.
- Initialize the result sequence as first job in sorted jobs.
- Do following for remaining $n - 1$ jobs
  - (a) If the current job can fit in the current result sequence without missing the deadline, add current job to the result. Else ignore the current job.
- Time complexity = O(n^2)

MINIMUM COST SPANNING TREES

- Kruskal's algorithm:
  - ➢ Find minimum spanning tree for weighted graph. If graph is not connected, then it finds a minimum spanning forest.
  - ➢ E = edges of graph and V = vertices of graph

    Kruskal's algorithm : O(E log E) or O(E log V).

    with heap : O(E log n)
- Prism Algorithm:
- It always forms a tree and smallest weight edge is chosen.

  Prism Algorithm : O(n^2)

  with heap = O(e log n)

  with fibonacci heap = O (e + log n) e-edge of graph.
- Optimal Randomized Algorithm also called as minimum weight spanning tree = [O(n + e)]

SINGLE SOURCE SHORTEST PATH (DIJKSTRA'S ALGORITHM)

- The shortest path is found to all vertices from source vertex in graph.
- This algorithm fail to give shortest path for some vertices if negative weight cycle is present in the graph.
- **Time Complexity:**

  Using Binary Min Heap: O((V + E) Log V)

  Using Fibonacci Heap: O(E +V Log V)

BELLMANN FORD ALGORITHM.

- Finds shortest path from source to all vertices in the graph.
- It suits well for distributed systems.
- If negative weight cycle is present then "negative weight cycle is reported" but distance is not calculated.
- Time Complexity = O (VE)

  For dense graph = $O(V^3)$

  For sparse graph = $O(V^2)$

Dynamic Programming

4

DYNAMIC PROGRAMMING ALGORITHMS

- Problem solving technique that solves the problem by dividing them into subproblems that are not independent.
- It is bottom-up mechanism.

1. **Longest Common Subsequence (LCS):**
   - Given two sequences, length of longest subsequence present in both of them is found.
   - Brute force approach solves LCS problem.
   - Recurrence Relation:
   - $$\text{LCS}(i,j) = \begin{cases} 0; & \textit{if } i = 0 \text{ (or) } j = 0 \\ i + \text{LCS}(i+1,\ j-1); & \textit{if } x[i] = y[j] \\ \max[\text{LCS}(i-1,\ j), \text{LCS}(i,\ j-1)]; & \textit{if } x[i] \neq y[j] \end{cases}$$
   - **Time complexity:**
     by Brute force = $O(2^m)$
     by Dynamic programming = $O(m*n)$
   - Space complexity = $O(mn)$; where m and n are length of two given sequences.
2. **0/1 Knapsack Problem:** Given weights and values of n items , these items are kept in a knapsack of capacity W to get the maximum total value in the knapsack.
   - 0/1 KS (M, N)

$$= \begin{cases} 0; & \text{if M} = 0 \text{ or N} = 0 \\ 0/1\ \text{KS (M, N} - 1); & \text{if } w[n] > \text{M} \\ \max\begin{Bmatrix} 0/1\ \text{KS(M} - \text{W}[n], \text{N} - 1) + \text{P}[n] \\ 0/1\ \text{KS(M, N} - 1) \end{Bmatrix}; & \text{otherwise} \end{cases}$$

- Time complexity = O(MN): If M value is very large then it behaves like an exponential and NP-complete problem.

3. **Travelling Salesperson Problem:** Given a set of cities and distance between every pair of cities, the problem is to find the shortest possible route that visits every city exactly once and returns to the starting point.
   - Time complexity = $0(2^n.n^2)$
   - It is NP hard.
4. **Matrix Chain Multiplication:** Given sequence of matrix; most efficient way to multiply them together is found out.
   - Time complexity = $0(n^3)$
   - Space complexity = $0(n^2)$
5. **Sum of subset Problem:** Given a non negative set of integers, and a value 'sum' if there is a subset of the given set with sum equal to given 'sum' is determined.
   - **Recurrence Relation:**

$$\text{SoS}(M, N, S) = \begin{cases} \textit{return}(S); & M = 0 \\ \textit{return}(-1); & N = 0 \\ \text{SoS}(M, N-1, S); & \textit{if } w[N] > M \\ \text{Min}\begin{Bmatrix} \text{SoS}(M - w[N], N-1, S \cup w[N]) \\ \text{SoS}(M, N-1, S) \end{Bmatrix} & \text{otherwise} \end{cases}$$

   - Time complexity by brute force = O(MN)
6. **Floyd-Warshall's: All pair shortest path** The problem is to find shortest distance between every pair of vertices in a given edge weighted directed graph.
   - $A^k(i, j)$= the min cost required to go from i to j by considering all intermediate vertices are numbered not greater than k.

$$A^0(i, j) = C(i, j)$$
$$A^k(i, j) = \min\{A^{k-1}(i, j), A^{k-1}(i, k) + A^{k-1}(k, j)\}$$

   - Time complexity = $O(n^3)$ with heap = $O(n^2 \log n)$.
     Warshall's algorithm will not work for negative edge cycle.

7. **Optimal Binary Search Tree:** Given a sorted array key [0...n – 1] of search keys and an array freq [0 ....n – 1] of frequency counts, where freq [i] is number of searches to keys [i]. A binary tree is constructed such that total cost of all the searches is as small as possible.
   - It is lexically ordered tree:
   - $\text{Cost}(i, j) = \min_{i < k \leq j} \{\text{cost}(i, k-1) + \text{cost}(k, j) + w(i, j)\}$

$$w(i, j) = p(j) + q(i) + w(i, j-1)$$
$$w(i, i) = q(i) \text{ and cost } (i, i) = 0$$

   - $\text{Cost} = \underbrace{\sum_{i}^{n} p_i \times \text{level } a_i}_{\text{(successful)}} + \underbrace{\sum_{i}^{n+1} q_i (\text{level } E_i - 1)}_{\text{(unsuccessful)}}$
   - Time complexity is O(n log n).

Graph Traversals, Hashing and Sorting

5

GRAPH TRAVERSALS

Graph traversal or graph search is process of visiting each vertex in a graph for checking and updating. They are classified by the order in which the vertices are visited.

1. **DEPTH FIRST SEARCH (DFS)**
   - Traverse the graph in depth ward motion.
   - Uses stack to remember the next vertex.
   - Preorder traversal of ordered tree average case : O $(n + e)$
   - Worst case adjacent matrix = O (n^2)
   - Computer number of paths between vertices, cycle and find articulation points.
   - Follows backtracking.
   - It traverse connected components thus identifying them and tests whether graph is connected.
2. **BREADTH FIRST SEARCH (BFS)**
   - Traverse connected components defining a spanning tree.
   - Level by level traversal of ordered tree running time of BFS is O(V + E).
   - Uses Queue for remembering next vertex.
   - Prim's and Dijkshtra's are based on BFS.
   - It tests whether graph is connected.
   - Computes spanning forest, a cycle in graph and for every vertex a path with minimum number of edges between start and current vertex.

HASHING

- Process of mapping large amount of data item to smaller table using hashing function.
- Searching is constant O(1).

- Uses indexing mechanism.

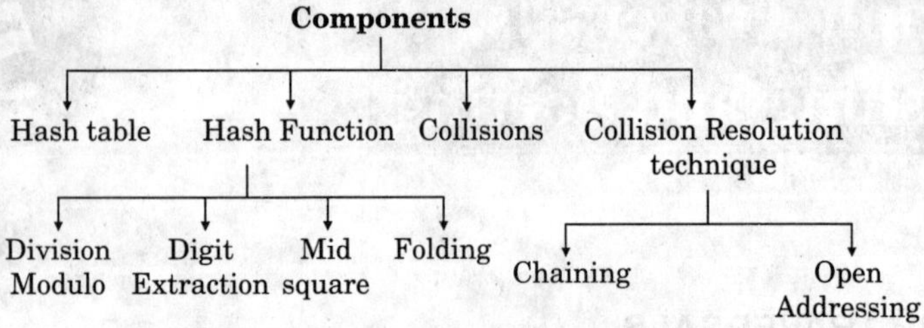

- Load Factor = $\dfrac{\text{Number of elements in hash table}}{\text{Hash table size}}$
- Hash table = Store data in associative manner, in array format.
- Direct Address table = Key is the address without manipulation .
  - ➢ Although keys are less in number; any key may contain 64 bits thus size of hash table should be $2^{64} - 1$.
  - ➢ Range of key determines the size direct address table.

HASH FUNCTIONS

(*i*) **Division modulo method:** H (X) = X % *m* (where *m* = size of hash table and X = Key)

(*ii*) **Digit Extraction method:** Selected digits are extracted from the key and used as the address.

(*iii*) **Mid Square method:** Some portion of the key is used instead of whole key used when is too large

(*iv*) **Folding method:** The key value is divided into parts whose size matched size of required address.

(*a*) **Fold shift:** Left and right parts are shifted and added with middle part

(*b*) **Fold boundary:** Left and right are folded on a fixed boundary and center number.

COLLISION RESOLUTION TECHNIQUE

When new element is mapped on already present element then collision occurs.

1. Open Addressing:

(*a*) **Linear Probing :** When collision is at L location then successive empty location is found.

Disadvantages: Primary clustering create long runs of filled slots near hash position of key.

(*b*) **Quadratic Probing:** Hash function = $h + i^2$.

Disadvantage: Secondary clustering long run of filled slots are created away from hash key position.

Maximum comparisons for successful search = size of largest cluster + 1.

All buckets are not compared because of Quadratic nature.

(*c*) **Random Probing:** A random number generator or RNG is present and no number should be repeated within random space.

$$Y_{new} = Y_{old} + C_{mod\ m}$$

Where; Y = seed value

C = constant

m = hash table size

Disadvantage: Random clustering.

(*d*) **Double hashing /Rehashing:** Uses non linear probing by computing different probe increments for different keys.

Avoids primary and secondary clustering

Disadvantage : Clustering is not completely avoided.

IMPORTANT POINTS:

- Load Factor (α) = n/m

  n = number of elements present in hash table

  m = Hash table size
- If α is less, Collisions are less
- $1 - \alpha$ = % of free space
- In open addressing scheme $0 \le \alpha \le 1$

2. Chaining:

- Linked implementation is used.
- Number of mapped = length of linked list elements .
- Complexity of deletion of element = deletion of single node in linked list.
- Maximum number of comparisons for successful search = size of largest linked list.
- No problem of overflow.
- Load factor $\alpha = \frac{n}{m}$ where $\alpha \ge O$

- Average number of probes:

Method	**Successful Search**	**Unsuccessful Search**
Linear Proving	$\frac{1}{2}+\frac{1}{2(1-\alpha)}$	$\frac{1}{2}+\frac{1}{2(1-\alpha)^2}$
Chaining	$\frac{(\alpha+1)}{2}$	$1+\frac{\alpha}{2}$

SEARCHING AND SORTING

	Best case	**Worst case**	**Average case**	***in*-place sorting**	**Stable Sorting**
Binary Search	O(1)	O(log*n*)	log(*n*)	–	–
Linear Search	O(1)	O(*n*)	O(*n*)	–	–
Bubble Sort	$O(n^2)$	$O(n^2)$	$O(n^2)$	✓	✓
Selection Sort	$O(n^2)$	$O(n^2)$	$O(n^2)$	✓	✗
Insertion sort	O(*n*)	$O(n^2)$	$O(n^2)$	✓	✓
Shell Sort	O(*n*)	$O(n\log^2 n)$	depends	✗	✗
Merge Sort	O(*n*log*n*)	O(*n*log*n*)	O(*n*log*n*)	✗	✓
Heap Sort	(Ω*n*log*n*)	O(*n*log*n*)	O(*n*log*n*)	✓	✗
Quick Sort	O(*n*log*n*)	$O(n^2)$	O(*n*log*n*)	✓	depends
Tree Sort	O(*n*log*n*)	$O(n^2)$	O(*n*log*n*)	✓	depends
Counting Sort	O(*n*)	O(*n*)	O(*n*)	✗	–
Bucket Sort	O(*n*)	O(*n*)	O(*n*)	✗	✓
Radix Sort	O(*n*)	O(*n*)	$\leq O(n^2)$	✓	✓

Complexity Classes: P, NP, NPH & NPC

6

COMPLEXITY THEORY

The purpose is to ascertain the amount of computational resource required to solve computational problems classying the problems according to their difficultly

Classes

P-space NP space P NP NP-Hard NP-Complete

1. **P-space (Polynomial space):** The language here represents its polynomial space complexity.
2. **NP space (non deterministic polynomial space):** The language here represents its non polynomial space complexity
3. **P-problem:** Class of problem solved by deterministic algorithms in a time polynomially related to size of problem instance.

   All the language accepted by deterministic turing machine are present that runs in polynomial time as a function of input length.

   Example:

   - 1 – SAT
   - Unary partition
   - 2-colour ability
   - Equivalence of DFA
   - Shortest Cycle in a graph
   - 2 – SAT
   - Shortest path
   - Eular Cycle
   - Min Cut
   - Sorting
4. **NP–problem (Non-deterministic polynomial time):** Problem class that can be solved by non deterministic algorithms in polynomial time related to size of respective problem instance.

   Problems are accepted by non deterministic turing machines with polynomial bound on the time along sequence of non deterministic choices.

   Example:

   1. Travelling sales person problem
   2. Sub-graph isomerism

5. **NP-hard problem (NP-H):**

   This problem is "at least as hard as any NP problem".

   Consider X language so that every Y language in NP can be reduced to X polynomialy and it is not possible to prove that X is in NP then it is not possible to prove that X is in NP then it is NP hard.

   Example: Turning Machine Halting

6. **NP-Complete Problem (NP-C):** When problem is both in NP and NP-hard then it is NP-C

   Problem X is NPC if; $\forall$ Y $\in$ NP; Y $\leq$ pX; X $\in$ NP.

   Example:
   - 3-SAT problem
   - Travelling sales man problem
   - Hamilton circuit problem
   - Vertex cover problem
   - Independent set problem
   - Chromatic number problem
   - Coloring Problem
   - Subgraph isomorphism problem
   - Edge cove problem
   - Knapsack problem
   - Max cut

REDUCTION

$P_1 \leq P_2$: Problem P_1 is reducible to problem P_2

$\Rightarrow$ P_2 is atleast as hard as P_1

Condition 1	**Condition 2**	**Implication**
$P_1 \leq P_2$	P_1 – undecidable	P_2 – undecidable
$P_1 \leq P_2$	P_2 – decidable	P_1 – decidable
$P_1 \leq P_2$	P_2 – recursive	P_1 – recursive
$P_1 \leq P_2$	P_2 – recursive enumerable	P_1 – recursive enumerable
$P_1 \leq P_2$	P_2 – P problem	P_1 – P problem
$P_1 \leq P_2$	P_2 – NP problem	P_1 – NP – Problem

* If NP complete is in P the P = NP

Computer Science

6

Theory of Computation

CONTENTS

Alphabet

1

- **ALPHABET:** An alphabet is a finite, non-empty set of symbols, Σ(sigma) is used to denote an alphabet
  e.g: Binary: $\Sigma = \{0, 1\}$
  All lower case letters: $\Sigma = \{a, b, c, \ldots z\}$
  Alphanumeric: $\Sigma = \{a - z, A - Z, 0 - a\}$
  DNA molecules letters: $\Sigma = \{a, c, g, t\}$
- **STRING:** A string over an alphabet set Σ is a finite sequence of symbols from Σ.
- **Notation:** Σ^* denotes the set of all strings (including empty string) over the alphabet set Σ.
  - Empty string is a string with no symbol over any alphabet. It is also called "Null string", denoted by ε(epsilon).
  - **Length of a string :** Length of a string w, denoted by '$|w|$', is equal to the number of (non = ε) characters in the string example $X = 0|0|\ 00$ $|X| = 6$
  - **Con-catenation:** The basic operation for string is binary concatenation operation. Let x and y be two strings in Σ^*. Let us form a new string Z by placing y after x, *i.e.*, $Z = xy$. The string Z is said to be obtained by con-catenation of x and y.
- **Property 1:** Con-catenation on set Σ^* is associative since for each x, y, z, in Σ^*, $x(yz) = (xy)z$
- **Property 2:** Identity element, The set Σ^* has an identity element Σ w.r.t. the binary operation of con-catenation as $x\,\Sigma = \Sigma\,x = x$ for every x in Σ^*
- **Property 3:** Σ^* has left and right cancellation

  $zx = zy$ implies $x = y$ (left cancellation)

  $xz = yz$ implies $x = y$ (right cancellation)
- **Property 4:** for x,y in Σ^*,

  $|xy| = |x| + |y|$

  $|x|, |y|, |x,y|$ denotes the length of string

- **Palindrome:** A palindrome is a string which is the same whether written forward or backward.

  Example: Malayalam.

Note : A palindrome of even length can be obtained by concatination of string and its transpose.

- **Prefix and suffix of a string:** A prefix of a string is a substring of leading symbols of that string. W is prefix of Y if there exist Y′ in Σ^* such that Y = W Y′

  Example: String 123 has 4 prefixes $\in$, 1, 12, 123

  Similarly, a suffix of a string is a substring of trailing symbols of that string. W is a suffix of Y is there exist Y′ in Σ^* such that Y = Y/W

  Example: 123 has 4 suffixes, $\in$ 3, 23,123.

- **Powers of Alphabet:**

  Let Σ be on alphabet, then

  $\Sigma^0 = |\in|$: zero length string

  $\Sigma^1 = \{a, b\}$: set of 1 length string

  $\Sigma^2 = \{ab,ab,aa,ba\}$: set of 2 length string

  Σ^k = the set of all strings of length k

  $\Sigma^* = \Sigma^0\, v\, \Sigma^1\, v\, \Sigma^2\, v ...$

  $\Sigma^+ = \Sigma^1\, v\, \Sigma^2\, v\, \Sigma^3\, v ...$

  Language: 'A language is a collection of sentences of finite length all constructed from a finite alphabet of symbols'.

  Example: Let $\Sigma = \{a,b\}$, Then language L = $\{ab, aab\}$

  Grammar: A phrase structure grammar (A grammar) is (V_N, Σ, P, S), where

  (*i*) V_N is a finite non-empty set whose elements are called variables.

  (*ii*) Σ is a finite non empty set whose elements are called terminals

  (*iii*) $V_N \cap \Sigma = \phi$

  (*iv*) S is a special variable (*i.e.*, an element of V_N) called the start symbol.

  (*v*) P is a finite set whose elements are $\alpha - \beta$, where α and β are strings on $V_N \cup \Sigma$, α has at least one symbol from V_N. Elements of P are called production or reproduction rules.

- **Automaton:** An automaton is defined as a system where energy materials and information are transformed, transmitted and used for performing same functions without direct participation of man.

In computer science "automaton means discrete automaton and is defined in more abstract way.

(*i*) **Automaton acts as Recognizer or Accepter:** An automaton is a machine that accepts or recognizes the strings of a language (L) over an input alphabet Σ.

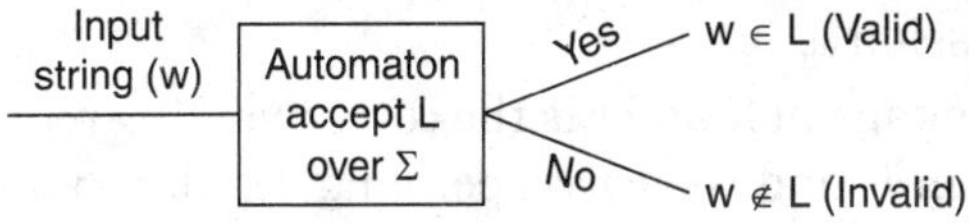

Recognizer/accepter

(*ii*) **Automaton Acts as producer or enumerator or transducer:** An automaton can also produce the output over any alphabet and for the given input alphabet Σ.

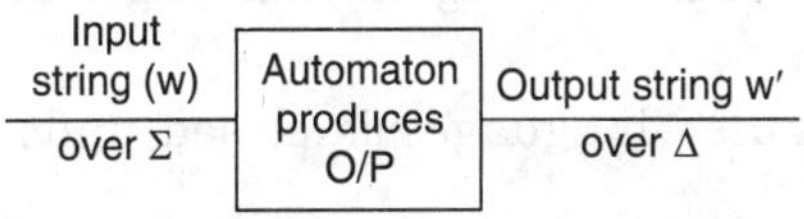

Equivalence of Language, Grammar and Automata

	Formal Languages	Grammars	Automata
1.	Regular languages	Regular grammars	Finite Automata
2.	Context Free Languages	Context Free Grammars	Push down Automata
3.	Context Sensitive Languages	Context Sensitive Grammars	Linear Bound Automata
4.	Recursive Enumerable Languages	Recursive Enumerable Grammar (unrestricted)	Turing Machines

Regular Expression and Languages: A regular expression is a formula, which defines a language using set theoretical union, denoted by +, concatenation and concatenation closure. These operations are combined according to a set of rules, adding parentheses when necessary.

R is the family of languages satisfying the following conditions:

- The language ϕ is in R and the corresponding regular expression is ϕ.
- The language (ε) is in R and the corresponding regular expression is ε.
- For each symbol a, the language $\{a\}$ is in R and the corresponding regular expression is a.

- L_1 and L_2 are languages in R_1 and r_1 and r_2 are the corresponding regular expression then.
  (*a*) The language $L_1 U L_2$ is in R and corresponding regular expression is $(r_1 + r_2)$
  (*b*) The language $L_1 L_2$ is in R and the corresponding regular expression is $(r_1 r_2)$.
- If L is a language in R and *r* is the corresponding regular expression. Then L* is in R and the corresponding regular expression is (r^*)
- Only language obtainable by using the above rules are in R.

Closure Properties of Regular Languages

- The set of regular languages is closed under the union operation.
- Finite union is closed for regular languages but infinite union is not closed.
- The set of regular languages is closed under the intersection operation.
- Regular languages are closed under finite intersection but not under infinite intersection.
- The set of regular languages is closed under the difference operation.
- The set of regular languages is closed under the complement operation.
- The set of regular languages is closed under the concatenation operation.
- The set of regular languages is closed under the kleene closure operation.
- The set of regular languages is closed under the positive closure operation.
- The set of regular languages is closed under the prefix operation as well as suffix operation.

  Init(L) = Prefix (L) = $\{u \mid uv$ is in regular language L$\}$

  Suffix(L) = $\{v \mid uv$ is in regular language L$\}$
- The set of regular languages is closed under the reversal operation.
- Half of a regular language is also regular: Let L is a regular language. Then Half(L) = $\{u \mid uv \in L \text{ and } |u| = |v|\}$.
- One third of a regular language is also regular: Let L is a regular language. Then one third (L) = $\{u \mid uvw \in L \text{ and } |u| = |v| = |w|\}$.
- Quotient of two regular languages is also regular :

$$L_1/L_2 = \{ x \mid xy \in L_1 \text{ for some } y \in L_2\}.$$

- Subsequence of a regular language is also regular language: Subsequence(L) = {w | w is obtained by removing symbols from anywhere of a string in L}.
- Sub-word of a regular language is also regular: Sub-word (L) = {v | for some u and for some w, uvw is in L}.
- Homomorphism of two regular languages is also regular.
- Inverse Homomorphism of two regular languages is also regular.
- Substitution of two regular languages is also regular.
- Shuffle of two regular languages: Shuffle(L_1, L_2) = ($x_1 y_1 x_2 y_2 ... x_k y_k$ | $x_1 x_2 ... x_k$ is in L_1 and $y_1 y_2 ... y_k$ is in L_2} is also regular.
- Symmetric difference of two regular languages is also regular.
- If L is regular then $\sqrt{L}$ is also a regular language: $\sqrt{L}$ = {w | ww in L}.
- If L is regular then Max(L) is also a regular language.
- If L is regular then Min(L) is also regular. Min(L) = {w | $w \in$ L and there is no proper prefix of w is in L}.
- Regular languages are not closed under subset, superset, infinite union as well as infinite intersection. *i.e.*, a subset or superset of a regular language need not be regular. Infinite union and infinite intersections of regular languages need not be regular.

Decision Properties of Regular Language

- **Membership:** It is decidable.
- **Emptiness (Is L empty?):** Checking whether the given regular language is empty or not. It is decidable.
- **Finiteness (Is L finite?):** Checking whether the given language is finite or not. It is decidable.
- **Equivalence of two Regular Languages (Is L1 ≅ L2?):** Checking whether the given two regular languages are equal or not. It is decidable.
- **Subset Operation over Two Regular Languages (Is L1 ⊆ L2?):** Checking whether the regular language L1 is subset of a regular language L2 or not. (L1 ⊆ L2) ≅ (L1 ∩ L2 = ϕ). It is decidable.

- **Chomsky Hierarchy:** All formal languages are divided into 4 classes by chomsky and those class hierarchy as "Chomsky-Hierarchy".

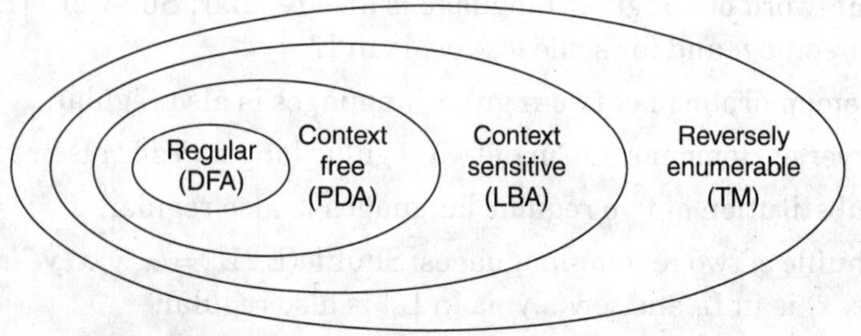

Types of Automaton:

(*i*) Finite Automaton (FA):

A state diagram that comprehensively captures all possible states and transitions that a machine can take while responding to a stream or sequence of input symbols. Works as recogniser or for "regular languages".

Types of FA:

- Deterministic Finite Automata (DFA)
  The machine can exist in only one state at any given time
- Non- Deterministic Finite Automata (NFA)
  The machine can exist in multiple states at the same time

(*ii*) Push Down Automata (PDA): A PDA consists of

- A finite non-empty set of states denoted by Q,
- A finite non-empty set of input symbols denoted by Σ,
- A finite non-empty set of pushdown symbols denoted by Γ,
- A special state called the initial state denoted by q_0,
- A special pushdown symbol called the initial symbol on the pushdown store denoted by z_0.
- The set of final states, a subset of Q denoted by F, and.
- The transition function δ from $Q \times \{\sum v\ (\varepsilon)\} \times \Gamma$ to the set of finite subset of $Q \times \Gamma^*$.

Symbolically a PDA is $(Q, \Sigma, \Gamma, \delta, q_0, z_0, F)$

Types of PDA

(*a*) Deterministic PDA (DPDA)

(*b*) Non-Deterministic PDA (NPDA or PDA)

- **Linear Bound Automata (LBA) :** An automaton that accepts content sensitive language is called a "LBA".
- **Turing Machine :** It is a theoretical computing machine to serve as an idealized model for mathematical calculation. ATM consist of a line of cells known as a "tape" that can be moved back and forth, an active element known as "Head" that possesses a property known as "colour" of active cell under neath it.

Types of TM:

(*a*) Deterministic TM (DTM)

(*b*) Non-Determininstic (NTM)

L (NTM) = L (DTM)

- **Types of Grammars:**

(*i*) **Regular Grammar (RG) or Type 3:** A regular grammar is a mathematical object G, with four components, G = (N, Σ, P, S), where

- N is a non-empty set, finite set of non terminal symbols,
- Σ is a finite set of terminal symbols, or alphabet, symbols,
- P is set of grammar rules each of one having one of the forms
- $A \rightarrow a\ B$
- $A \rightarrow a$
- $A \rightarrow \varepsilon$, for $A,B \in N_1$ $a \in \Sigma$ and ε the empty string and
- $S \in N$ is the start symbol.

Note

A grammar is regular grammar iff it is either left linear grammar or right linear grammar. Regular grammar is a grammar where all rules are restricted as following

either $V \rightarrow V\ T^* \mid T^*$ [Left linear grammar]

or $V \rightarrow T^*\ V \mid T^*$ [Right linear grammar]

(*ii*) **Context Free Grammar (CFG) or Type 2:** Every rule of (CFG is restricted as $V \rightarrow (VUT)^*$

(*iii*) **Context Sensitive Grammar (CSG) or Type 1:** Rule $X \rightarrow Y$ where $|X| \leq |Y|$, X ε $(VUT)^*$ and Y ε $(VUT)^*$ and X must contain atleast one variable.

Note

If NULL productions are present in the grammar, it may or may not be CSG.

(iv) Recursive Enumerable Grammar (REG) or Type 0: Rule $X \rightarrow Y$, where $X \in (VUT)^*$, $Y \in (VUT)^*$ and X must contain atleast one variable.

Finite Automata (FA): Broadly FA can be categorised in the following two types:

1. **Finite Transducer (FA with output):** Finite transducer can further be classified in two types: Mealy and Moore Machines act as language generator but not language recogniser
   (a) Mealy Machines: In finite automata, if output symbol is associated with transition (State and input) then such automata is called as Mealy Machine.
   (b) Moore Machine: In finite automata if output symbol is associated with each state then such automata is called as Moore Machine.
   - Specification of Mealy and Moore Machines:
     $M = (Q, \Sigma, \Delta, \delta, \lambda, q_0)$ is a 6-tuple notation where.
     Q is set of finite states,
     Σ is input alphabet contains finite number of input symbols.
     Δ is output alphabet which contains output symbols.
     δ is transition function, $\delta: Q \text{ X } \Sigma \rightarrow Q$.
     λ is output function : $\lambda : Q \rightarrow \Delta^*$ (Moor Machine)
     $\lambda : Q \text{ X } \Sigma \rightarrow \Delta^*$ (Mealy Machine)
     q_0 is initial state or state of Moore Machine, $q_0 \, \varepsilon \, Q$
2. **Finite Acceptor (FA without output):** It can be divided with the classification of Deterministic and Non-Deterministic.
   (a) Deterministic Finite Automata:
   DFA = $(Q, \Sigma, \delta, q_0, F)$ is 5-tuple notation where. Q is set of finite states,
   Σ is input alphabet contains finite number of input symbols
   δ is transition function defined over transitions of FA for state and *i/p*.
   $\delta : Q \times \Sigma \rightarrow Q$.
   q_0 is initial state or start state of DFA, $q_0 \in$ QF is a set of final states of DFA

Note

For every input symbol of alphabet there is an exactly one transition from every state of finite automata is called as DFA,

- DFA covers transitions for all valid and invalid strings in the given regular language.
- For every valid string, DFA reaches to one of its final state and for every invalid string it reaches to non final state.

Non-Deterministic Finite Automata: It implies that the machine can exist in more than one state at the same time. The transition could be non-deterministic.

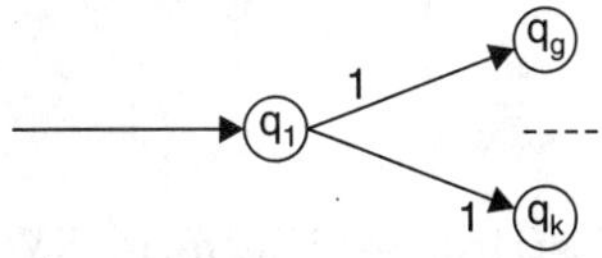

Each transition function therefore maps to a set of states

A Non-deterministic Finite Automaton (NFA) consists of:

- Q : A finite set of states
- Σ : A finite set of input symbols (alphabet)
- q_0 : A start state
- F : Set of accepting states
- δ : A transition function, which is a mapping between Q X Σ : subset of Q.

It can now be defined by 5 tuple: (Q, Σ, q_0, F, δ: NFA without Null moves.

WAY TO USE NFA

I/*p* : A word win Σ*

Condition: Is W acceptable by NFA

Steps:

- Start at the "start state" q_0
- For every input symbol in the sequence Wd_o
- Determine all possible next state from all current states, given the current input symbol in W and the transition function.
- If all symbols all consumed and if at least one of the current states is a final state then accept W.
- Otherwise, reject W.

EPSILON NFA (ε-NFA) or NFA

For every valid string there exist a path from initial state that reaches final state. ε-NFA is same as NFA but it can include epsilon transitions.

if ε-NFA = $(Q, \Sigma, \delta, q_0, F)$ is 5-tuple notation

where $S : Q \times \Sigma \cup (\varepsilon) \rightarrow 2^Q$.

Pumping Lemma: The pumping lemma is a property of all regular languages.

Let L be a regular language.

Then there exists some constant N such that for every string $W \in L$ ($|W| \geq N$), there exists a way to break W into there parts W = XYZ, such that.

- $Y \neq \Sigma$
- $|XY| \leq N$
- For all $k \geq 0$, all strings of the form $XY^k Z \in L$ (N is called the "Pumping Lemma Constant")

Examples: (Non regular languages)

$L = \{a^m b^m \mid i \geq 0\}$

$L = \{a^p \mid p \text{ is a prime}\}$

$L = \{a^m b^n \mid m > n\}$

$L = \{a^m b^n \mid m < n\}$

$L = \{a^m b^n \mid m! = n\}$

$L = \{w \mid w \ \varepsilon \ (a + b)^*\}$ and w has # a's equal to #b's}

$L = \{ww \mid w \ \varepsilon \ (a + b)^*\}$

$L = \{a^{n^2}\}$

$L = \{a^{2^n}\}$

$L = \{a^n b^n c^n\}$

Minimization of FA

Finite automata need to be minimized to reduce number of states of DFA.

- **Minimization Methods:** Partition method (state equivalence), table filing method and Myhill-Nerode theorem.
- **Myhill-Nerode Theorem:** Let L be a regular language, then it contains finite number of equivalence classes. Union of all Myhill-Nerode equivalence classes gives universal language. All

the strings of universal language partitioned into a finite number of Myhill-Nerode equivalence classes, if L is regular.

The number of Myhill-Nerode equivalence classes in a regular language ≡ Number of states in the unique minimal DFA corresponding to that language.

Applications of Automata:

(*i*) *Finite automata can be used in the following cases:*

(*a*) To design a lexical analysis of a compiler

(*b*) To recognize the pattern using regular expressions

(*c*) To design the combination and sequential circuits using Moore/Mealy machines.

(*ii*) *PDA can be used in the following cases:*

(*a*) To design the parsing phase of a compiler (syntax analysis)

(*b*) To implement stack applications

(*c*) To evaluate arithmetic expressions

(*d*) To solve the Tower of Hanoi problem

(*iii*) *Linear Bounded Automata can be used in the following cases:*

(*a*) To construct syntactic parse trees for semantic analysis of the compiler.

(*b*) To implement genetic programming

(*iv*) *Turing Machine can be used in the following cases:*

(*a*) To solve any recursively enumerable problem

(*b*) To understand complexity theory

(*c*) To implement neural nets

(*d*) To implement artificial intelligence

(*e*) To implement Robotic applications

Push Down Automata and CFLs

2

Definition: A context free grammar (CFG) consisting of a finite set of grammar rules is a quadruple (N,T,P,S) where

- N is a set of non-terminal symbols
- T is a set of terminals where $N \cap T$ = NULL
- P is a set of rules, $P : N \rightarrow (N \cup T)^*$ *i.e.*, the left hand side of the production rule P does have any right context or left context
- S is the start symbol.

Example:

- The grammar ({A}, {a, b, c}, P, A), $P : A \rightarrow a\ A$, $A \rightarrow a\ b\ c$

Generation of Derivation Tree

A derivation tree or parse tree is an ordered rooted tree that graphically represents the semantic information a string derived from a context-free grammar.

Representation Technique

Root vertex – Must be labeled by the start symbol

Vertex – Labeled by a non-terminal symbol

Leaves – Labeled by a terminal symbol or ε.

if $S \rightarrow X_1\ X_2 \ldots X_n$ is a prediction rule in a CFG, then the parse tree/ derivation will be as follows.

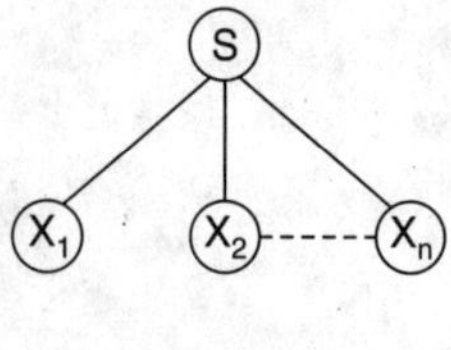

Sentential Form and Partial Derivation Tree: A partial derivation tree is a subtree of a derivation tree/parse tree such that either all of its children are in sub tree or none of them are in sub tree.

Example : If in any CFG the production ore

S → AB, A → aOA/ ε, B → Bb/ε.

The partial derivation tree can be the following.

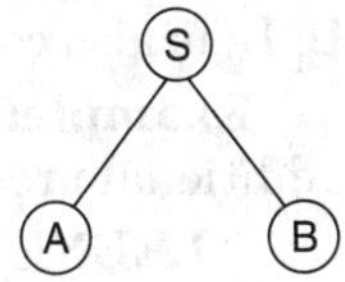

If the partial derivation tree contains the root S, it is called sentential form. The above sub tree is also in sentential form.

Derivation of a string:

- **Leftmost Derivation:** A left most derivation is obtained by applying production to the leftmost variable in each step.
- **Rightmost Derivation:** A rightmost derivation is obtained by applying production to the rightmost variable in each step.

Left and Right Recursive Grammar: In a CFG G, if there is a production in the form X → Xa where X is a non-terminal and 'a' is a string of terminal, it is called a left recursive production and the grammar is known as left recursive grammar.

And if in a CFG G, if there is a production is in the form X → aX where X is a non-terminal and 'a' is a string of terminals, it is called a right recursive production and the grammar is known as right recursive grammar.

Ambiguity in Context Free Grammars: If a context free grammar G has more than one derivation tree for some string W∈L (G), it is called an ambiguous grammar. There exist multiple rightmost or leftmost derivation for some string generated from that grammar.

CFL Closure Property

Context free languages are closed under.

- Union
- Concatenation
- Kleen Star Operation

UNION

Let L_1 and L_2 be two context free languages. Then $L_1 \in L_2$ is also context free

Example

Let L1 = $\{a^n\ b^n,\ n > 0\}$, corresponding grammar G1 will have P : S1 → a Ab/ab

Let L2 = $\{c^m\ d^m,\ n \geq 0\}$, corresponding grammar G2 will have P : S2 → C B b | ε.

Union of L_1 and L_2 = $\{a^n\ b^n\}$ U $\{c^m\ d^m\}$ additional production S → S1/S2

Con-catenation: If L_1 and L_2 are context free languages, then $L_1 L_2$ is also context free.

Example: Union of the languages L_1 and L_2, $L = L_1 L_2 = \{a^n b^n c^m d^m\}$ additional production S → S1 S2

KLEENE STAR: If L is a context free language, then L* is also context free

Let $L = \{a^n b^n, n \geq 0\}$, corresponding grammar G will have
P: S → aAb/ε.
kleene star $L_1 = \{a^n b^n\}^*$
additional productions S1 → SS1/∈.

Note
CFL are not close under Intersection, intersection with Regular Language, Complement.

Simplification of CFG: In a CFG, it may happen that all the production rules and symbol are not needed for the derivation of strings. Besides, there may be some null productions and unit productions. Elimination of these productions and symbols are called simplification of CFG and which consist of following steps:

- Reduction of CFG
- Removal of Unit productions
- Removal of Null productions

Reduction of CFG: CFG and are reduced in two phases:

Phase 1: Derivation of an equivalent grammar G', from the CFG G, such that each variable drives some terminal string.

Phase 2 : Derivation of an equivalent grammar, G", from CFG, G', such that each symbol appears in sentential form.

CHOMSKY NORMAL FORM

A CFG is in Chomsky Normal Form if the productions are in the following forms:

A → a

A → BC

S → ε

where A, B and C are non-terminals and a is terminal.

Algorithm to convert into chomsky normal form:

1. If the start symbol S occurs on some right side, create a new start symbol S' and a new production S' → S.
2. Remove Null productions.

3. Remove Unit production
4. Replace each production $A \rightarrow B_1 \ldots B_n$ where n > 2 with. $A \rightarrow B_1$ C where $C \rightarrow B_2 \ldots B_n$. Repeat this step for all productions having two or more symbols in the right side.
5. If the right side of any production is in the form $A \rightarrow aB$ where a is a terminal and A, B are non-terminal, then the production is replaced by $A \rightarrow XB$ and $X \rightarrow a$. Repeat the step for every production which is in the form $A \rightarrow aB$.

GREIBACH NORMAL FORM

A CFG is in Greibach Normal Form if the productions are in the following forms:

$A \rightarrow B$

$A \rightarrow b\ D_1 \ldots D_n$

$S \rightarrow \varepsilon$

Where A, $D_1 \ldots D_n$ are non-terminals and b is a terminal.

Algorithm to convert a CFG into Greibach Normal form

1. If the start symbol S occurs on some right side, create a new start symbol S′ and a new production $S' \rightarrow S$
2. Remove Null productions
3. Remove Unit productions
4. Remove all direct and indirect left recursion.
5. Do proper substitutions of productions to convert it into the proper form of GNF

PUSHDOWN AUTOMATA

A Pushdown automata is a way to implement a CFG in a way, DFA designed for regular grammar. A DFA can remember an infinite amount of information.

Pushdown automata can be described as the combination of finite state machine and a stack

PDA has three components:

- An input tape
- A control unit and
- A state with infinite size.

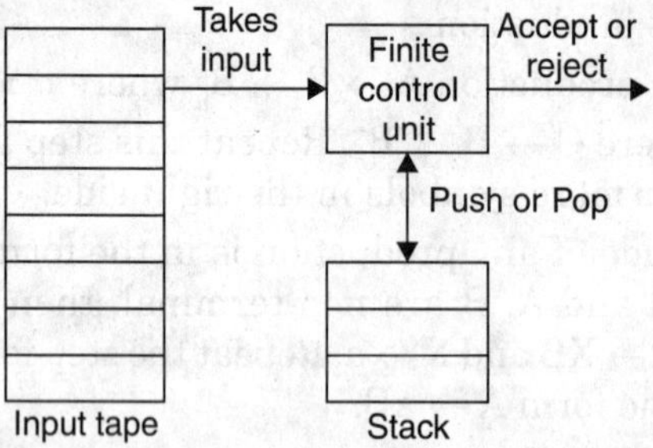

PDA Acceptance: There are two different ways to define PDA acceptability.

Final State Acceptability: In a final state acceptability, PDA accepts a string when, after reading the entire string, the PDA is in a final state. From the starting state, we can make moves that end up in a final state.

For a PDA (Q, Σ, S, δ, q_0, I, F), the language accepted by the set of final states F is →

L(PDA) = {W/(q_0, W, I) $\vdash^*$ (q_1, ε_1, x), $q \in$ F} for any input stack string X

Empty Stack Acceptability: Here a PDA accepts a string when, after reading the entire string, the PDA has emptied its stack.

For a PDA (Q, Σ, S, δ, q_0, I, F), the language accepted by the empty stack is:

L(PDA) = {W/(q_0, W, I) $\vdash^*$ (q, ε, ε) $q \in$ Q}

Non-CFLS Examples:

(*a*) L = $\{a^n b^n c^n \mid n \geq 0\}$

(*b*) L = $\{a^n b^m c^n d^m \mid m, n \geq 0\}$

(*c*) L = $\{a^{n^2} \mid n \geq 0\}$

(*d*) L = $\{a^{2^n} \mid n \geq 0\}$

(*e*) L = $\{a^n \mid n$ is prime$\}$

(*f*) L = $\{a^{n!} \mid n \geq 0\}$

(*g*) L = $\{a^{2^{n^2}} \mid n \geq 0\}$

(*h*) L = $\{a^i b^i c^k \mid i \leq j \leq k\}$

(*i*) L = $\{w w^R w^R \mid w \in (a + b)^*\}$

(*j*) L = $\{ww \mid w \in (a + b)^*\}$

(*k*) L = $\{0^p \mid p$ is composite$\}$

(*l*) L = $\{o^i 1^j \mid j = i^2\}$

(*m*) L = $\{a^n b^n c^i \mid i \leq n\}$

(*n*) L = $\{0^i 1^j o^k \mid j = \max(i, k)\}$

(o) L = $\{a^n b^n c^i \mid i \neq n\}$

(*p*) L = $\{ww^R w \mid w(a + b)^*\}$

Recursively Enumerable Sets and Turing Machine (TM)

3

TURING MACHINE

A Turing Machine is an accepting device which accepts the languages (recursively enumerable set) generated by type O grammars. It was invented in 1936 by Alan Turing.

Definition

A Turing Machine (TM) is a mathematical model which consists of an infinite length tape divided into cells on which input is given. It consists of a head which reads the input tape. A state register stores the state of Turing. After reading on input symbol, it is replaced with another symbol, its internal state is changed, and it moves from one cell to the right or left. If TM reaches the final state, the input string is accepted.

Example: Turing Machine (TM)

$$M = (Q, X, \Sigma, \delta, q_0, B, F) \text{ with}$$
$$Q = \{q_0, q_1, q_2, q_f\}$$
$$X = \{a, b\}$$
$$\varepsilon = \{1\}$$
$$q_0 = \{q_0\}$$
$$B = \text{blank symbol}$$
$$F = \{q_f\}$$

δ is given by-

Tape alphabet symbol	Present state 'q_0'	Present state 'q_1'	Present state 'q_2'
a	$\mid R_q \mid$	$\mid Lq_0 \mid$	$\mid L_{qf}$
b	$\mid L_q \mid$	$\mid Rq_1 \mid$	$\mid R_{qf} \mid$

Time and Space Complexity of Turing Machine: For a Turing, the time complexity refers to the measure of the number of times the tape moves when the machine is initialised for some input symbols and the spaces complexity is the number of cells of the tape written.

Time Complexity All Reasonable Functions

$$T(n) = O(n \log n)$$

TM's Space Complexity:

$$S(n) = O(n)$$

Accepted Language and Decided Language

A TM decides a language if it accepts it and enters into a rejecting state for any input not in the language. A language is recursive if it is decided by a Turing Machine.

There may be some cases where a TM does not stop. Such TM accepts the language, but it does not decide it.

Multi-Tape Turing Machine

Multi-Tape Turing Machine have multiple tapes where each tape is accessed with a separate head. Each head can move independently of the other heads.

Multi-Track Turing Machine

It is a specific type of Multi-tape Turing Machine, contains multiple track but just one tape head reads and writes on all tracks.

Non-Deterministic Turing Machine

In a Non- Deterministic Turing Machine, for every state and symbol, there is a group of actions the TM can here. So here the transitions are not deterministic.

Semi-Infinite Tape Turing machine

A Turing Machine with a semi- infinite tape has a left end but no right end. The left end is limited with an end marker. It is a two track up - upper track and lower track.

Language Decidability

A language is called decidable or recursive if there is a Turing Machine which accepts and halts every input string W. Every decidable language is Turing- Acceptable.

A decision problem P is decidable if the language L of all yes instances to P is decidable

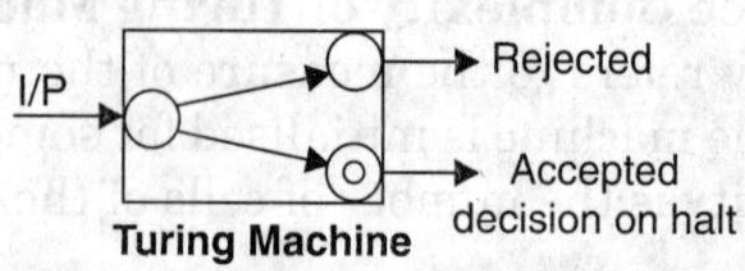

Undecidable Language

For an undecidable language, there is no Turing Machine which accepts the language and makes a decision for every input string W.

A decision problem P is called a "Undecidable" if the language L of all yes instances to P is not decidable. Undecidable language are not recursive language but some times, they may be recursively enumerable languages.

Turing Machine Halting Problem

Input: A Turing Machine and an input string w.

Problem: Does the Turing Machine finish computing of the string w in a finite number of steps ?

Proof: At first, it is assumed that such a Turing Machine exist to solve this problem. We will call this Turing Machine as Halting Machine that produces a 'Yes' or 'No' in a finite amount of time. If it finishes in a finite time, the output is Yes otherwise No.

Decidability Problems for Recursive Languages

1. Membership problem: Decidable.
2. Emptiness problem: Undecidable.
3. Finiteness problem: Undecidable.
4. Equivalence problem: Undecidable.
5. Subset problem: Undecidable.
6. Ambiguity problem: Undecidable.
7. Regularity problem: Undecidable.
8. Universality problem $L = \Sigma^*$?: Undecidable.
9. Disjointedness problem: Undecidable.

Some Decidability Problems Related to Halting Turing Machines (REC Languages)

1. Halting problem of a (halting) Turing Machine: Decidable.
2. Empty word halting problem for halting Turing Machine: Decidable.
3. State entry problem for halting Turing Machine: Decidable.

Rice Theorem

L = { ⟨M⟩ | L (M) ∈ P} is undecidable when, P, a non-trivial property of Turing Machine, is undecidaable. If the following two properties hold, it is proved as undecidable.

If M_1 and M_2 recognise the same language

1. Then either $\langle M_1\rangle \langle M_2\rangle \in L$ or $\langle M_1\rangle \langle M_2\rangle \notin L$ property for some M_1 and M_2 such that $\langle M_1\rangle \in L$ and
2. $\langle M_2\rangle \notin L$

Identification of Formal Languages

1. $a^{n^2} \rightarrow$ CSL
2. $a^n b^n c^n \rightarrow$ CSL
3. $\{ww \mid w \in (0, 1)^*\} \rightarrow$ CSL
4. $\{a^n b^m c^p \mid n = m = p\} \rightarrow$ CSL
5. $\{ww^R w \mid w \in (0, 1)^*\} \rightarrow$ CSL
6. $\{ww^R w^R \mid w \in (0, 1)^*\} \rightarrow$ CSL
7. $xww \mid xw \in (0, 1^+)\} \rightarrow$ CSL
8. $\{w \mid n_a(w) = n_b(w) = n_c(w)\} \rightarrow$ CSL
9. $\left\{w \,\middle|\, \frac{n_a(w)}{n_b(w)} = n_c(w)\right\} \rightarrow$ CSL
10. $\{a^n b^m c^n d^m\} \rightarrow$ CSL
11. $\{a^n b^m c^p \mid n = m \text{ and } m = p\} \rightarrow$ CSL
12. $a^n b^{n^2} \rightarrow$ CSL
13. $\{a^n b^{n+m} c^p\} \rightarrow$ DCFL
14. $\{w \mid n_a(w) + n_b(w) = n_c(w)\} \rightarrow$ DCFL
15. $\{a^m b^n c^m\} \rightarrow$ DCFL
16. $\{a^m b^n c^n\} \rightarrow$ DCFL
17. $\{a^n b^{n+m} c^m\} \rightarrow$ DCFL
18. $\{a^n b^n c^m d^{nj}\} \rightarrow$ DCFL
19. $\{a^n b^m c^m c^n\} \rightarrow$ DCFL
20. $\{wxw^R \mid w \in \{0, 1\}^* x \in \{0, 1\}\} \rightarrow$ DCFL

21. $\{ww^R \mid w \in (0, 1)^*\} \rightarrow$ CFL
22. $\{a^m b^n c^p \mid m = n \text{ or } n = p\} \rightarrow$ CFL
23. $\{wxw^R \mid x,w \in (0, 1)^*\} \rightarrow$ Regular
24. $\{wxw \mid x,w \in (0, 1)^*\} \rightarrow$ Regular
25. $\{wxw^R \mid x,w \in (0, 1)^+\} \rightarrow$ Regular
26. $a^* \rightarrow$ Regular
27. $a^* b^* \rightarrow$ Regular
28. $\{a^n b^n \mid n \leq 10000\} \rightarrow$ Regular
29. $\{a^n b^n c^n \mid n = 10\} \rightarrow$ Regular
30. $\left\{a^{n^2} / n \geq 0\right\}^* \rightarrow$ Regular
31. $\{xww \mid x,w \in (0, 1)^*\} \rightarrow$ Regular

4 Undecidability

Undecidablity/Decidability Table for Formal Languages

Problem	Regular Language	DCFL	CFL	Recursive Language	Recursively Enumerable Language
1. Is W in L? (membership problem)	✓	✓	✓	✓	×
2. Is L = ϕ? (emptiness problem)	✓	✓	✓	×	×
3. Is L = Finite? (finiteness problem)	✓	✓	✓	×	×
4. Is $L_1 = L_2$? (equivalence problem)	✓	✓	×	×	×
5. Is $L_1 \subseteq L_2$? (subset problem)	✓	×	×	×	×
6. Is 'L' regular? (regularity problem)	✓	✓	×	×	×
7. Is L ambiguous (ambiguity problem)	✓	×	×	×	×
8. Is $L = \Sigma^*$ (Universality problem)	✓	✓	×	×	×
9. Is $L_1 \cap L_2 = \theta$? (disjointedness problem)	✓	×	×	×	×

Problem	Regular Language	DCFL	CFL	Recursive Language	Recursively Enumerable Language
10. Is L = R? Where (R is given regular language	✓	✓	✗	✗	✗
11. Is the intersection of two languages is also a language of the same type?	✓	✗	✗	✓	✓
12. Is the compliment of a languages is also a language of the same type	✓	✓	✗	✓	✗

CLOSURE PROPERTIES TABLE

Property	Regular	DCFL	CFL	CSL	REC	RE
$\cup$	✓	☒	✓	✓	✓	✓
$\cap$	✓	☒	☒	✓	✓	✓
L^C	✓	✓	☒	☒	✓	☒
$\bullet$	✓	☒	✓	✓	✓	✓
L^*, L^+	✓	☒	✓	✓	✓	✓
L^R	✓	☒	✓	No information	✓	✓
$h(L)$	✓	☒	✓		No information	No information
$h^{-1}(L)$	✓	☒	✓			
$L_1 \cap R$	✓	✓	✓	✓	✓	✓
$L_1 - R$	✓	✓	✓	✓	✓	✓
$L_1 \cup R$	✓	✓	✓	✓	✓	✓
$L_1 - L_2$	✓	☒	☒	☒	✓	☒

Some Decidable Problem Related to Theory Machines:

1. State of TM after k(finite) steps? → Decidable
2. Will a string w be accepted by TM after k(finite) steps? → Decidable
3. Will a TM hang within k(finite) steps? → Decidable
4. Whether a given TM will ever make a left move? → Decidable
5. Whether a given TM will print some non-blank character? → Decidable
6. PCP and MPCP problems on unary alphabet → Decidable

Computer Science

7

Compiler Design

CONTENTS

Lexical Analysis

1

INTRODUCTION

A compiler translates the code written in one language to some other language without changing the meaning of the program. With the basic translation mechanism, compiler design works on error detection and recovery.

Before exploring the compiler, it is necessary to know the following concepts:

Preprocessor: A preprocessor, is a part of compiler, that produces input for compilers. It includes, macro-processing, augmentation, file inclusion, language extension etc.

INTERPRETER

Interpreter work is same as compiler, where high level language translated into low-level machine language. The main difference is the way they read the source code or input.

Compiler reads the whole source code at once, creates tokens, check semantics, generates intermediate code, execute the whole program. While interpreter reads a statement from the input, converts it to an intermediate code, execute it, then takes the next statement in sequence.

ASSEMBLER'S

Translator used for assembly language program is known as assembler which convert it into machine code. The output of an assembler is called an object file, which contains a combination of machine instructions as well as the data required to place these instructions in memory.

Linker: Linker is a program to link and merge, different object files together in order to make an executable file. The major task of a linker is to search and locate referenced module/routines in a program and to determine the memory location where these codes will be loaded, making the program instruction to have absolute references.

Loader: Loader is a part of operating system and is responsible for loading executable file into memory and execute them.

Cross-Compiler: A compiler that runs on platform(A) and is capable of generating executable code for platform(B) is called a cross-compiler.

Source to Source Compiler: A compiler that takes the source code of one programming language and translate it into the source code of another programming language is called a source to source compiler.

Phases of Compiler: Compiler works in following two phases:

1. **Analysis Phase:** The analysis phase generates an intermediate representation of the source program and symbol table, which should be fed to the synthesis phase as input.

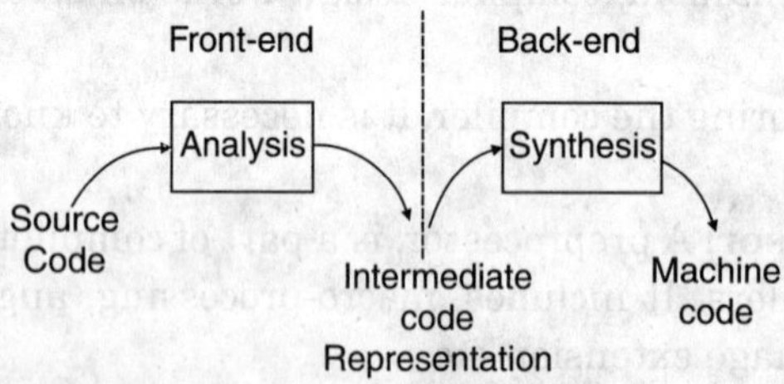

Synthesis Phase: It works as a back-end of the compiler the synthesis phase, generates the target program with the help of intermediate source code representation and symbol table.

COMPILER PROCESS

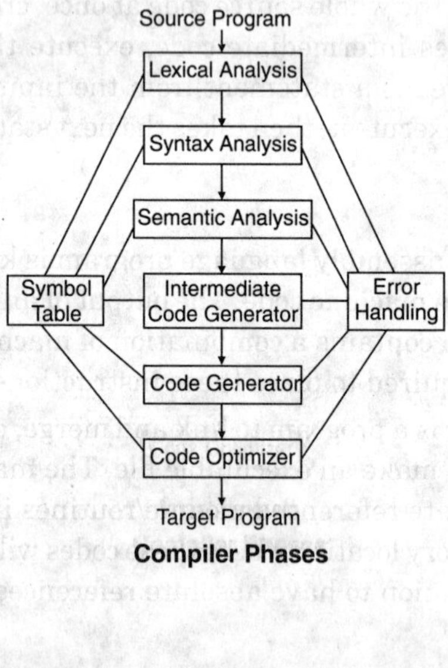

Compiler Phases

Language Processing System

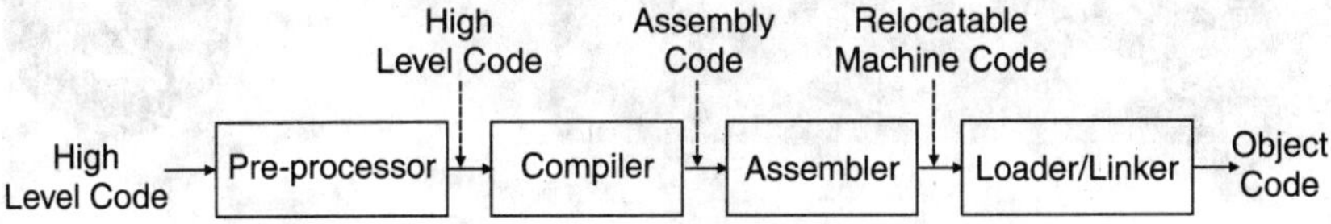

Language Processing System Using Compiler

Lexical Analysis: It is the first phase of any compilation process where it act like a text scanner. This phase scans the source code a stream of characters and converts it into meaning lexemes.

Lexical analyser represents these lexemes in the form of token as:

<token name, attribute-value>

A token can represent more than one lexeme, additional information should be held for that scientific lexeme. The additional information is called as attribute of the token.

If the lexical analyser finds a token invalid, it generates an error. The lexical analyser works closely with the syntax analyser. It reads character stream from the source code, check for legal tokens, and passes the data to syntax analyser.

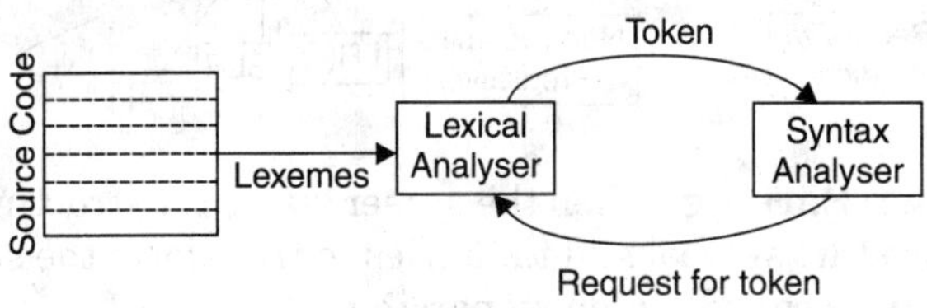

Parsing

2

INTRODUCTION

Syntax analyser is also known as parser. In it context-free grammar describes the production rules of syntax analyser.

The way the production rules are derived, can be categories into two types: top-down parsing and bottom-up parsing.

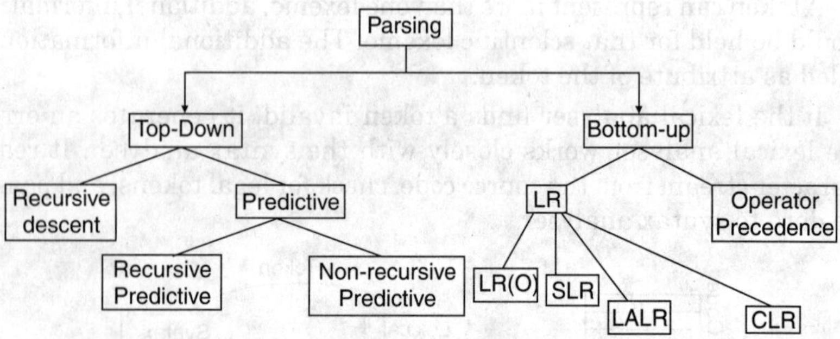

Top-down Parsing: When the parser starts constructing the parse tree from the start symbol and then tries to transform the start symbol to the input, it is called top-down parsing.

- **Recursive-Descent Parsing:** Follows Brute force mechanism and suffers from Backtracking.
- **Backtracking:** It means, if one derivation of production fails, the syntax analyser restart the process using different rules of same production. So this techniques process the input sting more than once to determine the right production.

Note: This technique recursively parses the input to make a parser tree, which may or may not require back-tracking. But the grammar associated with it (if not left factored) cannot avoid back-tracking.

Predictive parsing: A form of recursive-descent parsing that does not require any back-tracking is known as predictive parsing.

To accomplish its tasks, the predictive parser uses a look-ahead pointer, which points to the next input symbols. To make the parser back-tracking free, the predictive parses put some constraints on the grammar and accepts only a class of grammar known as LL(K) grammar.

Top-down parser
↓ Remove left recursion
↓ Left factored grammar
Recursive Descent
↓ Remove Back-tracking
Predictive Parser
↓ USE Table
↓ Remove Recursion
Non- Recursive predictive parser

LL PARSER

An LL parser accepts LL grammar. LL grammar is a subset of context free grammar but with some restriction. It can be implemented by means of both algorithm namely, recursive-descent or table driven.

LL parser is denoted as LL(K). The first L in LL(K) is parsing the input from left to right, the second L in LL(K) stands for left-most derivation and K itself represents the number of look aheads. Generally K = 1, So LL(K) may also be written as LL(1).

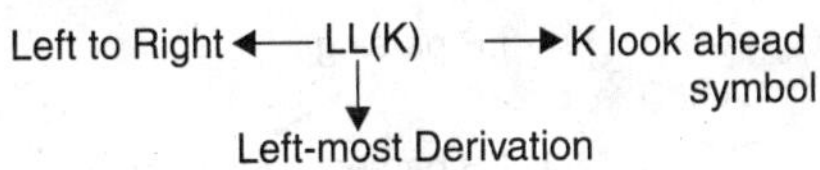

Configuration of LL(1) Parser:

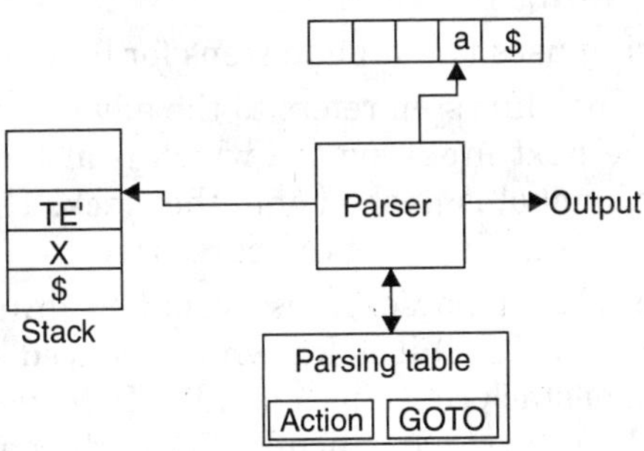

LL(1) Parsing Table Construction: LL(1) grammar is unambiguous, left factored and non left recursive first() and follows() sets are used to construct LL(1) parsing table.

For each rule A → α in grammar G:

(*i*) For each terminal '*a*' contained in FIRST(A) add A → α to [A, a] entry in parsing table if α derives '*a*' as the first symbol.

(*ii*) If FIRST(A) contain 'ε' for each terminal '*b*' in Follow(A) add A → ε to [A, *b*] entry in parsing table.

BOTTOM UP PARSING

Bottom up parsing starts from the leaf nodes of a tree and works in upward direction till it reaches to the root node in it production rules are applied in reverse manner in order to reach the symbol.

- **Handle:** The part of the string that matches with RHS of any production is called as handle.
- **Handle Pruning:** The process of finding the handle and replacing the handle by LHS of corresponding production is called "handle pruning".
- Bottom up parsing can be constructed for both ambiguous and unambiguous grammar, LR for unambiguous grammar and operator precedence parser (opp) for both ambiguous and unambiguous.
- Average time complexity is $O(n^3)$ and handle pruning is major overhead for bottom up parsing.

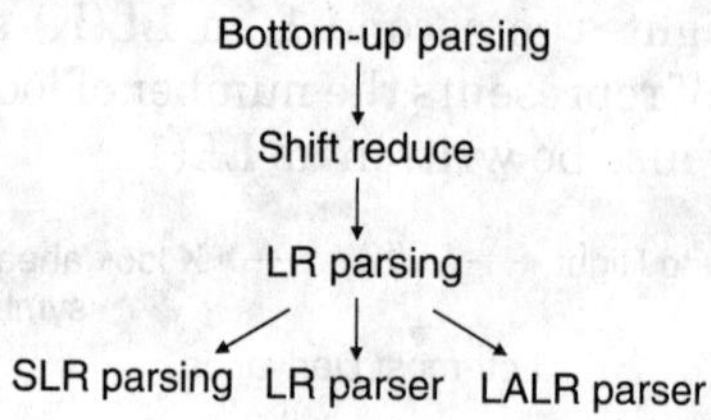

Shift-Reduce Parsing

Shift reduce parsing uses two unique steps for bottom-up parsing.

1. **Shift step:** The shift step refers to the advancement of the input pointer to the next input symbol,which is also called the shifted symbol. The symbol is pushed onto the stack. The shifted symbol is treated as a single node of the parse tree.
2. **Reduce step:** When parser finds a complete grammar rule (RHS) and replace it to (LHS) it is known as reduced step. This occurs when the top of stack contains a handle. To reduce a POP function is performed on the stack which POPS off the handle and replace it with LHS non-terminal symbol.

LR PARSERS

- **LR(0) Parser:**

(*i*) LR(0) parser is constructed for LR(0) grammar in which the parse table is free from multiple entries (conflicts).

(*ii*) **Conflict in LR(0) parser:**

(*a*) **Shift reduce (SR) conflict:** When the same state in DFA contains both shift and reduced items.

$A \rightarrow \alpha \cdot x\beta$ (shifting)

$B \rightarrow \gamma \cdot$ (reduced)

(*b*) Reduce Reduce (RR) conflict

$\left.\begin{array}{l} A \rightarrow \alpha\text{(reduced)} \\ B \rightarrow \gamma\text{(reduced)} \end{array}\right\}$ Both are in same state of DFA

(*iii*) Closure( ) and go to( ) functions are used to create canonical collection of LR items.

(*iv*) LR(0) parsing table construction:

(*a*) If go to $(I_i, a) = I_j$, then set action $[i, a] = S_j$ (shift entry)

(*b*) If go to $(I_i, A) = I_j$, then set action $[i, A] = j$ (state entry)

(*c*) If I_i contains $A \rightarrow \alpha \cdot$ (reduced production) then action [i, all entries] = R_P, (reduced entry), where 'P' is production number $(P : A \rightarrow \alpha)$

(*d*) If $S \rightarrow S$ is in I_i, then set action [i, \$] to accept.

(*v*) If a state contains either SR or RR conflicts then that state is called 'Inadequate State'.

- **Simple LR(1) Parser:**

(*i*) Conflicts in SLR(1) parser:

(*a*) Shift Reduce (SR) conflict:

$A \rightarrow \alpha \cdot x\beta$ (shift)

$B \rightarrow \gamma \cdot$ (reduce)

If $\text{FOLLOW(B)} \cap \{x\} \neq \phi$

(*b*) Reduce Reduce (RR) conflict:

$A \rightarrow \alpha.$

$B \rightarrow \gamma \cdot$ If $\text{FOLLOW(A)} \cap \text{FOLLOW(B)} \neq \phi$

(*ii*) SLR(1) parsing table construction:

(*a*) SLR(1) parsing table construction is same as LR(0) except reduced entries.

(b) If I_i contains $A \rightarrow \alpha$ (reduced production), then find FOLLOW(A) and for every a in FOLLOW(A), set action [*i*. *a*] = R_P{where P is production number}

(*iii*) SLR(1) is powerful then LR(0)

(*iv*) Size of SLR(1) parse table is same as size of LR(0) parse table.

(*v*) Every LR(0) grammar is SLR(1) but every SLR(1) need not be LR(0).

- **Canonical LR(1) or LR(1) Parser:**

(*i*) CLR(1) parsing table construction: Except reduced entries, remaining entries are same as SLR(1).

(*ii*) If I_i contains $A \rightarrow a, \$ \mid a \mid b$ then reduced entry (R_P) $A \rightarrow a$ in row '*i*' under the terminals given by look ahead ($, *a*, *b*) in LR(1) items [R_P entry entered into [*i*, $],[*i*, *a*] and [*i*, *b*]]

- **Look ahead LR(1) Parser:**

(*i*) It is constructed from CLR(1), if two states are having same productions but may contain different look aheads, those two states of CLR(1) are combined into a single state in LALR(1).

(*ii*) There is no chance of SR conflict but there may be chance for RR conflicts in LALR(1) after combining the states of CLR(1) parser.

(*iii*) Conflicts in CLR(1) and LALR(1)

(*a*) SR conflict: $A \rightarrow \alpha \cdot x\beta, a$

$B \rightarrow \gamma \cdot, x \mid y$

(*b*) RR conflict: $A \rightarrow \alpha \cdot, a \mid t_1$

$B \rightarrow \gamma \cdot, a \mid t_2$

(*iv*) Every LALR(1) grammar is CLR(1) but every CLR(1) grammar need not be LALR(1).

(*v*) LALR(1) parsers are often used in practice as parsing tables are smaller than CLR(1) parsing.

PARSERS COMPARISON

- OPP < LL(1) < LR(0) < SLR(1) ≤ LALR(1) ≤ CLR(1)
- Number of states (SLR(1)) =Number of states (LALR(1)) ≤ Number of states (CLR(1))

- LR(0) ⊂ SLR(1) ⊂ LALR(1) ⊂ CLR(1)
- LL(1) ⊂ LALR (1) ⊂ CLR(1)

IMPORTANT DEFINITIONS

1. **Ambiguous Grammar:** For a given input string if there exists 'more than one parse tree' then that grammar is called as "ambiguous grammar".
2. **Left Recursion:** The grammar: $A \to A\alpha \mid \beta$ is left recursive. Top down parsing cannot handle left recursive grammars. So we convert left recursive grammars into right recursive.
3. **Left Recursive Elimination:**
   Left recursive: $A \to A\alpha \mid \beta \Rightarrow A \to \beta A'$ (non left recursive)
   $A' \to \alpha A'/\varepsilon$

   Problem with left recursive grammar is that if such a grammar is used by top down parser (use left most derivation), then there is a danger of going into "infinite loop" while string is parsing.
4. To check whether given grammar is LL(1) or not:
   (*i*) if $A \to \alpha_1 \mid \alpha_2 \Rightarrow \{FIRST(\alpha_1) \cap FIRST(\alpha_2) = \phi\}$
   (*ii*) if $A \to \alpha \mid \varepsilon \Rightarrow \{FIRST(\alpha) \cap FOLLOW(A) = \phi\}$
   } is LL(1)
   - A grammar where its LL(1) parsing table has free from multiple entries is said to be LL(1) grammar.
   - A left recursive grammar cannot be a LL(1) grammar.
   - If a grammar is not left factored, it cannot be a LL(1).
   - An ambiguous grammar cannot be a LL(1) grammar.

Syntax Directed Translation

3

SEMANTIC

Semantics of a language provide meaning to its constructs, like tokens and syntax structure. Semantics help interpret symbols, their types and their relations with each other. The CFG with semantic actions is called as SDT or the translation rules placed in RHS of production.

CFG + Semantic rules = Syntax Directed Definitions

Example: $S \rightarrow AB$ {Print (*)

$A \rightarrow a$ {Print (1)}

Parse tree → SDT → Annotated Parse tree

The following tasks should be performed in semantic analysis

- Scope Resolution
- Type Checking
- Array Bound Checking

USAGE OF SDT

(*i*) SDT is constructed to store the information in symbol table.

(*ii*) It is used to verify the variable declaration.

(*iii*) SDT perform type checking, type conversion, type evaluation.

(*iv*) SDT evaluate algebraic expression etc.

Semantic Errors: There are some of semantic error which a semantic analyser needs to find out:

- Type Mismatch
- Undeclared variable
- Reserve identifies misuse

Multiple declaration of variable in a slope.

Accessing an out of scope variable

Actual and formal parameter mismatch

TYPES OF ATTRIBUTES

1. **Synthesized Attributes:** These attributes get values from the attribute values of their child nodes. To illustrate, assume the following production:

   $$S \rightarrow ABC$$

   If S is taking values from its child nodes (A, B, C) then it is said to be a synthesized attribute, as the values of ABC are synthesized to S.

2. **Inherited Attributes:** In this, inherited attributes can take values from parent or siblings.

   Example: $S \rightarrow ABC$

   A can get values from S, B and C. B can take values from S, A and C, likewise, C can take values from S, A and B.

- A parse tree which shows attribute at each and every node is called as ANNOTATED/DECORATED parse tree.

SDT (SYNTAX DIRECTED DEFINITION TREE)

S-attribute SDT: If an SDT uses only synthesized attributes, it is called as S-attribute SDT. These attributes are evaluated using semantic actions written after production.

S = E. Value + T. Value

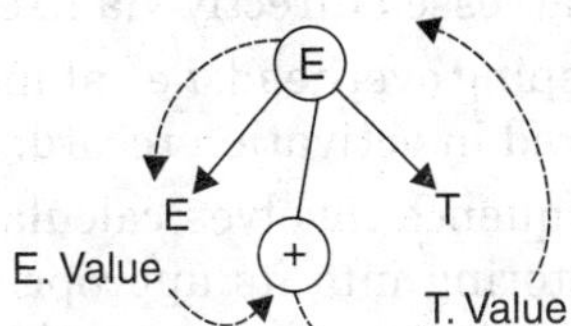

In this S-attribute SDTs are evaluated in bottom up parsing, as the values of parent nodes depend upon the values of the child nodes.

L-attribute SDT: This type of SDT use both synthesized and inherited attributes with restriction of not taking values from right siblings. No non-terminal can get values from the sibling to its right.

Example: $A \rightarrow BCD$ $\{C \cdot i = f(A \cdot i \text{ or } B \cdot i)\}$ or

$\{D \cdot i = f(A \cdot i \text{ or } B \cdot i \text{ or } C \cdot i)\}$ or

$\{B \cdot i = f(A \cdot i)$

Note

- Every L-attributed SDT need not be S-attribute SDT.
- SDT follows Depth First Search Notation.

Runtime Environment

4

Runtime means, a program in execution. Runtime environment is a state of the target machine, which includes software libraries, environment variables etc., to provide service to the process running in the system. Runtime support system is a package, mostly generated with the executable program itself and facilitates the process communication between the process and the runtime environment. It take care of memory allocation and de-allocation while the program is being executed.

Types of Runtime Environment

1. **Fully Static Runtime Environment:** Fully static runtime environment may be useful for the languages in which pointers or dynamic allocation is not possible in addition to no support for recursive function calls
   (*i*) Every procedure will have only one activation record which is allocated before execution.
   (*ii*) Variables are accessed directly via fixed addresses.
   (*iii*) Little book keeping overhead; *i.e.*, at most return address may have to be stored in activation record.
   (*iv*) The calling sequence involves calculation of each argument address and storing into its appropriate parameter location and saving the return address and then a jump is made.
2. **Stack based Runtime Environment:** In this, activation records are allocated (push of the activation records) whenever a function call is made. The necessary memory is taken from stack portion of the program. When program execution returns from function the memory used by the activation record is de-allocated (pop of the activation record). Thus, stack grows and shrinks with the chain of function calls.
3. **Fully Dynamic Runtime Environment:** Functional languages such as Lisp, ML, etc., uses this style of call stack management. Sailently, here activation records are de-allocated only when all references to them have disappeared, and this requires that activation records to dynamically freed at arbitrary times during execution. Memory manager (garbage collector) is needed.

The data structure that handles such a management is heap and thus this is also called as heap management.

ACTIVATION RECORDS

- Information needed by a single execution of a procedure is managed using a contiguous block of storage called "activation record".
- An activation record is allocated when a procedure is entered and it is de-allocated when that procedure is exited.
- It contains temporary data, local data, machine status, optional access link, optional control link, actual parameters and returned value.
  - (*i*) Program Counter (PC) whose value is the address of the next instruction to be executed.
  - (*i*) Stack pointer (SP) whose value is top of the (to of stack, tos).
  - (*iii*) Frame Pointer (FP) which points to the current activation record.

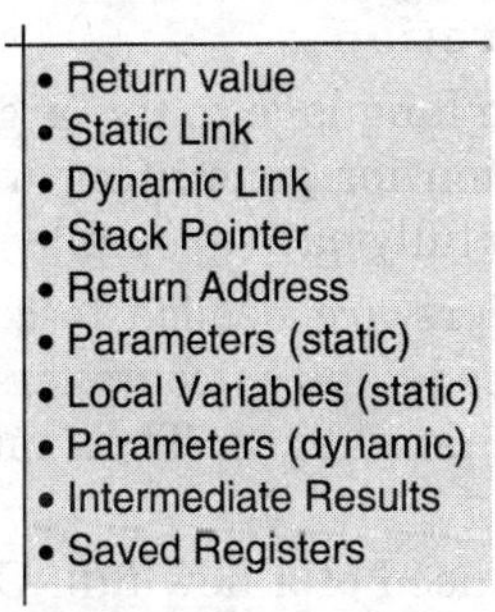

Activation Record Contents

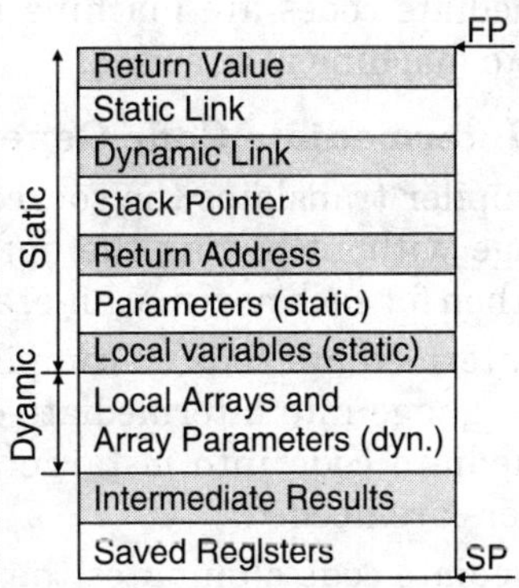

Activations Record

Note

- Activation records are allocated from one of static area (like Fortran 77), stack area (like C or Pascal) and heap area (like lisp).

Intermediate, Target Code Generation and Code Optimization

5

A source code can be directly translated into its target machine, then there is question arise about generating intermediate, which is then translated to machine code.

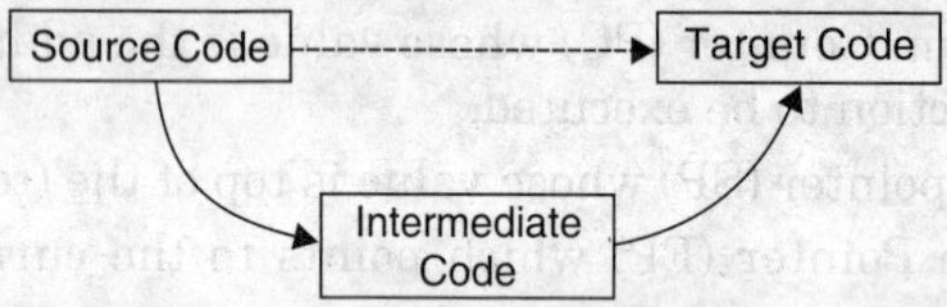

- Intermediate codes are machine independent codes, but they are closed to machine interaction.

Need for Intermediate Code Generation

- If a compiler translates the source language to its target machine language without having the option for generating intermediate codes, then for each new machine, a fully native compiler is required.
- With intermediate code, *n*-compilers are needed to convert each such language into intermediate code and *m*-compilers to convert intermediate code into *m*-target languages. Thus only $(n + m)$ compilers are needed.
- Intermediate code eliminates the need of a new full. Compiler for every unique machine by keeping the analysis portion same for all the compilers.
- Now with intermediate code, it becomes easier to apply the source code modification to improve code performance by applying code. Optimization techniques on the intermediate code.

CODE REPRESENTATION

Intermediate codes can be represented in a variety of ways and they have their own benefits.

- **High Level Intermediate Code Representation:** It is very close to the source language itself. They can be easily generated from the source code and we can easily apply code modification to enhance performance. But for target machine optimization it is less preferred.

- **Low Level Intermediate Code Representation:** This one is close to the target machine, which makes it suitable for register and memory allocation, instruction set selection etc. It is good for machine dependent optimization.

THREE ADDRESS CODE

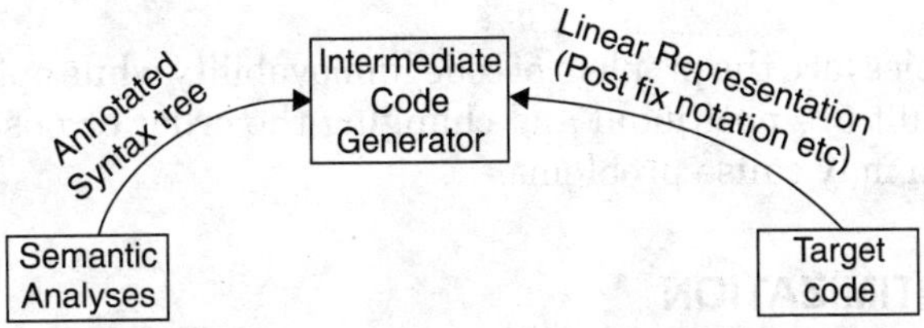

Intermediate code generator gets the input from semantic analyser in the form of an annotated syntax tree which is then converted into linear representation postfix notation. Intermediate code tends to be machine independent code, therefore code generator assumes to have unlimited number of memory storage (register) to generate code.

Example:

$$r_1 = c * d;$$
$$r_2 = b + r_1;$$
$$r_3 = r_1 + r_2;$$
$$a = r_3;$$

{r being used as register in target program}

A three-address code has at most three address location to calculate the expression. A three address code can be in two forms: quadruples and triples.

Quadruples: Each instruction in quadruples presentation is divided into four fields: operator, arg 1, arg 2, and result.

Example:

OP	arg 1	arg 2	Result
*	c	d	r_1
+	b	r_1	r_2
+	r_2	r_1	r_3
=	r_3		a

Triples: Each instruction in triples presentation has three fields: OP, arg 1 and arg 2.

Example:

OP	arg 1	arg 2
*	c	d
+	b	(0)
+	(1)	(0)
=	(2)	

Note: Triples face the problem of code immovability while optimization, as the result are positional and changing the order or position of an expression may cause problems.

CODE OPTIMIZATION

- Optimizations applied on target code (assembly code) is machine dependent optimization.
- Optimization applied on 3-address code is machine independent optimization.
- **Basic Block:** Sequence of consecutive statements in which context enters at beginning and leaves at end without halt or possibility of branching except at the end.
- The optimization which is performed within the block is local optimization.

Machine Independent Optimizations

1. **Loop Optimization:** Process of optimizing within the loop.
   Characteristics of loop optimization.
   (*i*) Code motion/Loop invariant elimination/Frequency reduction:
   Reduce the evaluation frequency of expressions.
   Bring loop-invariant statements out of the loop.
   (*ii*) *Loop Unrolling:* To execute less number of iterations.
   (*ii*) *Loop Jamming/Loop Fusio/Loop Combining:* Combine the bodies of two loops whenever they are sharing same index variable.
2. **Constant Folding:** Replacing the value of constant during compilation is called as folding.
3. **Constant Propagation:** Replacing the value of an expression during compile time is known as constant propagation.

Computer Science

8

Operating System

CONTENTS

1 Processes and Threads

PROCESS CONCEPT

Process

- It is program in execution or an instance of a program.
- It is active entity residing in main memory and program is passive one present on disk.

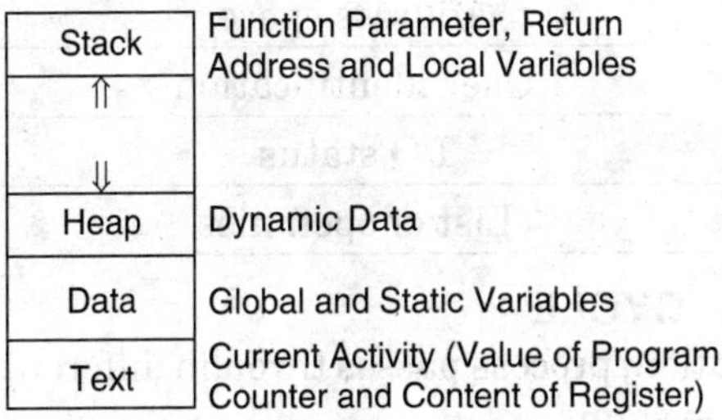

ABSTRACT VIEW OF PROCESS

- Operations
  - ➢ Creating the process.
  - ➢ Scheduling/running
  - ➢ Block, suspend or resume
  - ➢ Termination

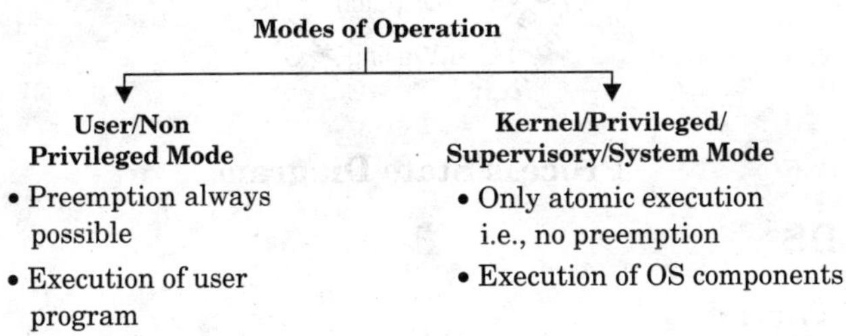

PROCESS CONTROL BLOCK (PCB)

- It is data structure maintained by operating system for every process.
- It is identified by process ID (PID)
- It is maintained throughout its lifetime (till process is terminated)

ATTRIBUTES

Pointer
Process ID
State
Program counter
CPU registers
CPU scheduling information
Memory management information
Accounting information
Address space
User identification
I/O status
List of open files

PROCESS LIFE CYCLE

- During execution; process passes through different states that differ in operating systems.

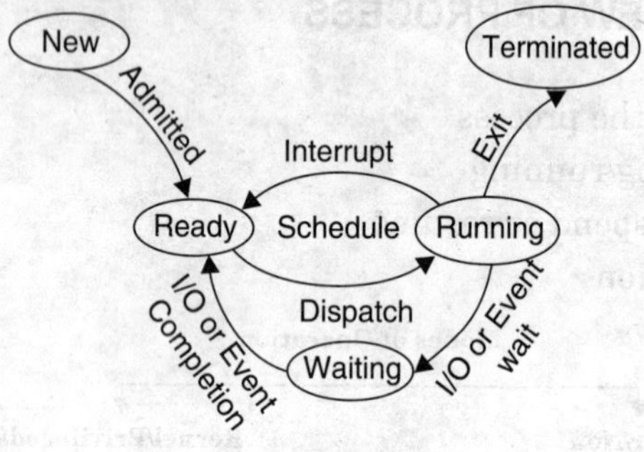

Process State Diagram

THREADS

Need of Thread

There were few problems with traditional processes.

(*i*) Separate address space.

(*ii*) Expensive process creation and switching.

(*iii*) Non-trivial memory sharing among processes.

Concept

- Thread is flow of execution through the process code.
- It has its own program counter, keeping track of next executable instruction, system registers holding current variables and stack with execution history.
- Thread contains shareable information like code segment, data segment and open files.
- These are lightweight process that improves application performance through parallelism.
- Each thread belongs to exactly one process and no thread can exist outside a process.
- It enables parallel execution of application on shared memory multiprocessors.

Types of Thread	
User Level Thread (ULT)	**Kernel Level Thread (KLT)**
• Implemented by thread library at user level. • Faster to create and manage • Generic in nature *i.e.*, can run on any operating system. • Entire process gets blocked when a thread requires an throughout device or any system call.	• Implementation is supported by operating system. • Slower to create and manage. • Specific to operating system. • Only specific thread that require throughout will be blocked.

Benefits

- Provides concurrency within a process.
- Efficient communication.
- Utilization of multiprocessor architecture.
- Resource sharing.

Multithreading

- Combined user level and kernel level thread.
- Multiple threads within the same application can run in parallel on multiple processors.
- A blocking system call need not block the entire process.

Multithreading models

1. **Many-to-one:**
   - Maps many user threads to one kernel thread.
   - Management is done in user space.
2. **Many-to-Many:**
   - Multiplexes any number of user threads onto an equal or smaller number of kernel threads.
3. **One-to-one:**
   - Maps each user thread to kernel thread.
   - **Disadvantage:** Each user thread requires its corresponding kernel thread.

Note: Difference Between Thread and Process

Thread	Process
• Light weight, takes less resources	• Heavy weight, resource intensive
• No need of interaction with OS	• OS interaction is necessary
• Can share same set of open files, child processes	• Each process has own memory and file resources
• While one thread is blocked and waiting; another thread in same task can sun	• If one process is blocked then no other can execute till first one is unblocked.
• A thread can read, write or change another thread's data	• Each process operates independently in multiple process.

IPC, Concurrency and Synchronization

2

IPC–INTER PROCESS COMMUNICATION

- It is a mechanism provided by operating system to allow the process to share data.
    - ➤ **Independent processes:** Processes that can execute independently without affecting the output with execution order.
        - No shared states.
        - Scheduling order is not significant.
    - ➤ **Co-operating processes:** Processes that affects or get affected by execution of other.
        - An IPC mechanism is required for information and data exchange like messages, shared memory, shared variable.
        - Advantages: Shared resources, speed up and modularity.
    - ➤ **Competing processes:** Processes that race to access a shared resource concurrently or simultaneously.

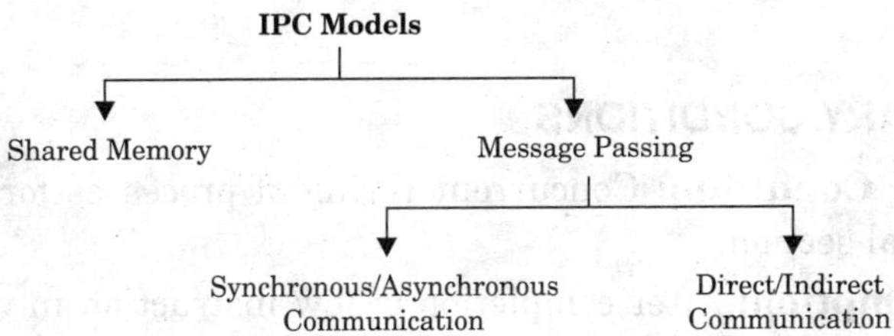

CONCURRENCY

- It is execution of several instructions sequence at the same time.
- Response time of application is better.
- Better performance and resource utilization.

SYNCHRONIZATION

- Mechanism that ensures that concurrent processes do not simultaneously execute some particular program segment called critical section.
- **Critical section:** Code segment accessing shared variable and executed as an atomic action.

- **Critical section problem:** In a group of cooperating processes, at a given point of time, only one process must be executing its critical section

do {

Entry section	← Controls entry and locks the resource
Critical section	← Critical part
Exit section	← Unlocks Resource
Remainder section	← Rest of section

} while (True);

Solution to Critical Section Problem

1. **Mutual Exclusion:** A process mutually excludes itself from competition and agrees to wait whenever the resource is not free.
2. **Progress:**
   (*i*) For first process to progress, resource must be initially free
   (*ii*) Release of lock should make one of the waiting process to access the resource
3. **Bounded Waiting:** Process should have definite waiting time due to mutual exclusion which is done by writing release of locks.

NECESSARY CONDITIONS

(*i*) **Race Condition:** Concurrent racing of processes for accessing critical section.

(*ii*) **Preemption:** After completion of few instruction in user mode, running processes can be preempted.

Synchronization lock can result in:

- Inconsistency
- Data loss
- Deadlocks

Locking Mechanism

- Test and set operation
- Busy Waiting
- Spin locks

Principle of Mutual Exclusion

- It states that no two processes can be simultaneously present in critical section at same time.

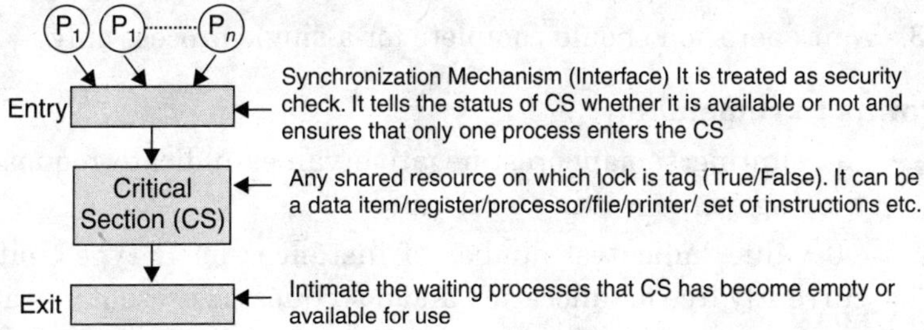

SEMAPHORES

- It is protected integer variable to facilitate and restrict access to shared resources.
- Its value indicate information about lock.

Operations on semaphores	
Wait/(P)/(Down)	**Signal/(V)/Up)**
• Used before entering critical section. • Decrement semaphore value by 1.	• Used after critical section to release acquired lock. • Increment semaphore value by 1.

Wait (P)
Access Critical Section
Signal (V)

Semaphore operations are atomically executed

Types of Semaphore	
Binary Semaphore	**Counting Semaphore**

• Implements mutual exclusion, also called Mutex.
• Initialized to 1 and take values only 0 and 1.
Semaphore *b*;
initial value *b* = 1;
wait (*b*) signal (*b*)
{ {
while (*b* == 0); *b* ++;
b – –;
} }
	• Implements bounded concurrency
	place current process in waiting queue;
	}
	}
	wake-up one waiting process on 'c';
	}
	}

Limitations of Semaphores (Binary)

1. Spin locks or busy wait.
2. Work on single instance of resource.
3. Wait operation should complete for a single process only .

Points to remember

- ➢ In counting semaphores; negative values indicate requests in waiting queue waiting on R type.

  ; 0 value indicates number of instances on R type that are currently free for allocation and no request is present in waiting queue.
- ➢ In Multiple semaphore; proper order of semaphore is very important.

Classical Problems on Synchronization using semaphores

1. **Bounded Buffer Problem:**
   - Or producer–consumer problem.
   - Solution is to create two counting semaphore ("full" and "empty") for keeping track of current number of full and empty buffers.
2. **Reader Writers Problem:** Here some processes called readers reads the shared data and never change it and another processes called writers change the data.

   (*i*) N readers are allowed simultaneously
   (*ii*) If a reader is reading
   (*a*) New reader is allowed
   } Shared Lock

   (*b*) New written is NOT allowed
   (*iii*) If a write is writing
   (*a*) New reader
   (*b*) New writer
   } Not allowed
   } Exclusive Lock
3. **Dining Philosopher Problem:**
   - Involves the allocation of limited resources from a group of processes in a dead lock free and starvation free manners.
   - Number of philosophers; $N \geq 2$

   Solution:

   (a) **(N – 1) and 1**

   Left then right fork ← → Right then left fork (Maximum concurrency)

(b)

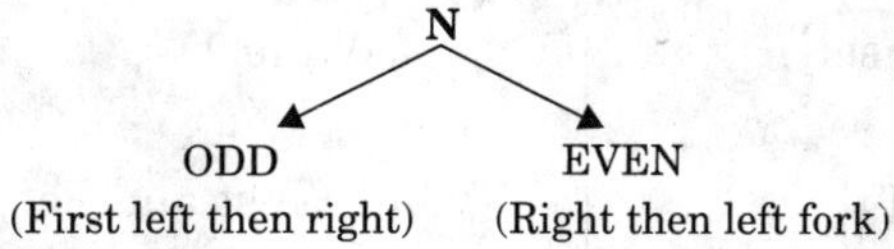

Peterson Solution

- Works only for 2 processes and 1 shared resource
- Requires intervention of operating system for letting only one waiting process to enter critical section.
- Drawback:
  - ➢ Busy wait or spin lock
  - ➢ Priority inversion problem

```
# define N 2
# define TRUE 1
# define FALSE 0
int turn;
int interested [N] = {FALSE};
void entry-section (int process)
{
int other;
other = 1 – process;
interested [process] ≡ TRUE;
turn = process;
while (interested [other] = = TRU0E && turn = = process)
}
Critical section
void exit section (int process)
{
interested [process] = FALSE;
}
```

Test and set Hardware Instructions :

Test: Check if resource is free or busy

Set: Locks the resource

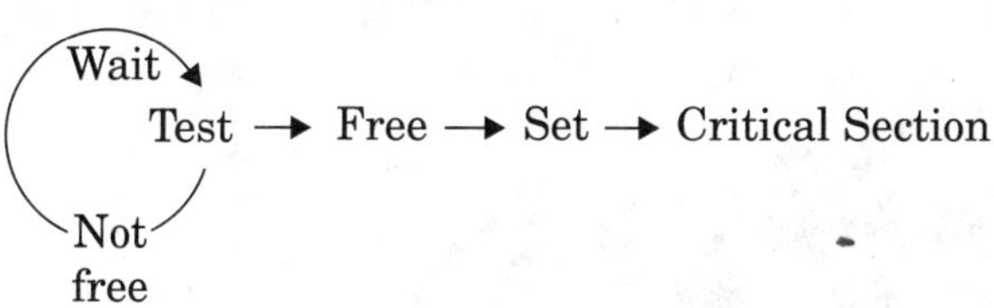

```
Boolean Test and set()
{
    if (Locked ==(T))  ⎫
    {                  ⎬ Test
    Return(T)          ⎭
else
{
    Locked = T  ⎫
                ⎬ Set
    Return(F)   ⎭
    }
}
```

```
    While(1)
{
while (Test and Set ())
    }
        Do-nothing
    }
  Access Critical Section
   Locked = F // Release of
                        Lock
    }
```

MONITOR

- A special module that includes variables and data structures grouped together.
- Processes running outside monitor do not have access to its variables and structures but they can activate the internal procedures.
- It follows rule that 'only one process can be active at any time'.
- It separates use locks for mutual 'exclusion' and 'condition variables for scheduling constraints'.
- Monitor is a lock that manages concurrent access to shared data, with zero or more conditional variables.
    - lock provides mutual exclusion to shared data
    - A conditional variable allows a queue of waiting processes while being inside a critical section.

3 Deadlock

INTRODUCTION

- Deadlock are a set of blocked processes each holding a resource and waiting to acquire a resource held by another process.
- Minimum 2 processes are required for deadlock.

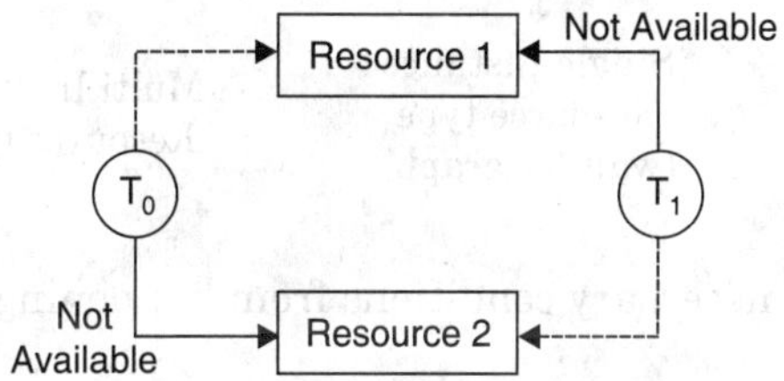

Necessary conditions for deadlock

These four conditions are simultaneously required for deadlock to happen.

1. **Mutual Exclusion:** Only one process at a time can use the source
2. **Hold and wait:** Process must be prevented from holding one or more resources while simultaneously waiting for other.
3. **No pre-emption:** A resource can only be released voluntarily by the process holding it after task completion.
4. **Circular wait:** Process should request resources only in strictly increasing or decreasing order.

   Let $P_0, P_1, \ldots, P_n$ be the processes and $R_0, R_1, \ldots, R_n$ be the resources P_0 is holding R_0 and waiting for R_1 which is held by P_1.

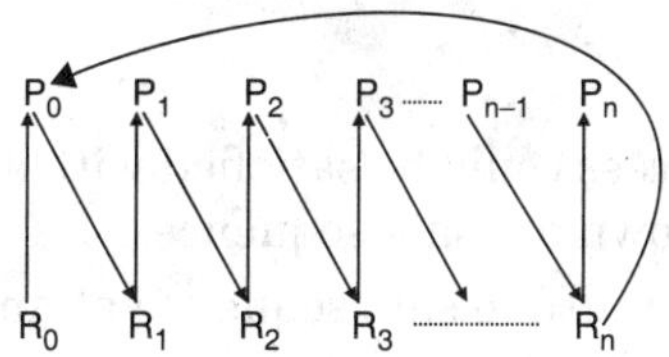

EXCEPTION

If RAG (Resource Allocation Graph) has only single or only multiple or single and multiple instances then; cycle is only necessary condition for deadlock.

Handling Deadlock

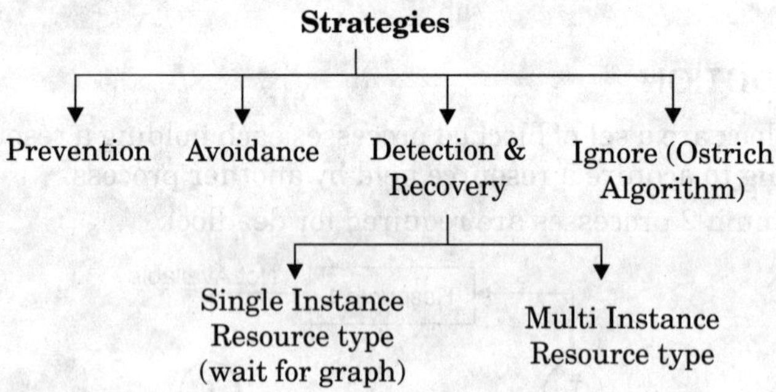

Prevention

Present any four necessary conditions from happening

It involves:

- Infinite resources
- No sharing
- No waiting
- Preempt resource
- Allocate all resources at the beginning
- Make every one use the same ordering in accessing resources.
- A combination of techniques.

AVOIDANCE

- System dynamically considers every request and decides whether it is safe or not.
- 2 algorithms are:
  1. Resource allocation graph algorithm: Handles 1 instance of each resource type.
  2. Banker's algorithm: Handles multiple instance of each resource type.
- System is safe if;
  - ➢ Need of all process could be satisfied with available resources in some order known as "safe sequence".
  - ➢ There may be multiple safe sequence at any given time.
  - ➢ Need = Max – Allocation.

DETECTION AND RECOVERY

- Allow a system to inter deadlock than detect it and eliminate it.
- Following approach is followed:
  - ➢ Scanning of resource allocation graph
  - ➢ Detecting cycle in a graph
  - ➢ Recovery from deadlock

Detection on algorithm activation

– No or less CPU utilization.

– Most processes are blocked.

- Deadlock is examined whether it is present or not.

Recovery after detection; recovery is done by:

***(i)* Process Termination:**

(*a*) About all deadlocked processes.

(*b*) About one process at time until deadlock cycle is eliminated.

Disadvantage: Overheads present.

***(ii)* Resource preemption:** Incrementally preempt and re-allocate resources until circular wait is broken.

- ➢ **Select a victim:** Resource to be preempted.
- ➢ **Rollback:** Rollback to safe state and restart.
- ➢ **Starvation:** Pick victim only small (finite) number of lines.

$$r \geq P(n - 1) + 1$$

where; r = number of deadlock free available resources.

n = maximum number of resources needed by each process.

P = number of processes.

4 CPU Scheduling

INTRODUCTION

- CPU scheduling makes full use of CPU in efficient and faster manner by allowing a process to use CPU write execution of another process is on hold due to unavilability of resource.
- Multiprogramming: Maximizes CPU utilization with some process running at all times
- Time Sharing: Ensures that CPU is switched so frequently among processes that user can interact with each running program. Response time should be short.
- Scheduling queue

  There are 3 queue for scheduling.

  (*i*) **Job Queue :** process that enter the system is kept in this queue.

  (*ii*) **Ready Queue :** contains process residing in main memory and are waiting to execute.

  (*iii*) **Device Queue :** contains process waiting for a particular I/O device. Each process has its own device queue.

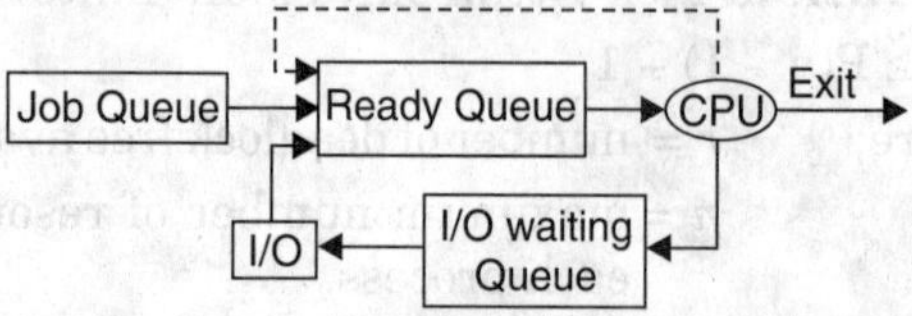

SCHEDULER

Special system software that handles scheduling. They select the job to be submitted into the system and decide which process to run.

Types		
Long-term (JOB SCHEDULER)	**Short-term (CPU SCHEDULER)**	**Medium-term (SWAPPING)**
• Controls degree of multiprogramming. • Determine which programs are admitted to the system for processing.	• These are dispatchers and decides which process to execute next.	• Handles process swapping by removing process from memory and later reentering it to continue the execution.

Context Switch

- Mechanism to store and restore the state or content of a CPU in PCB so that execution of process can be resumed from same point,
- Enables multiple process to share CPU hence supporting multitasking.
- It is pure overhead as system does no useful work while switching.

Dispatcher

- Module that gives CPU control to the process selected by CPU scheduler.
- Functions are switching content, switching to user mode are jumping to proper location in user program to restart it.
- **Dispatch Latency:** Time taken by dispatcher to stop one process and start another running.

Scheduling Criteria

1. **CPU Utilization:** CPU should be working most of the time. So it should be as busy as possible.
2. **Throughput:** Total number of processes completed per unit time.
3. **Turn around time:** Amount of time taken to execute a process Completion Time-Arrival Time.
4. **Waiting time:** Amount of time a process has been waiting in the ready queue to get CPU.
   Turnaround Time–Burst Time
5. **Response time:** Amount of time taken by process when request was submitted until the first response is produced.
   First Response Time–Arrival Time.

CPU SCHEDULING ALGORITHM

Algorithms are classified as:

- Priority /Non priority
- Premptive/Non preemptive.

1. **First come First serve (FCFS)/First-in First-out (FIFO)**
   - Execution of jobs are on first come, first served basis and implements FIFO queue.
   - Non preemptive algorithm
   - Easy to understand and implement.

   Drawback
   - Poor performance due to high average waiting time
   - **Convoy effect:** Slowing down of whole operating system because of few slow processes.

2. Shortest Job First (SJF/Shortest Job Next (SJN)

- Non-preemptive algorithm that favours shorter jobs first.
- Implemented in systems where CPU time required is known in advance.
- Minimize waiting time.

Draw Back

- Impossible to implement in interactive process where required CPU time is not known
- Starvation

3. Shortest Job Remaining Time First (SRTF)

- Preemptive SJF is SRTF
- Processor is allocated to the job closest to completion but can be preempted by never ready job with shorter completion time.

4. Priority Based Scheduling

- Processes are assigned a priority and one with highest priority is executed first.
- It is non–preemptive and most commonly used same priority processes are excuted on basis of FCFS

  Drawback: Starvation-low priority processes wait indefinitely

  Solution to starvation

  Aging: It increase priority of processes that have been waiting for a long time.

5. Round Robin Scheduling

- Preemptive algorithm designed for time sharing system.
- CPU is allocated to each process for certain time interval called Time Quantum or Time Slice.
- Content switching is used to save states of preempted processes.

6. Highest Response Ratio Next

- Non-preemption algorithm
- Process with higher response ratio is executed first.
- Response Ratio = $\dfrac{\text{Waiting time + Service time}}{\text{Service time}}$

7. Multilevel Queue Scheduling

- They use other existing algorithms to group and schedule jobs.
- Multiple queues are maintained for processes with common characteristics.
- Each queue can have its own scheduling algorithms.

- Priorities are assigned to each queue.

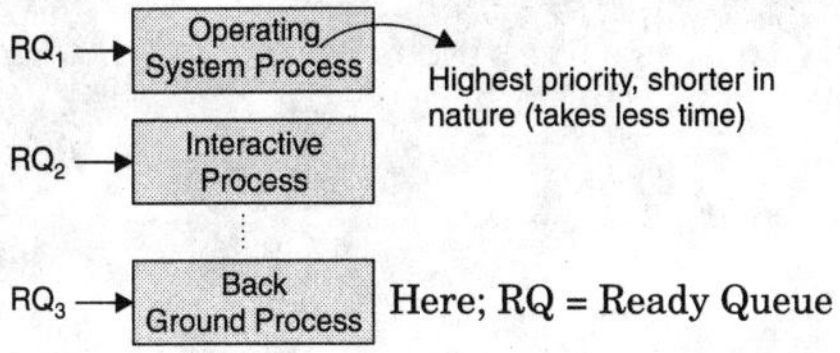

8. Multilevel Feedback Queue Scheduling

- It allows process to move between queues.
- It adjusts priority of each job hence avoiding starvation in following manner
  - Job starts in highest priority queue.
  - If time slice expires; job is dropped by one level.
  - If time slice is not expired; job is pushed up by one level.

9. Lottery Scheduling

- Adaptive scheduling addressing fairness problem of multi-level feed back queues.
- Here, every job is given some lottery ticket number then, on each time slice, a winning ticket is picked randomly.
- On average;

  Allotted CPU Time = Number of tickets given to each job.

Memory Management and Virtual Memory

5

MEMORY MANAGEMENT

- It handles or manages primary memory and moves processes back and furth between main memory and disk during execution.
- Keeps track of each and every memory location.

Dynamic loading

- Library is loaded into the memory during load or run time.
- A routine is not loaded until all of them are in "relocatable format".

Dynamic linking

- Linking is done during load or runtime and not during exe creation.
- Operating system support is needed.
- DLL–dynamic link library – links dynamically

Static linking

- All modules of a program are stored in memory before calling.

Static loading

- At time of loading, the absolute program is loaded into memory in order for execution to start.

MEMORY MANAGEMENT TECHNIQUES

Memory Management Techniques	
Contiguous (CG)	**Non-contigous (NCG)**
Program is stored at only one place. This approach is centralized.	Program is not centralized, it is distributed memory as per availability.
1. Multiprogramming with Fixed Task (MFT).	1. Paging
2. Multiprogramming with Variable Task (MVT).	2. Segmentation
3. Overlays	3. Segmented paging
4. Buddy system (Dynamic Merging)	4. Virtual memory (Demand paging)

PARTITIONS

- Main Memory is divided into multiple partitions, usually contigous areas of memory.
- The functions that can be used are:
  1. Allocation
  2. Protection-using limit registers.
  3. Free space management
  4. Deallocation

Goals:

- Fragmentation: minimum wastage of memory.
- Run larger programs in smaller memory area.

CONTIGUOUS MEMORY ALLOCATION

- The goals of partitions are supported by overlays and virtual memory hence increasing degree of multiprogramming resulting in more CPU utilization and increased throughput.

OVERLAYS

- Focus on a single process information retained in RAM at a time.
- Supports sequencing problem but not multitasking and multiprogramming.
- Possible when program is divided into independent modules.

MULTIPROGRAMMING WITH FIXED TASK

- Maximum process size $\propto$ Maximum partition size.
- Degree of multiprogramming $\propto$ Number of partitions.
- Suffers from both Internal External fragmentation.

MULTIPROGRAMMING WITH VARIABLE TASK:

- Degree of multiprogramming varies.
- Suffers from only External Fragmentation.
- Worst Fit is the best allocation policy.

BUDDY SYSTEM:

- Allocates memory from a fixed size segment with physically contigous pages.
- The adjacent buddies are quickly combined to form larger segment by technique called 'coalescing'.

ALLOCATION POLICIES

1. **First Fit:** Allocation of first available free space that is big enough.
2. **Best Fit:** Allocation of smallest available free space that is big enough and best for program
3. **Worst Fit:** Allocation of largest available free space.

FRAGMENTATION

The loading and removal of process from memory lead to broken pieces of free memory space.

It leads to non allocation of memory due to small size thus memory blocks remains unused. This problem is known as Fragmentation.

Types of Fragmentation	
External Fragmentation	**Internal Fragmentation**
• Total memory space is enough to satisfy a request or reside a process but is non contiguous so remain unused.	• Assigned memory block is bigger therefore some portion remains unused as other process cannot use it.
• Can be reduced by compaction or shuffling memory contents to place all memory together in one large block. Or non contiguous memory allocation.	• Can be reduced by effectively assigning the smallest partition that is big enough for process.

Compaction:

- Processes are on one side and free space is on other side in the memory.
- During memory compaction.
  (*i*) Block processes for compaction.
  (*ii*) Move them towards lower address space.
  (*iii*) Allocate memory for pending request.
  (*iv*) Resume blocked process w.r.t. compaction.
- It consumes CPU time (overhead).
- Program need to support the dynamic allocation.

NON–CONTIGOUS ALLOCATION

- Size of Logical address space (LAS) (CPU) generated ≥ physical address space (Main memory generated).
- Larger programs can run in smaller memory areas thus efficient use of multiprogramming.

PAGING

- Technique in which process address space is broken into blocks of same size called pages.
- Size of page – 2^n (between 512 bytes and 8192 bytes)
- Process size = Number of pages.
- Main memory is divided into small fixed sized blocks of memory called Frames whose size is same as page size to avoid External Fragmentation.

Logical Address Space

- Logical Address Space is divided into equal size pages.
- Page size (PS) is generation of power of 2.
- Number of pages in LAS (N) = $\frac{\text{LAS}}{\text{PS}}$.
- Page No (P) bits = $[\log_2 N]$.
- Page offset depends on page size.
- Page No dependents on number of pages.
- Page offset (d) bits = $[\log_2 \text{PS}]$.

Physical Address Space

- Physical Address Space is divided into equal size frames (Page frames).
- Frame size = Page size
- Number of frames (M) = $\frac{\text{PAS}}{\text{PS(FS)}}$
- Frame No (f) bits = $[\log_2 M]$
- Frame offset = Page offset = d

Page Table

- Keeps track of the relation between a page of a process to a frame in physical memory.
- Organised as series of entries.
- Number of page table entries = Number of pages in logical address space
- Its entry contain frame number.
- A 4-bit per page table entry is maintained:
  - ***(i)*** **Use bit:** Set when page is referenced cleared by clock algorithm.
  - ***(ii)*** **Modified bit:** Set when page is modified cleared when page is written to disk.
  - ***(iii)*** **Valid bit:** Set when program can make legitimate use of this page table entry.

***(iv)* Read only:** Set for program to read the page but do not modify it.

- Pagetable (PT) size in bytes = N × *e*; *e* = page table entry size in bytes ($e \geq 1$).
- 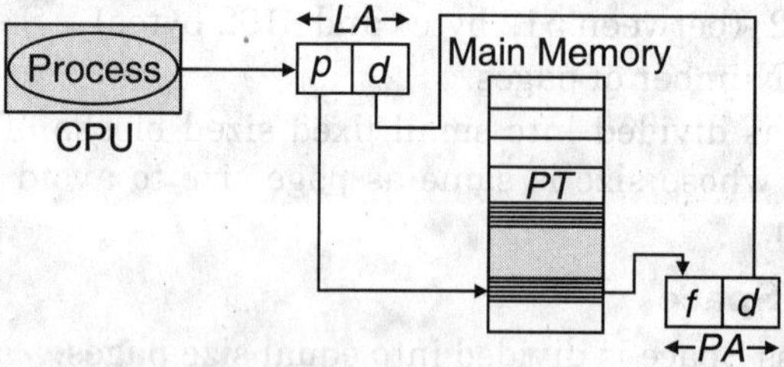

Performance of Paging

- TLB – Translation look a side buffer – cache used to improve virtual address translation speed:
- **Paging without TLB:**
  (*i*) Main Memory Access Time = '*m*'
  (*ii*) Effective Memory Access Time (EMAT) = '2*m*'
- **Paging with TLB:**
  (*i*) TLB Access Time = '*c*' [$c <<< m$]
  (*ii*) TLB Hit Ratio $(x) = \frac{\text{Number of hits}}{\text{Total References}}$
  (*iii*) EMAT $= x\,(c + m) + (1 - x)(c + 2m)$

MULTILEVEL PAGING

- Large page table is not desirable because they take lot of memory.
- Reducing page table size:
  (*i*) Increase page size-leads to internal fragmentation
  (*ii*) Multilevel paging.
- Optimal size of page:
  LAS = '*s*' bytes
  Page table entry size ='*e*' bytes
  Page size (PS) = P
  Page table (PT) size $= \frac{S}{P} \times e$
- Internal Fragmentation (IF) = P/2
- Total overhead = PT size + IF $= \left(\frac{P}{2} + \frac{S}{P} \times e\right)$ = Should be minimum

- Differentiating w.r.t to P

$$\frac{d}{dp}\left(\frac{P}{2}+\frac{S}{P}\times e\right) \Rightarrow \frac{1}{2}+\left(\frac{-1}{P^2}\times Se\right)=0$$

$$\Rightarrow \qquad \frac{Se}{P^2}=\frac{1}{2}$$

$$\Rightarrow \qquad P=\sqrt{2Se}$$

- Performance of multilevel paging:

$$\textbf{EMAT} = x(c+m)+(1+x)\,(c+(n+1)\,m)$$

where n is number of levels in paging, c is cache access time and m is memory access time.

Difference between Paging and Segmentation

Paging	Segmentation
• Contiguous range of memory addresses mapped to physical memory.	• An independent address space. Each segment has address in range from O to max value.
• Only one linear address space	• Many address spaces
• No sharing of procedures between users.	• Procedures are shared
• It is a physical unit	• It is logical unit
• Page is of fixed size	• Segment is of arbitary size
• Internal fragmentation in last page	• No internal fragmentation
• No external fragmentation	• External fragmentation present.

VIRTUAL MEMORY

- Memory that appears to exist as main storage although most of it is supported by data held in secondary storage.
- It given an illusion to the programmer that huge amount of memory is available.

Page Faults

- An interrupt occurred when program request data that is not in real memory. The data is fetched from virtual memory and loaded into RAM.
- More page faults, more page fault service time leading to increased execution time and decreased throughput.

Services

(*i*) Process gets blocked

(*ii*) Change the mode bit
Virtual Memory Manager (VMM) runs in kernel mode

(*iii*) VMM → Device Manager → Device Driver → Disk(Device)

(*iv*) Cases:
(*a*) Empty frame may be available
(*b*) No empty frame is available ⇒ Use page replacement algorithm

Performances of Virtual Memory

Effective Memory Access Time (EMAT):

$$\mathbf{EMAT_{DP} = P \times \boldsymbol{s} + (1 - P)\boldsymbol{m}}$$

Main Memory Access Time = '*m*' [in *n* sec/μsec]

PFST = '*s*' [*s* >>> *m*](in msec)

Page fault rate = 'P'

Page hit ratio = 1 – P

Implementing Virtual Memory

DEMAND PAGING

- Pages of data are copied from disk to RAM only when they are needed.
- The page tables need to sometimes point to the disk locations as opposed to memory locations.
- An additional valid or present bit is needed.
  → If present → page table entry points to page in memory.
  → If not present → a reference to an invalid (page fault) will cause hardware to trap.
- The OS performs following steps while running another process in meantime.
  (a) Choose an old page in memory to replace
  (*b*) If the old page has been modified, write contents back to disk
  (*c*) Change the corresponding page table entry and TLB entry
  (*d*) Load new page into memory from disk
  (*e*) Update page table entry
  (*f*) Continue the process
- It provides large virtual memory and more efficient use of memory.
- No limit on degree of multiprogramming.
- Drawback: Number of tables and amount of overhead for page handling are greater.

PAGE REPLACEMENT

- Technique that helps to decide which memory pages to swap out, write to disk when a page of memory needs to be allocated
- Minimizes total page miss balancing it with cost of primary storage and processor time of the algorithm itself.
- **Page Reference String:** Set of successively unique pages referred in given list of logical address or virtual address
- **Frame Allocation Policies:** All frames are not allocated, less than maximum demand are allocated.

  Total number of frames '*m*'

  Total number of processes = '*n*' [P_1, P_2, ..., P_n]

  Total demand of all processes = S = $\sum_{i=1}^{n} s_i$ $(s >>> m)$

Important

If process requires '*n*' frames and all frames are allocated at once by operating system then; No need of page replacement algorithm.

PAGE REPLACEMENT ALGORITHMS

First-in-First-Out (FIFO)

- Oldest page in main memory is replaced.
- Easy to important
- In general; with increase in number of page frames, page fault should decrease out sometimes they increase leading to unnatural behaviour called "Belady's Anamoly".

Optimal Page

- Lowest page faults rate
- Replace the page that will not be used for longest period of time.
- Does not follow Beladys Anamoly.
- Usually used as Benchmark for measuring performance of other algorithms.

Least Recently Used (LRU)

- Replace the page which has not been used for the longest time in main memory.
- Performance is closer to optimal.
- Time of reference is criteria

Most Recently Used (MRV)

- Replace the page that is used most recently.
- Time of Reference is criteria of selection.

COUNTING ALGORITHMS

LFU	MFU
Least Frequently Used	Most Frequently Used

LRU Approximation

- Variation of LRU.
- Approximation to the behaviour of LRU but are not exactly LRU.
- Reference bit
  - 0 [Page is not referred so far during current time period]
  - 1 [Page is referred atleast once during current time period]

Clock Algorithm

- Also called as Second Chance Algorithm
- FIFO replacement algorithm.
- Criteria – Arrival time and reference bit
- Page given a second chance can be replaced only after all other pages have been replaced (FIFO) or given second chance.

ENHANCED SECOND–CHANCE ALGORITHM

- Preference is given to those pages which have been modified to reduce the number of I/OS required.
- Criteria: Reference Bit and Modify/Dirty Bit.
- Modify Bit
  - 0 [Page is Clean]
  - 1 [Page is modified]

THRASHING

- In virtual memory when excessive paging takes place, it is called Thrashing.
- System spends more time paging then executing.
- Occurs when memory is over committed and pages are tossed out while still needed.

- CPU utilization is very low.

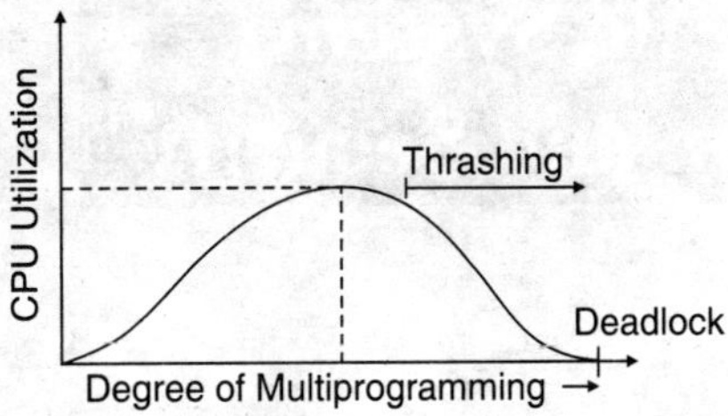

Reasons of Thrashing

- **Primary Reason**

  (*a*) lack of memory frames

  (*b*) high degree of multiprogramming.

- **Secondary reason**

  (*a*) Page replacement policy

  (*b*) Page size
  - → small: more page fault
  - → large: less page fault but internal fragmentation.

Control Strategies

Prevention
- Controlling the degree of multiprogramming

Detection
- Low CPU utilization
- High degree of multiprogramming
- High paging disk utilization

Recovery
- Process suspension
- Increase RAM

INVERTED PAGE TABLE (IPT)

- Global page table that is only one table in entire system.
- It is linear array that stores one entry per physicall frame.
- The page table entry is:

  < pid (process id), P (virtual page number) >

  and Index of each location is address of physical frame.

I/O and File Systems, Protection and Security

6

FILE SYSTEM

File

- A named collection of related information recorded on secondary storage. It is sequence of bits, bytes, lines or records.
- It is Data Structure having definition, structure, operation and attributes.
- **Structure**
  → Flat (series of bytes)
  → Records (Pull and Push, Read and Write)
  → Tree (B, B^+ trees)
- **Operation:** Create, Open, Read, Write, Modify, Seek, Copy, Move, Rename, Close, Delete.
- **Attributes:** Name, Type, Size, Owner, Path, Location etc.
- **Directory:** Metadata of files *i.e.*, files containing information about files.

FILE USAGE PATTERN

- Most files are small and are referenced mostly.
- Large files account for most of the bytes transferred between memory and disk, using up most of the disk space.

FILES ACCESS MECHANISMS

- Manner in which record of files may be accessed.
  (*i*) **Sequential Access:** records are accessed in some sequence.
  (*ii*) **Direct/Random Access:** records are directly accessed by their address.
  (*iii*) **Indexed Sequential Access:** Index for each file is created which is then searched sequentially.

COMPONENTS

- **Disk Management:** Organises disk blocks into files
- **Naming:** Provides file names and directories to users, instead of track and sector numbers.
- **Protection:** Keeps information secure from other users.
- **Reliability:** Protects information loss due to system crashes.

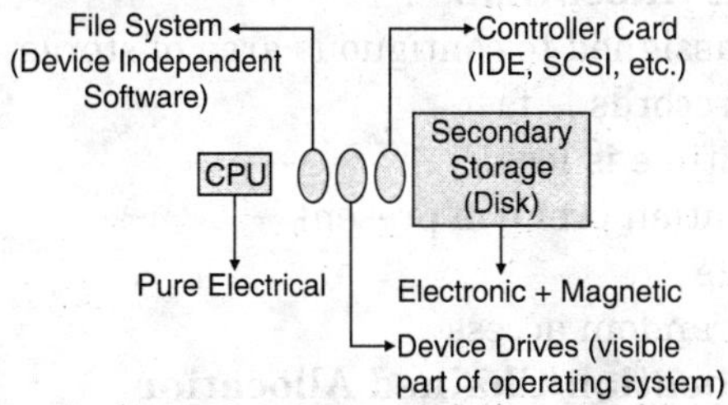

FILE SYSTEM STRUCTURE

- File system allows the data to be stored, located and retrieved easily.
- Certain defined structure is there for every file.
  - (*i*) **Text File:** Sequence of characters organised into lines.
  - (*ii*) **Source File:** Sequence of procedure and function.
  - (*iii*) **Object File:** Sequence of bytes organized into blocks
- **Levels of file system:**

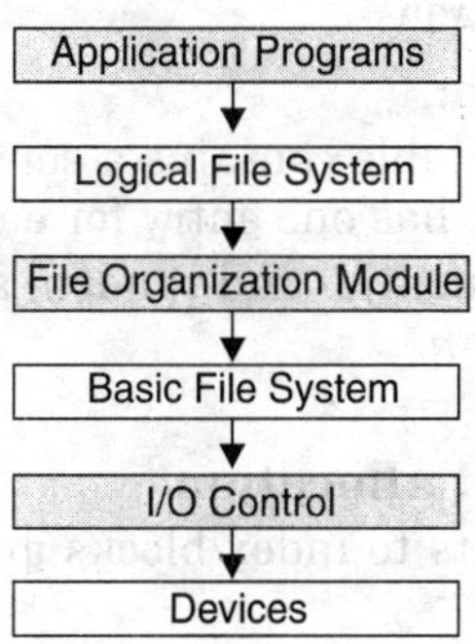

LOGICAL STRUCTURE OF DISK

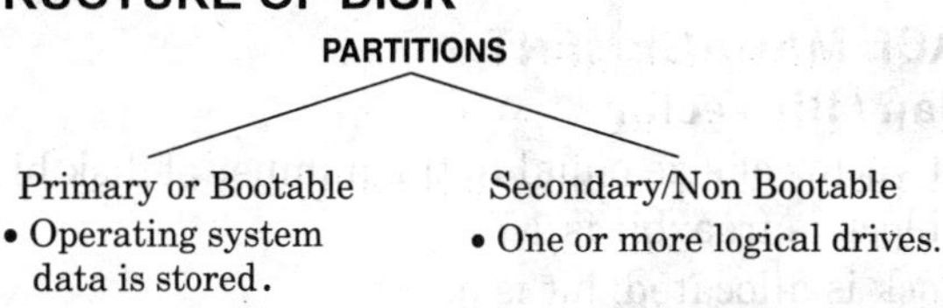

FCB–FILE CONTROL BLOCK:

Contains file information like ownership, permission and location.

(*i*) **UNIX:** UNIX FILE SYSTEM

(*ii*) **Windows:** FAT, FAT32, WTFS.

(*iii*) **Linux:** Extended file system

Allocation Methods

(*i*) **Contiguous Allocation:**
- Files are assigned to contiguous area of storage
- Access of records is fast
- Disk seek time is less
- Fragmentation problem present
- Not flexible
- Supports random access

(*ii*) **Linked Allocation/Chained Allocation:**
- Disk based version of linked list.
- Pointer of first and last block is available in directory and each block has pointer to next one.
- Flexible.
- Effective for sequential access but seek time is long.
- Extra storage space is required for pointers.
- Less reliable as pointer may loss/damage.
- Suffers from external fragmentation.
- MS-DOS file system implement linked list files by using File Attribute Table (FAT).

(*iii*) **Indexed Allocation:**
- The file allocation table contains a separate one-level index for each file and index has one entry for each portion allocated.
- Supports both sequential and random access.
- No fragmentation
- Flexible.

(*iv*) **Multilevel Indexed Allocation:**
- Index entries points to index blocks and first pointer points to data blocks.
- Single Indirect Block-contains additional pointers to data block.
- Double indirect Block-contain pointers to single indirect blocks.

FREE SPACE MANAGEMENT

1. **Bit Map / Bit Vector**
   - A bit vector of size equal to the number of disk block is used.
   - If a block is free; bit is 1.
   - If block is allocated; bit is 0.

Advantages:

- Simple and Efficient to find free blocks.
- Useful when kept in main memory, but not suitable for larger disk size.
- To find non-zero value;

  Block number = (Number of bits per word) × (number of zero words) + offset of first 1 bit.

Consider a disk with 'B' blocks, 'F' free, 'D'–Disk Block Address (DBA), 'S'–Disk Block size in Bytes (DBS).

$$\left.\begin{array}{l}\text{Actual Disk size} = \text{BS} \\ \text{Maximum possible Disk size} = 2^{\text{D}} \times \text{S}\end{array}\right\} \therefore \boxed{\text{B} \leq 2^{\text{D}}}$$

Condition in which free list uses less space than BitMap.

BitMap → 'B' bits

Free List → F × D bits $\boxed{\text{FD} < \text{B}}$

2. **Linked list Approach**
   - All free disk blocks are linked together.
   - Traversing the free list is difficult.
3. **Grouping**
   - Address of n-free blocks are stored in first free block.
   - First $n - 1$ of these blocks are actually free.
   - Last block contains address of another n block.
   - Address of large number of free blocks can be quickly found.
4. **Counting:** We usually allocate and free a number of contiguous blocks at the same time.
   (*a*) Rather than have the free-space list contain just block numbers.
   (*b*) The free-space list can contain paris (block number, count).
   (*c*) Although each entry is larger, the list, in general, will take less space.

DISK SCHEDULING

- It schedules I/O requests arriving for disk hence enhancing disk seek time.
  Also called I/O scheduling.

- **Seek time:** Time taken to locate the disk arm to a specified track where data is to be read or write.
- **Rotational latency:** Time taken by desired disk sector to rotate into a position so that it can access read/write heads.

- **Transfer time:** Time to transfer the data.
- Disk access time = Seek time + Rotational latency + Transfer time.

ALGORITHMS

1. **FCFS-First Come First Serve:**
   - Requests are addressed in order of their arrival in disk queue.
   - Every request fair chance.
   - No indefinite postponement.
   - It does not optimize seek time.
   - Does not provide best possible service.
2. **SSTF-Shortest Seek Time First:**
   - Requests with shortest seek time is executed first.
   - Seek time is calculated in advance resulting in execution of request near disk arm.
   - It increase the throughput and decreases Average response time.
   - Overheads are present.
   - Can cause starvation.
3. **Scan-Elevator Algorithm:**
   - The disk arm moves in particular direction servicing any request in the path and after reaching at end, direction is reversed and requests are serviced again.
   - Midrange requests are more serviced than those behind disk arm.
   - High throughput and average response time.
4. **C-Scan-Circular Scan:**
   - Here disk arm instead of reversing the direction goes to other end of the disk and then service the request.
   - Disk arm moves in circular manner.
   - Uniform wait time.
5. **Look:**
   - Similar to SCAN.
   - Disk arm goes to the last request to be serviced and not to the end.
   - Prevents extra delay.
6. **C Look-Circular Look:**
   - Similar to CSCAN.

PROTECTION AND SECURITY

Protection

- Mechanism and policy to enforce specified policy.
- Prevents accidental or intentional misuse of a system.

Security

- Providing protection to computer system resources.
- Aims at preventing intentional misuse of system.

Three goals to accomplish:

(*a*) **Data confidentiality:** Confidential data should be kept secret like password, Bank details.

(*b*) **Data Integrity:** Unauthorised users should not be able to modify data without owner's permission.

(*c*) **System availability:** System should not be made unusable.

Three security components:

(*a*) **Authentication:** Identify responsible user.

(*b*) **Authorization:** Identify which user is allowed to access and perform action.

(*c*) **Enforcement:** Ensuring that people do only what they are supposed to do.

Security Attacks

1. **Eavesdropping:**
   - Listener approach
   - One can tap into the serial line on the Ethernet, and see everything typed in as everything goes unencrypted over the network.
2. **Privilege Abuse:**
   - When user performs action he was not supposed to perform.
3. **Imposter:**
   - Pretending to be someone else.
   - Behavioral monitoring helps counter measure this attack.
4. **Trojan horse:**
   - A program that secretly performs some maliciousness alongwith visible action.
   - Counter measure: Integrity check.

5. **Salami Attack:**
   - When small attacks add up to one major attack that can go undetected.
   - Counter measure – code review frequently.
6. **Logic Bombs:**
   - Set of instructions secretly incorporated into a program so that harms the system when particular condition is satisfied.
   - Counter measure – code review.
7. **DOS or Denial-of-Service:**
   - Attempt to make system unavailable to intended user.
   - A handful of compromised machines can flood a victim machine with network packets disrupting its normal use.

Computer Science

9

Database

Contents

ER-Model and Relational Model

1

ER-MODEL

- Defines conceptual view of a database.
- Described by entity-relationship diagram.
- Implementation details are not induced.

  Entity: Any object, place, person. They have some unique attributes or properties that help in their identification

  Entity Set: Collection of similar types of entities
  - Need not be disjoint
  - Entities may contain attributes sharing similar value.

  Attributes: Properties of entities.

  Relationship: Association among entities.
  - Their attributes are called descriptive attributes.

  Relationship Set: Set of similar type relationship

  Super Key: Set of attributes that collectively identifies an entity in an entity set.

  Candidate Key: A minimal super key.

  Primary Key: It is candidate key that uniquely identify the entity set.

  Weak Entity Set: It does not have sufficient attributes to form a primary key.

  Strong Entity Set: Entity set having primary key.

STRUCTURAL CONSTRAINTS

- Degree → Number of entities participating
- Cardinality constraints → Cardinality defines number of entities in entity set
  - one-to-one
  - one-to-many
  - many-to-many
- Participation Constraints → Total or Partial.

E-R DIAGRAM SYMBOLS

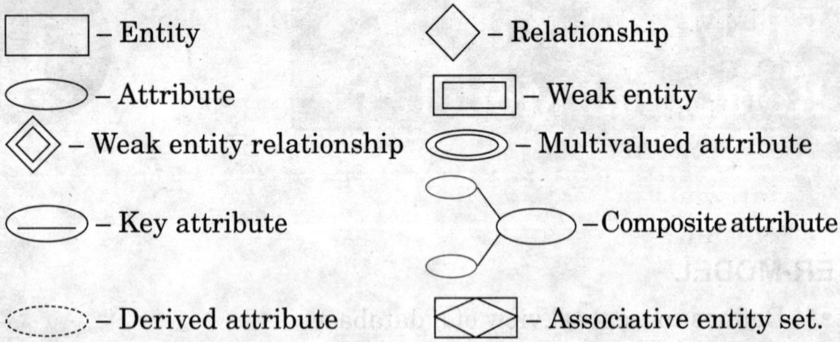

CARDINALITY

- Number of instance of an entity from a relation that can be associated with the relation.
- For one to many/many to one; relational table can be mixed with other tables involved
- For many to many; any two tables can be mixed
- For one to one and total participation of one entity; The entity and relation table can be mixed

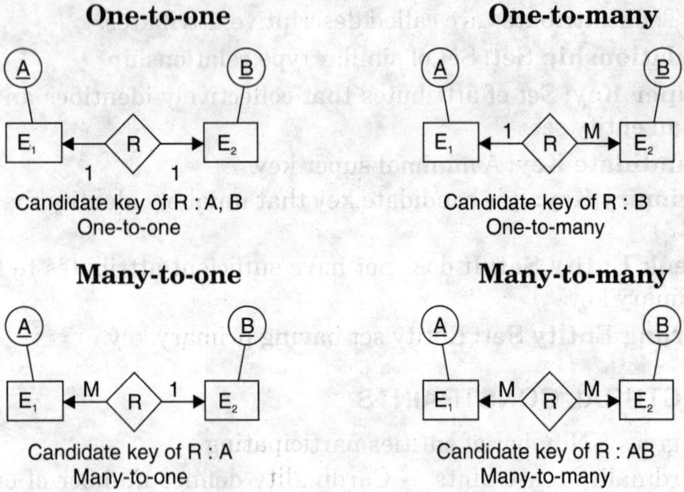

COMMANDS

DDL Commands

CREATE, ALTER, DROP, GRANT, REVOKE, TRUNCATE AND COMMENT.

DOL Commands

COMMIT, SAVEPOINT, ROLLBACK, AND SET TRANSACTION.

DML Commands

SELECT, INSERT, UPDATE, DELETE, CALL, LOCK TABLE AND EXPLAIN PLAN.

Relational Commands

Cartesian Product (×)

- Deg (R × S) = deg (R) + deg(S) and
- $|(R \times S)| = |R| \times |S|$

Natural Join (⋈)

- It is same as cross product + $\sigma_{\text{equality of common attribute}}$
- $\deg(R_1 \bowtie R_2) = \deg(R_1) + \deg(R_2)$ – number of common attribute
- Number of n-ary relation that can be formed over n-domains having elements: n^n
- Number of equivalent representation of a relation having degree m and cardinality n are $m! \times n!$

Order by

Default ascending order.

Aggregation Operations

SUM, COUNT, AVG, MIN, MAX

Selection Operation (Restriction) (σ)

- $\deg(\sigma_c(R)) = \deg(R)$ (Number of attributes)
- $0 \le |\sigma_c(R)| \le |R|$ (No. of tuples)
- $\sigma_{c1}(\sigma_{c2}(R)) = \sigma_{c2}(\sigma_{c1}(R)) = \sigma_{c1,c2}(R)$

Projection Operation (π)

- $0 \le \deg(\pi_A(R)) \le \deg(R)$
- $|\pi_{Ai}(R)| = |R|$

Rename (ρ)

Deg $(\rho_s(R))$ = degree(R) and $|(\rho_s(R))| = |R|$

Union Operation

- Two relations are union compatible if they are of same degree and same domain
- $\deg(R \cup S) = \deg(R) = \deg(S)$
- $\max(|R|, |S|) \le |R \cup S| < (|R| + |S|)$

Intersection Operation

- Two relation should be union compatible.
- deg $(R \cap S)$ = deg (R) = deg (S)
- $0 \leq |R \cap S| \leq \min(|R|, |S|)$

Set Difference (–)

- Two relation should be union compatible
- deg $(R - S)$ = deg(R) = (S)
- $0 \leq |(R - S)| \leq |R|$

Operation	Relational Algebra	Tuple Relational Calculus
Selection	$\sigma_{cond}(R)$	{T | R(T) AND Cond (T)}
Projection	$\Pi_{A_1, A_2, \ldots, A_k}(R)$	{T | T.A1, T.A2,..., $T.A_k$ | R(T)}
Cartesian Product	$R \times S$	{T | ∃T1 ∈R, ∃T_2 ∈R ($T.A_1$=$T_1.A_1$ AND,..., $T.A_n$ = $T_1.A_n$ AND $T.B_1$ = $T_2.B_1$ AND),..., $T.B_m$ = $T_2.B_m$)}
Union	$R \cup S$	{T | R(T) AND S(T)}
Set Difference	$R - S$	{T | R(T) AND ∀T1∈S, (T_1 <> T)} where T <> T_1 is T.A1 <>T_1A_1 OR ... $T.A_n$ <> $T_1.A_n$

Database Design

2

INTRODUCTION

Database systems manage large information bodies. The design basically involves design of database schema.

Limitation of File System

- It is necessary to know physical details of data to access database
- Concurrency control fails with large database
- Once access is given, whole file system can be accessed.

Goals of database design

- No redundancy
- Loss–less join
- Dependency preservation

Primary key versus Alternate key

Primary key	Alternate key
• Only one key for a relation	• More than one
• No null values	• Null values accepted
• Designs primary key	• Designs alternative key
• Unique key	• Not unique

Super key

- Combination of columns that uniquely identifies any row within a database.
- Differentiate super set of candidate key.

  Example: Let R be the relational schema with n-attributes, $R(A_1, A_2 \ldots A_n)$.

  Number of super keys possible

  (a) With only candidate key $A_1 \rightarrow 2n–1$

  (b) With only candidate key A_1, A_2 $2^{n-1} - 2^{n-2} + 2^{n-1}$

  (c) With only candidate key A_1A_2, $A_3A_4 \rightarrow 2^{n-2} - 2^{n-4} + 2^{n-2}$

FUNCTIONAL DEPENDENCY

- Relationship between two attributes basically between primary key and other non-key attributes within the table.

Types

Trivial
If $x \supseteq y$ then $x \rightarrow y$ is trivial dependency.
Example:
- Sid → Sid
- Sid Same → Sid

Non trivial
If $x \cap y = \phi$ and if then $x \rightarrow y$ satisfy functional dependency definition.
Example:
- Cid → Cname

ARMSTRONG'S AXIOMS

- Set of rules that when applied repeatedly; generates a closure of functional dependencies.
  1. Reflexive : if $x \supseteq y$ then $x \rightarrow y$
  2. Transitivity : if $x \rightarrow y$ and $y \rightarrow z$ then $x \rightarrow z$
  3. Argumentation : if $x \rightarrow y$ the $xz \rightarrow yz$
  4. Splitting : If $x \rightarrow yz$ then $x \rightarrow y$, $x \rightarrow z$
  5. Union : If $x \rightarrow y$ and $x \rightarrow z$ then $x \rightarrow yz$
  6. Pseudo transitivity : if $x \rightarrow y$, $yw \rightarrow z$ then $xw \rightarrow z$

Attribute Closure (x^+)

Set of all attributes functionally determined by X.

Example: R(ABCD) {A → B, B → C, C → D}

$$(A)^+ = \{ABCD\}$$

Functional Dependency Set Closure (F^+)

Set of all trival and non-trivial FD's derived from given FD set F.

$x \rightarrow y$ is logically applied in given FD set F only if x^+ should determine y.

Let R be the relational schema decomposed into R_1 and R_2. Given decomposition is loss-less only if

1. $R_1 \cup R_2 = R$
2. $R_1 \cap R_2 \neq \phi$
3. $R_1 \cap R_2 \rightarrow R_1$ or $R_1 \cap R_2 \rightarrow R_2$.

Example:

R(ABCDE)

{A → BC, CD → E, B → D, E → A}

D = {ABC, ACDE} → Loss-Less.

PROPERTIES OF DECOMPOSITION

1. **Loss-Less Join Decomposition**
   - When we can recover original relations from decomposed one.
   - There should not be generation of any additional tuples

     i.e $$R \equiv R_1 \bowtie R_2$$
2. **Dependency preserving decomposition**
   - The decomposition of schema R with functional dependencies F into schema with attribute dependencies F into schema with attribute set X and Y is dependency preserving if

     $(Fx \cup Fy)^+ = F^+$
   - No loss of any dependency should be there.

NORMALIZATION

Types of anomalies

(*i*) **Update Anomalies:** If data items are scattered and are not linked to each other properly, then it could lead to complex situation.

(*ii*) **Deletion Anomalies:** When deleting record, but part of it less left undeleted because of unawareness, the data is also saved somewhere else.

(*iii*) **Insert Anomalies:** When trying to insert data in a record that does not exits at all.

Besides these, are join anomalies also which need to normalize.

Note : Goals of normalization is to provide integrity and to maintain records.

First Normal Form

- All the attributes in a relation must have atomic domains.

Second Normal Form

- Every non-prime attribute should be fully functionally dependent on prime key attribute
- R should be in 1NF
- R should not contain any partial dependency.

Partial Dependency

Let R be the relational schema and X, Y, A are non-empty set of attributes

X : Any candidate key

A : Non-prime attribute

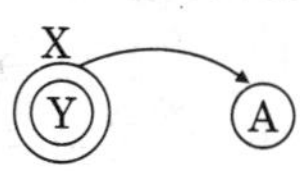

Y : Proper subset of any candidate key A should be non-prime attribute (Where A is said to be partial dependency)

Note

Prime attribute: An attribute which is a part of the prime key is known as prime attribute

Non-prime attribute: An attribute, which is not a part of prime key is said to be a non-prime attribute.

Third Normal Form:

- It must be in second normal form.
- No non-prime attribute is transitively dependent on prime key attribute.
- For any non-trivial functional dependency, $X \rightarrow A$ then either –X is a super key or A is prime attribute.

BCNF (Boyce – codd Normal form)

- BCNF is an extension of third normal form where
- For any non-trivial functions dependency, $X \rightarrow A$, X must be a super key.
- 4 NF → Let R be the relational schema. F be the single and multivalued dependency

  $x \rightarrow\rightarrow y$ is in 4 Nf

  iff:
- X : Candidate key or super key or

  XUY = R

Multivalued Dependency:

R be the relational schema X, Y, Z, attribute sets over R and t_1, t_2, t_3, t_4 are tuples over R.

X →→ Y only if

$$t_1 . x = t_2 . x = t_3 . x = t_4 . x$$
$$t_1 . y = t_2 . y = t_3 . y = t_4 . y$$
$$t_1 . z = t_2 . z = t_3 . z = t_4 . z$$

Complement Rule

If X →→ Y

then X →→ R – (XUY)

⇒ X →→ Z

A multivalued dependency X →→ Y is said to be trivial multivalued dependency:

if X ≥ Y or XUY ≡ R

Equality of FD set

FD sets F and G are said to be equal iff

(*a*) F covers G and

(*b*) G covers F.

Minimal Cover OR Canonical Cover:

- F can be its over minimal cover also known as canonical cover. A canonical cover of F is O "minimal".
- Set of functional dependencies equivalent to F, having no redundant dependencies or redundant parts of dependencies.
- There can be serval minimal covers of F.
- Formally GC is the minimal cover of F if
  - ➢ GC = F
  - ➢ The dependent (RHS) in every FD is GC is singleton attribute., This is called standard ot canonical form.
  - ➢ No FD in GC is redundant, In other words if any FD in GC is disabled, then GC would be no longer equivalent to F.
  - ➢ The determinant (LHS) if every FD in GC is irreducible, In other words, if any attributes is disabled from the determinant of any FD in GC, then GC would be no longer equivalent to F

REFERENTIAL INTEGRITY CONSTRAINTS

Foreign Key

Foreign Key is a set of attributes that references primary key or alternative key of the same relation or other relation.

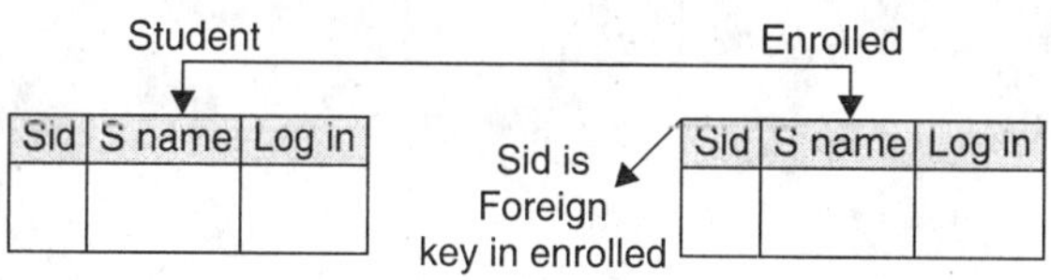

Referenced Relation

1. **Insertion:** no violation
2. **Deletion:**

   (*a*) *On delete no action:* Means if it causes problem on delete then not allowed to delete.

(*b*) *On delete cascade:* If we want to delete primary key value from referenced table then it will delete that value from referencing table also.

(*c*) *On delete set null:* If we want to delete primary key from referenced table then it will try to set the null values in place of that value in referencing table.

3. Updation:

(*a*) On update no action

(*b*) On update cascade

(*c*) On update set null

Referencing Relation

- **Insertion:** may cause violation
- **Deletion:** No violation
- **Updation:** May causes violation

Example:

A	C
2	4
3	4
4	3
5	4
6	2

C is foreign key referencing A Delete (2,4) and on delete cascade

A	C
3	4
4	3
5	4

SQL

3

INTRODUCTION

- SQL or Structured Query language is language to access and manipulate database.
- It is an ANSI (American National Standards Institute) standard.
- It has several language elements like:
  - **Clauses:** Constituent component of Statements and Queries
  - **Expressions:** Produce scalar values or tables
  - **Predicates:** Specify conditions
  - **Queries:** Retrieve the data on basis of specific criteria
  - **Statement:** Effects schema and data and controls
  - **Semicolon:** Statement terminator.

FUNCTIONS

- Executes user queries in a database
- Insert, update, retrieve, delete data/records in a database
- Creates new databases, new tables, new views, new procedures and also set permissions on them.

RDBMS

- Relational Database Management System.
- It is basis for SQL and other database like MS SQL Server, IBM DB2, Oracle, My SQL and Microsoft Access.
- It is based on relational model.
- It is most commonly used database with number of tables each with its own primary key.

TYPES OF SQL

(*i*) **DDL :** Data Definition language → define the database structure or table.

(ii) **DML:** Data Manipulation Language → manages data within table object.

(iii) **DCL:** Data Control Language → it gives privileges to access limited data

(iv) **TCS:** Transaction Control Statement → it apply changes permanently.

(v) **SCS:** Session Control Statement → Manage properties dynamically of a user session.

SQL Process Flow

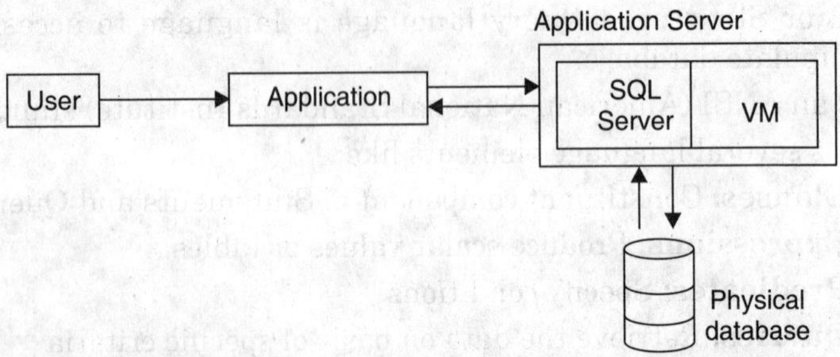

On Query execution; it is send to SQL server the SQL server manages database, load balancing, transaction management etc. It calls physical database and return the result.

SQL Statements

1. **Insert Into:** Insert table record into database
   SYNTAX :
   INSERT INTO table-Name Values (value 1, value 2...)
   Example:
   INSERT INTO users-INFO Values (1, 'opal kole', '6th avenue', '7714154').
2. **Insert All:** Insert more than one record into table
   SYNTAX:
   INSERT ALL
   INTO Table-Name [Column-Name 1, Column-Name 2,...] Values (record 1-value 1, record 1-value 2...)
   INTO Table-Name [Column-Name 1, Column-Name 2,...). Values (record 2-value1,...). Select * from dual ;

UPDATE

- Update table record within database.

> **Note**
> All table row or data can be updated by matching only conditional "WHERE" Clause.

SYNTAX: Update table–Name
SET Column– name 1 = value 1, column-name 2 = value 2,...;
Example: Update demo 1 SET contact no = 91;

Update Conditionally use WHERE Clause:
Syntax: Update table name
SET column-name 1 = value 1, column-name 2 = value 2....
[Where condition];
Example: UPDATE Demo 1 SET ADDRESS = '10 Two',
WHERE NO = 10;

DELETE

- To remove one or more than one row from table.

> **Note**
> This statement can be applied on entire row as well as can be applied on only specific table row.

(*i*) Remove only specific table row
Syntax: DELETE from table-Name.
[WHERE condition]
[LIMIT number];

(*ii*) Remove all TABLE rows
Syntax: DELETE FROM table-Name;
Example: DELETE FROM demo 1;

SELECT Statement

- Used for viewing data from the table. As a result return list of table format table data.
- *(asterisk) sign is used to fetch all table instead of. writing all column name.
  Syntax: SELECT * FROM table-name;
  Example: SELECT * FROM users-info;

Select all rows and selected columns.

Syntax: SELECT column_name 1, column_name 2... FROM table_name;

Example: Select no, name, address FROM users_info;

Only selected rows and all columns

Syntax: SELECT * FROM users-info WHERE no = 3;

Selected rows and selected columns

Syntax: SELECT column-name 1, column-name 2...FROM table-name [WHERE Condition];

SELECT DISTINCT STATEMENTS

Distinct statement is used for eliminating duplicate rows from selected column in table. DISTINCT statement can be added in multiple columns.

(*i*) Select with Distinct on all columns.

Syntax : SELECT DISTINCT * FROM Table_name

(*ii*) Select with Distinct on two columns

Syntax: SELECT DISTINCT column_name 1, column_name 2...FROM table name;

(*iii*) Select with Distinct one column

Syntax : SELECT DISTINCT column_name 1...FROM table_name;

WHERE CLAUSE

- Defines what records are to be included in the query, it is optional
- Uses operations:

(*a*) = , >,> =, < = ! = (< >).

(*b*) Between X and Y.

(*c*) IN (list)

(*d*) Like '% string' ('%' is a wild-card)

(*e*) IS NULL

(*f*) NOT (BETWEEN/IN/LIKE/NULL)

AND and OR

- "AND" demands all conditions to be true for the record.
- "OR" demands at least one condition to be true for the record.

ORDER BY Statement

- Represent the way of sorting the records.
- Generally order is taken in ASC (Ascending) order as default.

GROUP FUNCTIONS

- Performs common mathematical operations on a group of records.
- Must define what constitutes a group by using the GROUP BY clause.

LIKE OPERATOR

- It is used in "WHERE" clause to search for a specific pattern occurred in record.

  Syntax: SELECT column-name(S) FROM table_name

  WHERE column-name LIKE Pattern;

IN OPERATOR

- It is used in "WHERE" clause to specify multiple values in the record.

  Syntax: Select column-name(S) FROM table_name

  WHERE column_name IN (value 1, value 2,...)

BETWEEN OPERATOR

- It defines range of values for the selection, which can be numbers text or dates etc.

  Syntax: Select column_name(S) FROM table_name WHERE column_name BETWEEN value 1 and value 2;

SELECT SYNTAX

SELECT [DISTINCT/ALL]

Column_name 1, column_name 2, aggregate_function (column_name)

[FROM table_name]

[WHERE condition]

[GROUP BY group by-column-name 1,...]

[HAVING having-clause]

[ORDER BY [order-column name 1 [ASC | DESC],...];

SQL Alias

- An assigned temporary name to avoid long and complex table/column names.

- It makes the table/column more readable.
- When joining one or more table, then assigning alias name of a table or a column name becomes basis to read.

  Syntax: Column-name As alias_column_name and table-name alias_table_name.

JOINING TABLES

- Where there is a need to make a table, collecting data from different rows of different tables, there join is used.
- Joints between tables are usually based on primary/foreign keys.

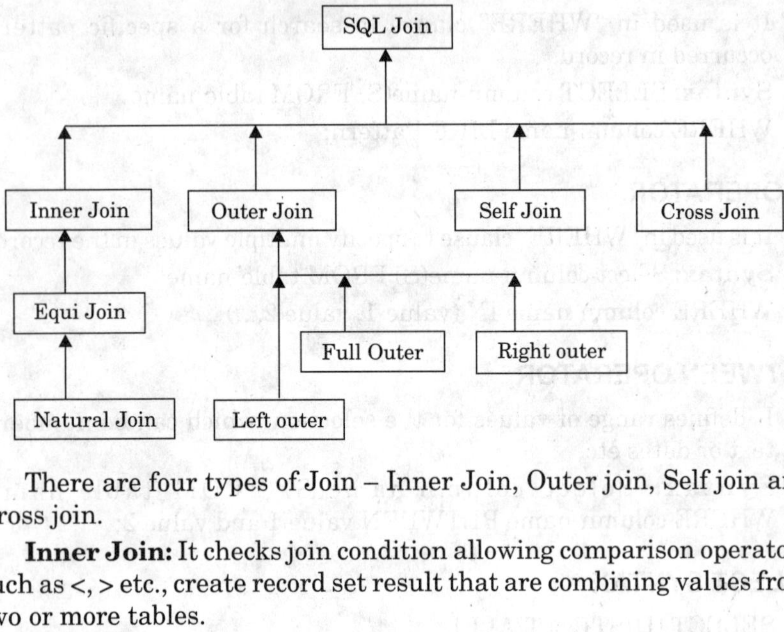

There are four types of Join – Inner Join, Outer join, Self join and Cross join.

Inner Join: It checks join condition allowing comparison operators such as <, > etc., create record set result that are combining values from two or more tables.

Equi Join: It is same as inner join but only specific type comparisons are allowed which exclude operators such as <, > etc.

Natural Join: Natural join is same as equi join but it allows only one column for each pair of same column named.

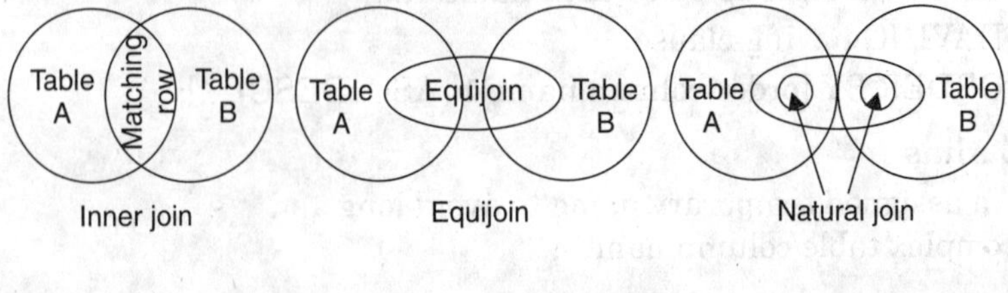

Outer Join

- To join two tables involving common attributes from two tables. But tables does not require to have a matching value to other table.

Left join/Left outer join: Left outer join always contains all records of left table (Table A) even of join condition does not find any matching record in right table (Table B).

Right join/Right outer join: Right outer join always contains all records of right table (Table B) even of join condition does not find any matching record in left table (Table A).

Full join/Full outer join: Full outer join always contains all records of left table (Table A) and right (Table B) even of join condition does not find any matching record in both left or right table. Returned result contains set NULL value for all column that are lack of value in matching rows.

Self Join: Joining table of itself.

Cross Join: To join table rows and return Cartesian product.

ALTER TABLE STATEMENT

- Used to rename table name, Add new column, Modify existing column, Drop the table column.
- SQL ALTER TABLE statement is a powerful statement to add, manage or update table structure.

(i) **TABLE RENAME**

SYNTAX: ALTER TABLE table_Name.

RENAME To new_ table_name;

(ii) **ADD NEW Column in Table**

Syntax : ALTER TABLE table-name

ADD column-name data type [(size)];

(iii) **ADD Multiplc column in table**

Syntax: ALTER TABLE table-name

ADD (column-name1) data type [(size)],

Column-name 2 data type [(size)].......,);

(*iv*) **MODIFY EXISTING COLUMN in table**

Syntax: ALTER TABLE table_name

MODIFY Column-name column_data type [(size)];

(*v*) **RENAME COLUMN in table**

Syntax: ALTER TABLE table_name

RENAME COLUMN old_column_name TO new-column_name;

(*vi*) **DROP column in table**

Syntax: ALTER TABLE table_name

DROP COLUMN column_name;

SQL Constraints

- Constraints are the rules which are applied on table columns to store valid data and prevent the users to enter/store invalid date into table columns.
- SQL constraints helps to enter limited size data. For example Postal Code India.

Type of Data Constraints

- **Input/Output Constraints:** It determines the speed of which data are inserted or extracted from database table. Eg. Primary, Foreign key constraints.
- **Business Rule Constraints:** These rules are applied to data before inserting into the table column. Eg. Not NULL, Default constraints.

Define Constraints

Oracle SQL allows programmers to define constraints at:

- Column level
- Table level

Column Level Constraints: Defined on single column along with other column attributes.

Syntax: Column-name data type [(size)] [NULL/NOT NULL [Constraint-name];

Table level Constraints: Defined after all table columns define.

Types of SQL Constraints

- **Primary key:** Value must be unique for each row in a table and not a NULL. Primary key used to identify individual records.

- **Foreign key:** Value in specified column must have reference in another table.
- **NOT NULL:** Column value must not be NULL.
- **UNIQUE:** Check column value must be unique across the given field in table.
- **Check:** Specified condition is given, which must evaluate to true for constraints to be specified.
- **Default:** Default value assign if none of the value specified in given field.

AGGREGATE FUNCTIONS

(*i*) Aggregate functions perform a calculation on a set of values and return a single value.

(*ii*) Aggregate functions return the same value any time that they are called by using a specific set of input values.

(*iii*) Aggregate functions can be used as expressions only in the following:

(*a*) The select list of a SELECT (either a subquery or an outer query).

(*b*) A HAVING clause.

- **AVG ( ) Function:**

  The AVG ( ) function returns the average value of a numeric column.

  Syntax : SELECT AVG (column_name) FROM table_name

- **COUNT ( ) Function:**

  The COUNT ( ) Function returns the number of rows that matches a specified criteria.

  COUNT (column_name) syntax:

  It returns the number of values (NULL values will not be counted) of the specified column:

  SELECT COUNT (column_name) FROM table_name;

  COUNT (*) Syntax:

  It returns the number of records in a table:

  SELECT (DISTINCT column-name) Syntax:

It returns the number of distinct values of the specified column:

SELECT COUNT (DISTINCT column_name) FROM table_name;

- **MAX( ) Function:**

  The MAX( ) function returns the largest value of the selected column.

  Syntax: SELECT MAX (column-name) FROM table_name;

- **MIN( ) Function:**

  The MIN( ) function returns the smallest value of the selected column.

  Syntax: SELECT MIN (column_name) FROM table_name;

- **SUM( ) Function:**

  The SUM( ) function returns the total sum of a numeric column.

  Syntax: SELECT SUM (column_name) FROM table_name;

- **LEN( ) Function:**

  The LEN ( ) function returns the length of the value in a text field.

  Syntax: SELECT LEN (column-name) FROM table-name;

HAVING Clause: The HAVING clause was added to SQL because the WHERE keyword could be used with aggregate functions.

GROUP BY Statement: The GROUP BY statement is used in conjunction with the aggregate functions to group the result_set by one or more columns.

File Structures (B and B$^+$ Trees)

4

SEQUENTIAL FILE

- Blocking factor: $\left\lfloor \dfrac{\text{Block size}}{\text{Record size}} \right\rfloor$
- Number of record blocks: $\left\lceil \dfrac{\text{Total number of records}}{\text{Blocking factor}} \right\rceil$
- Average number of blocks accessed by linear search:
  $$\left\lceil \frac{\text{\# of record blocks}}{2} \right\rceil$$
- Average number of blocks accessed by binary search:
  $$\lceil \log_2 \text{\# of record blocks} \rceil$$

INDEX FILE

- Index blocking factor = $\left\lceil \dfrac{\text{\# of record blocks} + 1}{2} \right\rceil$
- First (Single) level index blocks: $\left\lceil \dfrac{\text{\# of record blocks}}{\text{Index blocking factor}} \right\rceil$
- Number of block accesses = $\lceil \log_2 (\text{first level index blocks}) \rceil + 1$

Indexing Types

1. **Single level index:**
   (*a*) Primary index (sparse): Ordered with key field.
   (*b*) Clustered index (sparse): Ordered with non key field.
   (*c*) Secondary index (dense): Ordered with either key or non key field.
2. **Multilevel Index:**
   (*a*) Indexed sequential access method
   (*b*) B-tree index
   (*c*) B$^+$-tree index

SINGLE LEVEL INDEX

Dense Index

- For every data base record there exists entry in the index file.
- Number of data base records = Number of entries of the index file.

Sparse Index

- For set of database records there exists single entry in the index files.
- Number of index file entries < Number of database records
- Number of index file entries = Number of database blocks.

Clustered Index

- Search key should be used to physically order the DB.
- Search key is non-key.
- Atmost one clustering index is possible.
- Single level index blocks:

$$\left\lceil \frac{\text{No. of distinct values over non key field}}{\text{Index blocking factor}} \right\rceil + 1.$$

- Number of block accesses: $\lceil \log_2 (\text{single level index blocks}) \rceil + 1$

Secondary Index

- Search key is used to non ordered the DB file.
- Search key is primary or alternative key.
- Dense indexing is used.
- Number of block accesses $\lceil \log_2 (\text{single level index blocks}) \rceil + 1$
- Index blocking factor same for all indexes.

MULTILEVEL INDEX (STATIC LEVEL INDEX)

- Second level index is always sparse.
- Level 1 = "first level index blocks" computed by index.

$$\text{Level } 2 = \left\lceil \frac{\text{\# of blocks in level (1)}}{\text{Index blocking factor}} \right\rceil$$

$$\text{Level } n = \left\lceil \frac{\text{\# of blocks in level } (n - 1)}{\text{Index blocking factor}} \right\rceil = 1$$

- Number of levels = n
- Number of blocks = $\sum_{i=1}^{n}$ (Number of blocks in level i)
- Number of blocks access = $n + 1$

B-TREE (BAYES'S/BALANCED SEARCH TREE)

- **Root node:** 2 to n children (pointers)
- **Internal node:** $\lceil n/2 \rceil$ to n children
- Leaf nodes are all at same level.
- **Block Size** = $p \times$ (Size of block pointer) + $(p - 1) \times$ (Size of key field + size of record pointer)
- Minimum number of nodes = $1 + \left(\dfrac{2[(p/2)^h - 1]}{(p/2) - 2} \right)$
- Maximum number of nodes = $\dfrac{p^{h+1} - 1}{p - 1}$
- Minimum possible height = $\lceil \log_p \ell \rceil$ (ℓ : number of leaves)
- Maximum possible height = $\lfloor 1 + \log_{p/2} \ell/2 \rfloor$

B⁺TREE

- It is same as B-tree.
- All the records are available at leaf (last) level.
- It allows both random and sequential access, but in B-tree only random access allowed.
- All the leaf nodes are connected to next leaf node by block pointers [every leaf node has one block pointer]
- Order of non-leaf Node: [$p \times$ size of block pointer] + [$(p - 1) \times$ size of key field] $\leq$ Block size.
- Order of Leaf Node: [$(p_{leaf} - 1) \times$ (size of key field + size of record pointer) + $p \times$ (size of block pointer) $\leq$ Block size.]

TRANSACTION AND CONCURRENCY CONTROL

Introduction: A transaction is the basic logical unit of execution in an information system. It is a sequence of operations that must be executed as a whole, taking a consistent database state into another consistent database state;

Desirable Properties of ACID Transactions

Atomicity: A transaction is either performed entirely or not at all.

Consistently: Database should be consistent before and after the execution of the transaction.

Isolation: The updates of a transaction must not be made visible to other transaction until it is committed.

Durability: If a transaction changes the database and is committed. The changes must never be last because of subsequent failure.

Serializability: Transaction are considered serialisable if the effect of running them in on interleaved fashion is equivalent to running them serially in some order.

- **Schedule:** A chronological execution sequence of a transaction is called a schedule. A schedule can have many transactions in it, each comprising of a number of instructions/task.
- **Serial Schedule:** It is a schedule in which transactions are aligned in such a way that one transaction is executed first.
- Transaction are ordered one after another

States of Transactions

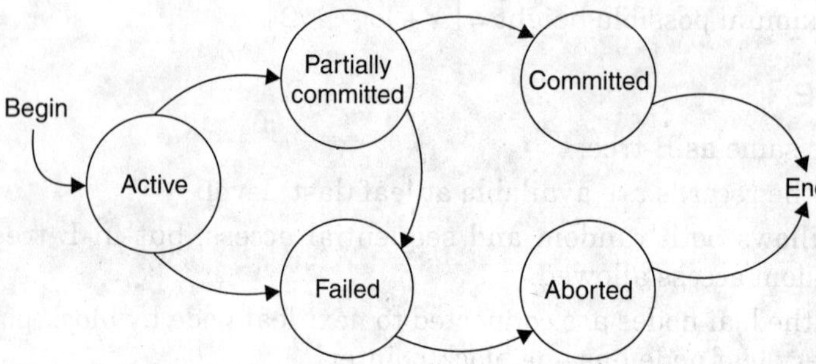

Concurrency

In a multiprogramming environment where multiple transactions can be executed simultaneously

Conflicts in Concurrent Execution

- **WR problem:**

T_i	T_j
W(A)	⋮
⋮	R(A) → Uncommitted read

- **RW problem:**

T_i	T_j
R(A)	⋮
⋮	W(A)

- **WW problem:**

T_i	T_j
W(A)	⋮
⋮	W(A)

Classification of Schedule based on Serializability Control with locks

- **Serializability:** A schedule is serialisable if it is equivalent to a serial schedule.
  (*i*) Conflict serialisability
  (*ii*) View serialisability
- **Conflict Serialisability:** Instructions I_i and I_j of transactions T_i and T_j respectively, conflict if and only if there exists some item Q accessed both I_i and I_j, and at least one of these instructions wrote Q.
  (*i*) I_i = read (Q), I_j = read (Q). I_i and I_j don't conflict.
  (*ii*) I_i = read (Q), I_j = write (Q). They conflict.
  (*iii*) I_i = write (Q), I_j = read (Q). They conflict.
  (*iv*) I_i = write (Q), I_j = write (Q). They conflict.
- **Conflict Equivalent:** If a schedule S can be transformed into a schedule S' by a series of swaps of non-conflicting instructions, we say that S and S' are **conflict equivalent**.
- **Conflict Serialisable:** We say that a schedule S is conflict serialisble if it is conflict equivalent to a serial schedule.
- **View Serialisability :** Let S and S' be two schedules with the same set of transactions. S and S' are view equivalent if the following three conditions are met:
  (*i*) For each data item Q, if transaction T_i reads the initial value of Q in schedule S, then transaction T_i must, in schedule S', also read the initial value of Q.
  (*ii*) For each data item Q if transaction T_i executes **read** (Q) in schedule S, and that value was produced by transaction T_j (if any), then transaction T_i must in schedule S' also read the value of Q that was produced by transaction T_j.
  (*iii*) For each data item Q, the transaction (if any) that performs the final write (Q) operation in schedule S must perform the final **write** (Q) operation in schedule S'.

Remember

- Every conflict serialisable schedule is also view serialisable.
- Every view serialisable schedule that is not conflict serialisable has blind writes.

- **Irrecoverable Schedule:** Its not possible to roll back after the commitment of a transaction as the initial data is no where.

Example:

	T_1	T_2
Roll back↑	R (A) W (A)	
Failed ←	⋮	R (A) Commit

- **Recoverable Schedule:** A schedule is recoverable if a transaction T_j reads a data items previously written by transaction T_i, the commit operation of T_i appears before the commit operation of T_j.

Example:

T_i	T_j
R (A)	
W (A)	
⋮	R (A)
Commit	W (B)
	Commit

- **Cascadeless Recoverable Schedule:** For each pair of transactions T_i and T_j such that T_j reads a data item previously written by T_i the commit operation of T_i appears before the read operation of T_j. Every cascadeless schedule is also recoverable.

Example:

T_i	T_j
R (A)	
W (A)	
⋮	
Commit	
	R (A)
	Commit

Cascading rollback: A single transaction failure leads to a series of transaction rollbacks.

- **Strict Recoverable Schedule:** If transaction T_i updates the data item A, any other transaction T_j not allowed to R(A) pr W(A) until commit or roll back of T_i.

  Example:

T_i	T_j
W (A)	
Commit or rollback	
	R (A) or W(A)

- **S:** $r_3(x)\ r_1(x)\ w_3(x)\ r_2(x)\ w_1(y)\ r_2\ (y)\ w_2(x)\ c_3c_1c_2$ is recoverable schedule but not cascadeless schedule.
- **S:** $r_1(x)\ \ r_2(z)\ \ r_1(z)\ \ r_3(x)\ \ r_3(y)\ \ w_1(x)\ \ w_3(y)r_2(y)w_2(z)\ \ w_2(y)c_1c_2c_3$ is irrecoverable.
- Serializability checking:

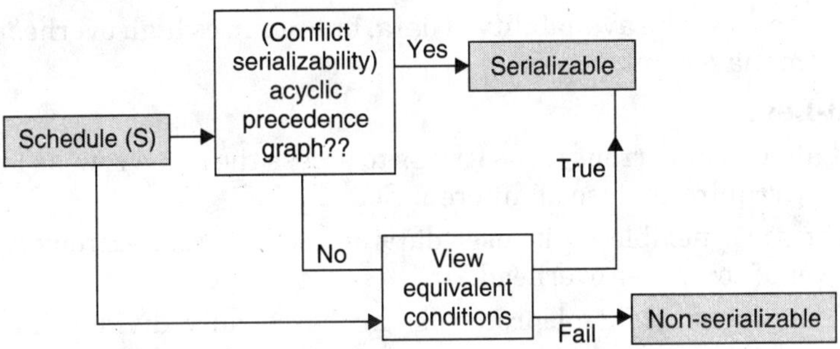

CONCURRENCY CONTROL WITH LOCKS

- Lock guarantees current transaction exclusive use of data item.
- Acquires lock prior to access.
- Lock released when transaction is completed.
- A locking protocol is a set of rules followed by all transaction while requesting and releasing locks.
- Locking protocols restrict the set of possible schedules.

Lock Granularity

Lock granularity indicates level of lock use: database, table, page, row of field (attribute).

Database Level

- The entire database is locked.
- Good for batch processes, but unsuitable for online multi-user DBMSs.

Table Level

- The entire table is locked.
- If a transaction requires access to several tables, each table may be locked.
- Table-level locks are not suitable for multi-user DBMSs.

Page Level

- A page has a fixed size and a table can span several pages while a page can contain several rows of one or more tables.
- Page-level lock is currently the most frequently used multi-user DBMS locking method.

Row-Level

- It allows concurrent transactions to access different rows of same table even if the rows are located on the same page.
- It improves the availability of data, but requires high overhead cost for management.

Field-Level

- It allows concurrent transactions to access the same row, as long as they require the use of different fields.
- The most flexible multi-user data access, but cost extremely high level of computer overhead.

  Concurrency control protocols can be broadly divided into two categories.

  - Lock based protocols
  - Timestamp based protocols

LOCK BASED PROTOCOLS

It is a mechanism by which any transaction cannot read or write data until it acquires an appropriate lock on it.

Binary Locks :

- It has two states for data items; locked or unlocked.
- Locked objects are unavailable to other objects
- Unlocked objects are open to any transaction.
- It locks before use of data item and release the lock after performing operation.

CONS: Irrecoverability, Deadlock and Low Concurrency Level

- **Shared/Exclusive:** This type of mechanism differentiate the locks based on their uses.

  (*i*) **Shared (S Mode):** Applied when concurrent transaction requires grant of reading.

  (*ii*) Produces no conflict for read-only transactions.

Exclusive (X mode)

(*i*) Exists when WRITE access is granted

(*ii*) Used when potential for conflict exists

Request *j* ↓ / Hold *i* →	S	X
S	Y	N
X	N	N

Lock-Compatability Matrix:

- A transaction may grants a lock on item if the requested lock is compatible with locks already held on item by other transactions.
- Any number of transactions can hold shared lock on an item, but if any transaction holds an exclusive on the no other transaction may hold any lock on the item.

Problems With Locking

- Transaction schedule may not be serialisable : managed through two-phase locking.
- Schedule may create deadlocks : Managed by using deadlock detection and prevention techniques.

Two-Phase Locking (2PL)

It has two phases:

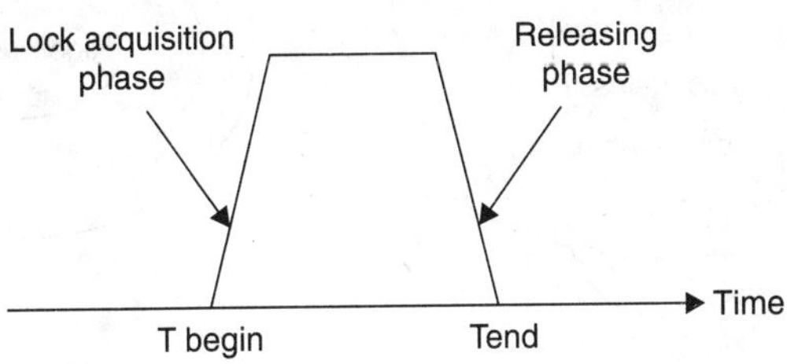

(*i*) Growing: All the locks are being required by the transaction. Once all locks have been acquired, the transaction is in its locked point.

(*ii*) Shrinking Phase: Second phase is shrinking, where locks held by the transaction are being released

It governs following rules

(*i*) Two transaction cannot have conflicting locks.

(*ii*) No unlock operation can precede a lock operation in the same transaction.

(*iii*) No data will be affected until all locks are obtained.

Basic 2PL Protocol

- Equal serial schedule based on lock point
- **Problems with basic 2PL:** Irrecoverability, Deadlock and Staturation.

Strict 2PL Protocol

In contrast to 2PL, strict 2PL does not release a lock after using it. Strict 2PL holds all the locks until the commit point.

Rigorous 2PL Protocol

- Basic 2PL with all locks (S/X) should be hold until commit.
- Equivalence serial schedule based on order of commit.

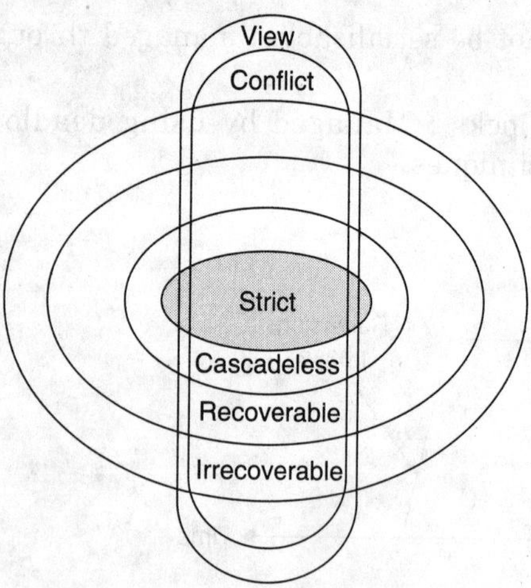

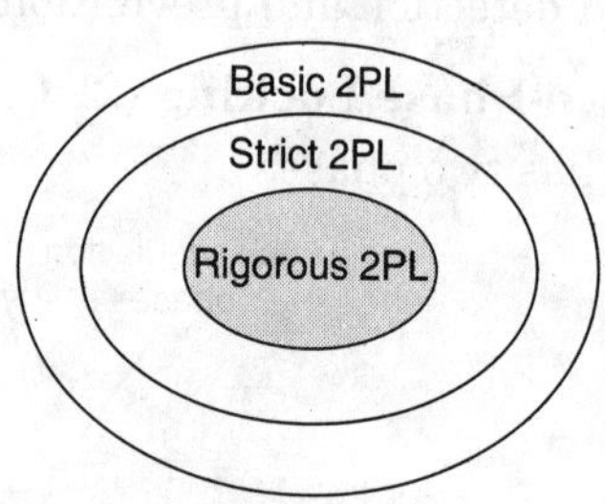

Timestamp-based Protocols

The most commonly used concurrency protocol is the time-stamp based protocol. This protocol uses either system time or logical counter as a timestamp.

Every transaction has a timestamp associated with it, and the ordering is determined by the age of transaction.

Timestamp Ordering Protocol

Timestamp ordering protocol ensures socializability among transactions in their conflicting read and write operations.

This is the responsibility of the protocol system that the conflicting pairs of tasks should be executed according to the timestamp values of transaction.

Basic Timestamp Ordering Protocol

1. **Transaction T issues R(A) option:**
   (*a*) If WTS(A) > TS(T) then roll back T
   (*b*) Otherwise allow to execute R(A) successfully.
   Set RTS(A) = max {TS(T), RTS(A)}
2. **Transaction T issues W(A) operation:**
   (*a*) If RTS(A) > TS (T) then roll back
   (*b*) If WTS (A) > TS (T) then roll back
   (*c*) Otherwise execute W(A) option set WTS (A) = {TS(T)}

Thomas Write Rule Stamp Ordering Protocol

1. **Transaction T issues R(A) option:**
   (*a*) If WTS (A) > TS (T) then roll back T
   (*b*) Otherwise execute successfully
   Set RTS (A) = max {TS (T), RTS (A)}
2. **Transaction T issues W (A) operation:**
   (*a*) If RTS (A) > TS (T) then roll back T.
   (*b*) If WTS (A) > TS (T) then ignore W(A) and continue execution of trans T.

Strict Time Stamp Ordering Protocol

A Transaction T_2 that issues a R(A) or W(A) such that TS(T_2) > WTS (X) has its read write option delayed until the transaction T_1 that write the value X has committed or rolled back.

Wait Die Protocol

- Write the transaction in ascending order of time stamp values.
- If T_1 required resource that is hold by T_2, T_1 wait for T_2 to unlock.
- If T_2 required resource that is hold by T_1, then roll back T_2 and restart with same time stamp value.

Wound Wait Protocol

- Write the transaction in ascending order of TS values.
- If T_1 required resource that is hold by T_2 then roll back T_2 and restart with same time stamp value.
- If T_2 required resource that is hold by T_1 than T_2 wait for T_1 to unlock.
- Both wait die and wound wait protocols may have starvation.

Computer Science

10

Software Engineering Gate

Contents

Information Gathering, Requirement & Feasibility Analysis

1

SOFTWARE ENGINEERING

Software engineering is concerned with the theories, methods and tools for developing, managing and evolving software products. At the first conference on software engineering in 1968, Fritz Bauer defined software engineering as "The establishment and use of sound engineering principles in order to obtain economically developed software that is reliable and works efficiently on real machines".

Due to increase in cost of maintaining software, objective is now shifting to produce quality software that is maintainable, delivered on time, within budget, and also satisfies its requirements.

Feasibility Study

It is the process of evaluation or analysis of the potential impact of a propose project or program.

Five Common Factors (TELOS)

Technical feasibility: Is it technically feasible to provide direct communication connectivity through space from one location of globe to another location?

Economic feasibility: Are the project's cost assumption realistic?

Legal feasibility: Does the business model realistic?

Operational feasibility: Is there any market for the product?

Schedule feasibility: Are the project's schedule assumption realistic?

Types of Requirements

1. A condition of capability needed by a user to solve a problem or achieve an objective
2. A condition or a capability that must be met or possessed by a system ... to satisfy a contract, standard, specification, or other formally imposed document."
    1. **Known Requirements:** Something a stakeholder believes to be implemented

2. **Unknown requirements:** Forgotten by the stakeholder because they are not needed right now or needed only by another stakeholder
3. **Undreamt requirements:** Stakeholder may not be able to think of new requirement due to limited knowledge

A Known, Unknown and Undreamt requirements may functional or non functional:

- **Functional requirements:** describe what the software has to do. They are often called product features. It depends on the type of software, expected users and the type of system where the software is used.
- **Non Functional requirements:** are mostly quality requirements. That stipulate how well the software does, what it has to do. These define system properties and constraints *e.g.* reliability, response time and storage requirements, Constraints are I/O device capability, system representations, etc.
- **User requirements:** Statements in natural language plus diagrams of the services the system provides and its operational constraints.
- **System requirements:** A structured document setting out detailed descriptions of the system's functions, services and operational constraints. Defines what should be implemented so may be part of a contract between client and contractor.

Requirements Engineering

- The process of finding out, analyzing, documenting and checking these services and constraints called requirement engineering
- RE produces one large document, written in a natural language, contains a description of what the system will do without how it will do?
- Input to RE is problem statement prepared by the customer and the output is SRS prepared by the developer
- The requirements themselves are the descriptions of the system services and constraints that are generated during the requirements engineering process

Requirements Engineering processes

The processes used for RE vary widely depending on the application domain, the people involved and the organization developing the requirements. However, there are a number of generic activities common to all processes

- Requirements elicitation
- Requirements analysis
- Requirements documentation
- Requirements review

Crucial Process Steps of Requirement Engineering

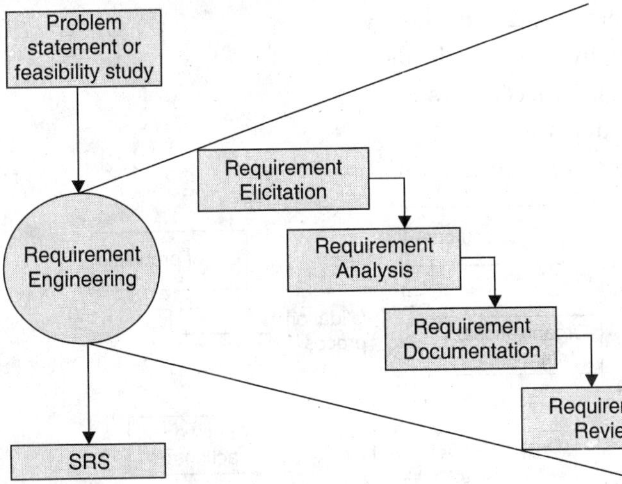

- **Requirement Elicitation:** known as gathering of requirement. Here requirement are identified with the help of customer and exiting system processes, if they are available.
- **Requirement Analysis:** analysis of requirement stars with Requirement Elicitation. Requirements are analyzed in order to identify inconstancy, defects etc.
- **Requirement Documentation:** this is the end product of requirement elicitation and analysis. Documentation is very important as it will be the foundation for the design of the software. The documentation is known as SRS.
- **Requirement Review:** review process is carried out to improve the quality of the SRS. it may also called verification. It should be a continuous activity that is incorporated into the elicitation, analysis, documentation. The primary output of requirement engineering process is requirement specification (SRS).

Need for Software Requirement Specification (SRS)

- The problem is that the client usually does not understand software or the software development process, and the developer often does not understand the client's problem and application area.

- This causes a communication gap between the parties involved in the development project. A basic purpose of software requirements specification is to bridge this communication gap.

Requirements Validation

Requirement Validation is used for checking the document:-

- Completeness & consistency
- Conformance to standards
- Requirements conflicts
- Technical errors
- Ambiguous requirements

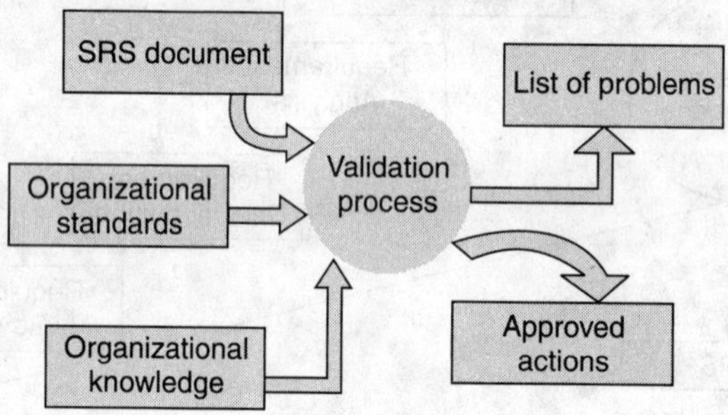

I/O Design, Process Life Cycle

2

SOFTWARE ENGINEERING PROCESS

Concept of the Software Engineering has evolved in 1986 by BOHEM to reduce the effect of his software crisis because software engineering defined as scientific and systematic approach to develop , operate and maintain software project to meet a given specific object it beautifully envisages the concept of life cycle of any software project through following five phase:-

- Requirement analysis
- Design
- Coding
- Testing
- Maintenance

Software Development Life Cycle (SDLC) Models

Software-development life-cycle is used to facilitate the development of a large software product in a systematic, well-defined, and cost-effective way. An information system goes through a series of phases from conception to implementation. This process is called the Software-Development Life-Cycle.

Various reasons for using a life-cycle model include:

- Helps to understand the entire process
- Enforces a structured approach to development
- Enables planning of resources in advance
- Enables subsequent controls of them
- Aids management to track progress of the system

Classical Waterfall Model

Classical waterfall model divides the life cycle into the following phases as shown in fig:

1. Feasibility Study
2. Requirements Analysis and Specification

3. Design
4. Coding and Unit Testing
5. Integration and System Testing
6. Maintenance

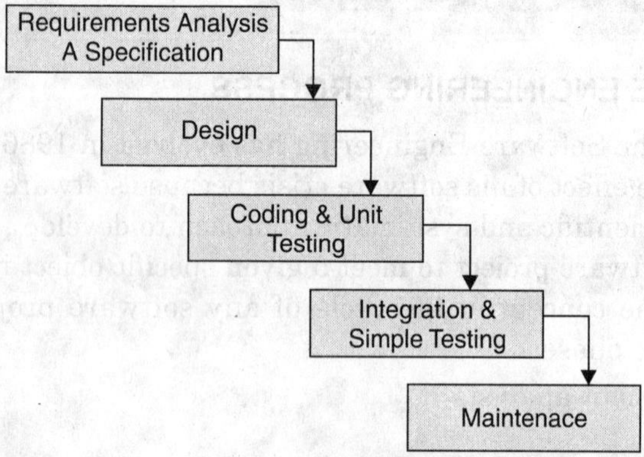

Classical Waterfall Model

Prototype Model

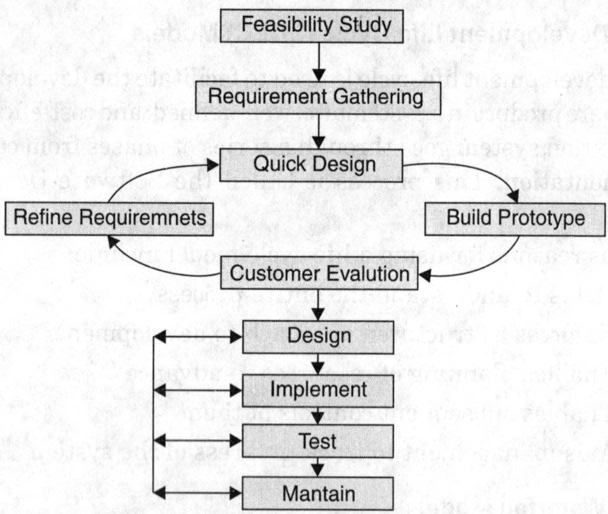

1. The new system requirements are defined in as much detail as possible. This usually involves interviewing a number of users representing all the departments or aspects of the existing system.
2. A preliminary design is created for the new system.

3. A first prototype of the new system is constructed from the preliminary design. This is usually a scaled-down system, and represents an approximation of the characteristics of the final product.
4. The users thoroughly evaluate the first prototype, noting its strengths and weaknesses, what needs to be added, and what should to be removed. The developer collects and analyzes the remarks from the users.
5. The first prototype is modified, based on the comments supplied by the users, and a second prototype of the new system is constructed.
6. The second prototype is evaluated in the same manner as was the first prototype.
7. The preceding steps are iterated as many times as necessary, until the users are satisfied that the prototype represents the final product desired.
8. The final system is constructed, based on the final prototype.
9. The final system is thoroughly evaluated and tested. Routine maintenance is carried out on a continuing basis to prevent large-scale failures and to minimize downtime.

Spiral Model

Each phase in this model is split into four sectors (or quadrants). The following activities are carried out during each phase of a spiral model.

First Quadrant (Objective Setting)

- During the first quadrant, it is needed to identify the objectives of the phase.
- Examine the risks associated with these objectives.

Second Quadrant (Risk Assessment and Reduction)

- A detailed analysis is carried out for each identified project risk.
- Steps are taken to reduce the risks. For example, if there is a risk that the requirements are inappropriate, a prototype system may be developed.

Third Quadrant (Development and Validation)

- Develop and validate the next level of the product after resolving the identified risks.

Fourth Quadrant (Review and Planning)

- Review the results achieved so far with the customer and plan the next iteration around the spiral.

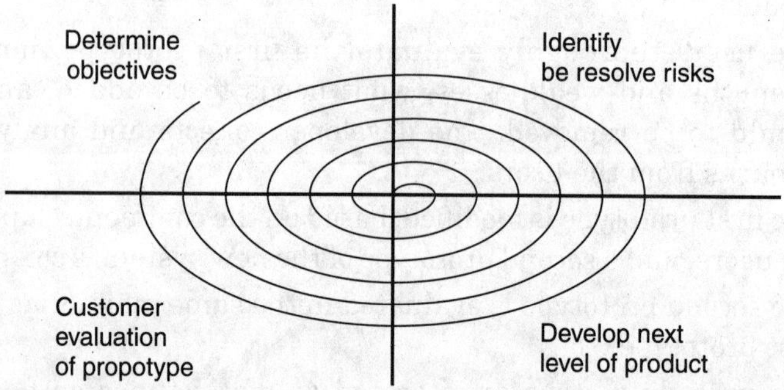

Rapid Development Application Model (RAD)

The process is stared with rapid prototype and is given to user for evolution. In that model user feedback is obtained and prototype is refined. SRS and design document are prepared with the association of users. RAD becomes faster if the software engineer uses the component's technology (CASE Tools) such that the components are really available for reuse.

RAD Phases

- **Requirements planning phase** (a workshop utilizing structured discussion of business problems)
- **User description phase:** automated tools capture information from users
- **Construction phase:** productivity tools, such as code generators, screen generators, etc. inside a time-box. ("Do until done")
- **Cutover phase:** installation of the system, user acceptance testing and user Training

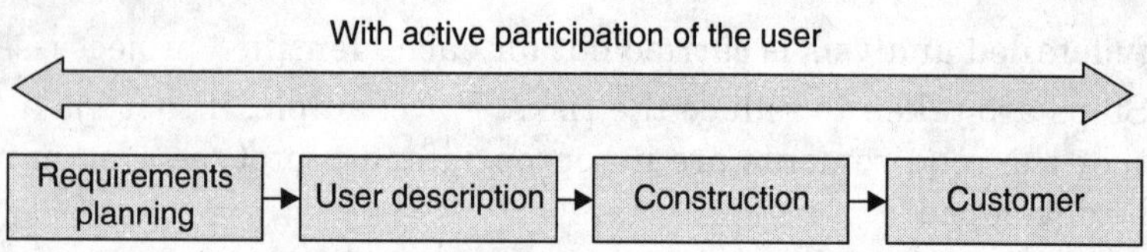

Evolutionary Process Model

In evolutionary development, requirements are implemented by category rather than by priority.

Main characteristics:

- The phases of the software construction are interleaved
- Feedback from the user is used throughout the entire process
- The software product is refined through many versions

Types of evolutionary development:

- Exploratory development
- Throw-away prototyping

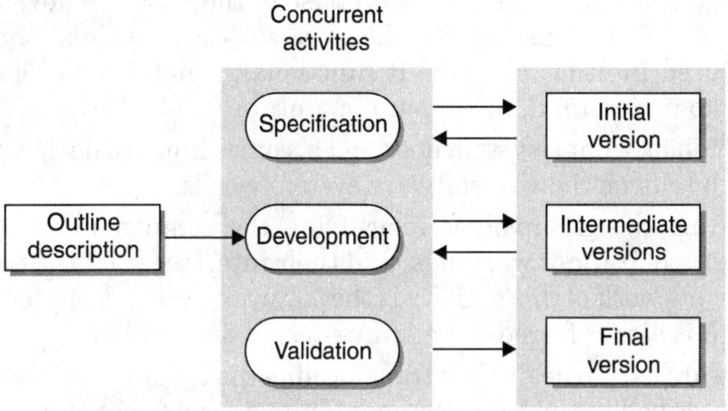

AGILE DEVELOPMENT APPROACHES

Agile Methodology which is used to convert the classical development models to a quickly and easily moveable process. Agile is known as an adaptive and empirical process which works on following principles:

- Individual and interaction over process and tools.
- Working software over comprehensive documentation.
- Customer collaboration over contract negotiation.
- Responding to change over following a plan.
- Agile methodology welcomes changing in requirement during the time of development. The main focus of agilest is to continuously deliver the software or it can be stated that Agile Methodology promotes sustainable development. The main requirement of this methodology is technical excellence and good design. In this approach, information is conveyed face to face and requirements are captured quickly because at the time of development customer is also involved.

Design

3

SOFTWARE DESIGN

- Design is the highly significant phase in the software development where the designer plans "how" a software system should be produced in order to make it functional, reliable and reasonably easy to understand, modify and maintain.
- SRS tell us what a system does and becomes input to design process, which tells us "how" a software system works.
- Software design involves identifying the component of software design, their inner workings, and their interface from the SRS. The principle work of this activity is the software design document (SDD) which is also referred as software design description
- Software design deals with transforming the customer requirements, as described in the SRS document, into a form (a set of documents) called software design document that is suitable for implementation in a programming language.

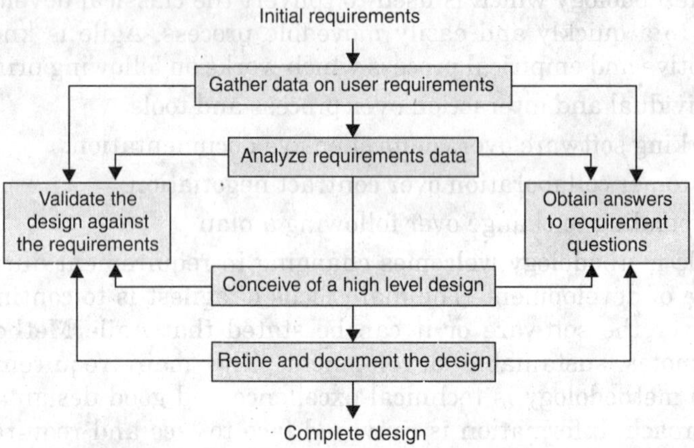

Design framework

Conceptual and Technical Design

- Conceptual design describe the system in language understandable to the customer. It does not contain any technical jargons and is independent of implementation

- By contrast the technical design describe the hardware configuration, software needs, communication interface, input and output of system, network architecture that translate the requirement into the solution to the customer's problem

Conceptual Design and Technical Design

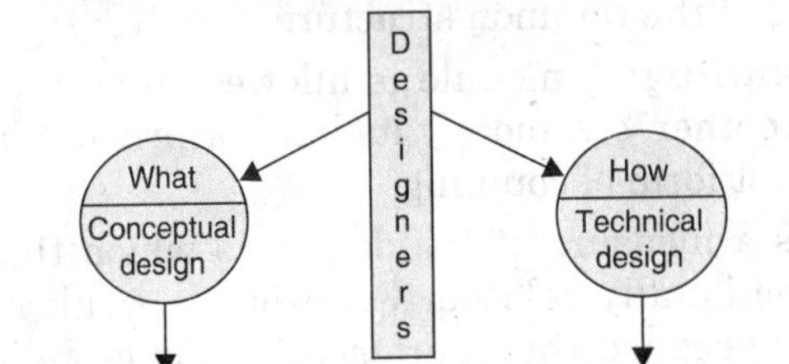

A two part design process

Software Design Principle

Abstraction

It is a tool that permits a designer to consider a component at abstract level; without worrying about the detail of the implementation of the component.

Encapsulation

It is the grouping of related ideas into one unit, which can thereafter be referred to by a single name.

Single name is here the key word to get an insight of what encapsulation is about: a subroutine (or *function* as we call it nowadays), for example, is a name that refers to a unit of code. Something that instead of being repeated over and over in the source code is factored out in a single place.

Information Hiding

Information hiding gives the designer the freedom to *modify* how the responsibility is fulfilled by a module/object.

This is especially valuable at points where the design (or even the requirements) are likely to change.

Coupling and Cohesion Measures

Coupling: It is the measure of the degree of interdependence between modules. Coupling is highly between components if they depend heavily on one another, (*e.g.*, there is a lot of communication between them).

Types of Coupling:

1. **Data coupling:** communication between modules is accomplished through well-defined parameter lists consisting of data information items.
2. **Stamp coupling:** Stamp coupling occurs between module A and B when complete data structure is passed from one module to another.

3. **Control coupling:** a module controls the flow of control or the logic of another module. This is accomplished by passing control information items as arguments in the argument list.
4. **Common coupling:** modules share common or global data or file structures. This is the strongest form of coupling both modules depend on the details of the common structure
5. **Content coupling:** A module is allowed to access or modify the contents of another, *e.g.* modify its local or private data items. This is the strongest form of coupling.

Cohesion: It is a measure of the degree to which the elements of a module are functionally related. Cohesion is weak if elements are bundled simply because they perform similar or related functions. Cohesion is strong if all parts are needed for the functioning of other parts (*e.g.*, Important design objective is to maximize module cohesion and minimize module coupling.

Types of Cohesion:

1. **Functional cohesion :** A and B are part of a single functional task. This is very good reason for them to be contained in the same procedure or achieved when the components of a module cooperate in performing exactly one function, *e.g.*, POLL_SENSORS, GENERATE_ALARM, etc.
2. **Sequential cohesion :** Module A outputs some data which forms the input to B. This is the reason for them to be contained in the same procedure.
3. **Communicational cohesion :** is achieved when software units or components of a module sharing a common information or data structure are grouped in one module.
4. **Procedural cohesion :** is the form of cohesion obtained when software components are grouped in a module to perform a series of functions following a certain procedure specified by the application requirements.
5. **Temporal cohesion :** Module exhibits temporal cohesion when it contains tasks that are related by the fact that all tasks must be executed in the same time-span. Examples are functions required to be activated for a particular input event, or during the same state of operation.
6. **Logical cohesion :** refers to modules designed using functions who are logically related, such as input/output functions, communication type functions (such as send and receive).
7. **Coincidental cohesion :** Coincidental cohesion exists in modules that contain instructions that have little or no relationship to one another.

Data Flow Diagrams

DFD show the flow of data through the system.

- All names should be unique
- It is not a flow chart
- Suppress logical decisions
- Defer error conditions & handling until the end of the analysis

Symbol	Name	Function
	Data flow	Connect process
	Process	Perform some transformation of its input data to yield output data.
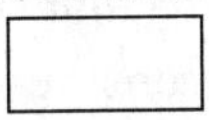	Source or sink	A source of system inputs or sink of system outputs.
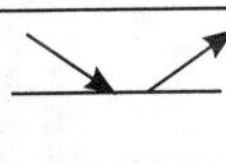	Data store	A repository of data, the arrow-head indicate net input and net outputs to store.

LEVELING

DFD represent a system or software at any level of abstraction. A level 0 DFD is called fundamental system model or context model represents entire software element as a single bubble with input and output data indicating by incoming & outgoing arrows.

Data Dictionaries are simply repositories to store information about all data items defined in DFD.

Includes:

Name of data item

Aliases (other names for items)

Description/Purpose

Related data items

Range of values

Data flows

Data structure definition

Planning and Managing the Product

4

INTRODUCTION

After finalizing SRS, next part is to estimate size, cost and development time of the project. Also, in many cases, customer may like to know the cost and development time even prior to finalization of the SRS.

In order to conduct a successful software project, we must understand:

- Scope of work to be done
- The resources required
- The cost to be expended
- The risk to be incurred
- The task to be accomplished
- The schedule to be followed

Software planning begins before technical work starts, continues as the software evolves from concept to reality.

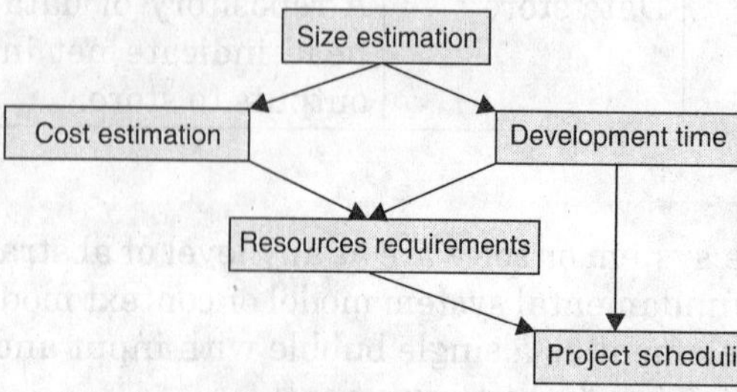

Fig. Activities during Software Project Planning

SIZE ESTIMATION

Lines of Code (LOC)

"A line of code is any line of program text that is not a comment or blank line, regardless of the number of statements or fragments of statements on the line. This specifically includes all lines containing program header, declaration, and executable and non-executable statements". This is the predominant definition for lines of code used by researchers. By this definition, figure shown has 17 LOC.

```
int. sort (int × [ ]. int n)
{
int i, j, save, im1;
/*This function sorts array x in ascending order*/
```

```
If (n < 2) return 1;
for (i = 2; i < = n; i ++)
{
im 1 = i – 1;
for (j = 1; J < = im; j++)
if (X[i] < X[j])
{
Save = X[i];
X[i] = X[j];
X[j] = save;
}
}
return 0;
}
```

FUNCTION COUNT

Alan Albrecht while working for IBM, recognized the problem in size measurement in the 1970s, and developed a technique (which he called Function Point Analysis), which appeared to be a solution to the size measurement problem.

The principle of Albrecht's function point analysis (FPA) is that a system is decomposed into functional units.

- **Inputs :** information entering the system
- **Outputs :** information leaving the system
- **Enquiries :** requests for instant access to information
- **Internal logical files :** information held within the system
- **External interface files :** information held by other system that is used by the system being analyzed

The FPA functional units are shown in figure given below.

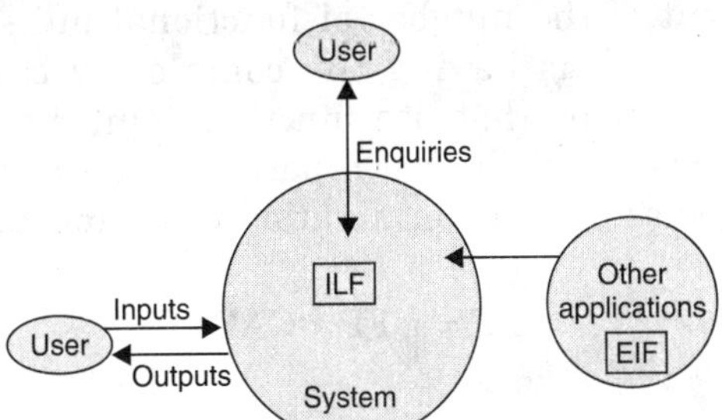

Special Features

- Function point approach is independent of the language, tools, or methodologies used for implementation; i.e., they do not take into consideration programming languages, data base management systems, processing hardware or any other data base technology.
- Function points can be estimated from requirement specification or design specification, thus making it possible to estimate development efforts in early phases of development.

Function points are directly linked to the statement of requirements; any change of requirements can easily be followed by a re-estimate.

Counting Function Points

Functional Units	Weighting Factors		
	Low	Average	High
External Inputs (EI)	3	4	6
External Output (EO)	4	5	7
External Inquiries (EQ)	3	4	6
External Logical Files (ILF)	7	10	15
External Interface Files (EIF)	5	7	10

The procedure for the calculation of UFP in mathematical form is given below:

$$\text{UFP} = \sum_{i=1}^{5} \sum_{J=1}^{3} Z_{ij} W_{ij}$$

Where i indicates the row and j indicates the column of table.

W_{ij}: It is the entry of the ith row and jth column of the table.

Z_{ij}: It is the count of the number of functional units of Type i that have been classified as having the complexity corresponding to column j. Organizations that use function point methods develop a criterion for determining whether a particular entry is Low, Average or High. Nonetheless, the determination of complexity is somewhat subjective.

$$\text{FP} = \text{UFP} * \text{CAF}$$

Where CAF is complexity adjustment factor and is equal to $[0.65 + 0.01 \times \Sigma F_i]$. The F_i ($i = 1$ to 14) are the degree of influence and are:

Rate each factor on a scale of 0 to 5.

0	1	2	3	4	5
No influence	Incidental	Moderate	Average	Significant	Essential

Number of factors considered (F_i)

1. Does the system require reliable backup and recovery?
2. Is data communication required?
3. Are there distributed processing functions
4. Is performance critical?
5. Will the system run in an existing heavily utilized operational environment?
6. Does the system require on line data entry?
7. Does the on line data entry require the input transaction to be built over multiple screens or operations?
8. Are the master files updated on line?
9. Is the inputs, outputs, files or inquiries complex?
10. Is the internal processing complex?
11. Is the code designed to be reusable?
12. Are conversion and installation included in the design?
13. Is the system designed for multiple installations in different organizations ?
14. Is the application designed to facilitate change and ease of use by the user?

Cost Estimation

A number of estimation techniques have been developed and are having following attributes in common:

Project scope must be established in advance

- Software metrics are used as a basis from which estimates are made
- The project is broken into small pieces which are estimated individually

To achieve reliable cost and schedule estimates, a number of options arise:

Delay estimation until late in project

- Use simple decomposition techniques to generate project cost and schedule estimates
- Develop empirical models for estimation
- Acquire one or more automated estimation tools

Static, Single Variable Models

Methods using this model use an equation to estimate the desired values such as cost, time, effort, etc. They all depend on the same variable used as predictor (say, size). An example of the most common equations is:

$$C = a \text{ L } b$$

C is the cost, L is the size and *a, b* are constants

$$E = 1.4 \text{ L } 0.93$$

$$DOC = 30.4 \text{ L } 0.90$$

$$D = 4.6 \text{ L } 0.26$$

Static, Multivariable Model

These models are often based on equation (*i*), they actually depend on several variables representing various aspects of the software development environment, for example method used, user participation, customer oriented changes, memory constraints, etc.

$$E = 5.2 \text{ L } 0.91$$

$$D = 4.1 \text{ L } 0.36$$

The productivity index uses 29 variables which are found to be highly correlated to productivity as follows:

$$I = \sum_{i=1}^{29} W_i X_i$$

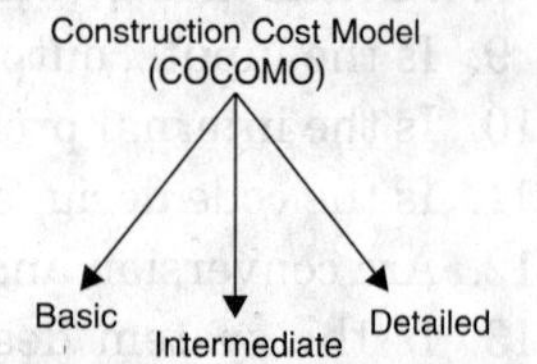

Model proposed by B.W. Boehm's

COCOMO work on the following models

(*i*) Organic Mode

(*ii*) Semidetached Mode

(*iii*) Embeded Mode

Basic Model

Basic COCOMO model takes the form

$$E = a_b (\text{KLOC})^{b_b}$$

$$D = C_b\,(E)^{d_b}$$

Where E is effort applied in Person-Months and D is the development time in months. The coefficients a_b, b_b, c_b and d_b are given in the following table:

Software project	a_b	b_b	c_b	d_b
Organic	2.4	1.05	2.5	0.38
Semidetached	3.0	1.12	2.5	0.35
Embedded	3.6	1.20	2.5	0.32

Coding, Testing Implementation and Maintenance

5

CODING STYLES

Coding guidelines provide only general suggestions regarding the coding style to be followed.

1. **Do not use a coding style that is too clever or too difficult to understand:** Code should be easy to understand. Clever coding can obscure meaning of the code and hamper understanding. It also makes maintenance difficult.
2. **Avoid obscure side effects:** The side effects of a function call include modification of parameters passed by reference, modification of global variables, and I/O operations. An obscure side effect is one that is not obvious from a casual examination of the code. Obscure side effects make it difficult to understand a piece of code.
3. **Does not use an identifier for multiple purposes:** Programmers often use the same identifier to denote several temporary entities. There are several things which are wrong with this approach and hence should be avoided. Some of the problems caused by use of variables for multiple purposes are as follows:
   - Each variable should be given a descriptive name indicating its purpose. This is not possible if an identifier is used for multiple purposes. Use of a variable for multiple purposes can lead to confusion and make it difficult to read and understand the code.
   - Use of variables for multiple purposes usually makes future enhancements more difficult.
   - **The code should be well-documented:** As a rule of thumb, there must be at least one comment line on the average for every three source lines.
   - **Do not use goto statements:** Use of goto statements makes a program unstructured and very difficult to understand.

Verification and Validation

Verification is the process of evaluating a system or component to determine whether the products of a given development phase satisfy the conditions imposed at the start of that phase.

Validation is the process of evaluating a system or component during or at the end of development process to determine whether it satisfies the specified requirements .

Testing = Verification + Validation

Software Testing

- Software testing is the process of testing the software product.
- Testing strategy provides a framework or set of activities which are essential for the success of the project they may include planning, designing of test cases, execution of program with test cases, interpretation of the outcome and finally collection and management of data.
- Testing is the process of executing a program with the intent of finding errors.
- Effective software testing will contribute to the delivery of high quality software product, more satisfied users, lower maintenance cost, more accurate and reliable result.
- Hence software testing is necessary and important activity of software development process.

Coding Guidelines

- Package name should be in lower case (mypackage, edu.iitk.maths)
- Type names should be nouns and start with uppercase (Day, DateOfBirth,...)
- Var names should be nouns in lowercase; vars with large scope should have long names; loop iterators should be *i, j, k*...
- Const names should be all caps
- Method names should be verbs starting with lower case (*e.g.*, getValue())
- Prefix *is* should be used for boolean method

Error, Mistake, Bug, Fault and Failure

- People make errors. A good synonym is mistake. This may be a syntax error or misunderstanding of specifications. Sometimes, there are logical errors.
- When developers make mistakes while coding, we call these mistakes "bugs"

- A fault is the representation of an error, where representation is the mode of expression, such as narrative text, data flow diagrams, ER diagrams, source code etc. Defect is a good synonym for fault.
- A failure occurs when a fault executes. A particular fault may cause different failures, depending on how it has been exercised.

Test Case

This is the triplet [I, S, O], where I is the data input to the system, S is the state of the system at which the data is input, and O is the expected output of the system.

Test Suite

This is the set of all test cases with which a given software product is to be tested. The set of test cases is called a test suite. Hence any combination of test cases may generate a test suite.

Test Data

Inputs which have been devised to test the system Test cases Inputs to test the system and the predicted outputs from these inputs if the system operates according to its specification.

Test Case ID	
Section-I (Before Execution)	**Section-II (After Execution)**
Purpose:	Execution History:
Pre condition: (If any)	Result:
Inputs:	If fails, any possible reason (Optional):
Expected Outputs:	Any other observation:
Post conditions:	Any suggestion:
Written by:	Run by:
Date:	Date:

Levels of Testing

There are 3 levels of testing:

(*i*) Unit Testing

(*ii*) Integration Testing

(*iii*) System Testing

- Unit testing (or module testing) is the testing of different units (or modules) of a system in isolation.

- In order to test a single module, a complete environment is needed to provide all that is necessary for execution of the module. That is, besides the module under test itself, the following steps are needed in order to be able to test the module.

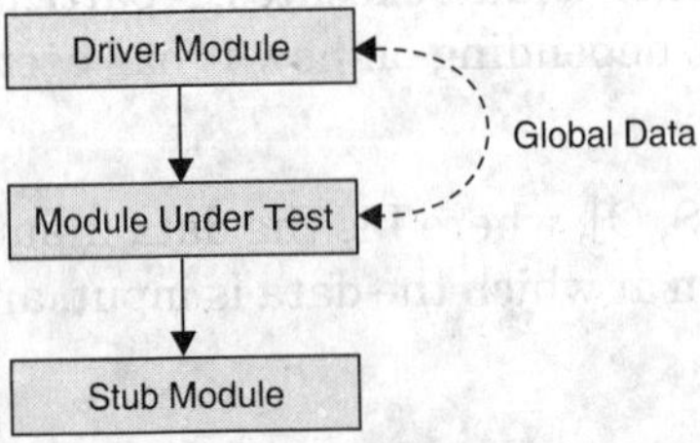

Integration Testing: Integration is the process by which components are aggregated to create larger components. Integration Testing is testing done to show that even though the components were individually satisfactory (after passing component testing), checks the combination of components are incorrect or inconsistent.

- Focuses on interaction of modules in a subsystem.
- Unit tested modules combined to form subsystems.
- Test cases to "exercise" the interaction of modules in different ways.

Purpose of Integration: Testing is to identify bugs of following Types: These are protocol-design bugs, input and output format bugs, inadequate protection against corrupted data, wrong subroutine call sequence, call-parameter bugs, misunderstood entry or exit parameter values. The entire system is viewed as a collection of subsystems (sets of classes) determined during the system and object design.

Goal: Test all interfaces between subsystems and the interaction of subsystems

There are four types of approaches used in integration testing:

(*i*) Top down integration testing
(*ii*) Bottom up integration testing
(*iii*) Sandwich testing
(*iv*) Big bang testing

System Testing

During system testing, we should evaluate a number of attributes of the software that are vital to the user. These represent the operational correctness of the product and may be part of the software specifications.

There are following attributes to be checked while system testing:

Usable	Is the product convenient, clear, and predictable?
Secure	Is access to sensitive data restricted to those with authorization ?
Compatible	Will the product work correctly in conjunction with existing data software and procedures?
Dependable	Do adequate safeguards against failure and methods for recovery exists in the product?
Documented	Are manuals complete, correct and understandable?

Alpha, Beta and Acceptance Testing

The term **Acceptance Testing** is used when the software is developed for a specific customer. A series of tests are conducted to enable the customer to validate all requirements. These tests are conducted by the end user customer and may range from adhoc tests to well planned systematic series of tests.

The terms **alpha and beta testing** are used when the software is developed as a product for anonymous customers. Alpha Tests are conducted at the developer's site by some potential customers. These tests are conducted in a controlled environment. Alpha testing may be started when formal testing process is near completion. Beta Tests are conducted by the customers / end users at their sites. Unlike alpha testing, developer is not present here. Beta testing is conducted in a real environment that cannot be controlled by the developer.

Functional Testing (Black Box Testing)

In the black-box testing, test cases are designed from an examination of the input/output values only and no knowledge of design, or code is required. The following are the main approaches to designing black box test cases.

1. Boundary value analysis
2. Equivalence class portioning
3. Cause Effect graphing

1. Boundary value analysis

- Test cases that are close to boundary value condition have a higher chance of detecting an error.
- Boundary condition means, an input value may be on the boundary, just below the boundary (upper side) or just above the boundary (lower side).

- Programmers often fail to see the special processing required by the input values that lie at the boundary of the different equivalence classes.

  For example, programmers may improperly use < instead of <=, or conversely <= for <. Boundary value analysis leads to selection of test cases at the boundaries of the different equivalence classes.
- Suppose we have an input variable x with a range from 1–100 the boundary values are 1,2,99 and 100. Equivalence Class Partitioning
- In this approach, the domain of input values to a program is partitioned into a finite number of equivalence classes, so that if the program works correctly for a value then it will work correctly for all the other values in that class.
- This partitioning is done such that the behavior of the program is similar for every input data belonging to the same equivalence class.
- The main idea behind defining the equivalence classes is that testing the code with any one value belonging to an equivalence class is as good as testing the software with any other value belonging to that equivalence class.
- Equivalence classes for a software can be designed by examining the input data and output data.
- The following are some general guidelines for designing the equivalence classes

Cause effect graphing

- One weakness with the equivalence class partitioning and boundary value methods is that they consider each input separately. That is, both concentrate on the conditions and classes of one input.
- One way to exercise combinations of different input conditions is to consider all valid combinations of the equivalence classes of input conditions.
- For example, if there are *n different input conditions, such that a* combination of the input conditions is valid, we will have 2^ test cases.

Structural Testing (White Box Testing)

- A complementary approach to functional testing is called structural / white box testing.

- It permits us to examine the internal structure of the program.
- In the white-box testing approach, designing test cases requires thorough knowledge about the internal structure of software, and therefore the white-box testing is called structural testing.

Various criteria of structural testing

1. **Path Testing:** Path based testing strategy requires us to design test cases such that all linearly independent paths in the program are executed at least once. A linearly independent path can be defined in terms of the control flow graph (CFG) of a program.

   This type of testing involves:

   - generating a set of paths that will cover every branch in the program.
   - finding a set of test cases that will execute every path in the set of program paths.

   Basically two types of graph are designed through path testing:

   (*i*) **Control flow graph:** The control flow of a program can be analyzed using a graphical representation known as flow graph. The flow graph is a directed graph in which nodes are either entire statements or fragments of a statement, and edges represents flow of control. If I and j are nodes in the program graph ,there is an edge from node I to node j if the statement (fragment) corresponds to node j can be executed immediately after the statement.

   Flow graph representation is the first step of path testing

   - Second step is to draw the DD graph from the flow graph
   - DD path graph is known as decision to decision path graph in which on concentrate decision nodes.
   - The nodes of flow graph which are sequence are combined into single node.
   - Hence DD graph is directed graph in which nodes are sequence of statements and edges show control flow between nodes
   - The DD path graph is used to find independent path.
   - Execute all independent path at least once.

Cyclomatic Complexity

- Is also known as structural complexity because it gives internal view of code
- For more complicated programs it is not easy to determine the number of independent paths of the program.
- McCabe's cyclomatic complexity defines the number of linear independent paths through a program. Also, the McCabe's cyclomatic complexity is very simple to compute.
- The McCabe's cyclomatic complexity metric provides a practical way of determining the maximum number of linearly independent paths in a program. Though the McCabe's metric does not directly identify the linearly independent paths, but it informs approximately how many paths to look for. There are three different ways to compute the cyclomatic complexity.

Method 1: Given a control flow graph G of a program, the cyclomatic complexity V(G) can be computed as:

$$V(G) = E - N + 2(P)$$

where N is the number of nodes of the control flow graph and E is the number of edges in the control flow graph.

Method 2: An alternative way of computing the cyclomatic complexity of a program from an inspection of its control flow graph is as follows:

$$V(G) = \text{Total number of bounded areas} + 1$$

In the program's control flow graph G, any region enclosed by nodes and edges can be called as a bounded area.

Method 3: The cyclomatic complexity of a program can also be easily computed by computing the number of decision statements of the program. If N is the number of decision statement of a program, then the McCabe's metric is equal to N + 1.

Mutation Testing

- Software is first tested by using an initial test suite built up from the different white box testing strategies.
- After the initial testing is complete, mutation testing is taken up.
- Mutation testing is a fault based technique.
- The idea behind mutation testing is to make few arbitrary changes to a program at a time.
- Multiple copies of a program are made, and each copy is altered; this altered copy is called a mutant. Mutants are executed with test data to determine whether the test data are capable of detecting the change between the original program and the mutated program

- A major disadvantage of the mutation-based testing approach is that it is computationally very expensive, since a large number of possible mutants can be generated.
- Mutation testing should be used in conjunction of some testing tool which would run all the test cases automatically.

Performance Testing

- Performance testing is carried out to check whether the system needs the nonfunctional requirements identified in the SRS document.
- There are several types of performance testing. Among of them nine types are discussed below. The types of performance testing to be carried out on a system depend on the different non-functional requirements of the system documented in the SRS document. All performance tests can be considered as black-box tests.
  - Stress testing
  - Volume testing
  - Configuration testing
  - Compatibility testing
  - Regression testing
  - Recovery testing
  - Maintenance testing
  - Documentation testing
  - Usability testing

Software Maintenance

Software Maintenance is a very broad activity that includes error corrections, enhancements of capabilities, deletion of obsolete capabilities, and optimization. Software maintenance is needed to correct errors, enhance features, port the software to new platforms, etc. 70 percent of the cost of software is devoted to maintenance.

Need for Software Maintenance:

- Software Maintenance is a very broad activity that includes error corrections, enhancements of capabilities, deletion of obsolete capabilities, and optimization.
- Software maintenance is needed to correct errors, enhance features, port the software to new platforms, etc.

- 70 percent of the cost of software is devoted to maintenance

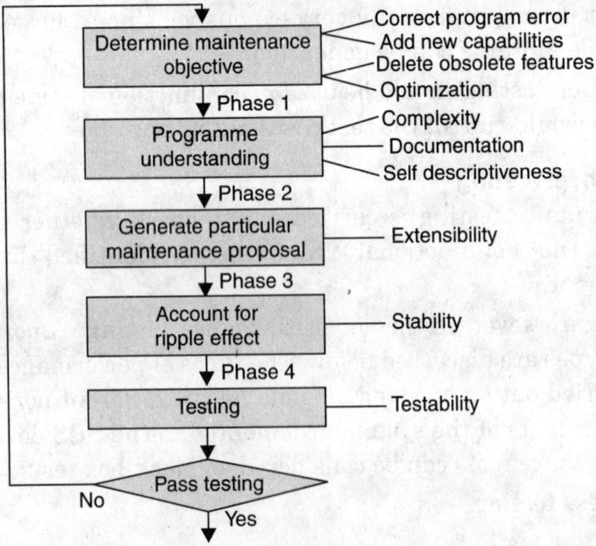

Types of Maintenance

Corrective: Corrective maintenance of a software product is necessary to rectify the bugs observed while the system is in use.

Adaptive: A software product might need maintenance when the customers need the product to run on new platforms, on new operating systems, or when they need the product to interface with new hardware or software.

Perfective: A software product needs maintenance to support the new features that users want it to support, to change different functionalities of the system according to customer demands, or to enhance the performance of the system.

Estimation of maintenance cost

- Maintenance Effort is very significant and consume about 40–70% of the cost of entire life cycle
- It is advisable to invent more effort in early phase of software life cycle to reduce the maintenance cost
- The defect repair ratio increase heavily from analysis phase to implementation phase

- Good software engineering techniques such as precise specification, loose coupling and configuration management all reduce maintenance cost.

Phase	Ratio
Analysis	1
Design	10
Implementation	100

Software Configuration Management

Configuration management (CM) is the process of controlling and documenting change to a developing system. As the size of an effort increase, so does the necessity of implementing effective CM. Software configuration management (SCM) is a set of activities that are designed to control change by identifying the work products that are likely to change, establishing relationships among them. The process of software development and maintenance is controlled is called configuration management. The configuration management is different in development and maintenance phases of life cycle due to different environments.

Configuration Management Activities: The activities are divided into four broad categories.

1. The identification of the components and changes.
2. The control of the way by which the changes are made .
3. Auditing the changes.
4. Status accounting recording and documenting all the activities that have take place.

Functions of SCM

- **Identification** identifies those items whose configuration needs to be controlled, usually consisting of hardware, software, and documentation.
- **Change Control** establishes procedures for proposing or requesting changes, evaluating those changes for desirability, obtaining authorization for changes, publishing and tracking changes, and implementing changes. This function also identifies the people and organizations who have authority to make changes at various levels.

- **Status Accounting** is the documentation function of CM. Its primary purpose is to maintain formal records of established configurations and make regular reports of configuration status. These records should accurately describe the product, and are used to verify the configuration of the system for testing, delivery, and other activities.
- **Auditing** Effective CM requires regular evaluation of the configuration. This is done through the auditing function, where the physical and functional configurations are compared to the documented configuration. The purpose of auditing is to maintain the integrity of the baseline and release configurations for all controlled products.
- **Redocumentation** is the recreation of a semantically equivalent representation within the same relative abstraction level.
- **Design recovery** entails identifying and extracting meaningful higher level abstractions beyond those obtained directly from examination of the source code. This may be achieved from a combination of code, existing design documentation, personal experience, and knowledge of the problem and application domains.

Computer Science

11

Computer Network

CONTENTS

OSI Stack, LAN Technologies (Ethernet, Token Ring)

1

OSI MODEL

Open System Interconnection (OSI) is a well defined conceptual communication model that is developed by for **International Organization of Standardization or ISO** to ensure data communication compatibility. It is a seven layer architecture. It is a layered model with seven layers and each layer being designated to well-defined part of communication system with various protocols defined at each layer.

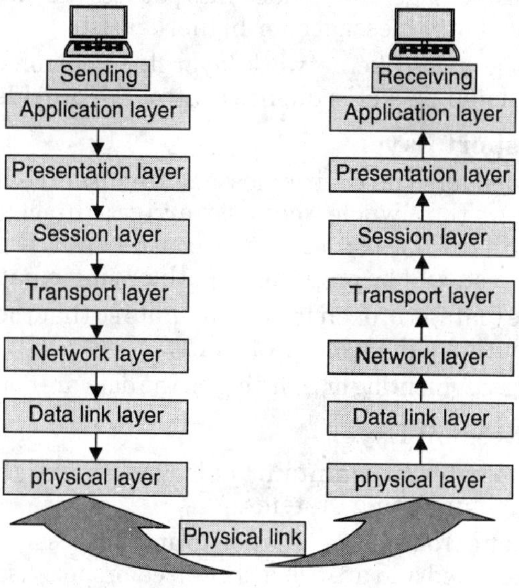

Functions of Different Layers

Layer 1: The Physical Layer:

- It is the basic layer of the OSI Model. It is responsible for activating, maintaining and deactivating the physical connection.
- It deals with raw unstructured data, encoding the data and converting the digital/analog bits into electrical signal or optical signals.
- Voltages and data rates needed for transmission is defined in the physical layer.

Layer 2: Data Link Layer

- It is a logical layer between two nodes in a network.
- It is handles synchronization of data to be transmitted over the physical layer and Transmission and receiving of data frames sequentially. It sends and expects acknowledgements for frames received and sent respectively.
- This layer is to make sure that data is transferred error free from one node to another and manages the Frame traffic control over the network.

Layer 3: The Network Layer

- This layer deliver packets from source to destination across multiple links (networks). If two system are connected on the same link then network layer is not required. The signal is routed through different channels to the other end as a network controller.
- The outgoing messages are divided into packets the incoming packets are assembled into messages for higher levels.
- Connection services like network layer flow control, network layer error control and packet sequence control are provided.

Layer 4: Transport Layer

- This layer delivers the entire message from source to destination. It make sure that whole message arrives intact and in order, ensuring both error control and flow control level. It decides if data transmission should be on parallel path or single path.
- the message (data)is broken into small units so that they are handled more efficiently by the network layer .
- Multiplexing, Segmenting or Splitting on the data are done by this layer.

Layer 5: The Session Layer

- This layer establish, maintain and synchronize the interaction between communicating systems.
- Transfer of data from one destination to another session layer streams of data are marked and are resynchronized properly, so that the ends of the messages are not cut prematurely and data loss is avoided.

Layer 6: The Presentation Layer

- This layer takes care of the syntax and semantics of the information exchanged between two communicating systems and the data is sent in such a way that the receiver will understand the information (data) and will be able to use the data.
- This layer act as role translator as two systems can have different language.
- It performs Data compression, Data encryption, Data conversion etc.

Layer 7: Application Layer

- It is the top most layer of OSI Model.
- It deals with data Manipulation enabling user or software access to the network.
- Some services provided by this layer includes: E-Mail, transferring of files, distributing the results to user, directory services, network resource etc.
- This layer mainly holds application programs to act upon the received and to be sent data.

Merits of OSI reference model

- It distinguishes well between the services, interfaces and protocols.
- Protocols are very well hidden & can be replaced by new protocols as technology changes.
- Supports both connection oriented & connectionless service.

Demerits of OSI reference model

- Model was devised before the invention of protocols.
- Fitting of protocols is tedious task.
- It is just used as a reference model.

PROTOCOLS	
Application	NNTP, SIP, SSI, DNS, FTP, Gopher, HTTP, NFS, NTP, SMPP, SMTP, DHCP, SNMP, Telnet, Netconf
Presentation	MIME, XDR, TLS, SSL
Session	Named Pipes, NetBIOS, SAP, SIP, L2TP, PPTP
Transport	TCP, UDP, SCTP, DCCP
Network	IP (IPv4, IPv6), ICMP, IPsec, IGMP, IPX, Apple Talk
Data Link	ATM, SDLC, HDLC, ARP, CSLIP, SLIP, PLIP, IEEE 802.3, Frame Relay ITU-T G.hn DLL, PPP, X.25
Physical	EIA/TIA-232 EIA/TIA-449 ITU-T VSeries, I.430, I431 POTS, PDH, SONET/SDH PON, OTN, DSL, IEEE 802.3 IEEE 802.11 IEEE 802.15, IEEE 802.16, IEEE 1394, ITU-T, G.hn, PHY USB Bluetooth

TOKEN RING (IEEE 802.5)

- Star-wired ring topology
- Connectionless communication
- Token-passing access method
- Shielded and unshielded twisted-pair cabling
- Baseband transmission

Operation

- When a station wishes to transmit, it must wait for token to pass by and seize the token.
  - **One approach:** change one bit in token which transforms it into a "start-of-frame sequence" and appends frame for transmission.
  - **Second approach:** station claims token by removing it from the ring.
- The data frame circles the ring and is removed by the transmitting station.
- Each station interrogates passing frame. If destined for station, it copies the frame into local buffer.

Token Holding Time

Token Rotation Time (TRT):

$$TRT \le \text{Active Nodes} * THT + \text{Ring Latency}$$

$$THT = \text{Ring Latency} - \text{Token Circulation Time}$$

Frame Format

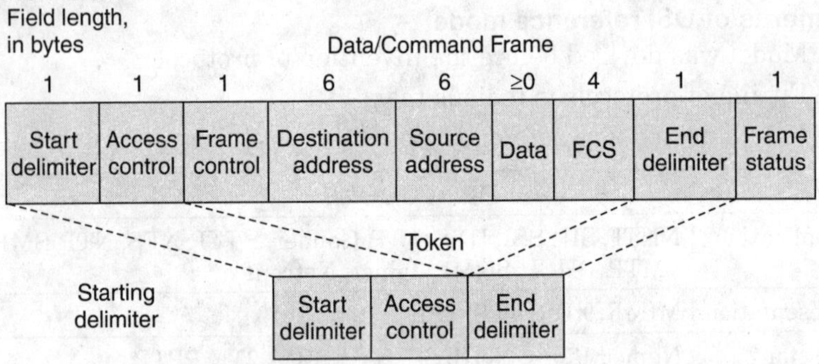

- **SD = Starting Delimiter(1 octet):** Indicates start of the frame
- **AC = Access Control(1 octet):** Indicates the frame's priority and whether it is a token or a data frame
- **FC = Frame Control (1 Octet):** Contains either Media Access Control information for all computers or "end station" information for only one computer
- **DA = Destination Address (2 or 6 Octets):** Indicates the address of the computer to receive the frame
- **SA = Source Address (2 or 6 Octets):** Indicates the computer that sent the frame
- **DATA = Information 0 or more octets up to 4027:** Contains the data being sent
- **FRC =** Frame check sequence **(4 Octets)** Contains CRC error-checking information
- **ED = Ending Delimiter (1 Octet):** Indicates the end of the frame

- **FS=Frame Status(1 octet):** Tells whether the frame was recognized, copied, or whether the destination address was available
- J, K = Code Violation
- T = Token; T = 0 for Token & T = 1 for Frame
- P = Priority bit; indicate tokens priority.
- M = Monitor bit; prevent a token whose priority is greater than 0 or any frame from continuously circulating on the ring.
- R = Reserved bits; allow station with high priority Frames to request that the next token be issued at the requested priority.
- The MSB (Most Significant Bit) is always transmitted first
- **Minimum Token size:** propagation delay = transmission delay

Field	Format	Description
Starting delimiter	J K 0 J K 0 | 0 | 0	J, K non-data symbols (line code)
Access control	P P P | T | M | R R R	PPP Priority, T Token bit M Monitor bit; RRR Reservation
Frame control	F F | Z Z Z Z Z Z	FF frame type ZZZZZZ control bit
Ending delimiter	J K I J K I | I | E	I intermediate-frame bit E error-detection bitg
Frame status	A | C | XX | A | C | X X	A address-recognized bit xx undefined C address-copied bit

A (Destination)	C (Frame Acceptance)	Remark
0	0	Destination not present & frame not accepted
0	1	Not possible
1	0	Destination present & frame not accepted
1	1	Destination present & frame accepted

- Ring Latency (RL): Time taken for a bit to travel around ring.

$$RL = \frac{d}{v} + \frac{Mb}{R} \text{ (seconds)} = \frac{dR}{V} + Mb \text{ (bits)}$$

where d: Length of link (in meters)

v: Velocity (m/sec)

M: Number of station

R: Data rate of link (bps)

- Data transfer rate = $\dfrac{f}{t_1 + t_2 + \dfrac{f}{b}}$;

  where f: Frame length
  B: Channel capacity or bandwidth
  t_1: Ring latency time
  t_2: token observing time

- Length of link (in bits) = $R \times \dfrac{d}{v}$

$$\text{Utilization} = \frac{T_1}{T_1 + T_2}$$

$$= \frac{1}{1 + \dfrac{a}{N}}; \text{ if } a < 1$$

$$= \frac{1}{a\left(1 + \dfrac{1}{N}\right)}; \text{ if } a > 1$$

where T_1: Average time to transmit a data frame
T_2: Average time to pass a token]
N: Number of stations

- **For Minimum Token Size :** Propagation delay = Transmission delay
- **Types of Control Frame**
  - (*i*) **Becon Frame:** (000010) to find major faults in ring
  - (*ii*) **Claim Token:** (000011) used in election process of monitor
  - (*iii*) **Purge:** (000100) used to clear unwanted singnals
  - (*iv*) **Active monitor present:** (000101) to inform all the stations that monitor is alive
  - (*v*) **Stand by monitor present:** (000110) to carryout neighour identification process
  - (*vi*) **Duplicate address test:** (000000) for virtual PC, physical address may change

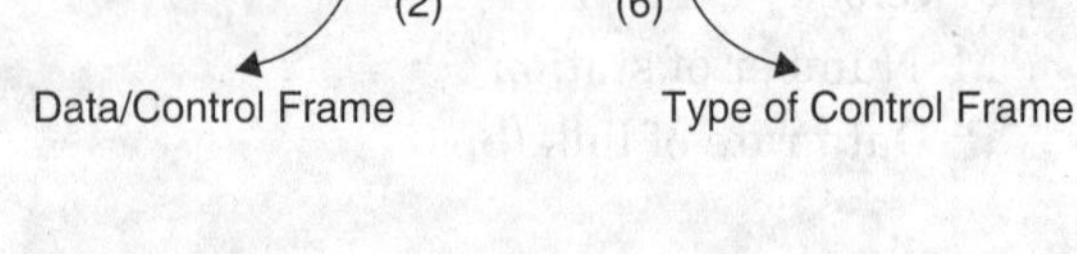

Delay Token Ring Reinsertion Strategy (DTR)	Early Token Ring Reinsertion Strategy (ETR)
(*a*) Token is reinserted after getting the entire data packet	(*a*) Token is reinserted as soon as data transmission is over
(*b*) Efficiency is low and always only one packet is available on the link	(*b*) Efficiency is high and many packets can be available on the link
(*c*) Reliability is high. THT = 10 ms	(*c*) Reliability is low, no meaning of THT
(*d*) It is used under no load conditions	(*d*) It is used under high load conditions
(*e*) Cycle time = $a + b + c + d$	(*e*) Cycle time = $a + c + d$ a: Packet transmission time b: Ring latency c: Token transmission d: Propagation delay between stations

ETHERNET (IEEE 802.3)

- It is basis of the Ethernet standard.
- Popular LAN technology
- Defines the carrier sense multiple access collision detect (CSMA/CD) protocol
- Relatively inexpensive &reasonably fast,
- Provides connectionless communication
- It defines the MAC layer for bus networks

FRAME FORMAT

IEEE 802.2

Field length, in bytes	7	1	6	6	2	46-1500	4
	Preamble	SOF	Destination address	Source address	Length	802.2 header and data	FCS

SOF = Start-of-frame delimiter
FCS = Frame check sequence

- **Preamble :** each byte have the bit pattern 10101010. Manchester encoding is employed that enables the receiver's clock to synchronize with the sender's and initialize itself.
- **Start of Frame Delimiter :** contains a byte sequence 10101011. Denotes the start of the frame.
- **Destination Address :** address where message has to be delivered. 2-byte local address and 6-byte, local or global address
- **Source Address :** address from where message is generated. 2-byte local address and 6-byte, local or global address

- **Length :** it tells number of bytes in the data field, from a minimum of 0 to a maximum of 1500.
- **Data :** This field can be split up into two parts - Data(0-1500 bytes) and Padding(0-46 bytes).
- **Frame Checksum :** contains CRC error-checking information
- **Multicast :** Sending to group of stations. This is ensured by setting the first bit in either 2-byte/6-byte addresses to 1.
- **Broadcast :** Sending to all stations. This can be done by setting all bits in the address field to 1.All Ethernet cards(Nodes) are a member of this group.

Reasons for having a minimum length frame:

1. To prevent a station from completing the transmission of a short frame before the first bit has even reached the far end of the cable, where it may collide with another frame

   Transmission time > 2*propagation time between two farthest nodes

2. When a transceiver detects a collision, it truncates the current frame, which implies that stray bits and pieces of frames appear on the cable all the time. Hence distinguish between valid frames and garbage,

Minimum Ethernet Frame Size :

DA + SA + Length + Data (mn) + CRC

= 6 + 6 + 2 + 46 + 4 bytes = 64 bytes

Maximum Ethernet Frame size :

DA+ SA + Length + Data(max) + CRC

= 6 + 6 + 2 + 1500 + 4 bytes = 1518 bytes

- Channel efficiency (utilization η) = $\dfrac{1}{1+\dfrac{2BLe}{vf}} = \dfrac{1}{1+5.44a}$

$$a = \frac{\text{Propagation delay}}{\text{Transmission delay}} = \frac{d/v}{f/B}$$

If length of packet increases η also increases

f: Frame length

v: Speed of signal propagation

e: Contention slots/frame

L: Cable length (d)

B: Network bandwidth

a: Propagation delay

2T: Duration of each slot = 2 × Propagation delay

A: Slot probability ($1/e$)

- The probability of one station succeeding in putting its traffic on a network of 'n' stations is given as $nP(1-P)^{n-1}$
- **CSMA/CD for ethernet:**

Utilization $\eta = \dfrac{1}{1+6.44a}$ [used when ack information is not provided]

$$\text{C.P.} = \text{Number of slots} \times \text{Slot duration}$$

$$= e \times 2 \times \frac{d}{v}$$

$$\text{Utilization} = \frac{\text{T.P.}}{\text{T.P.} + \text{C.P.}} = \frac{\left(\dfrac{1}{2a}\right)}{\left(\dfrac{1}{2a}\right)+\left(\dfrac{1-A}{A}\right)}$$

where, $\dfrac{1}{2a}$ = Transmission Interval

$\dfrac{1-A}{A}$ = Contention Interval

$$A = \left(1-\frac{1}{N}\right)^{N-1} ; \text{N = Number of stations}$$

Flow and Error Control

2

Flow Control: It coordinates that amount of data that can be sent before receiving acknowledgement.

Error Control: It is methods of error detection and retransmission that ensures that data arrives at the destination error free.

In the data link layer, it is based on ARQ (automatic repeat request) that is; retransmission of specific frame whenever error is detected in an exchange.

To ensure reliable communication, there needs to exist flow control and error control. Together Flow and error control needs to be done at several layers.

- For node-to-node links, flow and error control is carried out in the data-link layer.
- For end-point to end-point, flow and error control is carried out in the transport layer.

Flow and Error control:

- Error Detection and ARQ (error detection with retransmissions) must be combined with methods that intelligently limit the number of 'outstanding' (unACKed) frames.

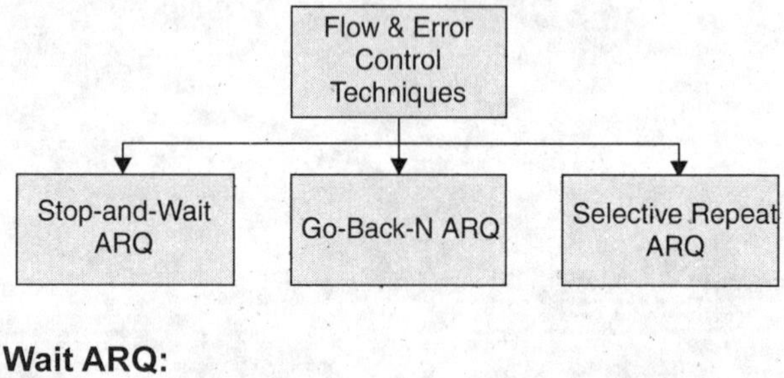

Stop and Wait ARQ:

- Include re-transmission of data in case of lost or damaged framer.
- It is addition to the basic flow control mechanism with re-transmissions.

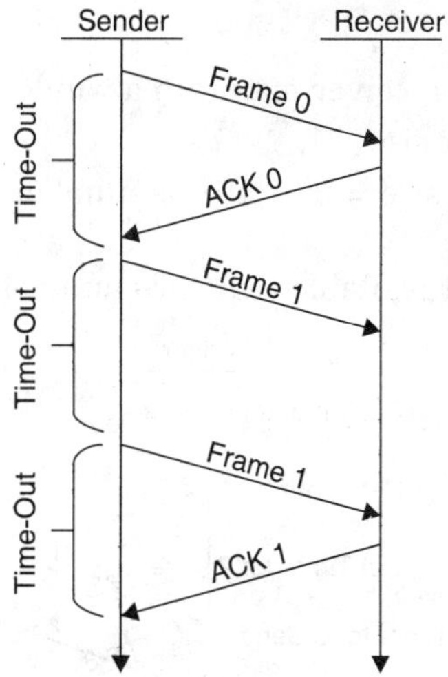

- The sender maintains a timeout counter.
- When a frame is sent, the sender starts the timeout counter.
- If acknowledgement of frame comes in time, the sender transmits the next frame in queue.
- If acknowledgement does not come in time, the sender assumes that either the frame or its acknowledgement is lost in transit. Sender retransmits the frame and starts the timeout counter.
- If a negative acknowledgement is received, the sender retransmits the frame.
- **Piggybacking:** In bidirectional communications, both parties implement flow control. Outstanding ACKs are placed in the header of information frames, piggybacking save bandwidth by combining the overhead from a data frame and an ACK frame (addresses, CRC, etc) into just one frame.
- Efficiency $\eta = \dfrac{t_{\text{transmit}}}{(t_{\text{transmit}}) + (2t_{\text{propagation}})}$

$$= \frac{t_{\text{transmit}}}{t_{\text{transmit}} + \text{Round Trip time (RTT)}}$$

$$= \frac{f/\text{B}}{f/\text{B} + \text{RTT}} = \frac{1}{1 + 2a} \qquad \left[\because a = \frac{t_{\text{propagation}}}{t_{\text{transmission}}}\right]$$

- **Throughput = 1 window/RTT = 1 packet/ RTT**

Go-back-n ARQ

- both sender and receiver maintain a window.
- Receiver window size = 1.
- Sender Window size = $2^k - 1$ (k is number of bits received in the header)
- $W_S + W_R \leq$ ASN (available sequence number)

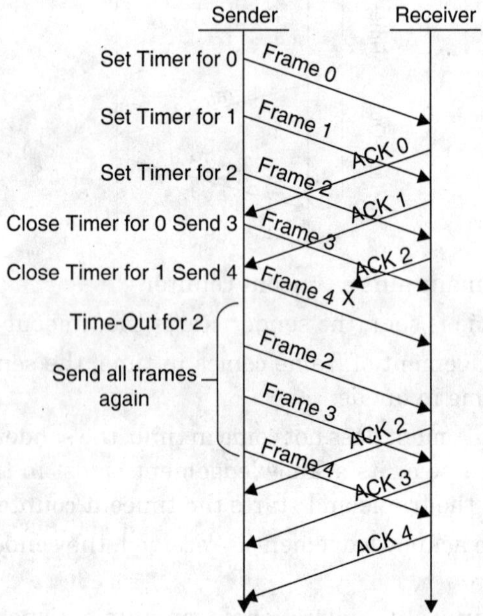

- Multiple frames are sent without previous acknowledgement (ACK).
- The sequence number of incoming frames is tracked at receivers end & it sends positive ACK back.
- After transmitting all the frames, sender checks up to which sequence number positive acknowledgements are received.
- If any acknowledgement is not received, it retransmits all the frames after which it does not receive any positive ACK.
- This is done so because the receiver does not have any buffer space for its window size and has to process each frame as it comes.
- It uses Cumulative ACK: The ACK N message acknowledges all frames with sequence number <= N
- Efficiency = $(2^K - 1) \times \dfrac{t_{\text{tranmission}}}{t_{\text{tranmission}} + \text{RTT}}$

Selective Repeat ARQ

- The receiver while keeping track of sequence numbers, buffers the frames in memory and sends NACK for only frame which is missing or damaged.
- It uses Selective ACK: The ACK N message acknowledges only the frame with sequence number N

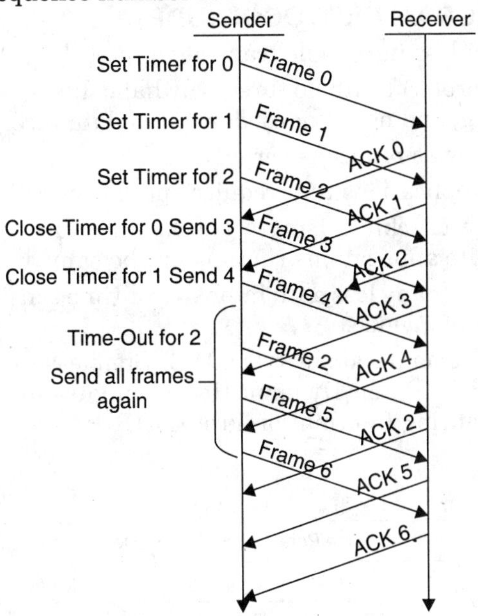

- $W_S = W_R = N/2$; N = maximum ASN(2^K)
- Uses piggybacking

  Piggyback throughput: (2 x packet) / RTT

$$\text{Efficiency} = (2^{K-1}) \times \frac{t_{\text{transmit}}}{t_{\text{transmit}} + \text{RTT}}$$

3 TCP/UDP and Sockets

USER DATAGRAM PROTOCOL (UDP)

- Connectionless unreliable transport protocol.
- Simplest protocol with no three-way handshake, no flow control, no sequencing, and no acknowledgment of data receipt.
- Less latency as reduced overhead
- Ideal for applications that require speed over reliability.
- Basic error-checking using a checksum & uses port numbers to differentiate applications running on the same host.
- Efficient for many less data intensive or time sensitive applications like streaming video.
- Example: Domain Name server (DNS), Simple Network Management Protocol (SNMP), the Dynamic Host Configuration Protocol (DHCP) and the Routing Information Protocol (RIP).

UDP FORMAT

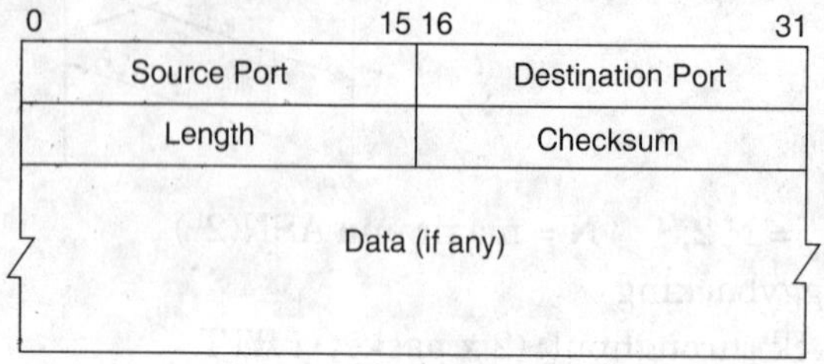

Field Length Description

Source Port: 16 bits → Source UDP Port
Destination Port: 16 bits → Destination UDP Port
Length: 16 bits → Length of the header and the data that is entire packet
Checksum: 16 bits → Used for Error-Checking
Data: The user data to be transmitted.

TCP-TRANSMISSION CONTROL PROTOCOL

- Connection- oriented transport protocol.
- Reliable delivery.
- Connection establishment involves an agreed upon mechanism.

- It employs a three-way handshake to form a connection.
- Stream-oriented transport protocol.
- Segment the data into smaller pieces & assign a sequence number to them.
- Provides flow control.
- Employs a *sliding* window mechanism.
- **Example:** File Transfer Protocol (FTP), HyperText Transfer Protocol (HTTP), Post Office Protocol (POP), Simple Mail Transfer Protocol (SMTP).

TCP Packet Structure

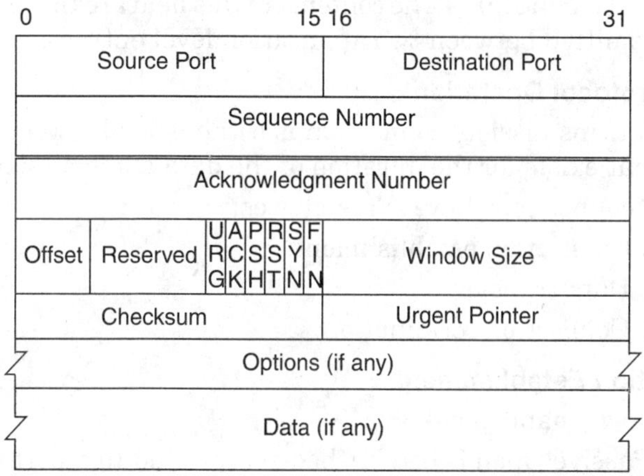

- **Source port: (16 bits)** → Identifies the sending application.
- **Destination port: (16 bits)** → Identifies the destination application.
- **Sequence number : (32 bit)** → Used for assembling segmented data in the proper order at the receiving end.
- **Acknowledgement number: (32 bit)** →The sequence number that the sender (the receiving end) expects next.
- **Data offset: (4 bit)** → The size of the TCP header and the offset from the start of the TCP packet to the data portion.
- **Reserved: (6 bit)** → Reserved for future use, should be set to zero.
- **Flags: (6 bit)** → (also known as control bits): indicate the type of transmission the packet represents and how the packet should be interpreted. contains six 1-bit flags:
  - URG—Urgent pointer field is significant.
  - ACK—Acknowledgement field is significant.
  - PSH—Push function.

- RST—Reset the connection.
- SYN—Synchronize sequence numbers.
- FIN—No more data from sender.

- **Window: (16 bit)** → The number of bytes the sender is willing to receive starting from the acknowledgement field value.
- **Checksum: (16 bit)** → error-checking of the header and data.
- **Urgent pointer: (16 bit)** → If the URG flag is set, then it is an offset from the sequence number indicating the last urgent data byte.
- **Options: (variable)** → Additional header fields may follow the urgent pointer.
- **Data: (variable)** → The contents of this field are the user data being transmitted between two application level entities.

Basic Protocol Operation

For data transmission, connection is established between the two end points that exists for the duration of the data transmission

TCP connections have three phases:

1. Connection establishment
2. Data transfer
3. Connection termination

Connection Establishment

Uses a 3-way handshake.

- 1st: Passive Open is established-server bind to a port to open it up for connections.
- 2nd: Active open is initiated by the client
- 3rd: acknowledgement is sent to client by the server . At this point, both the client and server have received an acknowledgement of the connection.

Data Transfer

Then the data is transferred by ensuring following features:

- Error-free data transfer : checksum is calculated and matched
- Ordered-data transfer: sequence number of packets ensures the correct order
- Retransmission of lost packets: lost packets are sent again is an acknowledgement is not received within a specified time period
- Discarding of duplicate packets
- Congestion throttling or flow control : a timer is set that help control congestion

Connection Termination

Uses four-way handshake with each side of the connection terminating independently.

- 1st: packet with flag is transmitted indicating it is finished
- 2nd: at other end; flag is acknowledge.
- this two-phase handshake from both ends of the connection terminates the connection.

SOCKET

- A *socket* is one endpoint of a two-way communication between two programs running on the network.
- An endpoint is a combination of an IP address and a port number. Every TCP connection can be uniquely identified by its two endpoints that enables multiple connections between the host and the server.
- A server runs on a specific computer and has a socket that is bound to a specific port number. The server just waits, listening to the socket for a client to make a connection request.
- On the client-side: The client knows the host name and port number of the server . It then establish connection with server.
- Server then binds client to a local port number accepting the connection.

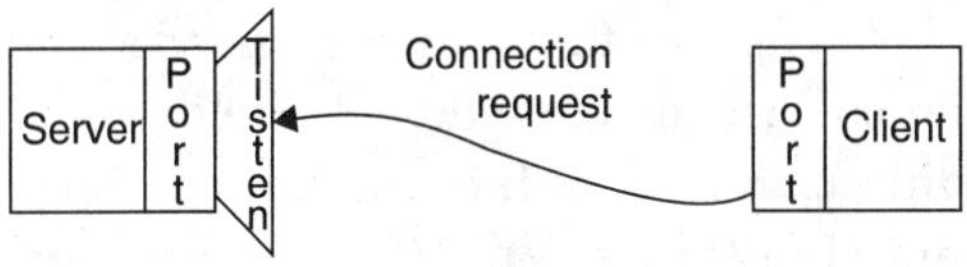

- A new socket is bounded to the address & port of the client. The client use the socket to communicate with the server.
- The new socket enables the original socket to listen to any other connection requests.

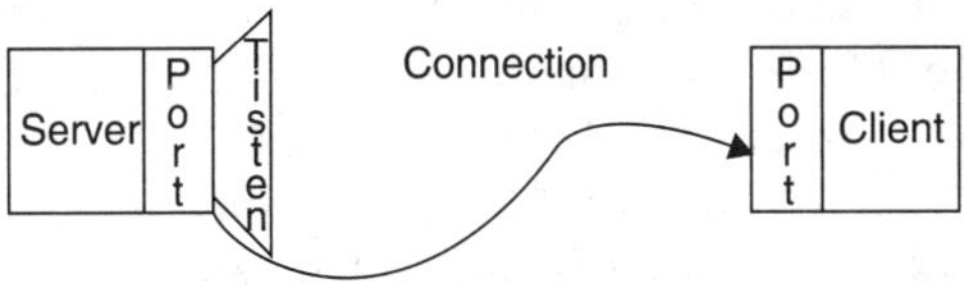

IPV4, Application Layer Protocol

4

Internet Protocol

- It is data-oriented protocol used for communicating data across a network.
- It is a best effort protocol;
- it does not guarantee delivery & correctness of data.
- Results in duplicate or out-of-order packets.

The IP Packet Structure

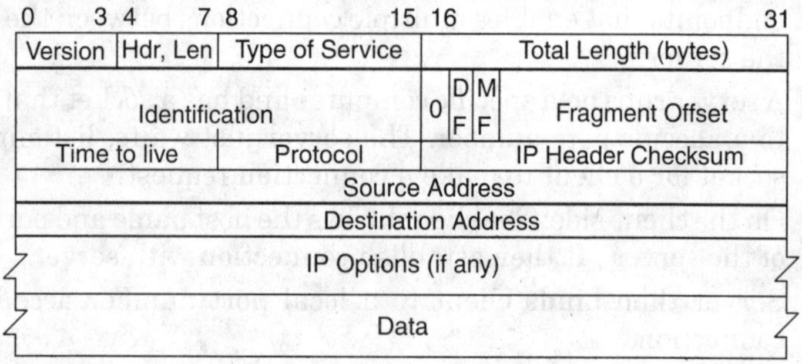

- An IP packet consists of two sections; header and data.
- The header consists of 12 mandatory fields and 1 optional field:
    - **Version:** Version no. of Internet Protocol used (e.g. IPV4).
    - **Internet Header Length (IHL):** Indicates the total size of the IP packet header.
    - **Type of Service (TOS):** Defines delay, throughput and reliability requirement of the IP packet.
    - **Total Length:** Length of entire IP Packet (including IP header and IP Payload).
    - **Identification:** Used for uniquely identifying fragments of an original IP datagram.
    - **Flags:** Used to control or identify fragments.
    - **Fragment Offset:** This offset tells the exact position of the fragment in the original IP Packet.
    - Time To Live (TTL) The maximum number of hops a packet can traverse between the source and destination hosts.
    - **Protocol:** Identifies the protocol used in the data portion of the IP packet.

- **Header Checksum:** Used for error checking of the header.
- **Source Address:** IP address of the sender of the packet. This may not be the actual address of the sender if NAT is used.
- **Destination address:** IP address of the receiver of the IP packet.
- **Options:** This is optional field, which is used if the value of IHL is greater than 5. These options may contain values for options such as Security, Record Route, Time Stamp, etc.
- **Data:** The contents of the data field are specified in the protocol header field and can be any one of the transport layer protocols.

IP ADDRESS

Used for global unique identification.

- An IP address provides a hierarchical structure to both uniquely identify a host, and what network that host exists on.
- An IP address is comprised of four octets, separated by periods. Each octet is an 8-bit number, resulting in a 32-bit IP address.

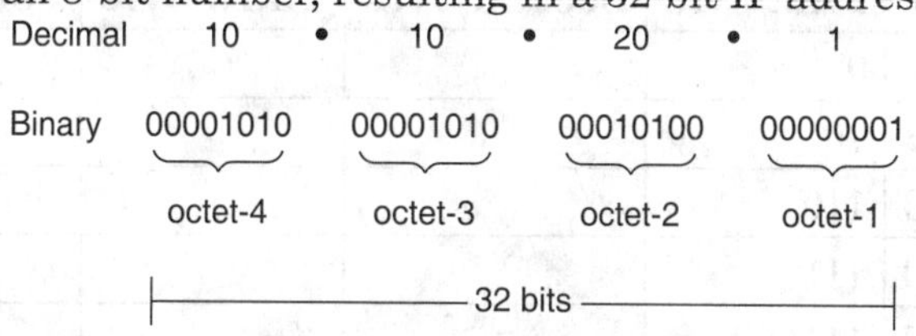

- The smallest possible value of an octet is 0, or 00000000 in binary.
- The largest possible value of an octet is 255, or 11111111 in binary.
- There are five classes of IP addresses – Class A, B, C, D, E.
- Class A acquires largest address space.

Class	Number of Addresses	Percentage
A	2^{31} = 2, 147, 483, 648	50%
B	2^{30} = 1, 073, 741, 824	25%
C	2^{29} = 536, 870, 912	12.5%
D	2^{28} = 268, 435, 456	6.25%
E	2^{28} = 268, 435, 456	6.25%

Address space

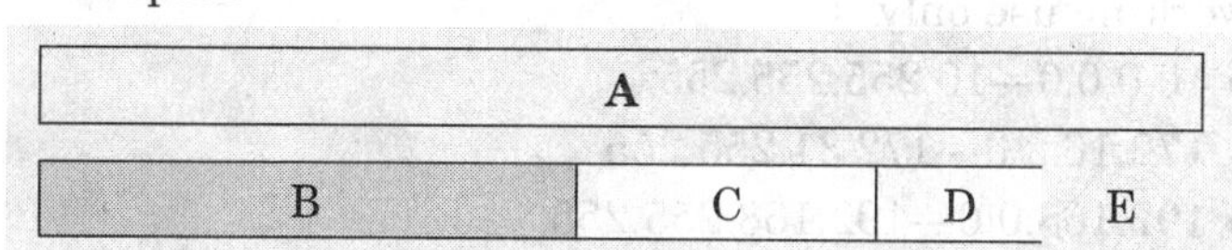

- IP address is divided into three sections:
  - **Class type:** Identifies the class type

- **Network Number:** Identifies the network.
- **Host-Number:** Identifies the host.

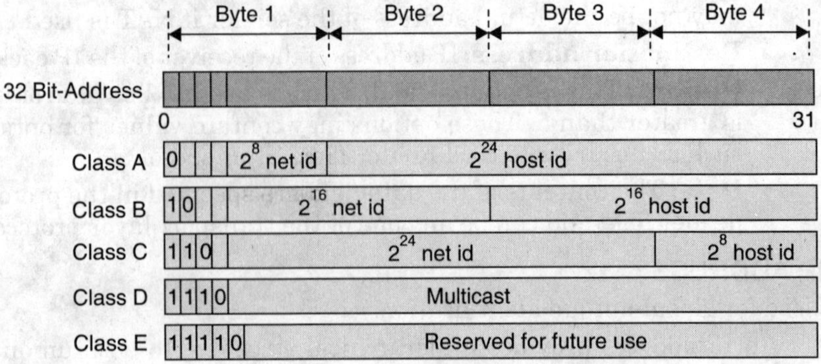

- Identification of class in binary notation:

	First byte	Second byte	Third byte	Fourth byte
Class	0			
Class B	10			
Class C	110			
Class D	1110			
Class E	1111			

- Identification of class in decimal notation:

Class A 1.0.0.0 to 126.255.255.255
Class B 128.0.0.0 to 191.255.255.255
Class C 192.0.0.0 to 233.255.255.255
Class D 224.0.0.0 to 239.255.255.255

Private IP Addresses

- Network hosts that do not need to have their addresses visible on the public Internet can be assigned private IP address.
- These addresses cannot be used to route data outside of a private network.
- There are four address ranges that are reserved for private networking use only.
  - 10.0.0.0—10.255.255.255
  - 172.16.0.0—172.31.255.255
  - 192.168.0.0—192.168.255.255
  - 169.254.0.0—169.254.255.255

Special Addresses

Special Address	Netid	Hostid	Source or Destination
Network address	Specific	All 0s	None
Direct broadcast address	Specific	All 1s	Destination
Limited broadcast address	All 1s	All 1s	Destination
This host on this network	All 0s	All 0s	Source
Specific host on this network	All 0s	Specific	Destination
Loopback address	127	Any	Destination

Limitations

- A large part of the available addresses were wasted
- No flexibility
- Lack of security

Solution

Subnetting	Supernetting
(*i*) Dividing a network into multiple subnets is subnetting.	(*i*) Aggregation of two or more n/ws to generates single IP address for the group is supernetting
(*ii*) Bits are borrowed from host id	(*ii*) Bits are borrowed from network id.
(*iii*) It is applicable for single network	(*iii*) It is applicable for two or more networks
(*iv*) Number of 1s in subnet mask is always equal to more than network id bits	(*iv*) Number of 1s always less than *n*/*w* id bits
	(*v*) It reduces routing table entries.
	(*vi*) Network ids of the network must be in sequence.

CIDR-CLASSLESS INTER DOMAIN ROUTING

- The primary concern with classful addressing is the lack of flexibility in assigning a block of addresses.
- Instead of assigning fixed network prefixes of 8, 16, or 24 bits, CIDR uses prefixes that can range from 13 to 27 bits.
- The blocks of addresses can be assigned to networks as small as 32 hosts or to those with over 500,000 hosts.
- This allows address assignments to more closely match the needs of an organization.
- A CIDR address looks very similar to a classfull IP address.
- It uses the standard 32-bit dotted-quad notation.

APPLICATION LAYER PROTOCOL

SMTP (Simple Mail Transfer Protocol):

- Most popular network service is electronic mail (e-mail) which is supported by Simple Mail Transfer Protocol (SMTP).
- It transfers messages from senders' mail servers to the recipients' mail servers using TCP connections.
- It provides services for mail exchange between users on the same or different computers.
- Components:
  - **UA:** user agent
  - **MTA:** mail transfer agent
  - **MIME:** multipurpose internet mail extension
  - **MAP:** mail access protocol: POP3 & IMAP4

TELNET (Terminal Network)

- TELNET is client-server application that allows a user to log onto remote machine and lets the user to access any application program on a remote computer.
- Uses the NVT (Network Virtual Terminal) system to encode characters on the local system.
- On the server (remote) machine, NVT decodes the characters to a form acceptable to the remote machine.
- TELNET is a protocol that provides a general, bi-directional, eight-bit byte oriented communications facility.

FTP (File Transfer Protocol)

- FTP is the standard mechanism for copying a file from one host to another.
- it establishes 2 connections between hosts.
- built on a client-server architecture and uses separate connections for:
  - data transfer,
  - control information (commands and responses).
- It transfer data reliably and efficiently.

POP (Post Office Protocol)

- POP is also called as POP3 protocol.
- It is used by a mail server in conjunction with SMTP to receive and holds mail for hosts.
- POP3 mail server receives e-mails and filters them into the appropriate user folders. When a user connects to the mail server to retrieve his mail, the messages are downloaded from mail server to the user's hard disk.

HTTP (Hypertext Transfer Protocol)

- This is used to access data on the World Wide Web (www).
- It is the Web's main application-layer protocol
- Arepository of information spread all over the world and linked together.
- The HTIP protocol transfer data in the form of plain text, hyper text, audio, video and so on.
- HTTP utilizes TCP connections to send client requests and server replies.
- Methods of operations:
  - *(i)* **Head:** Used to describe client
  - *(ii)* **Get:** Used to get resources from authorative servers
  - *(iii)* **Put:** Used to create object
  - *(iv)* **Post:** Used to modify the existing order or to enhance the object
  - *(v)* **Delete:** Used to remove the object
  - *(vi)* **Trace:** Used by developers only to check + debug the network
  - *(vii)* **Connect:** Offers secured services
  - *(viii)* **Options:** Optimises the website option *i.e.,* to design website

Domain Name System (DNS)

- To identify an entity, TCP/IP protocol uses the IP address which uniquely identifies the connection of a host to the Internet.
- DNS is a hierarchical system, based on a distributed database, that uses a hierarchy of Name Servers to resolve Internet host names into the corresponding IP addresses required for packet routing by issuing a DNS query to a name server.
- DNS is a system that can map a name to an address and conversely an address to name.
- It is protocol that can be used in different platforms.
- Domain name space is divided into three categories.
- **Generic Domain:** defines registered hosts according, to their generic behaviour. Each node in the tree defines a domain which is an index to the domain name space database.

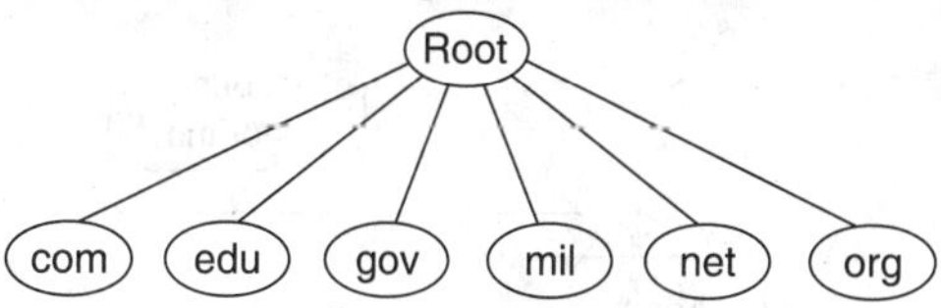

Generic domain

- **Country Domain:** uses 2 characters country abbreviations (e.g., US for United States) in place of 3 characters.
- **Inverse Domain:** The inverse domain is used to map an address to a name.

Routing Algorithm and Congestion Control

5

ROUTING ALGORITHMS

- The path to be travelled by the message from its source to its destination is determined by the routing algorithm. The routing algorithm chooses the next port and channel on which to send out the message.
- Uses graph theory to present algorithms
  - **nodes:** routers (are assigned IDs)
  - **edges:** links between routers (can be directed or undirected)
  - weights on edges: any cost measure of using that link (distance, congestion, capacity)
  - **shortest path:** minimum number of links (hops)
  - **least cost path:** minimum total cost, regardless of hops
- **Adaptive algorithms**
  - They change their routing decisions to reflect changes in the topology, and usually the traffic as well.
  - Adaptive algorithms differ in where they get their information, when they change the routes, and what metric is used for optimization (e.g., distance, number of hops, or estimated transmit time).
- **Non-adaptive algorithms**
  - They do not base their routing decisions on measurements or estimates of the current traffic and topology.
  - the choice of the route source to destination is computed in advance, off-line and downloaded to the route when the network is booted. This procedure is sometimes called static routing.

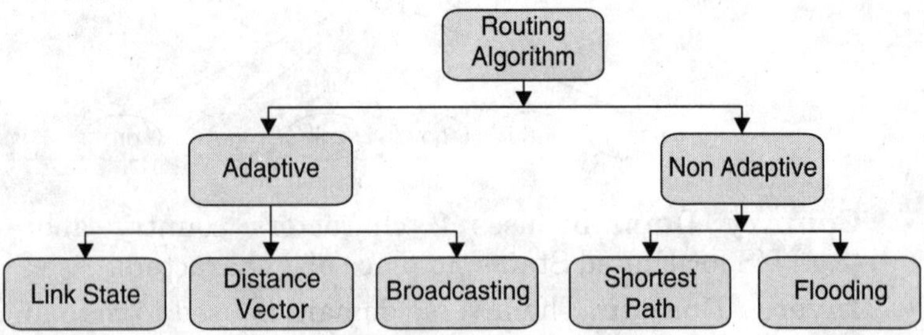

Link-State Routing

- Periodically do:
  - Discover neighbor addresses.
  - Determine costs to neighbor.
  - Broadcast neighbor information to routers.
  - Add received neighbor information to the graph.
  - Compute shortest paths.
- Link-state routing has two main variants:
  - Intermediate System-Intermediate System (IS-IS).
  - Open Shortest-Path First (OSPF)

Distance-Vector Routing

- Each router maintains a table with the best known distance to each destination and which line to use to get there. Tables updated by exchanging information with the neighbors
- Iterative shortest-path & path-independent.
- Routers update tables solely on cost.

Broadcast Routing

- Sending a packed to all destinations simultaneously is called Broadcasting.
- Point-to-point simulated broadcast is simple and inefficient.
- Multi destination routing is a more efficient point-to-point simulation.
- Each packet contains multiple destination addresses.
- Flooding.
- Every incoming packet is sent out on every outgoing line except the one it arrived from.
- Always finds the quickest route.
- No routing information required.
- Failure resistant.

Shortest Path Routing

- Routing decision are taken on the basis of cost between source and destination.
- Hop count plays major role.
- uses various algorithms to decide a path with minimum number of hops.

Hierarchical Routing

- Larger networks use more resources for all routers.
- The big network is partitioned into smaller *regions* (or *areas*, or *zones*, or ...).
- The regions are linked together by a new parent *area* (or *zones*, or *segments*, or ...).
- Define autonomous systems (AS) as logical grouping of routers.
- Inter-AS routing is routing from one AS to another.
- Intra-AS routing is routing within an AS.
- They can use different routing methods.
- Routers at the AS "edge" are called gateway.
- Gateways communicate with other gateways to implement inter-AS but run routing methods for both inter- and intra-AS.

Multicast Routing

- Application that require separate processes access and ability to work on the same data.
- Small group can use point-to-point messaging to accomplish this task.
- Need a mechanism that would send messages to well-defined groups that are numerically large in size but small compared to the network as a whole.
  - Sending a message to a such a group is called multicasting.
  - Corresponding routing algorithm is called multicast routing.
- Generalizes multi destination routing.

CONGESTION CONTROL

- Congestion is a situation when too many packets are present in a subnet or approaching the same link. The incoming packets are more than the capacity of the network resulting in collapsed performance and no packet delivery.
- **Causes:**
  - **bursty traffic:** when network fail to cope up with sudden increase of traffic
  - slow processor or routers
  - insufficient storage space at receiver
  - less bandwidth
  - ill configuration

TECHNIQUE

Different techniques for resolving Congestion are present.

- **Open-loop:** try to prevent congestion occurring by good design
- **Closed-loop:** monitor the system to detect congestion, pass this information to where action can be taken, and adjust system operation to correct the problem (detect, feedback and correct)

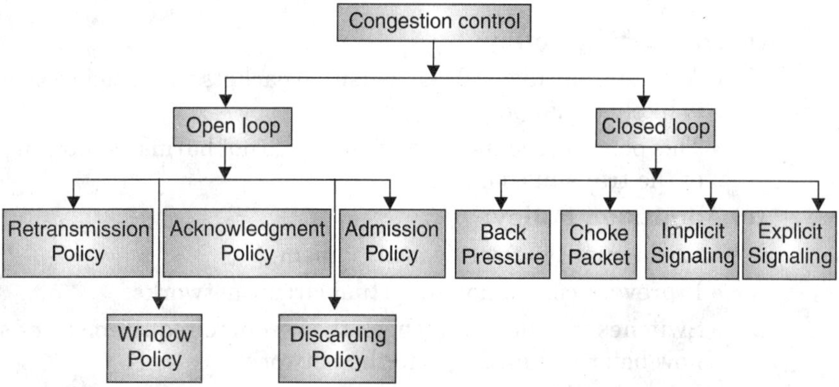

Types of Congestion Control Methods

1. **Open-loop Congestion Control:**
    - It prevents the congestion before it happens.
    - Congestion control is handled either by the source or by the destination.

   ***(i)* Retransmission Policy:**

   - The sender retransmits a packet, if it feels that the packet it has sent is lost or corrupted.
   - The retransmission policy and the timers need to be designed to optimize efficiency and prevent the congestion.

   ***(ii)* Window Policy:**

   - Selective reject window method is used for congestion control.
   - When timer for a packet times out, the specific lost or damaged packets are send back.

   ***(iii)* Acknowledgement Policy:**

   - If the receiver does not acknowledge every packet it receives it may slow down the sender and help prevent congestion.
   - Acknowledgments add to the traffic load on the network. Thus, by sending fewer acknowledgements we can reduce load on the network.

- Approaches to implement it are:
  - A receiver may send an acknowledgement only if it has a packet to be sent.
  - A receiver may send an acknowledgement when a timer expires.
  - A receiver may also decide to acknowledge only N packets at a time.

(*iv*) Discarding Policy:

- A router may discard less sensitive packets when congestion is likely to happen.
- This policy prevents congestion and do not harm the integrity of the transmission.

(*v*) Admission Policy:

- It is a quality-of-service mechanism
- It prevent congestion in virtual circuit networks.
- Switches in a flow first check the resource requirement of a flow before admitting it to the network.
- A router can deny establishing a virtual circuit connection if there is congestion in the "network or if there is a possibility of future congestion.

2. Closed Loop Congestion Control:

- It try to remove the congestion after it happens.
- The various methods used for closed loop congestion control are:

(*i*) **Backpressure:** Backpressure is a node-to-node congestion control that starts with a node and propagates, in the opposite direction of data flow in which the congested node stops receiving data from the immediate upstream node or nodes.

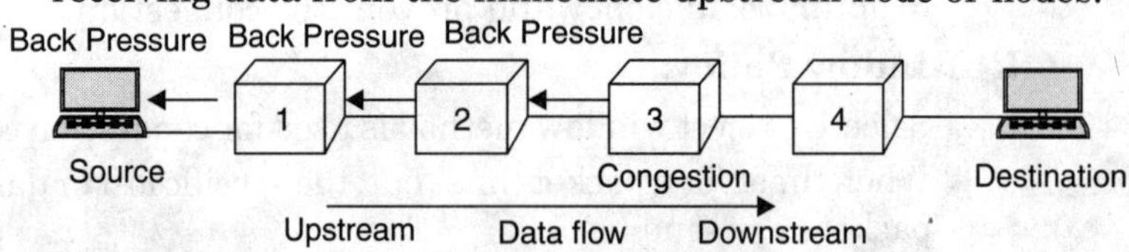

Backpressure Method

(*ii*) **Choke Packet:** The congested router or node sends a special type of packet called choke packet to the source to inform it about the congestion, not informing the intermediate nodes through which it has travelled.

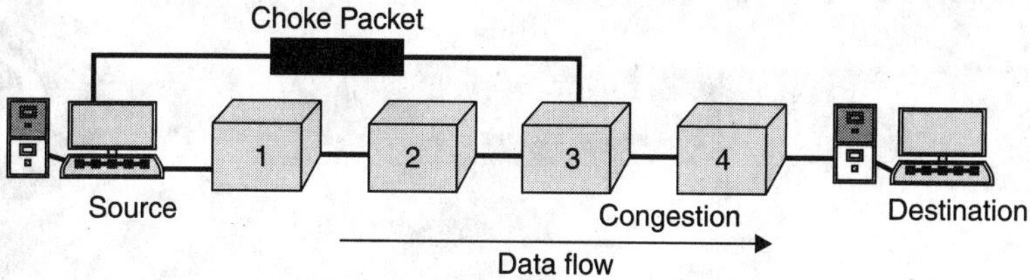

Choke Packet Method

(*iii*) Implicit Signaling:

- There is no communication between the congested node or nodes and the source.
- The source guesses that there is congestion somewhere in the network when it does not receive any acknowledgment. Therefore the delay in receiving an acknowledgment is interpreted as congestion in the network.
- On sensing this congestion, the source slows down.
- This control policy is used by TCP.

(*iv*) Explicit Signaling:

- the congested nodes explicitly send a signal to the source or destination to inform about the congestion.
- Here, the signal is included in the packets that carry data.
- It can occur in either the forward direction or the backward direction.
  - **Backward signaling:** a bit is set in a packet moving in the direction opposite to the congestion. It warns the source about the congestion and informs the source to slow down.
  - **Forward signaling:** a bit is set in a packet moving in the direction of congestion. It warns the destination about the congestion. The receiver uses policies such as slowing down the acknowledgements to remove the congestion.

Networking Devices

6

HUB

- It is an electronic connection device used to connect workstation and server in a network.
- Perform broadcasting: repeat any signal that comes in one port & copy it to the other ports.
- It Operates at physical layer.
- Contains multiple ports.
- Simple, low in cost and no software requirement.
- Performance is low when traffic is high.
- 2 types of hub are:
  - **Active Hub:** They are smarter than the passive hubs. They provide the path for the data signals & regenerate, concentrate and strengthen them.
  - **Passive Hub:** Works as connector. Connects the wire coming from different branches.

REPEATER

- It regenerates the signal over the same network before the signal becomes too weak or corrupted by copying it bit by bit.
- They do no amplify the signal.
- Remove unwanted noise from the signal.
- Operates at physical layer.

SWITCH

- It is a device connecting network segments.
- It is a multi port bridge with a buffer.
- Large number of ports imply less traffic.
- High efficiency and performance.
- It works at data link layer.
- Perform error checking thus forwarding only good packets to correct port.

- It switch divides collision domain of hosts, but broadcast domain remains same.

BRIDGE

- A bridge is a repeater, with add on functionality of filtering content by reading the MAC addresses of source and destination.
- It is used for interconnecting two LANs working on the same protocol.
- It has a single input and single output port, thus making it a 2 port device.
- It operates at data link layer.
- Uses table for filtering decisions & mapping address to ports.

ROUTER

- They routes data packets based on their IP addresses.
- It is a Network Layer device.
- They connect LANs and WANs together.
- Have a dynamically updating routing table based on which, decisions on routing the data packets are taken.
- Router divide broadcast domains of hosts connected through it.

BROUTER

- A bridge router or brouter is a network device that has Combined features of bridges and routers.
- It routes packets for known protocols and simply forwards all other packets as a bridge would.
- It operate at both the network layer for routable protocols and at the data link layer for non-routable protocols.

GATEWAY

- It is a passage to connect two networks together that may work upon different networking models.
- They works as the messenger agents that take data from one system, interpret it, and transfer it to another system.
- They are also called protocol converters.
- Operates at network layer.

- They are more complex than switch or router

N/W Element	Operating Layer	Forms of Data	Connectivity	Type of device (hardware/software)	Device type
Repeater	Physical Layer	Bits	Nearest LANS of same type	Fully hardware (Amplifier)	2 port device
Hub	Physical Layer	Bits	Nearest LANS of same type	Fully hardware (Amplifier)	Multiport repeater passive device
Switch	Data Link Layer (Physical address provided by vender)	Frame	Nearest different LANS	More hardware less software	8P/16P/32P active device
Bridge	Data Link Layer (Physical address provided by vender)	Frame	Nearest different LANS	More hardware less software	8P/16P/32P active device
Router	Network Layer (Logical address)	Packet	Faraway LANS (LAN -WAN) interconnect different similar networks	Less hardware more software (routing)	Sophicticated electronic device
Gateway	All layers (upto 7 layer)	Message	Different WANS (WAN -WAN)	Fully software	Protocol converter

Networking Security Basic Concepts

7

Network Security is the process of taking physical and software preventative measures to protect the underlying networking infrastructure from unauthorized access, misuse, malfunction, modification, destruction, or improper disclosure, thereby creating a secure platform for computers, users and programs to perform their permitted critical functions within a secure environment.

CRYPTOGRAPHY

- It is the science and art of transforming messages to make them secure and immune to attacks.
- It means secret writing

  Terminology:
- P → Plaintext: The original intelligible message
- C → Ciphertext: The transformed message
- Cipher: An algorithm for transforming an Plaintext into ciphertext by transposition or substitution
- Key: Some critical information used by the cipher, known only to the sender and receiver
- E → Encryption (encode):The process of converting plaintext to ciphertext
- D → Decryption (decode): The process of converting ciphertext back into plaintext

Modes:

Symmetric Key Cryptography	Asymmetric Key Cryptography
1. The same algorithm with the same key is used for encryption and decryption	1. One algorithm is used for encryption and decryption with a pair of keys, one for encryption and one for decryption.
2. The key must be kept secret.	2. One of the two keys two must be kept secret

3. It may be impossible or at least impractical to decipher a message if no other information is available	3. It may be impossible or at least impractical to decipher a message if no other information is available.

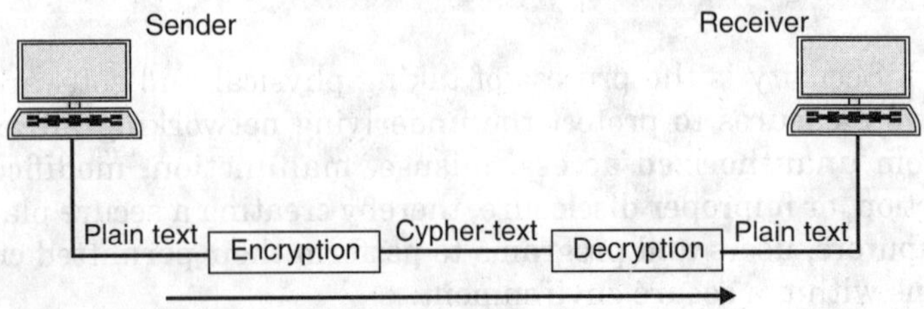

Secret Key Encryption

- Both sender and receiver have one secret key.
- Data is encrypted at sender's end using the key.
- Encrypted data is sent on the public domain to the receiver.
- The encrypted data packets are decrypted by the receiver using same key.
- **Example:** Data Encryption Standard (DES).
- There is a separate key for each host on the network making it difficult to manage.

Public Key Encryption

- Here, every user has its own Secret Key and it is not in the shared domain. The secret key is never revealed on public domain.
- Along with secret key, every user has public key, which is always made public and is used by Senders to encrypt the data.
- When the user receives the encrypted data, decryption is done using its own Secret Key.
- **Example:** Rivest-Shamir-Adleman (RSA).

DIGITAL SIGNATURES

- A digital code (generated and authenticated by public key encryption) which is attached to an electronically transmitted document to verify its contents and the sender's identity
- It can be used with any kind of message, whether encrypted or not, so that reciever can be sure of the senders identity & that the message arrived intact

METHOD

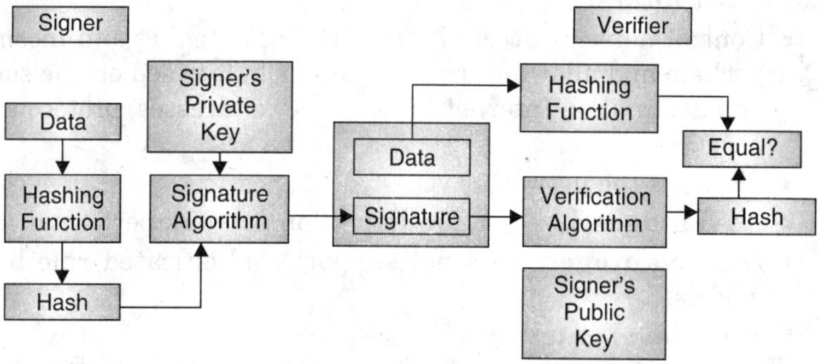

- Each person has a public-private key pair.
- The private key used for signing is referred to as the signature key and the public key as the verification key.
- Signer feeds data to the hash function and generates hash of data.
- Hash value and signature key are then fed to the signature algorithm which produces the digital signature on given hash. Signature is appended to the data and then both are sent to the verifier.
- Verifier feeds the digital signature and the verification key into the verification algorithm. The verification algorithm gives some value as output.
- Verifier also runs same hash function on received data to generate hash value.
- For verification, this hash value and output of verification algorithm are compared. Based on the comparison result, verifier decides whether the digital signature is valid.
- Since digital signature is created by 'private' key of signer and no one else can have this key; the signer cannot repudiate signing the data in future.

FIREWALL

- A firewall is a hardware or software system that prevents unauthorized access to or from a network
- It is a barrier between (LAN) and the Internet. It allows keeping private resources confidential and minimizes the security risks.
- It controls network traffic, in both directions.
- There are two types of Firewall system:
    - works by using filters at the network layer
    - works by using proxy servers at the user, application, or network layer.

Firewall Techniques are:

1. **Packet filters:**
   - Control network access by monitoring outgoing and incoming packets and allowing them to pass or halt based on the source and destination Internet Protocol (IP) addresses, protocols and ports.
   - Works at the network level.
   - **Advantages:** low cost, low impact on network performance.
   - **Disadvantages:** does not support sophisticated rule based models.
2. **Circuit level gateways:**
   - Work at the session layer
   - It monitor TCP handshaking between packets to determine whether a requested session is legitimate
   - **Advantages:** relatively inexpensive , hiding information about the private network
   - **Disadvantages:** they do not filter individual packets
3. **Application level gateways:**
   - Work at the application layer.
   - Incoming or outgoing packets cannot access services for which there is no proxy & log user activity and logins.
   - Filter application specific commands.
   - **Advantages:** a high level of security.
   - **Disadvantages:** having a significant impact on network performance, not transparent to end users and require manual configuration of each client computer.
4. **Stateful multilayer inspection firewalls:**
   - Work at the application, session, network layer.
   - Filter packets at the network layer, determine whether session packets are legitimate and evaluate contents of packets at the application layer. Can log user activity and logins.
   - They allow direct connection between client and host.
   - They rely on algorithms to recognize and process application layer data
   - **Advantages:** a high level of security, good performance, transparency to end users
   - **Disadvantages:** expensive and complex.

Computer Science

12

Web Technologies

CONTENTS

HTML

1

- Hyper Text Mark Language or HTML used to create web page and its elements from the building blocks of all website.
- The predefined tags are interpreted by browser.
- It is formatting or presentation language written in plaintext making it hardware and software independent.
- It is standardized by WWWC (World Wide Web Console).
- It is a markup language and not a programming language.

TAGS

HTML uses various tage that are enclosed within angle braces ⟨tag name⟩. Except few, these tags have their corresponding closing tags.

ATTRIBUTES

- Define the characteristics of an HTML element.
- They are placed inside the elements's opening tag.
- They have two parts–'Name' (property that user set) and 'value' (value of the property to be set).

ELEMENTS

- Define by starting tag and if other content is present with elements then it ends with a closing tag.

  e.g. <p> paragraph content </P>.

BASIC HTML TAGS

Tags that are essential part of the documents.

<HTML>: Main container for HTML pages.

<HEAD>: Container for page header information.

<TITLE>: Title of the page.

<BODY>: Main body of the page.

BODY TAGS

- Tags used in body part that formats the body.
- Also called as formatting tags.

(*i*) <*b*>: 'Bold'-specifies bold text

(*ii*) <*br*>: 'break'-produces line break in text

(*iii*) <big>: specifies big text

(*iv*) <basefont>: specifies the basic font size.

(*v*) <center>: specifies centered text

(*vi*) <comment>: puts a comment in the document

(*vii*) <del>: specifies deleted text

(*viii*) <div>: specifies a section in a document

(*ix*) <*dl*>: definition list

(*x*) 〈*dt*〉: definition term

(*xi*) 〈embed〉: specifies container for an external application

(*xii*) 〈font〉: specifies text font, size and colour.

(*xiii*) 〈frame〉: specifies a sub window

(*xiv*) 〈frame-set〉: specifies set of frame

(*xv*) 〈hr〉: horizontal rule

(*xvi*) 〈h_1〉 to 〈h_6〉: header 1 to header 6

(*xvii*) 〈*i*〉: italicise the text

(*xviii*) 〈ins〉: inserted content

(*xix*) 〈ing〉: image insertion

(*xx*) 〈no script〉: specifies non script section.

(*xxi*) 〈plaintext〉: tells browser to treat all the text as plain text.

(*xxii*) 〈*p*〉: paragraph- starts the paragraph, followed by closing tag 〈/*p*〉

(*xxiii*) 〈pre〉: performatted text

(*xxiv*) 〈*q*〉: short quotation or in-line quotation

(*xxv*) 〈*s*〉: strike through text

(*xxvi*) 〈sup〉: superscript

(*xxvii*) 〈sub〉: subscript

(*xxviii*) 〈small〉: small text

(*xxix*) 〈strong〉: strong text

(*xxx*) 〈*tt*〉: teletype text

(*xxxi*) 〈td〉: table cell

(*xxxii*) 〈th〉: 〈table heading〉

(*xxxiii*) ⟨*u*⟩: 'underline' (mainly used to specify hyperlinks)

(*xxxiv*) ⟨var⟩: variable

(*xxxv*) ⟨wbr⟩: word break point.

(*xxxvi*) ⟨xmp⟩: Example text or performatted text

LIST AND TABLE TAGS

(*i*) ⟨Li⟩ & ⟨/Li⟩: Opening and closing of a individual item of a list.

(*ii*) ⟨UL⟩ & ⟨/UL⟩: Un-numbered list.
Each item appears as a bullet point.

(*iii*) ⟨OL⟩ & ⟨/OL⟩: Ordered or numbered list.
Each item appears as numbered point on a separate line.

(*iv*) ⟨table⟩ ⟨/table⟩: Beginning and end of the table.
Each table have data arranged into rows and columns of cell.

(*v*) ⟨tr⟩ ⟨/tr⟩: Row starting and row closing.

(*vi*) ⟨td⟩ ⟨td⟩: Individual cell within row.
Text, images, links, forms etc, can be inserted.

(*vii*) ⟨table border⟩ ⟨/table⟩: Closing and ending of table with border.
It makes table presentable.

Form Tags

(*i*) ⟨form action ="path/file" method = "post"⟩ ⟨/form ⟩:

- Opening and closing of the form.
- When form is submitted, the listed file will be executed (in a sub-directory of cgi-bin).
- The target = new attribute is optional and output of CGI program will be sent to a browser window.

(*ii*) ⟨text area rows = "06" cols = "80" name = "parameter"⟩ ⟨/text⟩.

- Text box of 6 row height and 80 column wide is created.
- Text present in the box will be printed as it is.

(*iii*) ⟨select name = "parameter"⟩ ⟨option⟩ Label 1 ⟨/option⟩:

- drop down box is created.
- 'selected' statement causes that option to be the default.
- the label between the option tag is sent as the value of named parameter on selecting an option.
- 'multiple' word is written in select tag for multiple values.

(*iv*) ⟨input type = "check box" name = "parameter"⟩:

- Check box is created
- True value is given on checking the box.

XML

2

INTRODUCTION

- Extensible Markup Language or XML, a text based markup language.
- XML carries the data and store it. It does not present the data. It is hardware and software independent.
- XML is an open standard defined by W_3C or world wide web consortium.
- XML tags are user defined and case sensitive language.
- XML is used for off-loading and reloading the database.

Difference between HTML and XML

HTML	XML
• Hyper Text Markup Language	• Extensible Markup Language
• Designs the data thus focussing on formatting and layout	• Transport and store the data with focus on what data is.
• It is markup language or presentation language	• It provides framework for defining markup language and is neither programming nor presentation language
• Predefined tags and case insensitive	• User defined tags and case sensitive

Syntax

⟨? xml version = "1.0"?⟩
⟨contact-info⟩
⟨name⟩ Sahil Aggarwal ⟨/name⟩
⟨phone⟩ 1234956 ⟨/phone⟩
⟨/contact-info⟩

Attributes

Specifies a single property for the element, using name/value pair. An XML-element can have one or more attributes.

e.g., ⟨a href = "http://www. facebook.com/"⟩ Facebook! ⟨/*a*⟩

Here, 'href' is attribute name and "http:www.facebook.com/" is attribute value.

Syntax Rules

1. Root tag must be present in every XML document.
2. Tags or attributes name are case sensitive.
   e.g., href and HREF are two different attributes.
3. There is closing tag for every opening tag.
   e.g., ⟨name⟩ Ajit Sharma ⟨/name⟩
4. Tags must be property nested.
   e.g., ⟨*b*⟩ ⟨*i*⟩ Heading ⟨/*i*⟩ ⟨/*b*⟩
5. Attribute names are defined without quotation mark and Attribute value must be enclosed in double quotes.
   e.g., ⟨*a b* = "*x*" *c* = "*y*"⟩ ... ⟨/*a*⟩
6. Same attribute cannot have two values in a syntax.
   e.g., ⟨*a b* = "*x*" *c* = "*y*" *b* = "*z*"⟩ ... ⟨/*a*⟩: Incorrect as *b* has 2 values.

XML PARSER

It is a library that provides an interface for client application to work with XML documents.

It checks proper format and validate the document.

Syntax rules

- **Document should be well-formed** → XML parser can extract data only when XML document follows proper syntax.
- **Valid document:** XML scheme defines the structure of the document and if it follows the structure then document is valid.

LANGUAGES DEVELOPED FORM XML

- **WML** – Wireless Markup Language
  – develop web pages using mobiles phones
- **WAP** – Wireless Application Protocol
  – access websites using mobile phones

- **RDF** – Resource Description Framework
  – share the resources like audio, video, ebook etc.
- **RSS** – Really Simple Syndicate
  – share news in the web
- **SMIL** – Synchronized Multimedia International Language
- – develops multimedia applications

  e.g., Flex, silver light.

LANGUAGES MEANT FOR XML

1. **XSL** – XML Style Sheet → defines how to display XML data.
2. **XSLT**– XML Style Sheet Transformation
3. **XSL-FO** – XML Style Sheet Formatting Object

   } XML to HTML (2 and 3)
4. **X-Query** – Retrieve data from multiple XML documents.
5. **X-path** – Retrieve data from single XML document.
6. **X-link** – Defines relationship between XML document.
7. **X-pointer** – Define relationship within same XML document.

DOCUMENT TYPE DEFINITION (DTD)

DTD describes XML language precisely. It checks vocabulary and validity of the structure of XML document.

e.g., ⟨!DOC TYPE email⟩.

[

⟨!ELEMENT email (to, from, subject, body)⟩

⟨!ELEMENT to (≠ PC DATA)⟩

⟨!ELEMENT from (≠ PC DATA)⟩

⟨!ELEMENT subject (≠ PC DATA)⟩

⟨!ELEMENT body (≠ PC DATA)⟩

]⟩

Building Blocks of DTD

1. ELEMENT → Used to define tag and tells parser to parse the document from root element.
2. ATTLIST → defines attributes and it is always name-value pair.

3. ENTITY → short cuts for special symbols. It starts with '&' and ends with ';'. They are placeholders in XML.

   5 built in entities is well formed XML;

   (*i*) & amp; → ampersand (&)

   (*ii*) & apos; → single quote (' ')

   (*iii*) & gt; → greater than (>)

   (*iv*) & lt; → less than (<)

   (*v*) & quote; → Double quote (" ")

   * HTML entities can be used in XML.

   We can define our entity in DTD and use them in XML.

   e.g., In DTD: ⟨!ENTITY WHO "Word Health Organization"

   In XML: ⟨org⟩ and WHO; ⟨org⟩

4. CDATA → Character Data.

   Few section in XML contains non-parsing characters.

5. PC DATA → Parsed Character Data.

   All characters /text/data will be parsed inside XML tags.

Types of Elements/Tags

1. **Empty Element:** Do not contain any data with single attribute present. Keyword 'EMPTY' is used.

   e.g., ⟨!DOCTYPE hr [

   ⟨!ELEMENT address EMPTY⟩

   ]⟩

   ⟨address/⟩

2. **Children Element:** Any number of element type can be placed in another element type.

   These can be:

   - **Optional child element:** Child is optional.

   eg. ⟨product⟩

   ⟨!ELEMENT product (name, cost/price)⟩

   ⟨!ELEMENT name (# PC DATA)⟩

   ⟨!ELEMENT cost (# PC DATA)⟩

   ⟨!ELEMENT price (# PC DATA)⟩

   ⟨product/⟩

- **Multiple occurrence of a child element:** Child element appears more than once.

  eg. ⟨student⟩

  ⟨name⟩ Ajit ⟨/name⟩

  ⟨phone no.⟩ 12344861 ⟨/phone no.⟩

  ⟨phone no.⟩ 48912307 ⟨/phone no.⟩

  ⟨/student⟩

Note

- '+' → one or more → child element can occur one or more time inside perent element.
- '*' → zero or more → child element can occur zero or more times.
- '?' → zero or one → child element can occur zero or one time.

XML SCHEMA

- Like DTD file; XML schema file contains only metadata.
- It contains description of element types.
  - Attributes
  - Definition and structure of elements and attributes.
- It defines XML document and written in form of XML.
- It is reusable and helps in mapping of data from database to XML document because of support for data types.
- Avoid name conflict by providing name spaces.
- Imposing data restriction and pattern refinement is not possible.

Basic Concepts of Client-Server Computing

3

CLIENT SERVER MODEL

- In client server model; Client application program running on a local machine sends service request to server application program running on remote machine, which in turn sends result to client.
- Server is not client specific. It provides service to any client.
- Here software is of major importance.

Elements of Computing

- Request-Response process in finite process which can be repeated several times.

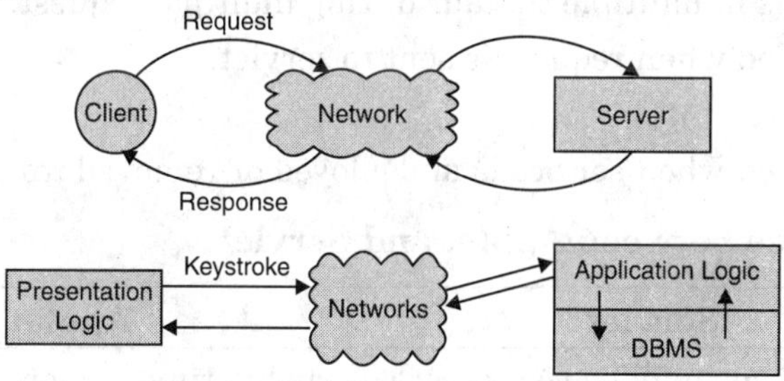

Client-Server Model

- It is a distributed access.
- It uses data base server where request for data is accepted, and result is sent back after retrieval of data from database.

Server Side Programming

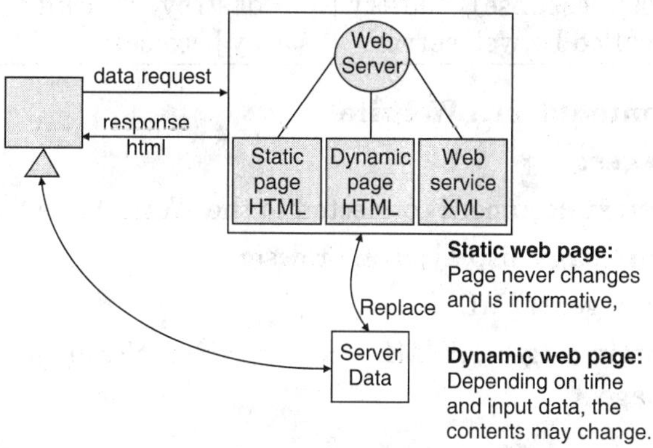

Servlet

- Java program running within the context of web servers.
- It enables single process to run and no IPC mechanism.
- Servlet container – runtime environment.
  – 2 containers
  (*i*) generic servlet → any protocol.
  (*ii*) http servlet → http protocol.

Servlet methods

(*i*) init ( ):
- starts and initialise the servlet.
- called when servlet is deployed.

(*ii*) Service ( ):
- runs in multiple threads during multiple request.
- called when request is sent to servlet.

(*iii*) Destroy ( ):
- called when service is undeployed or removed from the servet.

Difference between Applet and Servlet

Servlet	Applet
(1) Lifetime may be years	(1) Lifetime is more than 1 day
(2) Servlet runs inside the web server to generate dynamic html or server side	(2) Applet runs inside the browser to make the page dynamic or server side
(3) Methods init ( ), service (request, response), destory ( ) are called by web server	(3) Methods init (), start (), stop (), destroy (), paint () are called by browser

Types of contents on a Website

(*i*) **Webpages:**
- Hypertext document connected to the World Wide Web.
- Primary page displayed on browser.
- Static page: HTML
- Dynamic page: HTML + Server Side Script/programming language

- Client side dynamic: HTML + javascript
- Both dynamic: HTML + programming language, javascript + server side script.

(*ii*) Images |Audio| Video: displayed or played on client side.

(*iii*) CSS or Cascading Style Sheet: It defines the styles of HTML tags hence improving HTML.

(*iv*) Script: It is embedded in HTML and executed by the browser.

Dynamic pages at client side are returned using Java script, VBscript whereas server side pages uses ASP, servlet, JSP, PHP and ASP· NET.

(*v*) XML: data representation language.

(*vi*) AJAX (Asynchronous Javascript XML: makes dynamic pages on both sides.

It enables multitasking with multiple scripts running the tasks.

(*vii*) Client side component

(*viii*) Server side component

Points to Remember

- **JAVA SCRIPT:**
  - Can fetch some data or information for updation from server but not complete HTML page.
  - It bypass the browser to request server but server responds in XML and Javascript then updates the data on the page.
- **Component:** Reusable piece of software reused at runtime. Functionality is given by set of functions called interface.

Features of Webservers

(*i*) **Generate response:**

- It depends upon the requested page.
- If static page → webserver sends the content of html file as response.
- If dynamic page → webserver executes the program, collects its output and then send it as response.

(*ii*) **Virtual Hosting:**

- Also known as Shared hosting or Dedicated hosting.
- Cost of webhosting is reduced by hosting more websites.
- Webserver identifies the required website thus using domain name and URL.

(*iii*) **Compression (gzip):** Page transfer between server and client and vice versa takes place in compressed form.

(*iv*) **Authentication:** Process where credentials are compared to those on file in database of authorized user's information.

It provides security to data.

(*v*) **SSL: Secure Socket Layer:** Standard security technology that provides an encrypted link between server and a client.

(*vi*) **Web statistic:** Keeps an account of people visiting, their place, number and problems faced by them.